THE ART OF
MARVELL'S POETRY

THE ART OF
MARVELL'S POETRY

J. B. Leishman

late Senior Lecturer in English Literature at the University of Oxford and Fellow of St. John's College

MINERVA PRESS

First American edition published in 1968
by arrangement with Hutchinson & Co. Ltd.

Library of Congress Catalog Card Number: 68-22181

Funk & Wagnalls, *A Division of* Reader's Digest Books, Inc.

Printed in the United States of America

CONTENTS

❧❧❧

PREFACE TO SECOND EDITION

The publication of this book coincided with the death of its editor, Professor John Butt, and it has accordingly fallen to me to introduce its second edition.

I have corrected its straightforward misprints. The checking of the quotations showed that Leishman sometimes signalised his revisions of their punctuation by means of a note, and sometimes not; in which case, I have let stand such punctuation as seems to have been changed deliberately. In a few instances Leishman did not specify the edition of a work he was quoting from, and when it has not been possible to deduce it from among those I have had access to, I have verified the wording of the quotation according to the standard edition of the work in question, though I have not thought it necessary to bring the punctuation and capitalisation into conformity with it.

In preparing the new edition I have been grateful for the expert help of Mr Anthony Burton. I am also grateful to Professor Pierre Legouis, who privately sent in a list of the misprints he noted while preparing his review of the book.

GEOFFREY TILLOTSON

London 1967

PREFACE TO FIRST EDITION

When J. B. Leishman died in August 1963 he was near to reaching the end of several years' work on a book about Marvell's non-satirical poetry. In beginning to organise his work for a book of this kind it was his custom to deliver a course of lectures on the subject in the Honours School. These lectures were written out in full, and thus provided him with a draft for expansion, refinement, and correction. This process of revision had been completed for chapters 2, 3, 4, and most of chapter 5, all of which were left in a state ready for typist and printer; but although the remainder of chapter 5, chapter 6, and chapter 1 still demanded further attention, they had already reached a stage of revision beyond the original lecture draft: the differences in quality, though perceptible, need not cause the reader trouble. My task has been to eliminate some unintentional repetition, to rewrite a few sentences left obscure in the original draft, and to correct an occasional error. I have also presumed to add a footnote about the knowledge of Marvell's poetry in the eighteenth century on which Leishman was misinformed.

Readers of his British Academy Warton Lecture, *Themes and Variations in Marvell's Poetry*, will recognise several passages in the pages that follow, and will be prepared for the kind of study to which the author invites them. Marvell's poetry is shown to be the work of a man living at a certain moment in history; it is poetry which could not have been written at any other time, and its affinities to the work of contemporary poets are clearly demonstrated. Just as it could have been written at no other time, so it could have been written by no one else. The claim is supported by showing Marvell's distinctive handling of poetic kinds, and his individual treatment of familiar topics. This is a mode of criticism for which Leishman was peculiarly well fitted by his exceptionally wide reading in European literature, his retentive memory, and his discriminating taste. He had already practised this mode in his books on Donne and on Shakespeare's *Sonnets*, and he was preparing a book of the same kind on Milton's minor poems. The present work may therefore be regarded as a characteristic production, perhaps the most characteristic production, of his mature scholarship.

In preparing this book for the press, I owe much to the skill of Mrs Jean Henson in deciphering a difficult manuscript, to Professors Geoffrey and Kathleen Tillotson for time generously given in advising me on numerous points of detail, and to Mrs E. E. Duncan-Jones to whose expert knowledge of Marvell's life and work the author himself bears grateful testimony in the pages that follow. The Delegates of the Clarendon Press have kindly granted permission to quote from H. M. Margoliouth's edition of *The Poems and Letters of Andrew Marvell*.

JOHN BUTT

Edinburgh 1964

MARVELL THE MAN

Sir Herbert Grierson, in the Introduction to his *Metaphysical Lyrics and Poems of the Seventeenth Century*, describes Andrew Marvell as 'the most interesting personality between Donne and Dryden, and at his very best a finer poet than either'. He is perhaps the most entirely delightful of seventeenth-century poets, whether dialectical or Jonsonian, and also one of the most difficult to generalise about. He is capable of a rare artistic perfection, and yet he often—though not perhaps so noticeably to an English reader as to the Gallic sensibility of his most elaborate commentator, Professor Pierre Legouis—displays a strange carelessness and amateurishness, especially in syntax and in inversions for the sake of rhyme. He reveals, often in varying degrees of combination, qualities which in other seventeenth-century poets, dialectical or non-dialectical, seem to predominate. He has much of Donne's love of sheer wit and paradox and hyperbole, and of Donne's ability, while almost dispensing with visual imagery, to make passionately poetical arguments out of abstract ideas, and many of his shorter poems have the sequacious and logical structure which distinguishes Donne and Herbert at their best. At the same time, visual imagery plays a much greater part in his poetry than in that of either Donne or Herbert. There is as much colour in it as in Crashaw's, or, for that matter, as in Milton's, shorter poems. There is as much of external nature in it as in Vaughan's, though only occasionally of nature moralised; for, while Marvell's moralising poem *On a Drop of Dew* does indeed remind us of Vaughan, his many descriptions of gardens and meadows in *Appleton House* and elsewhere remind us of Milton's *L'Allegro* and *Il Penseroso*, although the witty and ingenious manner of the descriptions themselves and of the reflexions and analogies which they suggest is quite unlike Milton. Unlike Donne, Marvell does not disdain occasional allusions to classical mythology; many of his poems are at least formally pastorals, and again and again in his poetry the trees and flowers of a personified nature crowd into a shade or crush into a bower or flashingly arise to honour master or mistress in a manner which, for all its greater ingenuity, elaboration and hyperbole, is not wholly dissimilar from that in which they behave in later pastorals; for here as elsewhere Marvell's wit had decided affinities with that of Pope and Prior. Then, although one tends to think of Marvell as being primarily a poet of the school of Donne, and although most of his lyric poetry, like that of the other dialectical poets, is private rather than public, has he not in the *Horatian Ode upon Cromwell's Return from Ireland* written perhaps the greatest public poem of the seventeenth century, as also the one nearest in form and content both to the graver Horace and to the poetic ideal towards which Ben Jonson seems to be always striving? Finally, by far the greater part of Marvell's lyrical verse is written in the octosyllabic couplet, that measure in which, though it was neglected by Donne and Herbert, so many seventeenth-century poets (I need only mention Vaughan, Crashaw and Milton) wrote some of their finest verse—that measure which during the first half of the seventeenth century became, as Aristotle would have said, what it had in it to be, and which is one of the chief of those common elements which immediately occur to the mind when one tries to think of seventeenth-century poetry in general rather than of poetry of the School of Jonson and poetry of the School of Donne.

I find it difficult to express my admiration for Marvell without involuntary exaggeration, without seeming to say that whatever any other seventeenth-century poet has done well Marvell has done better. It is true that in the art of making the purest poetry out of almost pure abstractions not even Donne has surpassed, or even, perhaps, equalled, Marvell's *Definition of Love*, but then, on the other hand, Marvell has nothing at all comparable with that tenderness which is no less characteristic of Donne's best love-poetry than its wit, nothing like

> I wonder by my troth, what thou, and I
> Did, till we lov'd?

nothing like

> All other things, to their destruction draw,
> Only our love hath no decay;

nothing like

> So, so, breake off this last lamenting kisse.

Marvell's moralising in *On a Drop of Dew* is no less beautiful than Vaughan's moralising in *The Water-fall*, but he has nothing comparable with the intense vision of *The World* or the white ecstasy of *The Retreate* and of many another poem. Some of Marvell's descriptions and images have both the colour and the crystalline purity of Crashaw's, but although he lacks Crashaw's not infrequent mawkishness and sentimentality, he also lacks both his childlike tenderness and his rapture. He often equals Herbert in structure, but he has none of his passionate personal drama. In fact, the true relation between Marvell and the poets I have mentioned is that, while he cannot equal any of them in their special intensities, he can rival each and all of them in variety and breadth. This is partly because he is, in comparison with them, singularly uncommitted, or, as M. Sartre would say, *désengagé*. His poetry is, so to speak, the poetry of a temperament rather than of any urgent personal experience, but of a temperament in which nearly all the most attractive virtues of the first half of the seventeenth century seem to be combined. He is the seventeenth-century poet *par excellence*: in no other do so many of the characteristic qualities of seventeenth-century poetry appear together.

Although a study of the facts of his life tells us nothing about the motive-power of his poetry, the peculiar virtues of his poetry are, I think, closely connected with that uncommittedness and independence which are the most striking features of his biography.

He was born in 1621, the son of a Cambridge graduate who was rector of Winestead-in-Holderness, near Hull, and who was later elected Town's Preacher and Master of the Charterhouse by the corporation of the town. In 1633, at the age of twelve, he was matriculated as a sizar from Trinity College, Cambridge, but the only interesting fact we know about his university career is that about 1639 he was converted to Roman Catholicism until his father discovered him in a London bookshop and sent him back to Cambridge, where he seems to have remained until about 1641, at the beginning of which year his father was drowned. When, many years later, Milton recommended his appointment as his assistant in the Latin secretaryship, he told the Council that Marvell had spent four years abroad, in Holland, France, Italy and Spain; we do not know for certain when he left England, but it was almost certainly in 1642, at the very beginning of the Civil War, two years after Milton had returned from his travels to support that cause which Marvell, as he said later in *The Rehearsal Transpros'd*, thought 'too good to be fought for', either for or against.

He probably returned to England in 1646,[1] but between then and the beginning of his employment in the household of Thomas Lord Fairfax in Yorkshire, probably early in 1651, we know nothing of him except what we can infer from four datable poems. From these it would appear that although he was in no sense a partisan, his sympathies were on the whole royalist, aristocratic and anti-puritan, but that although he disliked Cromwell as a democrat and leveller and because of his associates, he could nevertheless feel a disinterested and, as it were, artistic admiration for him as a man of destiny. The earliest of these poems are the Commendatory Verses he contributed to Lovelace's *Lucasta*, a book which, though not published until 1649, was licensed in February 1647–8, and which, apparently, had not yet been licensed when Marvell wrote his poem. 'Our times', he begins,

> are much degenerate from those
> Which your sweet Muse which your fair Fortune chose. . . .
> These vertues now are banisht out of Towne,
> Our Civill Wars have lost the Civicke crowne.
> He highest builds, who with most Art destroys,
> And against others Fame his owne employs. . . .
> The barbed Censurers begin to looke
> Like the grim consistory on thy Booke;
> And on each line cast a reforming eye,
> Severer then the yong Presbytery.

Then there is the unique copy in the library of Worcester College of

1. 'He met Fleckno in Rome in Lent, and our knowledge of Fleckno's movements fixes the meeting to the Lent of either 1645 or 1646.' (H. M. Margoliouth, *Review of English Studies*, April 1941, p. 217). The recent discovery by Mr John P. Cutts (*TLS*, 8 August 1952), in a British Museum Additional Manuscript (31432) containing some society songs in the autograph of William Lawes, of a version of Marvell's *Thyrsis and Dorinda*, might lead some to favour 1645 as the date of Marvell's return to England, since William Lawes was killed at the siege of Chester in September of that year. Is there, though, much difficulty in supposing that Marvell had written this presumably earliest (and perhaps already somewhat corrupted) version of the least distinctively Marvellian of his pastoral dialogues before he left England in or about 1642? It is, in any case, the earliest of his poems that can be dated, if only by means of a *terminus ante quem*; and the fact that it was set by two other composers, John Gamble (*Ayres and Dialogues*, Second Book, 1659) and Matthew Locke (Playford's *Choice Ayres*, 1675), that it appeared in a seventeenth-century miscellany (*A Crew of Kind London Gossips*, 1663, p. 92), and that it exists in three manuscripts (Margoliouth, *Poems and Letters*, 1927, I 221 and letter to *TLS*, 19 May 1950), suggests that it had been fairly widely circulated in manuscript. Is not this, perhaps, more likely to have happened before than after that disruption of literary society which followed the outbreak of the Civil War?

the anonymous *Elegy upon the Death of Lord Francis Villiers*, post-humous son of George Villiers, first Duke of Buckingham, who was killed in a skirmish near Kingston-on-Thames in July 1648. The elegy is inscribed 'by Andrew Marvell' in the handwriting of that excellent authority and benefactor to many Oxford libraries, George Clarke, 1660–1736. It is not a remarkable poem and consists mainly of rather conventional eulogy, but the political sentiments of its author may be gauged from the lines in which he exclaims, apostrophising Fame:

> Much rather thou I know expectst to tell
> How heavy *Cromwell* gnasht the earth and fell.
> Or how slow Death farre from the sight of day
> The long-deceived *Fairfax* bore away.

Then, sometime in the early summer of 1650, he wrote the great and extraordinary poem *Horatian Ode upon Cromwell's Return from Ireland*. I call it extraordinary because of its complete detachment and uncommittedness. With only the barest allusion to that religious and ecclesiastical conflict which for Milton and so many others was of the very essence of the Civil War, without any profession of faith either in monarchy or in republicanism, Marvell contemplates the rise of Cromwell as disinterestedly—one might almost say, as artistically—as if he were contemplating some classic hero in the pages of Plutarch.[1] Although, as the evidence of the other poems suggests, he was at this time temperamentally a royalist, he is fascinated by what Goethe would have called the daemonic element in Cromwell, just as Goethe himself was fascinated by it in Napoleon. One might perhaps be tempted to say that his humanistic education, largely founded as it was on a study of antiquity in which history was made by individuals and in which the sheer power and magnitude of the Greek and Roman heroes played so great a part, had predisposed him to admire the sheer colossality, the sheer *virtù*, of Cromwell: one might be tempted to say so, did one not remember that all Marvell's educated contemporaries of either party had been nourished on a similar conception of history. At the same time it is certainly true, I think, that what might be called classic

---

1. Indeed, it has been plausibly suggested (see Margoliouth, I 237) that Marvell's description of Cromwell's 'industrious Valour' (l. 33) and his breaking the clouds like lightning (ll. 13–16) may have been partly inspired by Lucan's description, in the first book of the *Pharsalia*, of that other 'man of destiny', Julius Caesar, who, with 'restlesse valour', 'breakes through the wounded aire' like lightning, and that, here and there, Marvell's diction may owe something to the translation of Lucan's poem by the despised Tom May.

republicanism, 'the known rules of ancient liberty', played no small
part in the formation of Milton's political views. Some eighteen months
before Marvell's Ode, in the *Tenure of Kings and Magistrates*, published
in February 1649, a fortnight after the King's execution, Milton had
defended those whom he regarded as tyrannicides with something
very like the dangerous argument that might is right. He exhorts
those who were beginning to tremble at what they had done as though
it were some great sin, and who were disputing precedents, forms, and
circumstances when the Commonwealth was nigh perishing for want
of deeds, 'not to startle from the just and pious resolution of adhering,
with all their strength and assistance, to the present parliament and
army, in the glorious way wherein justice and victory hath set them—
the only warrants through all ages, next under immediate revelation,
to exercise supreme power'—a parenthesis which comes very near
to saying that what is just is what is victorious and that what is victorious is what is just.[1] Milton then proceeds to declare, a page or
two later, no longer parenthetically but explicitly, that 'if all human
power to execute, not accidentally but intendedly, the wrath of God
upon evil-doers without exception, be of God; then that power,
whether ordinary, or if that fail, extraordinary, so executing that intent of God, is lawful, and not to be resisted'.[2] In Milton's defence it
might be pleaded that he was so convinced that Charles was a wicked
and malignant tyrant that he could not but assume that Cromwell,
his destroyer, was the instrument of God. Marvell's admiration for
Cromwell as a kind of superman, beyond good and evil, springs from
no such religious conviction or righteous indignation: it is, as I have
said, quite disinterested, and, as it were, aesthetic; it is as though he were
sitting in a theatre enjoying the performance of some tremendous
drama.

> 'Tis Madness to resist or blame
> The force of angry Heavens flame:
>   And, if we would speak true,
>   Much to the Man is due.
> Who, from his private Gardens, where
> He liv'd reserved and austere,
>   As if his highest plot
>   To plant the Bergamot,
> Could by industrious Valour climbe
> To ruine the great Work of Time,

1. Bohn's edn., II 5.   2. *op. cit.*, 8.

> And cast the Kingdome old
> Into another Mold.
> Though Justice against Fate complain,
> And plead the antient Rights in vain:
> But those do hold or break
> As Men are strong or weak.
> Nature that hateth emptiness,
> Allows of penetration less:
> And therefore must make room
> Where greater Spirits come.[1]

Marvell proceeds to suggest that Cromwell deliberately caused Charles to take flight in order to entrap him, and he appreciates this Macchiavellian stroke of 'policy',[2] as his contemporaries would have called it, with the same connoisseurship as he does the dignified bearing of Cromwell's victim upon the scaffold.

> And *Hampton* shows what part
> He had of wiser Art.
> Where, twining subtile fears with hope,
> He wove a Net of such a scope,
> That *Charles* himself might chase
> To *Caresbrooks* narrow case.
> That thence the *Royal Actor* born
> The *Tragick Scaffold* might adorn:
> While round the armed Bands
> Did clap their bloody hands.
> *He* nothing common did or mean
> Upon that memorable Scene:
> But with his keener Eye
> The Axes edge did try:
> Nor call'd the *Gods* with vulgar spight
> To vindicate his helpless Right,
> But bow'd his comely Head,
> Down as upon a Bed.[3]

---

1. *Horatian Ode upon Cromwell's Return from Ireland*, ll. 25–44.

2. In this connexion it is worth recalling that on 15 August 1656 James Scudamore, writing from Saumur, mentioned that among the English residents there was Cromwell's ward William Dutton, 'whose Governour is one Mervill, a notable English Italo-Machavillian'. (Letter to *TLS* from Elsie Elizabeth Duncan-Jones, 2 December 1949.)

3. ll. 47–64.

The fact that, although Marvell could admire Cromwell's career aesthetically, he still detested him and his followers politically, is proved by his verses on *Tom May's Death*, which cannot have been written before the middle of November 1650, that is to say, about five or six months after the *Horatian Ode*. 'Thomas May, 1595–1650, playwright, poet, historian, and translator of Lucan, made his reputation at the court of Charles I, and later attached himself to the Parliamentary cause, holding employment under the House of Commons. It appears that he had hoped to succeed Ben Jonson as poet laureate in 1637, and it was to chagrin at the appointment of Davenant that his enemies attributed the change in his political position.'[1] He died on 13 November 1650. According to Wood, 'going well to bed, he was therein found next morning dead, occasioned, as some say, by tying his nightcap too close under his fat chin and cheeks, which choked him when he turned on the other side.' Marvell gives a different explanation:

> As one put drunk into the Packet-boat,
> *Tom May* was hurry'd hence and did not know't.

The Council of State ordered him to be buried in Westminster Abbey, and Marvell makes the shade of Ben Jonson express bitter indignation at the intrusion of this 'Most servil' wit, and Mercenary Pen' into the company of Chaucer and Spenser.

> When the Sword glitters ore the Judges head,
> And fear has Coward Churchmen silenced,
> Then is the Poets time, 'tis then he drawes,
> And single fights forsaken Vertues cause.
> He, when the wheel of Empire, whirleth back,
> And though the World's disjointed Axel crack,
> Sings still of ancient Rights and better Times,
> Seeks wretched good, arraigns successful Crimes.
> But thou base man first prostituted hast
> Our spotless knowledge and the studies chast.
> Apostatizing from our Arts and us,
> To turn the Chronicler to *Spartacus*.[2]

Here Marvell condemns May as a hireling for not defending those 'ancient rights' which in the *Horatian Ode* Justice had vainly pleaded against Fate, and contemptuously refers to Cromwell, whom May had celebrated in his *Blessing of the History of the Parliament of England*

1. Margoliouth, I 239.   2. ll. 63–74.

(1650), as Spartacus, the leader of the revolting Roman slaves—Cromwell whom Marvell himself, a few months earlier, had celebrated as the Man of Destiny.

In the letter which he wrote to Bradshaw, President of the Council of State, in February 1652-3, recommending Marvell as his assistant in the Secretaryship for Foreign Tongues, Milton declared that he 'comes now lately out of the house of the Lord Fairfax, who was a Generall, where he was entrusted to give some instructions in the languages to the Lady, his daughter'. Thomas, third Baron Fairfax, was appointed Commander-in-Chief on 12 June 1650, with Cromwell, who had returned from Ireland, as his Lieutenant-General; but being unwilling to lead an attack on Scotland unless provoked by an invasion, Fairfax almost immediately resigned the Command and retired to his estate in Yorkshire. Although only thirty-eight he was now compelled by his wounds, an intermittent pain, and the gout to lead a sedentary life. He did not forget that he was a great-nephew of Edward Fairfax the translator of Tasso; he had received a good education, and he spent his time translating and writing verses. The internal evidence of his poems[1] suggests that it was early in 1651 that Marvell joined this household from which, in February 1653, exactly two years later, he had, as Milton wrote to Bradshaw, lately come. Lord Fairfax's daughter Mary, to whom he acted as tutor, was only thirteen when he first came there and did not, one may imagine, make very exacting demands upon his time. It was during these two years of leisure and detachment, among scenes that he loved and in the society of his cultured patron, that Marvell probably wrote almost the whole of the small body of poetry for which he is now chiefly remembered.

By 1653 the delights of retirement began to pall, and the formerly so detached and spectatorial Marvell sought for a post in the service of the Commonwealth. He had now become an ardent republican, and in his *Character of Holland* describes the new state as 'Darling of Heaven, and of Men the Care'. Milton's first recommendation for him for appointment as his colleague in the Latin Secretaryship was unsuccessful, but succeeded in 1657, after Marvell had acted for some time as tutor to one of Cromwell's wards, residing for the purpose mainly in the house of the Puritan divine John Oxenbridge, a fellow of Eton, who had twice visited the Bermudas. In 1655 he published anonymously his poem on *The First Anniversary of the Government under his Highness the Lord Protector*, which breathes unbounded admiration for Cromwell

1. See Margoliouth's note on *Epigramma in Duos Montes, Poems and Letters*, I 229.

and complete confidence in his government, and after Cromwell's death he gave the same unwavering support to his son Richard. He was elected M.P. for Hull in Richard Cromwell's parliament (1659) and continued to represent the constituency until his death in 1678, but his political influence was due far more to his writings, both in verse and prose, than to his action in parliament. In a number of satires and pamphlets which were famous in their day he attacked the Court and the bishops, championed the dissenters, cried 'No-popery' with Shaftesbury and the Whigs, and held up the republics of Rome and Venice as patterns to England.

Perhaps no great poet—and I think he deserves to be called a great poet—seems to have been so little influenced by any other motive than the sheer love of writing poetry. He published, or allowed to be published, only three or four quite inconsiderable poems during his lifetime, and only his later political satires seem to have circulated at all extensively in manuscript. It may well be that, with the exception of *A Dialogue between Thyrsis and Dorinda*,[1] all the beautiful earlier poems would have been irrecoverably lost but for Marvell's housekeeper: after his death she took all the manuscripts she could find to a printer, passed herself off as Marvell's widow, and, let us hope, made a little money. Even so, the volume of *Miscellaneous Poems* published in 1681 seems to have passed almost unnoticed. Professor Pierre Legouis, a most industrious researcher, was able to discover only two brief allusions to Marvell as a poet during the whole of the eighteenth century, one in a private letter and one in a lecture on physiognomy.[2] Until well on in the nineteenth century it was not as a poet but as a politician, as an opponent of the Court and a champion of liberty, that

1. Which has survived in two MSS. (BM Additional MS 29921 and Rawlinson Poet. MS 81) and among the 'Ingenious Poems' added to *A Crew of Kind London Gossips*, 1663 (a reprint of S. Rowlands's *A Whole Crew of Kind Gossips*, 1609), pp. 92–4.

2. Later, in *RES*, X (1934), 447–50, Professor Legouis showed that Addison had borrowed, without acknowledgement, from Marvell's *Coy Mistress* and that he was therefore presumably acquainted with the whole of the 1681 folio. In *Spectator* 89 (12 June 1711) Addison has an amusing paper on those whom he calls 'demurrers', women 'who are for spinning out the time of courtship to an immoderate length'. The paper as a whole is characteristically Addisonian, and were it not for a couple of sentences towards the end it would have been impossible to maintain with any confidence that the original inspiration had come from Marvell. These sentences, however, are decisive: 'Were the age of man the same that it was before the flood, a lady might sacrifice half a century to a scruple, and be two or three ages in demurring. Had she nine hundred years good, she might hold out to the conversion of the *Jews* before she thought fit to be prevailed upon.'

Marvell was remembered. It was not until 1801 that two poems of his, in abridged and expurgated versions, appeared in an anthology, and the earliest known appreciation of him as a poet, a very brief one, was written in 1806 by Bowles in a note in his edition of Pope.[1] He was in fact, like Herrick, one of those neglected earlier poets whom the nineteenth century rediscovered, and the three men who played the

1. [This account of Marvell's reputation in the eighteenth century needs qualification. It is true that he was remembered chiefly as a politician and a controversialist, but his non-satirical poems were not entirely neglected. In the bibliography of his *André Marvell: poète, puritain, patriote*, which seems to have been compiled after the book itself was completed, Professor Legouis draws attention (p. 472) to a selection from the poems in the first two volumes of the last edition of *Dryden's Miscellanies* (1727). This consists of *The Nymph, Young Love, Daphnis and Chloe, Damon the Mower, Ametas and Thestylis* (a poem from which Johnson quotes in his *Dictionary* under the word *nor*), *Musicks Empire, The Garden, On Mr Milton's Paradise Lost*, and *Senec. Traged. ex Thyeste Chor*. 2. *Translated. The Nymph, Daphnis and Chloe*, and *The Garden* were not published entire, as Thomas Cooke, Marvell's first editor, pointed out in the preface to his two-volume edition published the same year. It is clear that Cooke was principally interested in the satirical poems: apart from the poem on *Paradise Lost*, he specially commends only *On Blood's stealing the Crown* and *A Dialogue between two Horses*; but he allows that there are few of Marvell's poems 'which have not something pleasing in them, and some he must be allowed to have excelled in. Most of them seem to be the effect of a lively genius, and manly sense, but at the same time seem to want that correctness he was capable of making.'

Cooke's edition was reprinted in 1772. Four years later appeared *The Works of Andrew Marvell, Esq. . . . with a new life of the author*, by Capt. Edward Thompson, in three quarto volumes. This is primarily an edition of Marvell's writings in prose, but it may be claimed that for all its deficiencies the half-volume containing the poems is still the most sumptuous edition of them we possess. Thompson was an enthusiast. He discovered in the poems 'the warm effusions of a lively fancy', found *To his Coy Mistress* 'sweet, natural and easy', drew attention to *The Gallery* and *Thyrsis and Dorinda*, and considered 'the English language does not boast a more elegant elegiach poem' than *A Poem upon the Death of Oliver Cromwell*. Thompson furthermore was the first editor to give currency to the *Horatian Ode upon Cromwell's Return from Ireland*, which had previously appeared only on cancelled leaves of the 1681 folio.

Marvell ('a witty droll in the seventeenth century') is accorded five double-column folio pages in the fifth volume of *Biographia Britannica* (1760). His poems are mentioned, but none is singled out for critical attention. More significant of his reputation as a poet is his inclusion in *The Lives of the Poets of Great Britain and Ireland* (vol. IV, 1753), attributed to Theophilus Cibber, but in fact the work of Robert Shiels. The account covers twenty-one pages. As was to be expected, the source of this life was Cooke's biography and the emphasis was placed on the witty controversialist; but of the two poems quoted one is *A Dialogue between the Resolved Soul and Created Pleasure*, and that this was not a mere random choice is shown by the prefatory remarks: 'It is written with a true spirit of poetry, the numbers are various, and harmonious, and is one of the best pieces, in the serious way, of which he is author.' This does not amount to fame, but it falls short of total disrepute. (This note had gone to press before the publication of Professor Legouis' *Andrew Marvell: Poet, Puritan, Patriot*, Oxford, 1965. See Chapter VIII, 'After Death'.) J.B.]

chief part in that rediscovery, who put him, so to speak, on the map, were, it is pleasant to recall, Lamb, Tennyson and Palgrave. It was probably Tennyson, whose knowledge of our older poets was both wide and discerning, who communicated his admiration for Marvell to Palgrave, and led him to include the *Horatian Ode*, *The Garden* and *The Bermudas* in the *Golden Treasury*. Tennyson particularly admired *To his Coy Mistress*, and Palgrave greatly regretted that Victorian prudery made it impossible for him to include that too.[1]

It was, I have said, during the two halcyon years he spent with the Lord General Fairfax in Yorkshire that Marvell probably wrote almost the whole of that small body of poetry by which he is now chiefly remembered. And, so far as we can tell, he wrote it for no other reason and from no other motive than to please himself and Fairfax. It was a combination of circumstances no less fortunate than that which brought Wordsworth and Coleridge together during 1797 and 1798, and a literary partnership no less fruitful, if much more one-sided. The more one considers it, the more astonishing and admirable, and yet, at the same time, the more characteristic and appropriate it seems—the fact that some of the most beautiful seventeenth-century poetry should have been written as a result of the chance encounter of two cultivated gentlemen in remote Yorkshire country houses while the Civil War was raging in the world outside.

> How with such rage shall beauty hold a plea,
> Whose action is no stronger than a flower?

But beauty did. And perhaps the example should lead us to reflect a little upon the concepts of doing good, doing one's duty, and (as Dr Johnson declared it was a writer's duty to do) leaving the world better than one found it. For while one can say with complete certainty and without any fear of contradiction that the world is the better for the possession of Marvell's poetry, it would perhaps be very difficult to maintain that it either was or is the better for his later political and satirical activities. By the generations for whom Charles II was first and foremost a reprobate, a creature of the French King, and a concealed Papist, Marvell was remembered as a great patriot and champion of Civil Liberty, but to many who have studied more carefully the

---

1. [See further Colin J. Horne, 'Palgrave's "Golden Treasury"', in *English Studies* 1949, p. 60, and Kathleen Tillotson, 'Donne's Poetry in the Nineteenth Century', in *Elizabethan and Jacobean Studies Presented to Frank Percy Wilson* (1959), p. 322. J.B.]

political history of those years his post-Restoration activities may appear
as in many respects rather philistine and ill-informed. We may indeed
honour Marvell (as we honour Milton) for defending what he *believed*
to be the cause of liberty, but we may be permitted to murmur with
Hölderlin

> Was bleibet aber, stiften die Dichter,
>
> ('That which remains is the gift of poets.')

And for those who are still inclined to speak of the later seventeenth and
of the eighteenth century as an Age of Prose and Reason, and who, in
spite of all that can be and all that in recent times has been said in favour
of that age and of its literature, are still inclined to regret the depersonal-
isation of its poetry and what seems to them its excessive preoccupation
with man in his political and social capacity, there will always remain
something sadly symbolic about the career of Marvell. The poetry he
wrote round about 1650 may be regarded as one of the finest flowers
of a culture, a civilisation, which vanished after the Civil War.[1] Those
poets who, from Donne onwards, were content, usually without any
thought of publication, to write for their own pleasure and to circulate
their poems in manuscript among their friends, may often, as it seems
to us, have set too high a value upon mere ingenuity and mere clever-
ness, but about their practice of poetry there was a disinterestedness
and a detachment which it is impossible not to admire. They communicated, they did not preach and lecture at one another. What Mr Eliot
called 'a dissociation of sensibility' was really, I think, as one can see
so clearly both with Marvell and with his friend Milton, a result of the
constricting and dehumanising influence of party politics. It was
during the Restoration period that the sharp distinction between serious
and light poetry really began: Dryden's satires on the one hand, the
lyrics of Rochester and Sedley on the other. The serious business of the
poet was to expose knaves and fools, to represent the continuance
of civilisation as being dependent on either the government or the
opposition, or, it might be, on the poet himself and a few of his friends;
to attack Whigs or Tories, Papists or dissenters, Scotsmen, Irishmen,
Welshmen, Frenchmen, placemen, proud gamesters, the vulgar rich,
affected women, pedants, Grub-street authors—in fact, to be perpetually finding somebody or something to abuse, although in his
lighter moments he might condescend to address playful verses to a

---

1. [It is argued in a later chapter that some of this poetry may have been written
after the Restoration (see pp. 113-14). This passage might therefore have been
revised when the author came to reconsider it. J.B.]

member of the Fair Sex. Sir Herbert Grierson's remark that 'Milton's whole thought was too polemical in character to attain satisfying wisdom'[1] is one that applies to many later poets. In recent times a good case has been made out for the variety of Pope's poetry, for his sensibility and for his sense of beauty, and there is much in Dr Leavis's contention that he has as much claim to be regarded as the last poet of the seventeenth century as the first of the eighteenth. Nevertheless, the fact remains that for the attainment of satisfying wisdom Pope's mind, or, what amounts to the same thing, his mind under the influence of his time, was too polemical, too much like that of Mrs Coleridge, which, as her husband complained, 'in all disputes uniformly *projects itself forth* to recriminate, instead of turning itself inward with a silent self-questioning'. Pope, in fact, like so many post-Restoration poets, and in contrast to the earlier Marvell, and, one may add, the earlier Milton, devotes a disproportionate attention to matters which wisdom would dismiss with, at the most, a weary smile. Perhaps one of the chief problems for a poet, at any rate for a great, or potentially great, poet, is to achieve a sufficiently detached and philosophic attitude towards those whom Shakespeare on a certain occasion referred to as 'all these'.[2] About even Pope, let alone about Dryden, one feels that 'all these' were too much with him. Those whom we may call the manuscript poets of the earlier seventeenth century wrote as though 'all these' did not exist—or, at any rate, as though they were habitually aware of the existence only of cultivated contemporaries like themselves, who shared their own disinterested interest in wit and poetry and the act of making something out of nothing, or almost nothing. These brilliant amateurs knew of no sharp and, as one may be tempted to say, rather priggish and self-righteous distinction between 'pure description' and 'moralised song', and under such blissfully favourable conditions even quite minor poets occasionally wrote exquisite verse. But by the end of the Civil Wars these little academes and demi-paradises had been dissolved. Pope, indeed, had a garden and a real capacity to enjoy it, but he was distracted by a perpetual awareness of 'all these' strutting and fretting outside the gate, or even looking over the hedge. It was too much for him—he 'stoop'd to Truth and moralis'd his Song'.

Let us now try to analyse some of the peculiar virtues of those poems which Marvell wrote before 'all these' became too much with him. That detachment and uncommittedness which so distinguishes his

1. *Criticism and Creation*, 1950, p. 45.
2. 'Tired with all these, for restful death I cry.'

pre-republican phase also seems to be one of the most remarkable characteristics of his poetry. I have already remarked that the passionate intensity, the passionate vision, the tenderness, the ecstasy of Donne and Herbert, Vaughan and Crashaw, are absent from his poetry. It is also very seldom that he is so wholly serious as Donne is in his best love-poetry, or as Herbert, Vaughan and Crashaw almost always are— perhaps only in his verses *On a Drop of Dew* and in the *Dialogue between the Resolved Soul, and Created Pleasure*. On the other hand, he is never so wholly unserious, so sheerly and merely witty, as Donne often is. A certain balance between seriousness and light-heartedness, between gravity and wit, distinguishes nearly all his poems. Dr Johnson, who complained that he could not see that Gray's *Bard* promoted any truth, moral or political, would scarcely have known what to make of them. In a sense, most of them are exquisite trifles, but they are very far from trivial. *The Definition of Love*, like so many of Donne's poems, is a continuous piece of argument: so, too, is *To his Coy Mistress*, where, indeed, the argument is almost syllogistic in form: 'If we had time, I could court you at leisure; But our life only lasts for a moment; Therefore in order to live we must seize the moment as it flies.' The high-spirited exaggeration is also like Donne:

> I would
> Love you ten years before the Flood:
> And you should if you please refuse
> Till the Conversion of the *Jews*.
> My vegetable Love should grow
> Vaster than Empires, and more slow.

Like Donne, and yet also like Dryden. Sometimes when reading Marvell I almost feel that I am reading a more sensitive, a more essentially poetic Dryden: there is that same masculinity which Hopkins praised, that same stress on the naked thew and sinew of the English language, and something of the same 'long majestic march and energy divine'. Something, too, which suggests how delicately and precariously balanced, how easily oversettable, was that peculiar combination of qualities which makes Marvell's best poety what it is. Consider *The Character of Holland*, which he probably wrote in February 1653, just after he had left Nunappleton and had become a whole-hearted supporter of the Commonwealth and of that very unjust and unnecessary war with Holland for which the City merchants had clamoured.

Holland, that scarce deserves the name of Land,
As but th'Off-scouring of the Brittish Sand;
And so much Earth as was contributed
By English Pilots when they heav'd the Lead;
Or what by th'Oceans slow alluvion fell,
Of shipwrackt Cockle and the Muscle-shell;
This indigested vomit of the Sea
Fell to the Dutch by just Propriety.

   Glad then, as Miners that have found the Oar,
They with mad labour fish'd the Land to Shoar;
And div'd as desperately for each piece
Of Earth, as if't had been of Ambergreece;
Collecting anxiously small Loads of Clay,
Less then what building Swallows bear away;
Or then those Pills which sordid Beetles roul,
Transfusing into them their Dunghil Soul.

   How did they rivet, with Gigantick Piles,
Thorough the Center their new-catched Miles;
And to the stake a strugling Country bound,
Where barking Waves still bait the forced Ground;
Building their watry Babel far more high
To reach the Sea, then those to scale the Sky.

   Yet still his claim the Injur'd Ocean laid,
And oft at Leap-frog ore their Steeples plaid:
As if on purpose it on Land had come
To shew them what's their Mare Liberum.[1]
A daily deluge over them does boyl;
The Earth and Water play at Level-coyl;[2]
The Fish oft-times the Burger dispossest,
And sat not as a Meat but as a Guest;[3]

---

1. 'The title of a book by Grotius published in 1609. It was written against the Portuguese claim to private possession of Eastern waters; the doctrine gained importance later in the disputes between England and Holland about the English Channel. Selden in Mare Clausum (1632) set out to refute Grotius's doctrine of the freedom of the seas. The Commonwealth Government claimed the Channel as British, and required foreign ships to salute the English flag.' (Margoliouth)

2. Lève-cul, 'hitch-buttock', which OED defines as 'a rough, noisy game, formerly played at Christmas, in which each player is in turn driven from his seat and supplanted by another'.

3. Was Marvell here profanely appropriating and satirically applying to Holland an ingenious fancy which Donne had delivered from a pulpit in Holland? It occurs at the conclusion of the second of the two sermons into which Donne, as he said,

And oft the *Tritons* and the *Sea-Nymphs* saw
Whole sholes of *Dutch* serv'd up for *Cabillau*;[1]
Or as they over the new Level rang'd
For pickled *Herring*, pickled *Heeren* chang'd.
Nature, it seem'd, asham'd of her mistake,
Would throw their Land away at *Duck* and *Drake*.

This, the most brilliant and readable of all Marvell's political satires, is still more obviously like Dryden, the so often burlesque and lampooning Dryden of *Mac Flecknoe* and of certain passages in the Satires. It may be compared, for example, with the following passage from *Absalom and Achitophel*, describing, under the name of Shimei, a certain Sheriff Bethel:

If any leisure time he had from Power,
(Because 'tis Sin to misimploy an hour;)
His bus'ness was by Writing, to Persuade,
That Kings were Useless, and a Clog to Trade:
And, that his noble Stile he might refine,
No *Rechabite* more shund the fumes of Wine.
Chaste were his Cellars, and his Shrieval Board
The Grossness of a City Feast abhor'd:
His Cooks, with long disuse, their Trade forgot;
Cool was his Kitchen, tho his Brains were hot.
Such frugal Vertue Malice may accuse;
But sure 'twas necessary to the *Jews*:
For Towns once burnt, such Magistrates require
As dare not tempt Gods Providence by fire.
With Spiritual food he fed his Servants well,
But free from flesh, that made the *Jews* Rebel:
And *Moses*'s Laws he held in more account,
For forty days of Fasting in the Mount.[2]

'digested' what must have been the enormously long sermon he had preached at the Hague on 19 December 1619 on St Matthew's verses about the Calling of Simon and Andrew to be fishers of men: 'This is the net, with which if yee be willing to bee caught, that is, to lay downe all your hopes and affiances in the gracious promises of his Gospel, then you are fishes reserved for that great Mariage-feast, which is the Kingdome of heaven; where, whosoever is a dish, is a ghest too; whosoever is served in at the table, sits at the table; whosoever is caught by this net, is called to this feast.' (*The Sermons of John Donne*, ed. Potter and Simpson, II 309–10. The two Hague sermons had been printed in *LXXX Sermons*, 1640.)
   1. Dutch *Kabeljauw* (French *cabillaud*), cod-fish.
   2. First Part, ll. 612–29.

In *The Character of Holland* that intellectual robustness and toughness which we are nearly always aware of beneath the exquisitely graceful and artificial surface of Marvell's poetry here suddenly emerges, just as, though in a more serious and distinguished manner, it does in the *Horatian Ode*. But *The Character of Holland* also suggests that even in the Marvell of *Appleton House*, of *The Garden*, of *To his Coy Mistress* there was potentially present a much cruder and more limited kind of poet, a mere political satirist and lampooner. After the Restoration Marvell turned to satire: there is no positive proof that he had written all his non-satirical poems, his trifles, as he had perhaps now come to regard them, before then, but it seems reasonable to suppose that he had. His satires have their moments, but they do not, I think, contain anything so good or so memorable of its kind as those lines I have quoted from *The Character of Holland*, and they cannot be compared with Dryden's. The thought suggests itself: had Marvell been born some twenty years later, had he missed the particular social and intellectual climate in which he grew up, had he been the exact contemporary of Dryden, would he have reached no higher poetical rank than that of a second-rate satirist? Professor George Williamson has said of him that

> Compared with a poet like Milton, who created his own literary medium, Marvell is a supreme example of the poet who discovers his talent in the current of a literary tradition.[1]

One might amplify this statement. One might declare that Marvell, unlike Milton, and like so many poets of the earlier seventeenth century, was a brilliant amateur, one of the many for whom the writing of poetry was almost as much a social as a purely literary activity, and that the kind of poetry which had been, and to some extent still was being, written and circulated around him largely determined the kind of poetry which he himself wrote. Perhaps the only poems of Milton which may be regarded as belonging in some degree to this tradition of social and amateur poetry are his two most characteristically seventeenth-century poems, *L'Allegro* and *Il Penseroso*, and, as I shall suggest later, it seems not improbable that a reading of them in the 1645 volume may have had no inconsiderable influence on some of Marvell's poetry. For Milton, though, these and other earlier poems were but a kind of *parerga*. It was not on the taste and practice of his cultivated contemporaries, but on the Latin and Greek classics and their

1. *The Donne Tradition*, Cambridge, Mass., 1930, p. 151.

Italian imitators and interpreters that his eyes were really fixed, and, in spite of his political preoccupations during the Commonwealth, after the Restoration he did not, like Marvell, turn to satire but returned to the heroic poem. Although he had made some concessions, and although many have wished that he had made more, poetry had never been for him, as it had been for those whom we may most appropriately refer to as the manuscript poets, and as it was, I suppose, for many Chinese and Japanese poets, a kind of refined pleasure, a gentlemanly accomplishment, a social grace. Intense literary ambition and moral ardour had been and remained his driving forces. He had no inclination to murmur, consciously or subconsciously, '*Nous n'irons plus au bois, les lauriers sont coupés.*' It is unprofitable to attempt to explain or interpret Milton's poetry, or, perhaps, that of any poet of Milton's eminence in terms of the Spirit of the Age. On the other hand, Marvell's earlier poetry, like that of the manuscript poets in general, was the result of a partnership between the poet and a particular social and cultural tradition which vanished after the Restoration.[1] Never in England has there been a time when poetry, even the practice of poetry, was so much part of the education and accomplishments of a gentleman. In the Preface to his reprint of that agreeable minor poet William Hammond, who was born in 1614, who published his poems in 1655, and who was the uncle of another agreeable minor poet and notable classical scholar, Thomas Stanley[2]—in his Preface to this reprint Sir Egerton Brydges remarked that 'a laudable spirit of literature seems then to have prevailed among the gentilitial families' of Kent; and, after naming some of them, he continued: 'The effects of example are so obvious, that it is easy to account for this honourable ambition having been so generally spread in a narrow neighbourhood when once excited. It seems to have expired with that generation; and I know not that it ever revived again.' But, as the numerous manuscript collections reveal, it was not only in Kent that such poetical circles were to be found, and we have already devoted some attention to a very small but very notable circle in Yorkshire. It is true that after the Restoration there was a mob of gentlemen who wrote with ease, but they were gentlemen of a different kind, gentlemen, many of them, who had returned from an uncomfortable exile and were now mainly intent upon having a good

---

1. [See note 1, p. 21]

2. Stanley's tutor had been William Fairfax, eldest son of the translator of Tasso. The Lord General wrote a poem 'Upon Mr Stanley's Booke of Philosophers supposing itt the worke of his Tutor W: Fa:' (Bodleian MS Fairfax 40, p. 611).

time. They lacked the stable background, the courtly and scholarly tradition, the controlling awareness of an ideal which had made their predecessors what they were. They tended, in comparison, to be mere men of fashion, mere men of wit and pleasure about town, distinguished for the wild debauchery and quickness of wit in repartee which for Dryden seem to have been inseparably connected with the idea of a gentleman, and which, as he said, Beaumont and Fletcher imitated far better than Shakespeare. It might perhaps be pleaded in Pope's defence that he longed for that ideal community in and out of which so many of the earlier seventeenth-century poets had written, and that it was the painful contrast between the ideal and the actual which drove him to satire. For the manuscript poets and their readers there had been, mainly, one another; for Pope, and, we may add, for Swift, there were, almost overpoweringly, 'all these'.

A PRELIMINARY SURVEY
OF MARVELL'S POETRY

The small collection of Marvell's non-satirical poetry, most of which was probably seen only by a few of his intimate friends and which has reached us almost by accident, is perhaps the most remarkable example we have of the interaction between what Mr Eliot, in a famous phrase, called Tradition and the Individual Talent. For, although Marvell's poetry is highly original and, at its best, unmistakably his own and no one else's, he is almost always acting upon hints and suggestions provided by earlier poets, and almost never writing entirely, as children would say, out of his own head. When he returned from his foreign travels in (as is probable) 1646, he seems to have bought and read attentively many of those notable volumes of verse by living or recently deceased poets which, from 1640 onwards, appeared in such rapid succession, often from the press of that most enterprising of publishers Humphrey Moseley. Particular borrowings or imitations prove that he had read (I mention them in order of publication) Carew's *Poems* (1640, 1642, 1651), Waller's *Poems* (1645), *The Poems of Mr John Milton* (1645), Crashaw's *Steps to the Temple* (1646, 1648), Cowley's *The Mistress* (1647), Cleveland's *Poems* (1647 and 1651), Lovelace's *Lucasta* (1649), and Davenant's *Gondibert* (1651). These and other poets, including the Ancients, were continually suggesting to Marvell new and amusing things to do. And how remarkable, considering the comparatively small number of his poems, is their variety! There is something in almost every one of them that recalls some other seventeenth-century poet, and yet perhaps no single one of them is really like a poem by anyone else.

How did Marvell begin? There are a few commendatory, elegiac, satirical, and political poems, all of them, except the great *Horatian Ode*, in the heroic couplet, and all of them, except for that ode, of small intrinsic importance, which can be assigned, because of their allusions to public events, to various dates between 1646 and 1650. When, though, we come to the unpublic, the lyrical, reflective, or descriptive poems, we have almost no external evidence to help us. A recently discovered manuscript proves that the pastoral *Dialogue between Thyrsis and Dorinda* must have been written before September 1645, and therefore probably before Marvell set out on his foreign travels in or about 1642. Since 'little T.C.' in *The Picture of little T.C. in a Prospect of Flowers* was probably, as Margoliouth suggested, the second Theophila Cornewall, who was baptised on 26 September 1644, that poem must have been written at some time after Marvell's return from his travels in or about 1646. It is impossible not to suppose that the poems *Upon the Hill and Grove at Bill-borow* and *Upon Appleton House*, both dedicated 'To the Lord Fairfax', and *Musicks Empire*, in which Fairfax is seemingly evoked in the last stanza, were written during the two years, 1651 to 1653, which Marvell spent with the retired Lord General at his estate of Nunappleton in Yorkshire, as tutor to his young daughter Mary. And it seems reasonable to suppose that the poem *Bermudas* was written some time after July 1653, when Marvell, together with his pupil, Cromwell's ward William Dutton, began his residence with John Oxenbridge, Fellow of Eton College, who had twice visited those islands. These, I think, are the only private poems for whose dates there is any kind of external evidence. I myself am inclined to believe that nearly all the best of what it seems convenient to call Marvell's private poems were written during those two years at Nunappleton, when he had infinite leisure and the society of a friend and patron who was both a lover of poetry and, in a small way, a poet himself. The affinity between *The Garden* and the poem on Appleton House is obvious, and it is difficult not to associate the predominantly pastoral or descriptive element in many other poems with Marvell's residence at Nunappleton: more important, though, as a common characteristic is that maturity and security which is equally apparent in poems otherwise so different as the *Horatian Ode*, *The Definition of Love*, *To his Coy Mistress*, *The Picture of Little T.C. in a Prospect of Flowers*, the Mower poems, *On a Drop of Dew*. I need not prolong the list: apart from certain careless amateurishnesses—an excessive use of inversion for the sake of rhyme, an excessive use of expletives such as 'do', 'did' and 'doth' to supply syllables—of which he never rid himself, one feels that in all these poems, and in those which seem to belong with them, Marvell knew exactly what he wanted to do before he began to write, and that in each poem he has completely realised his intention. I myself seem to be aware almost of a difference in kind between their assuredness, their maturity and security, their unmistakable Marvellianism, and what, in comparison, seems, at worst, the uncontrolled extravagance and, at best, the less characteristically individualised traditionality of nine poems which stand rather apart from the rest. Three of these poems, the pastoral dialogues *Clorinda and Damon* and *Thyrsis and Dorinda* and *A Dialogue Between the Resolved Soul, and Created Pleasure*, are agreeable and not specially characteristic essays in that popular musical form the dialogue, or, as we should call it, the duet. *Thyrsis and Dorinda*, which, as we have seen, was probably written before Marvell set out on his foreign travels in or about 1642, was no less than three times set to music, and it seems likely that the other two dialogues were written for the same purpose. In *Thyrsis and Dorinda* and *Clorinda and Damon* it is hard to detect anything specifically Marvellian or beyond the reach of dozens of minor seventeenth-century poets; and although *A Dialogue Between the Resolved Soul, and Created Pleasure*[1] is a much finer

1. Two resemblances in this poem to passages in *Paradise Lost* suggest that it may have been written after reading that poem in manuscript or print:

ll. 14–16, where Pleasure hails the Soul as 'Lord of Earth, and Heavens Heir', and bids it 'lay aside that Warlike Crest'

> And of Nature's banquet share:
> Where the Souls of fruits and flow'rs
> Stand prepar'd to heighten yours:

cf. *PL*, V 482–7 (Raphael to Adam):

> flowrs and thir fruit
> Mans nourishment, by gradual scale sublim'd
> To vital Spirits aspire, to animal,
> To intellectual, give both life and sense,
> Fancie and understanding, when the Soule
> Reason receives, and reason is her being.

ll. 51–4 (Pleasure to the Soul):

> All this fair, and soft, and sweet,
> Which scatteringly doth shine,
> Shall within one Beauty meet,
> And she be only thine:

cf. *PL*, IX 602–9 (Satan to Eve):

> Thenceforth to Speculations high or deep
> I turnd my thoughts, and with capacious mind
> Considerd all things visible in Heav'n
> Or Earth or Middle, all things fair and good;
> But all that fair and good in thy Divine
> Semblance, and in thy Beautys heav'nly Ray
> United I beheld; no Fair to thine
> Equivalent or second.

Although the resemblances are not so detailed or the ideas so peculiarly Miltonic as to make it absolutely necessary to suppose that Marvell must have read Milton's

achievement, it is not, like the presumably later and essentially unlyrical and unsingable *Dialogue Between the Soul and the Body*, which was certainly not written for music, distinctively and unmistakably Marvellian. Of these three dialogues, where Marvell is writing for a particular purpose and contentedly accepting an established tradition, further discussion may be reserved for a more appropriate place, but of the other six poems which I have in mind a more detailed examination seems appropriate in this preliminary survey: it will enable us to see more clearly with what tastes and allegiances Marvell began—or at least (since the chronology of his poems cannot be established with any certainty) what tastes and allegiances he reveals when he is not being distinctively Marvellian; and it will enable me to concentrate my attention upon more entirely characteristic poems in the chapters that follow.

All six of these poems have affinities with those two enormously popular and often closely related expressions of seventeenth-century sensibility or seventeenth-century wit, the emblem and the epigram. Three of them, *The Match, The Unfortunate Lover, The Gallery*, are predominantly and sometimes grotesquely emblematical or allegorical; and the other three, *Mourning, Eyes and Tears, The Fair Singer*, have a more obvious affinity with certain kinds of Renaissance Latin epigram than we find in Marvell's more characteristic poems. Of these six poems only three contain any kind of evidence for an approximate date of composition: in *The Unfortunate Lover* the imitation of a passage in Lovelace's *Lucasta* proves that it certainly cannot have been written earlier than 1646 and possibly not earlier than 1649;[1] in *The Gallery*

---

poem before he wrote his own, the frequency with which, in other poems, it can be demonstrated without question that he is remembering his reading makes it seem at least possible that he is doing so here. The fact remains, however, that this poem has the appearance of having been intended to be set to music, and I do not know whether post-Restoration composers were still setting 'dialogues' essentially similar to those which Henry Lawes and his contemporaries had set so frequently a generation before. It is, of course, just possible that Marvell, without any invitation from a composer, may have found pleasure in reviving an old form which he had practised more than twenty years ago. After all, his *Two Songs at the Marriage of the Lord* Fauconberg *and the Lady* Mary Cromwell, written as late as 1657, consisted of a duet and a trio.

1. The first two lines of the last stanza of this poem,

> This is the only *Banneret*
> That ever Love created yet,

were certainly suggested, as H. M. Margoliouth indicated in a note, by two lines in the poem *Dialogue—Lucasta, Alexis* in Lovelace's *Lucasta*, 1649, a volume to which Marvell contributed some commendatory verses:

there seems to be an allusion to a public event of July 1650; and in *Mourning* there is a stanza which may possibly have been suggested by one in a poem of Sir Henry Wotton's first printed in 1651.

I will begin with *The Unfortunate Lover*. In this extraordinary and unprecedented poem Marvell describes the Lover and his situation in a succession of huge and extravagant metaphors, emblems, or allegories. (Here, at any rate, the medieval definition of allegory as an extended metaphor is appropriate.) In the second stanza, to represent his predestined abjectness and rejectedness, the death of the Lover's mother in giving birth to him and the Caesarean operation by which he was delivered are described in terms of a shipwreck:

> 'Twas in a Shipwrack, when the Seas
> Rul'd, and the Winds did what they please,
> That my poor Lover floting lay,
> And, e're brought forth, was cast away:
> Till at the last the master-Wave
> Upon the Rock his Mother drave;
> And there she split against the Stone,
> In a *Cesarian Section*.

Thinking, no doubt, both of Prometheus chained to his rock in the Caucasus, where vultures devoured his liver, and of Andromeda chained to the sea-rock from which she was rescued by Perseus, Marvell represents him as for ever remaining on the sea-beaten rock (fit emblem for a cruel world). He received his tears from the sea and his sighs from the wind; black cormorants

> fed him up with Hopes and Air,
> Which soon digested to Despair.
> And as one Corm'rant fed him, still
> Another on his Heart did bill.

He is forced, like a gladiator, to contend all day before angry Heaven

---

> Love nee're his Standard when his Hoste he sets,
> Creates alone fresh-bleeding Bannerets.

Lucasta was licensed on 4 February 1647–8, and, if ll. 21–32 of Marvell's commendatory verses are taken to mean that the book had not yet been licensed, we may assume that Marvell wrote them at some time *before* that date and *after* his return from his travels in 1646 (see *Poems and Letters*, ed. Margoliouth, I 216). Is it, though, absolutely necessary to suppose that Marvell had read all the poems in the book before he commended it? For all we know the passage he has imitated may first have struck him after he had received or bought a copy of *Lucasta* in or after 1649.

with the Waves of Fortune, while tyrant Love attacks him with
'wing'd Artillery', and he, like mad Ajax, braves this double storm:

> See how he nak'd and fierce does stand,
> Cuffing the Thunder with one hand;
> While with the other he does lock,
> And grapple, with the stubborn Rock:
> From which he with each Wave rebounds,
> Torn into Flames, and ragg'd with Wounds.
> And all he saies, a Lover drest
> In his own Blood does relish best.

I have called this poem extraordinary and unprecedented because I
cannot point to any other sixteenth- or seventeenth-century poem
which it really resembles. Nevertheless, I think it may be regarded as
extraordinary in degree rather than in kind, and as simply carrying
to an unprecedented extreme that emblematisation of metaphor which
is one of the distinguishing characteristics of much seventeenth-century
poetry, especially English. For, just as the sixteenth- and seventeenth-
century emblem books, which, from the publication of Alciati's *Emblemata* in 1531, became so enormously popular, illustrated, pictorialised
and expanded various metaphors and allegories in short poems or
passages from Petrarch, Ovid, the Greek Anthology and other sources,
both secular and sacred, often making detailed and clearly visible
what in the original verse was perhaps no more than implicit, even so,
it might be said, various seventeenth-century poets, especially English
ones, emblematised their metaphors and similes, expanding them with
the detail and particularity of emblems, giving, as it were, 'Instructions
to a Painter' (or engraver). Indeed, some even of the epigrams in the
Greek Anthology are almost emblems, and among the fifty or so from
that source which, in Latin translations or imitations, Alciati included
among the 220 epigrams which he illustrated is one by Geminus on
Themistocles (VII 73; Alciati, no. 134), which must be among the
very earliest examples of the *genre* 'Instructions to a Painter' (or
sculptor, or architect):

In place of a simple tomb set Hellas, and on her set ships symbolic
of the destroyed barbarian fleet, and round the tomb's frieze depict
the Persian host and Xerxes: with these things bury Themistocles.
And as a pillar let Salamis stand thereon, telling of my deed. Why
do you lay me in my greatness in so small a space?

Alciati has used a suitably modified Latin version of this epigram to accompany an emblem of Giangalleazzo Visconti, first Duke of Milan, who, among other martial exploits, had repelled an attempted Turkish invasion of Italy: the Duke stands on a map of central Italy, and from his raised arm extends a scroll bearing, in Greek, the last line of the Greek epigram ('Why do you lay me in my greatness in so small a space?'). In the Planudean Anthology (AP XVI 115) there is an anonymous and presumably late epigram on the centaur Chiron, which concludes 'a horse is belching a man and a man is farting a horse'—a divine witticism which many of those hundreds of Renaissance Latin poets who achieved print, many cardinals and reverend fathers, must surely have contemplated with a despairing admiration. Alciati (no. 5) has applied a greatly expanded Latin adaptation of this epigram to an emblem in which there appears, not a centaur, but a kind of merman:

> Quid dicam? quonam hoc compellam nomine monstrum
>   Biforme, quod non est homo, nec est draco?
> Sed sine vir pedibus, summis sine partibus anguis,
>   Vir anguipes dici, & homiceps anguis potest.
> Anguem pedit homo, hominem eructavit & anguis:
>   Nec finis hominis est, initium nec est ferae.
> Sic olim Cecrops doctis regnavit Athenis:
>   Sic & gigantes terra mater protulit.
> Haec vafrum species, sed relligione carentem,
>   Terrena tantum quique curet, indicat.

(What should I say? With what name should I address this biform monster, which is neither man nor serpent, but a man without feet and a snake without upper parts, and may be called a snake-footed man and a man-headed snake? A man is farting a snake and a snake has belched a man. Its end is not that of a man nor its beginning that of a beast. Thus did Cecrops once rule learned Athens, thus did Mother Earth bring forth giants. This picture indicates man who is crafty but has no religion, and whosoever thinks only of earthly things.)

What, however charming it may be, makes much seventeenth-century poetry seem 'quaint' to us is this emblematisation of metaphor, this way in which the poet compels his reader to visualise all the detail of a metaphor or simile or personification, instead of giving, as it were, mere general directives to his imagination and allowing him to supply or withhold detail as he pleases. There are some examples of this kind of writing in Milton's Nativity Ode and in some other of his early poems, where they tend to stand out as uncharacteristic of him, because this was a contemporary manner which Milton quickly outgrew. Too often, like so many other stylistic peculiarities of seventeenth-century poetry, it has been described as 'metaphysical', although in Donne, who almost alone perhaps has some right to be regarded as 'metaphysical', it scarcely occurs at all. On the other hand, it is frequent in Crashaw, a much more visualising and descriptive poet than Donne, who, except for satirical purposes, makes little use of description. And, as I shall attempt to show, Marvell's poetry, in most of which description plays a great part, has far deeper affinities with Crashaw's than with Donne's.

Less astonishing and extravagant than *The Unfortunate Lover*, but also, it must be admitted, far less brilliant, is *The Match*, written in ten rather plodding and mechanical 8,6,8,6 quatrains, of which the argument may be briefly exhibited as follows: Nature laid up a treasure against her old age, but Likeness drew the separate parts of it together and they combined into Celia. Love collected a full supply or magazine to keep himself warm in his old age; its materials spontaneously ignited, and that fire am I:

> So we alone the happy rest,
> > Whilst all the World is poor,
> And have within our Selves possest
> > All Love's and Nature's store.

Midway between these two poems—less grotesquely extravagant than *The Unfortunate Lover*, more visibly pictorial than *The Match*—is *The Gallery*, where the poet invites Clora to come and view his Soul, which he has composed into a single gallery, containing nothing but pictures of herself: here as 'an Inhumane Murtheress', testing the power of her cruel attractions over human hearts, there as a still slumbering Aurora, surrounded by singing birds and springing roses; here as an enchantress in a cave, divining from her lover's entrails how long her beauty will last, there as Venus in her boat, accompanied by wave-calming halcyons. With these and a thousand other pictures his Gallery is filled:

> > But, of these Pictures and the rest,
> > That at the Entrance likes me best:
> > Where the same Posture, and the Look
> > Remains, with which I first was took.

> A tender Shepherdess, whose Hair
> Hangs loosely playing in the Air,
> Transplanting Flow'rs from the green Hill,
> To crown her Head, and Bosome fill.

While it is possible to maintain, and even, perhaps, to demonstrate, that some of Marvell's non-political poems are more successful or more characteristic than others, such occasional evidence for date as is provided by borrowings and allusions scarcely supports a conviction that the less successful poems must necessarily have been written earlier than the more successful. *The Unfortunate Lover* cannot have been written earlier than 1646, but, on the other hand, it may have been written at any time after the publication of Lovelace's *Lucasta* in 1649. And it is possible that *The Gallery* was not written before July 1650, for in the penultimate stanza of that poem Marvell declares that Clora's pictures will form within him

> a Collection choicer far
> Then or *White-hall's*, or *Mantua's* were,

and, as Margoliouth noticed, if *were* is intended to represent the past tense rather than the subjunctive, these lines at any rate must have been written after the Act of Parliament completing the sale and dispersal of Charles I's great collection of pictures at Whitehall (including those which the King had purchased from Vicenzo Gonzaga, Duke of Mantua) in July 1650. And even if Marvell had written these three emblematically allegorical poems before he came to Nunappleton in 1651, he still retained his taste for emblem and allegory, as is revealed by *Musicks Empire*, which concludes with a compliment, probably to the Lord General Fairfax. He retained it, too, even after he had achieved (or, perhaps one should rather say, resisting the temptation to assume a perpetually sustained progress, even after he took the trouble to achieve) complete stylistic assurance; for if, as I shall show later, the correspondence between literal and metaphysical in *Musicks Empire* is continually breaking down, in *On a Drop of Dew*, one of his most perfect poems, it is exquisitely preserved throughout. Indeed, the more I consider the matter, the more I am inclined to believe that the only non-political or non-satirical poems which Marvell had written before he came to Nunappleton were the pastoral dialogue *Thyrsis and Dorinda*, set to music by William Lawes and presumably written at his request, together, perhaps, with *Clorinda and Damon* and *A Dialogue*

Between the Resolved Soul, and Created Pleasure,[1] and that Marvell, not an ambitious poet, wrote only in response to some external stimulation: the stimulation of public events and 'emergent occasions', or the stimulation of a poetry-loving companion such as Fairfax. If I am right, such 'development' as we may think we can detect in his unpublic and unpolitical poetry must all, except for the three dialogues I have mentioned, have taken place between 1651 and 1653. Everything seems to suggest that it was only during those two years of leisure and congenial companionship that Marvell seriously (or continuously) devoted himself to the writing of this kind of poetry, and that within such a brief but concentrated career it is equally possible to regard what seem the less characteristic poems either as beginnings, or as lapses, or as experiments, contemporary with what seem to us the more characteristic poems, of a kind which he decided not to pursue.

But whenever Marvell really began to write significant 'private' poems, his taste for emblem and allegory (apparent both in the grotesque extravagance of *The Unfortunate Lover* and in the perfection of *On a Drop of Dew*), and for the elaborate comparison, or series of comparisons, running through an entire poem, reveals that he neither began nor ended as a disciple of Donne, of whose poetry this kind of writing (despite popular notions to the contrary) is quite uncharacteristic. Indeed, the impulse behind the three poems I have been considering may well have come to him as he was turning over the pages of various emblem books rather than from any particular literary examples. It is true that Marvell, like so many other English poets of the seventeenth century, occasionally employs a sustained, elaborate, sometimes almost scholastic and seldom more than half-serious kind of argumentation which both he and they probably learnt from Donne, but his predominantly descriptive and expository manner is quite unlike Donne's characteristic evocation and analysis of particular situations. The influence of Crashaw is much more pervasive, and behind the remaining three of those six less characteristic poems which I proposed to examine in this preliminary survey we may perceive the examples either of Crashaw or of those neo-Latin epigrammatists whom Crashaw often imitated.

Eyes and Tears was almost certainly suggested by Crashaw's *The Weeper*, although it is a more intellectual, more tightly constructed, less purely descriptive poem than Crashaw's.[2] Some of the fourteen stanzas

1. But see footnote on p. 31.
2. Its title seems to come from Shakespeare, *Venus and Adonis*, l. 962:

into which its fifty-six lines of octosyllabic couplets are divided might indeed be transposed, and perhaps one or two might be omitted without serious loss, but it is not, like *The Weeper*, a mere rosary, a mere string of picturesquely hyperbolical panegyrics. If it contains nothing quite so beautiful and memorable as Crashaw's finest stanzas, it contains nothing so weak (one might almost say, so mindless) as his inferior ones. And while Crashaw is concerned exclusively with the weeping Magdalene, Marvell's allusion to her is but one of the several antithetical analogies by means of which he supports his central argument or paradox, that weeping is superior to seeing, sorrow to joy, and tears to laughter. He begins with two stanzas which are, I think, more purely intellectual than anything in Crashaw's poetry:

> How wisely Nature did decree,
> With the same Eyes to weep and see!
> That, having view'd the object vain,
> They might be ready to complain.
>
> And, since the Self-deluding Sight,
> In a false Angle takes each hight;[1]
> These Tears which better measure all,
> Like wat'ry Lines and Plummets fall.

Then come a series of ingenious arguments from analogy, proving the fundamentality of tears: laughter turns to tears; the sun, after distilling the world all day, is left with nothing but moisture, which it rains back in pity; stars appear beautiful only as the tears of light, and so on. The eighth stanza,

> So *Magdalen*, in Tears more wise
> Dissolv'd those captivating Eyes,
> Whose liquid Chaines could flowing meet
> To fetter her Redeemers feet,

might almost be regarded as a complimentary allusion to Crashaw's weeping Magdalene, and at the end of his poem Marvell has added

---

> O how her eyes and tears did lend and borrow
> Her eyes seen in the tears, tears in the eyes:

and the penultimate line, 'and each the other's difference bears', owes something to *A Lover's Complaint*, stanzas 42–3, 'our drops this difference bore'.

1. Margoliouth refers to ll. 269–70 of *A Poem upon the Death of O.C.*:

> The tree ere while foreshortned to our view,
> When fall'n shews taller yet than as it grew.

a translation of this stanza into Latin elegiacs which would not have
been out of place in *Epigrammata Sacra*, the little collection of Latin
epigrams on sacred subjects which Crashaw published in 1634. During
the Counter-Reformation the form of the classical epigram was
extensively applied to sacred subjects, especially by the Jesuits, and
afforded an excellent means of giving printed expression to the various
antitheses and paradoxes of Christian theology. The Magdalene's
tears was a very favourite subject, and in his *Cannocchiale Aristotelico*
('The Aristotelian Perspective Glass'), 1655, Emanuele Tesauro takes
the weeping Magdalene washing Christ's feet as an example of a theme
from which endless witty arguments may be drawn. 'You have therefore to gather the Motions or circumstances of these four Opposite
Objects: LOVE, TEARS, FIRE, FROST: a thing which you will
find very easy, if you keep the order of the two said Tables.'Tesauro
then proceeds to illustrate all possible combinations of these conceits,
in a passage of which the following is a sufficient specimen:

> What is this prodigy? Water and Flame, once bitter rivals, are
> now reconciled like peaceful bedfellows in Magdalen's eyes . . . You
> will find in them a spring and a torch, you will draw fire from the
> water, water from the fire. Her eyes repeat the fabulous miracle of
> Mount Ætna on whose top the snow is espoused to the fire. Like a
> new bride, Magdalen carries the wonted offerings of fire and water
> on the threshold. Hail, eyes, dispensers of fiery springs. Come you,
> sick ones, to these hot baths healthier than the Leucadian fountain.
> Love the bath-keeper calls you, come.[1]

This should be enough to suggest, first, that ingenious conceits of
this kind, whether or no they may be appropriately termed 'metaphysical', are a European, not a distinctively English, phenomenon;
secondly, that what makes distinguished and memorable much of the
poetry of Crashaw, Marvell and other seventeenth-century poets in
which such conceits occur is not the conceits themselves but the phrasing and rhythm of their contexts, and sometimes (there are touches of
it in this poem of Marvell's) the shapeliness, tightness and continuity
given by that semi-scholastic kind of argumentation which so many of
these poets seem to have learnt from Donne. Ingenious conceits about
tears and sighs, often illustrated in the emblem books, must occupy
many hundreds of pages of sixteenth- and seventeenth-century poetry,
Latin and vernacular: Cupid blowing a furnace with sighs and distilling

1. Quoted by Mario Praz, *The Flaming Heart*, 1958, pp. 227–8.

tears into a limbeck; a lover tossed or shipwrecked by winds of sighs on seas of tears, or weeping a sea of tears and drowning in it. The Latin and English elegies on Edward King in the volume to which Milton contributed *Lycidas* are full of such ingenious fancies: the waters of the Irish Sea have drowned King and the waters of their tears are likely to drown his mourners; they are mere islands floating in a sea of tears; water is now accursed—if there is any in their composition, let them weep it away in tears. Again and again in reading six-teenth- and seventeenth-century poetry of this kind one is reminded of Mallarmé's reply to Degas, that poems are made not with ideas but with words. Of the countless thousands of neo-Latin epigrams it is very seldom that we find one that seems to possess any distinctively poetic merit; of most of them any clever schoolboy or undergraduate, had he been given the ideas, the conceits, could have supplied the versification with equal competence. And this is true of many of the more ingenious epigrams in the Greek Anthology which Alciati and others chose to emblematise.

I have professed to regard *Eyes and Tears* as one of the less completely characteristic of Marvell's poems; nevertheless, the neat paradoxical antithesis of the eleventh stanza,

> The Incense was to Heaven dear,
> Not as a Perfume, but a Tear.
> And Stars shew lovely in the Night,
> But as they seem the Tears of Light,

is very similar to that of a passage in that entirely characteristic poem *The Garden*:

> *Apollo* hunted *Daphne* so,
> Only that She might Laurel grow.
> And *Pan* did after *Syrinx* speed,
> Not as a Nymph, but for a Reed.

Only in poems where some kind of half-serious argument was being developed, or some kind of paradoxical proposition was being main-tained, could these two stanzas have occurred, and such argument was much more extensively cultivated by seventeenth-century English poets than by their European contemporaries and predecessors, vernacular or Latin. The syntactical structure, or pattern, or formula of these stanzas is identical, and, although the inversions which Marvell too often permitted himself cause the more brilliant and memorable stanza from *The Garden* to fall short of perfection, there is in both a wonderful unity of metre, rhythm, syntax and content, all co-operating to produce, with the utmost economy of means, a total poetic effect which could not have been produced in any other way. It is in such concentrated, darting, kingfisher-like brilliance, in such charming visualisations, vibrating with an intellect and wit which have expelled, or transformed, conventional prettiness, that the ultimately incomparable attractiveness of much of Marvell's poetry resides. We can point to many poets, poems and passages from which he has taken hints and suggestions, or even, at times, his initial inspiration; but, although we can identify many, perhaps most, of his ingredients, he has often blended them according to a secret recipe which he alone possessed.

While *Eyes and Tears* has affinities with Crashaw and with the more 'conceited' and ingeniously descriptive kind of neo-Latin epigram, *Mourning*, although it has some incidental affinities with the same tradition, belongs more fundamentally to a rather different one, that of the satirical epigram, for which Renaissance Latin poets found their models sometimes in the satirical epigrams of the Greek Anthology, which to us seem to be among the less valuable and characteristic constituents of that collection, but more frequently in those of Martial. Some of the very best of Martial's epigrams are, it is true, non-satirical, but the satirical ones are more numerous; it was Martial and some of his Roman predecessors who gave the satirical epigram such perfection as it was capable of receiving, and for many Renaissance epigrammatists, and for most of the numerous English ones of the sixteenth and seventeenth centuries, Martial's satirical epigrams were the models they chiefly had in mind. An occasional topic with Martial and a favourite one with Renaissance epigrammatists was that of feminine hypocrisy, and it may well be that the initial inspiration for Marvell's *Mourning* was an epigram by the French neo-Latin poet Étienne Pasquier (1529–1615) entitled *De Amœna Vidua*, 'On Amœna,[1] having lost her husband', which contains the lines:

> His tamen in lachrimis nihil est ornatius illa,
> Perpetuusque subest eius in ore nitor.
> Siccine, defunctum quae deperit orba maritum,
> Semper aget viduo fœmina maesta thoro?
> Quae flet culta, suum non luget, Amœna, maritum;
> Quid facit ergo? alium quaerit, Amœna, virum.

(Yet amid these tears, nothing could be handsomer than she and

1. Pasquier is using the adjective *amœna* ('lovely', 'charming') as a proper noun.

there lurks a perpetual brightness in her face. Will she, who pines in her bereavement for her dead husband, always be thus enacting the mourner on a widowed bed? One, Amœna, who weeps with elegance is not mourning her husband. What, then, is she doing? Amœna, she's looking for another.)[1]

Whether or no it was from Pasquier that Marvell derived the cynical notion of grief as something deliberately aroused by a woman in order to increase her attractiveness, he has combined it not only with something of that ingeniously metaphorical description of tears which he had used in the poem *Eyes and Tears* and which he had learnt from Crashaw, but also with a sustained, elaborate, mock-serious kind of argumentation such as we find only in certain English poets of the seventeenth century, and which, as I have suggested, those poets seem to have learnt from Donne. There is not, I think, anything at all like it in the neo-Latin epigrammatists, and although there are perhaps some approaches to it in the *Capitoli* of Berni and others and in Tasso's famous stanzas *Sopra la Bellezza*, the intellectual apparatus and resources there deployed are far less elaborate and, one might almost say, more schoolboyish. Moreover, while Berni and his like, and Donne in some of his Elegies, are obviously burlesquing scholastic argument and scholastic terminology, Marvell is here being mock-heroic rather than burlesque. Donne, in such a poem as *The Anagram*, proving that it is better to marry an old and ugly woman than a young and handsome one, is almost laughing, almost rollickingly high-spirited, but Marvell here preserves a wooden-faced gravity and writes a satirical poem which has the superficial appearance of being, and which to a simple-minded reader might seem to be, a celebration. And while Donne nearly always conveys the impression that he is addressing some imaginary listener, Marvell, although in his opening stanza he, as it were, looks up and addresses the astrologers, conveys in the rest of his poem the impression that he is uttering solitary and detached reflexions and bringing his whole mind to bear upon this weighty subject.

I

You, that decipher out the Fate
Of humane Off-springs from the Skies,
What mean these Infants which of late
Spring from the Starrs of *Chlora's* Eyes?

1. *Deliciae C. C. Poetarum Gallorum*, ed. R. Gherus (the anagrammatic pseudonym of Janus Gruterus), 1609, ii 875.

II

Her Eyes confus'd and doubled ore
With Tears suspended ere they flow,
Seem bending upwards to restore
To Heaven, whence it came, their Woe.

III

When, molding of the watry Sphears,
Slow drops unty themselves away;
As if she, with those precious Tears,
Would strow the ground where *Strephon* lay.

IV

Yet some affirm, pretending Art,
Her Eyes have so her Bosome drown'd,
Only to soften near her Heart
A place to fix another Wound;

V

And, while vain Pomp does her restrain
Within her solitary Bowr,
She courts her self in am'rous Rain,
Her self both *Danae* and the Showr.

VI

Nay others, bolder, hence esteem
Joy now so much her Master grown,
That whatsoever does but seem
Like Grief, is from her Windows thrown.

VII

Nor that she payes, while she survives,
To her dead Love this Tribute due,
But casts abroad these Donatives[1]
At the installing of a new.

VIII

How wide they dream! The *Indian* Slaves
That sink for Pearl through Seas profound,
Would find her Tears yet deeper Waves
And not of one the bottom sound.

---

1. 'A donation, gift, present; *esp.* one given formally or officially, as a largess or bounty' (*OED*). Cf. Donne, *Sermons*, ed. Potter and Simpson, IV 233, ll. 861–3:

IX

> I yet my silent Judgment keep,
> Disputing not what they believe:
> But sure as oft as Women weep,
> It is to be suppos'd they grieve.[1]

If, as seems possible, the ingenious conceit in the eighth stanza was suggested by a simpler one in a poem ascribed to Wotton, *Mourning* cannot have been written earlier than 1651. In a poem entitled *A Description of the Countreys Recreations*, which Izaak Walton printed in the *Reliquiae Wottonianae* (1651) among the poems 'found among the Papers of Sir *Henry Wotton*', and which he quoted in *The Compleat Angler* (1653) as 'a copy printed among some of Sir Henry Wotton's and doubtless made either by him or by a lover of angling', the penultimate stanza is as follows:

> Go, let the diving *Negro* seek
> For Gems hid in some forlorn creek;
> We all Pearls scorn,
> Save what the dewy morne
> Congeals upon each little spire of grasse;
> Which careless Shepherds beat down as they passe;
> And Gold ne're here appears,
> Save what the yellow *Ceres* bears.

It may well have been this not exceptionally ingenious conceit, that the pearls of dew upon the grass blades are more precious than the pearls which negroes dive for, which suggested to Marvell the much more ingenious one that Chlora's tears are deeper than the waters through which Indians dive for pearl. The relationship is not, I will admit, self-evident; nevertheless, the fact remains that in such tenuous evidence as it is possible to discover for the date of these six less wholly characteristic emblematical or epigrammatic poems there is nothing which forbids, and something which encourages, the supposition that they were all written at Nunappleton between 1651 and 1653.

The last of these three epigrammatic poems, one more completely within the tradition of the neo-classical epigram than are Marvell's

---

'If the King cast a *donative*, at his Coronation, will any man lie still and say, he meant none of that money to *me*?'

1. I have made various alterations in the often obscuring and confusing punctuation of this poem.

more wholly characteristic ones, is *The Fair Singer*, a poem which, had its first and third stanzas been equal to its second, would have been a perfect one. It would perhaps be more accurate to say that it is within the tradition of a characteristically English development of a certain kind of neo-classical epigram, one in which something of the ingenuity and intellectuality of Crashaw and his Jesuit masters in their epigrams on sacred subjects was applied to secular ones. In both kinds of poem there is an intense intellection, although the results which the two kinds of epigram achieve are very different and sometimes almost exactly opposite; for, while the sacred epigrammatists make either conceptions more perceptual or pictures more pictorial, the English celebrators of Fair Singers, Fair Dancers and so forth, achieve a kind of intellectual formula for a sensory experience, and try to express the essential *thisness* of something visible or audible in some thinkable but only limitedly picturable metaphor. I shall try to exhibit in some detail the different results achieved by these two kinds of intellection—an intellection more ingenious and concentrated than we find even in late Roman or Alexandrian epigrams, one which has led to the indiscriminate designation of almost all poetry where it occurs as 'metaphysical'.

Of the many collections of sacred epigrams, often accompanied by emblems, which the Jesuits and their imitators composed, many, though by no means the majority, attempt by various means such imaginative realisation of biblical, especially New Testament, scenes and incidents as St Ignatius recommended in his *Religious Exercises*. Of these biblical epigrammatists the most brilliant was Crashaw, all of whose *Epigrammata Sacra* are comments on New Testament texts, although many of the chosen texts are not descriptive but doctrinal. If we take those on texts which record scenes and incidents (the only ones which it is profitable to compare with the secular epigrammatic forms of which Marvell's *Fair Singer* is an example), and ask what exactly Crashaw is doing, the reply would seem to be that, in general, he is magnifying and expanding, sometimes by means of personification (often of a kind which has some affinity with classical personification of elements and natural forces, or even with that in certain Alexandrian epigrams), sometimes by means of allegorisation, and sometimes by, as it were, the inreading, or extraction, of unapparent paradoxes and antitheses.

Crashaw's most famous epigram, that on the miracle at Cana, is an elaborate personification:

JOANN 2

Aquae in vinum versae

Unde rubor vestris, & non sua purpura lymphis?
Quae rosa mirantes tam nova mutat aquas?
Numen (convivae) praesens agnoscite Numen:
Nympha pudica Deum vidit, & erubuit.

('Whence comes redness to your lymphs and purple not their own? What rosiness so new is changing the admiring waters? A divinity, guests, acknowledge a present divinity: the bashful nymph beheld God and blushed.')[1]

It has been plausibly maintained[2] that Crashaw's blushing water-nymph was suggested to him by the blushing rose in an epigram by the Jesuit Maximilianus Sandaeus, who in 1629 published a course of sermons on the Virgin as a 'mystic flower', each sermon being headed by an emblem and an epigram. The sermon entitled *Maria in Purificatione Rosa* is preceded by an emblem depicting, in the centre of a rose, the presentation in the Temple, beneath which is the couplet:

Vin' scire unde suum rosa candida traxerit ostrum?
Purgantem vidit Virginem et erubuit.

('Would you know whence the white rose drew its purple? It beheld the purifying Virgin and blushed.')

The conceit and the personification in Herrick's little poem *How Roses came red* may possibly have been inspired by Sandaeus or Crashaw or both of them:

Roses at first were white,
    Till they co'd not agree,
Whether my *Sapho's* breast,
    Or they more white sho'd be.

But being vanquisht quite,
    A blush their cheeks bespred;
Since which (beleeve the rest)
    The *Roses* first came red.

---

1. *The Poems of Richard Crashaw*, ed. L. C. Martin, p. 38.
2. See Martin's note on this epigram, pp. 429–30. Since Latin *rubescere* simply means 'to turn red', it is only when one can feel quite sure that there is personification that one is justified in citing any passage where it occurs as a precedent for Crashaw's use of it.

It seems, though, more likely that both Sandaeus and Herrick, and perhaps Crashaw too, were all independently inspired by some Alexandrian epigram or short Anacreontic poem which I have been unable to discover, and which declared, perhaps, that the white rose turned red when it found itself unable to compare with the hands, or feet, or breasts of Aphrodite. It is, at any rate, just the sort of pretty and ingenious conceit that we find in those late Greek poems which became so popular during the later Renaissance, and, whether or no it has a Greek original, is a good example of the way in which the Reverend Fathers, 'if haply they might save some', appropriated and consecrated the profane. Crashaw has again personified the water as a nymph in his epigram on Pilate washing his hands. It is one of several of the *Epigrammata Sacra* of which he made English versions, and it is the more impressive English version which I will quote:

> *To* Pontius *washing his blood-stained hands*
>
> Is murther no sin? or a sin so cheape
>   That thou need'st heape
> A Rape upon't? till thy Adult'rous touch
>   Taught her these sullied cheeks, this blubber'd face?
> She was a Nimph, the meadowes knew none such,
>   Of honest Parentage, of unstain'd Race,
> The Daughter of a faire and well-fam'd Fountaine
> As ever Silver-tipt the side of shady mountaine.
>
> See how she weeps, and weeps, that she appeares
>   Nothing but Teares;
> Each drop's a Teare that weeps for her own wast;
>   Harke how at every Touch she does complaine her:
> Harke how she bids her frighted Drops make hast,
>   And with sad murmurs chides the Hands that stain her.
> Leave, leave, for shame, or else (Good judge) decree
> What water shal wash this, when this hath washed thee.[1]

In his epigram on the pool at Bethesda, which became health-restoring only after an angel, from time to time, had descended and 'troubled' its waters, Crashaw first uses a simile (or implicit simile), comparing the inefficacy of the untroubled waters with those which eluded the thirst of Tantalus, and then, as it were, extracts and magnifies with

---

1. Martin, p. 94. I have made various changes in the punctuation. The Latin version is on p. 57.

metaphor the not immediately apparent paradox that the 'troubled' waters should be able to liberate from trouble:

JOANN 5

Ad Bethesdae piscinam positus

Quis novus hic refugis incumbit Tantalus undis,
    Quem fallit toties tam fugitiva salus?
Unde hoc naufragium felix? medicaeque procellae?
    Vitaque, tempestas quam pretiosa dedit?

(What new Tantalus reclines here on fleeing waters?
Whom does so fugitive health so often elude?
Whence this fortunate shipwreck? these medicinal storms?
And life, which a precious tempest has conferred?)[1]

The magnification and metaphorisation of the 'troubled' pool into a tempestuous sea by which the sufferer, as Marvell, undoubtedly recalling this passage, wrote in his *Dialogue Between the Soul and Body* (l. 30), is 'Shipwrackt into Health again', is perhaps as near as it would be possible to discover to some sort of poetical precedent for the extraordinary metaphors and personifications in *The Unfortunate Lover*; and, indeed, Marvell's indebtedness to Crashaw seems, on the whole, to have been greater than to any other single poet. Nevertheless, although in these three epigrams of Crashaw there is intense intellection, the result cannot properly be described, as can at any rate the middle stanza of Marvell's *Fair Singer*, as an intellectualisation.

I

To make a final conquest of all me,
Love did compose so sweet an Enemy,
In whom both Beauties to my death agree,
Joyning themselves in fatal Harmony;
That while she with her Eyes my Heart does bind,
She with her Voice might captivate my Mind.

II

I could have fled from One but singly fair:
My dis-intangled Soul it self might save,
Breaking the curled trammels of her hair.
But how should I avoid to be her Slave,
Whose subtile Art invisibly can wreath
My Fetters of the very Air I breath?

1. *Poems*, ed. Martin, p. 15.

III

It had been easie fighting in some plain,
Where Victory might hang in equal choice,
But all resistance against her is vain,
Who has th' advantage both of Eyes and Voice,
And all my Forces needs must be undone,
She having gained both the Wind and Sun.[1]

The middle stanza is a finer achievement than anything in similar
poems by Marvell's contemporaries; it has the appearance of having
been 'given' to him while the other two, though not without distinction, seem, in comparison, mere filling. It would not have been at
all surprising had Marvell appended a version of it in Latin elegiacs:
one recalls the three Latin epigrams *Ad Leonoram Romae canentem*,
which Milton, during his stay in Rome in the winter of 1638–9,
addressed to the famous singer Leonora Baroni, in whose honour,
according to Thomas Warton, a collection of poems in Greek, Latin,
Italian, French and Spanish was published with the title *Applausi
poetici alle glorie della Signora Leonora Baroni*; and one may perhaps be
tempted to wonder whether Marvell too may not have been inspired
by Leonora during his visit to Rome in 1645 or 1646. If so, no two
celebrations could well be more different, and the originality and
novelty of the English epigrammatic poems of this kind become
strikingly clear when we compare them—compare, even though its
first and third stanzas are inferior to its second, the sobriety of Marvell's whole poem, the plainness and precision of its language, the
absence of conventional allusion and decoration, the 'naturalness' of its
metaphors and similes, with the hollow pomposity of Milton's three
epigrams, all of them in that strain of ingeniously but more or less
meaninglessly hyperbolical flattery which was the current coin of
Renaissance compliment, and which appears in a more intellectual
and refined form in some of Donne's verse-letters to noble patronesses
and in a more gross one in Dryden's dedication of *The State of Innocence*
to Mary of Modena. In the first of these epigrams Milton declares
that, while others have only a guardian angel, Leonora's voice 're-
sounds a present deity', preparing mortals for the music of Heaven,
and that while God is mutely diffused through all other things, in her

---

1. A not uncommon military metaphor. Cf. Milton's *Areopagitica* (1644, p. 36):
'When a man hath . . . drawn forth his reasons, as it were a battell raung'd . . . calls
out his adversary into the plain, offers him the advantage of wind and sun.'

he speaks; in the second, that Tasso would have been far happier had
he lived in these days and loved Leonora Baroni instead of Leonora
d'Este, since, however madly he had loved her, her voice would have
restored his sanity; and in the third that the siren Parthenope is not
buried at Naples, as the city boasts, but alive in Rome, arresting both
men and Gods with her song. When he reads these and many similar
neo-Latin epigrams a modern reader may feel that he has wandered
into a society of overgrown schoolboys, for this was the kind of verse
which, until Dryden's day and later, the brighter boys at Westminster
and other schools were taught to write on given themes, such as the
visit of a patron or royal personage, a royal birthday, wedding or
funeral, the death of some nobleman or ecclesiastical dignitary. In
comparison with Milton's epigrams on Leonora, Marvell's epigram
(for as such it might be appropriately described) on the Fair Singer
seems incomparably more adult and mature, and, like so much of
the best Caroline verse, has the appearance of having been written by
a cultivated man of the world for other cultivated men of the world
rather than by a schoolboy for the approval of his master or by an
academic for the approval of his colleagues.

There are many delightful English 'epigrammatic' poems of this
kind, although most of them are concerned with seeing rather than
with hearing, especially with 'Seeing her Walking' (in the Snow, in the
Rain, in the Grass, in the Park, and so on). Marvell's friend Lovelace
(in his *Lucasta*, 1649) has a memorable though unequal poem on
Gratiana Dancing and Singing, of which the third stanza is justly famous:

> Each step trod out a lover's thought
> And the ambitious hopes he brought,
>   Chained to her brave feet with such arts,
> Such sweet command and gentle awe,
> As, when she ceased, we sighing saw
>   The floor lay paved with broken hearts.

And Robert Heath (in his *Clarastella*, 1650) has a poem on *Seeing her
Dancing*, which begins, in a manner reminiscent of Jonson's 'Still to be
neat, still to be drest',

> Robes loosely flowing, and aspect as free,

but in whose third stanza there is something of that intellectualisation
of sense-impression which, if the term 'metaphysical poetry' is to mean
anything at all, ought surely to be one of the things we mean by it, and

of which the second stanza of Marvell's *Fair Singer* is such a superb example:

> As when with steadfast eies we view the Sun,
> We know it goes, though see no motion;
>   So undiscern'd she mov'd, that we
>   Perceiv'd she mov'd, but did not see.[1]

Marvell's metaphor of 'fetters of air'[2] is some degrees more subtle, refined and intellectual than Lovelace's floor 'paved with broken hearts'; and one can see that it is more difficult, and requires more intellectuality and ingenuity, to describe singing in this epigrammatic fashion, by metaphor, not by simile, by saying what it does to one, not by saying what it reminds one of, than to describe dancing or walking; but this perhaps is why poems on Fair Singers are less frequent than poems on Fair Dancers, Walkers, Weepers and the like. For merely to describe the singer's voice in a series of expansive similes or comparisons, to say that it was like, or sweeter than, the sound of a nightingale, a fountain, a flute, and so on, would have been to break the rules of this difficult game and to forsake precise description for vague eulogy. Even Lovelace, in the fourth and last stanza of his poem, has to relapse into simile when, after devoting three stanzas to Gratiana's dancing, he comes to describe her singing:

> So did she move; so did she sing,
> Like the harmonious spheres that bring
>   Unto their rounds their music's aid;
> Which she performèd such a way
> As all the enamour'd world will say
>   'The graces dancèd, and Apollo play'd.'

Waller, so many of whose songs and shorter poems might be classified as descriptive epigrams, has at least four poems on Fair Singers and one on a Fair Dancer. They may well have helped to keep the topic before Marvell and other poets, but, although they are not without distinction, they are unsubtle and somewhat insipid in comparison

---

1. *Op. cit.*, p. 11.

2. *Alciati omnia emblemata* CLXXX, '*Eloquentia fortitudine praestantior*', in which Hercules is shewn leading prisoners on chains or fetters from his tongue, is probably the source of this phrase. Marvell has adapted Lucian's praise of eloquence (the source of this emblem, see Lucian, Loeb ed., vol. i, pp. 64-6) to praise his Fair Singer.

with Marvell's *Fair Singer*, or even with Lovelace's poem.[1] Indeed, Waller's poem *Of Mrs Arden*[2] may well have inspired Marvell to do better, for it shares with Marvell's poem the idea that the singer exercises a double power, that of her beauty and that of her voice. The first six lines, if not, perhaps, very memorable, are admirably neat, and it would have been better had Waller stopped there; unfortunately, though, as so often in all except his very best poems, he has been unable to resist the tendency to dilate and dilute, and has added another six lines containing a too expansively worked-out simile.

> Behold, and listen, while the fair
> Breaks in sweet sounds the willing air,
> And with her own breath fans the fire
> Which her bright eyes do first inspire.
> What reason can that love control,
> Which more than one way courts the soul?
> So when a flash of lightning falls
> On our abodes, the danger calls
> For human aid, which hopes the flame
> To conquer, though from heaven it came;
> But if the winds with that conspire,
> Men strive not, but deplore the fire.

This poem is immediately preceded by one *Of my Lady Isabella, playing on the Lute*,[3] in which Waller makes a less distinguished use of the same ideas, and concludes with a comparison of the 'fair tyrant' to Nero playing while Rome burned. On the other hand, in *To a Lady singing a Song of his own Composing*,[4] he has performed an original and ingenious

---

1. Waller's song 'Behold the brand of beauty tossed' (*Poems*, ed. Thorn Drury, I 126) will perhaps better stand comparison with Lovelace's poem on Gratiana than any of his singer poems will with Marvell's *Fair Singer*. It seems possible that his declaration, in the second stanza, that the sun and moon move to the music of their own spheres

> As this nymph's dance
> Moves with the numbers which she hears

may have suggested to Lovelace the stanza beginning:

> So did she move: so did she sing,
> Like the harmonious spheres that bring
> Unto their rounds their music's aid.

2. *Poems*, ed. Thorn Drury, I 91.   3. *op. cit.*, I 90.   4. *op. cit.*, I 105.

variation on the topic. It is an excellent poem, although, like many of Waller's best, it is characteristically neo-classical rather than characteristically earlier seventeenth-century, and is nearer, on the one hand, to the Renaissance Latin epigram and, on the other hand, to Prior and Pope, than to Marvell's *Fair Singer* and a few other seventeenth-century poems that have some affinity with Marvell's. The second stanza contains a 'conceit' which occurs in a fragment of Aeschylus and in various classical authors and which Waller seems to have used for the first time in English,[1] and the ingenious 'classical' conceit in the last stanza seems to have been of Waller's own invention.

> Chloris! yourself you so excel,
> When you vouchsafe to breathe my thought,
> That, like a spirit, with this spell
> Of my own teaching, I am caught.
>
> That eagle's fate and mine are one,
> Which, on the shaft that made him die,
> Espied a feather of his own,
> Wherewith he wont to soar so high.
>
> Had Echo, with so sweet a grace,
> Narcissus' loud complaints returned,
> Not for reflection of his face,
> But of his voice, the boy had burned.

In the fourth and last of these poems on female singers, 'While I listen to thy voice',[2] Waller contents himself with the rather commonplace hyperbole that the singer's voice anticipates the heavenly choir:

> Peace, Chloris! peace! or singing die,
> That together you and I
> To heaven may go;
> For all we know
> Of what the blessed do above,
> Is, that they sing, and that they love.

Even in *Of Mrs Arden*, the better of the two poems where Waller celebrates conjointly beauty of voice and beauty of appearance, he does not contrive to make the combination seem anything like so surprising and paradoxical as Marvell does; and this is also true of the second and better of Carew's two poems on *Celia Singing*:

1. See Thorn Drury's note, II 188–9.   2. *op. cit.*, I 127.

> You that thinke Love can convey
> 　　No other way
> But through the eyes into the heart
> 　　His fatall Dart:
> Close up those casements, and but heare
> 　　This Syren sing;
> 　　And on the wing
> Of her sweet voyce it shall appeare
> That Love can enter at the eare:
> 　　Then unvaile your eyes, behold
> 　　The curious mould
> Where that voyce dwels, and as we know
> 　　When the Cocks crow,
> 　　We freely may
> 　　Gaze on the day;
> So may you, when the Musique's done,
> Awake and see the rising Sun.[1]

Carew professes to be describing a paradox, but he scarcely succeeds, and neither perhaps does Waller, in making us feel it as such. Marvell's poem communicates far more of the tension that exists between the elements of a genuine paradox: partly because, like Donne, he uses the first person singular, and describes the effect of the Fair Singer not upon hearers and spectators in general but only upon himself, as though he were communicating an exciting piece of personal experience and self-discovery; still more, though, because his syntax is much more elaborate. Each stanza consists of a single complex sentence (the full stop at the end of the third line of the second stanza might well be replaced by a semi-colon, or even by a comma), and these long-breathed sentences seem to be outreaching further and ingrasping more than do the simple and shorter sentences (and shorter lines) of Waller and Carew, and are far more successfully able to transform what is really a simple antithesis into what produces the impression (or illusion) of astonishing paradox. And at the centre of his poem he exalts antithesis into paradox through a sheer command of poetic language and poetic invention far beyond the reach of Waller, and probably beyond that of Carew too.

> And with her own breath fans the fire
> Which her bright eyes do first inspire;

1. *Poems*, ed. Dunlap, p. 39. I have removed some superfluous commas.

This neat antithesis of Waller's scarcely communicates any sense of discovery or produces any shock of surprise; but Marvell's

> how should I avoid to be her Slave,
> Whose subtile Art invisibly can wreath
> My Fetters of the very Air I breath?

are among the most surprising lines in seventeenth-century poetry, and produce the illusion that what is so surprisingly described is indeed surprising to the point of paradox. As I shall attempt to show later,[1] Marvell in *The Definition of Love* is developing antitheses rather than paradoxes, but in that poem too he contrives, through sheer vigour of language, to give antithesis the appearance of paradox. He has a wonderful power of magnifying the comparatively small into the comparatively great. I can find no single phrase to describe it, and must content myself with such approximations as 'humorous gravity', 'measured hyperbole', 'serious burlesque'. He can treat a 'light' subject weightily without any trace of bombast, and can expand it in the most astonishing way without any suggestion of inflation. When we call a piece of verse bombastic or inflated we mean that there is a discrepancy between subject and treatment of which the author himself is apparently unaware. There is indeed often (perhaps nearly always) more or less of discrepancy between subject and language in these descriptive passages of Marvell's, but it is a discrepancy of which he himself is fully conscious, although he is, as it were, pretending, and inviting us to pretend, that there is no discrepancy at all. More perhaps than any other seventeenth-century poet, Marvell invites the reader to join him in a kind of highly sophisticated game.

Although the descriptive epigrams of Lovelace and Heath, Waller and Carew, are inferior to Marvell's *Fair Singer*, there is in all of them a comparatively sober precision which differs greatly from, on the one hand, such conventionally hyperbolical eulogy as we find in Milton's epigrams on Leonora, and, on the other hand, Crashaw's hectic hyperbolisation of the 'troubled' pool of Bethesda into a tempestuous sea by which the invalid is 'shipwrecked into health'. Marvell and some of his contemporaries would seem, like Wordsworth, to have discovered that 'the human mind is capable of being excited without the application of gross and violent stimulants'; in poems of this kind they indeed aimed at surprise, but at a surprisingly natural kind of surprise, and in

1. See pp. 68–70.

other kinds of poem Marvell's metaphors and hyperboles are normally extravagant only when he is deliberately aiming at a burlesque, or semi-burlesque, effect. In poems of which Marvell's *Fair Singer* is the supreme example, what they have given us, however ingenious and intellectualised, are still essentially descriptions, analytic and defining, precise and comparatively sober, of a sight or sound, which are simultaneously descriptions, often metaphorical, of its effect upon spectators or hearers. The thing described still remains for the poet the main thing, his real, not merely his ostensible, subject, and is not, as in so many Renaissance poems which might be roughly classified as epigrammatic, a mere topic for wit, or a more or less accidentally encountered emblem or symbol of some truth, idea, or experience which transcends it and which is the poet's real concern. The chief reason why I have called this manner of description 'intellectualised' is that it seems to be moving towards and to culminate in some compressed and satisfying formula which shall summarise the essence, the *thisness*, of what is being described: fetters of air, a floor paved with broken hearts, a perceived but unseen motion. There seems to me a remarkable affinity between this procedure and that of Rilke in many of the poems in his *Neue Gedichte* and elsewhere; and Marvell's wonderful lines about her

> Whose subtile Art invisibly can wreath
> My Fetters of the very Air I breath

together with his almost equally wonderful description, in *Musicks Empire*, of music as 'the Mosaique of the Air' recall some of the things Rilke himself has written about music: as when, after contemplating, in one of the *Sonnets to Orpheus* (II, X) the dehumanising triumph of technology, he speaks of the undesecrated marvels of existence that still remain:

> Und die Musik, immer neu, aus den bebendsten Steinen,
> baut im unbrauchtaren Raum ihr vergöttlichtes Haus

('Music, too, keeps building anew, with the insecurest stones, her celestial house in unusable space');

or as at the conclusion of that astonishing poem *The Island of the Sirens*:

> und sich blindlings in die Ruder lehnen,
> wie umringt

von der Stille, die die ganze Weite
in sich hat und an die Ohren weht,
so als wäre ihre andre Seite
der Gesang, dem keiner widersteht.

('and they blindly bend against their oars there
as hemmed in

'by that silence, wherein's all the misted
distance, and by which their ears are fanned
even as though its other side consisted
of the song no mortal can withstand.')

Many of Rilke's *Neue Gedichte*, those most unprecedented of European
poems, might be classified as descriptive epigrams, and, although they
are far more ambitious and diversified, their analytical, defining, intellectualised manner of description, in which precision, sobriety and
surprisingness are so often combined, seems to me to have a real
affinity with that of Marvell and his contemporaries in such poems as
The Fair Singer.

I remarked at the beginning of my discussion of them that the six
poems I have been attempting to analyse all have some more or less
close affinity with either or both of those two characteristic expressions
of seventeenth-century sensibility and seventeenth-century wit, the
emblem and the epigram, and I have several times incidentally observed
that we do not find such an affinity in the most characteristic poems of
Donne. If, like Professor Robert Ellrodt in a recent study,[1] we regard
Donne as the standard or norm of so-called 'metaphysical' poetry, then
it is perhaps only in the sustained and elaborate argumentation of
Mourning and in the analysis and intellectualisation of sense-impression
in *The Fair Singer* that these six poems may be said to contain anything
distinctively 'metaphysical'. What is absent from them all is that self-
involvement, that analysis of his own moods, feelings, relationships
and situations, actual or imagined, which M. Ellrodt, with some reason,
regards as the most distinctively 'metaphysical' characteristic of
Donne's poetry, and with which he can discern a real and striking
affinity only in the poetry of George Herbert. This introspective
analysis, or analytical introspection, may indeed in a sense be regarded
as the most essential and fundamental, as it was certainly the least

---

1. *Les Poètes métaphysiques anglais*, 1960.

imitable, characteristic of the best of Donne's *Songs and Sonets*: only, though, in a sense, for it was part of Donne's psychological rather than of his specifically poetic equipment, just as the subtle and sustained argumentation with which it is so often conducted was part of his intellectual equipment. It is his sheer verbal energy, his colloquial vigour, his mastery of rhythm, laying, as Hopkins wrote of Dryden, 'the strongest possible stress on the naked thew and sinew of the English language'—it is this, together with his so often vividly dramatic expression, that enables him to fuse the psychological and intellectual elements in the *Songs and Sonets* into such incomparable poetry. Donne was both an excellent poet and an excellent writer of prose, but, had he been, like Traherne, for example, a born prose writer rather than a born poet, had his sheer poetic gift been only moderate, his powers of introspective analysis and subtle argumentation would only have enabled him to write interesting but, on the whole, rather plodding and unexciting poems like those of his friend Lord Herbert of Cherbury.[1] There are indeed anticipations, faint pre-echoes, of Donne's colloquial vigour and plainness, his dramatic expression, and even, at times, of his dialectic, in some of Wyatt's songs,[2] and, though less strikingly (because of a certain formality and restriction imposed by the

---

1. Or (I am almost tempted to say) like his own *Extasie*, of which we have received so many ingenious and often contradictory interpretations. I am grateful to Miss Helen Gardner for having had the courage to remark, in the course of her own admirable essay on this poem, that 'at times it descends to what can only be described as a dogged plod', and that it contains too much argument and too little ecstasy ('The Argument about "The Ecstasy" ', in *Elizabethan and Jacobean Studies presented to F. P. Wilson*, 1959, pp. 303-4).

2. In his essay on 'Donne's Relation to the Poetry of his Time' (first published in *A Garland for John Donne*, 1931, and reprinted in *The Flaming Heart*, 1958, p. 196) Professor Mario Praz places side by side a passage from one of Petrarch's sonnets, which may perhaps have inspired them, and two stanzas from a poem of Wyatt's, stating and, from his own experience of it, lamenting, the paradoxical and miraculous fact that a lover who has lost his heart should still remain alive. These stanzas, though far from being among his best, do indeed, like others in Wyatt's songs, seem to anticipate some of Donne's *Songs and Sonets*, such as *The Paradox* or *The Broken Heart*, and what is most striking about them is the contrast between the comparative subtlety and sophistication of their argument and the apparent witlessness, the plain, colloquial, almost unliterary manner, in which that argument is expressed—expressed, moreover, in a verse form where we might expect to find, at most, only the simplest sort of *cri de cœur*. In the passage from Petrarch's sonnet there is no such piquant contrast between style and matter, and any novelty in the argument is (at least for a modern reader) obscured and, as it were, anaesthetised by the 'literariness' of its expression. It is not, perhaps, when he is writing in this way that Petrarch, who, when all deductions have been made, still remains one of the great poets of Europe, is at his best.

sonnet form) in Sidney's sonnets; and these, together with the dramatic
blank verse of Shakespeare and his contemporaries, may well have
suggested many new and interesting possibilities to Donne. Certainly,
he was the first English poet who made a really imposing and continuous use both of dramatic expression and of subtle and sustained
argumentation in lyrical poetry, and these things, superficially at least,
were more imitable than that introspective analysis which was part
of his psychological equipment, and they could be applied to subjects
which Donne would never have treated and combined with manners
and methods which he would never have used. How very few of his
Songs and Sonets have any affinity with emblem or epigram! Let us
briefly remind ourselves of the *kinds* of poem we find there—kinds
for the most part, it would seem, invented by Donne himself. It is
true that in many of these poems several of Donne's characteristic
methods—dramatic expression, analysis, demonstration, and so on—
are combined; nevertheless, if one attempted to decide what was the
predominant, most striking, most memorable characteristic of each
poem, one might arrive at some such classification as this: (1) Proclamations or announcements of discoveries about love: (a) exultantly
joyful, about the nature of the relationship between himself and a kind
of ideal partner, a relationship which he analyses and defines with
hyperboles in which one often seems to detect a certain self-ironical
humour, as though he knew that he was saying rather more than he
could, as yet, actually feel (*The good-morrow, The Sunne Rising, The
Canonization, The Anniversarie*); (b) more or less satirical or cynical
proclamations of discoveries or resolutions: that he has discovered
virtue in a woman and been able to love it (*The undertaking*), that he
has resolved to be a rake, even at the cost of ultimately falling in love
with a woman who loves him (*Loves Vsury*), that inconstancy is orthodox and constancy heretical (*The Indifferent*), that love is wholly un-
spiritual and that women are mindless (*Loves Alchymie*), that he has
succeeded in reducing love to a sport or an appetite entirely within
his control (*Loves diet*), that love is disgusting (*Farewell to love*). (2) Ex-
postulations: with Love, for having made him love one who does not
love him in return (*Loves exchange, Loves Deitie, The Will*), with a
disdainful woman (*The Dampe*), with himself, for having fallen in love,
written love-poems, and allowed them to be set to music (*The triple
Foole*), against the unnaturalness of confining a man's love to one
woman (*Confined Love*). (3) Imprecations: *The Curse, The Apparition.*
(4) Analyses: (a) of moods or conditions (*Twicknam garden, A nocturnall*

upon S Lucies day, *The Dissolution*); (b) of a metaphorically imagined situation (*The Legacie*). (5) Combinations of analysis and demonstration: *Aire and Angels* (on the difference between men's and women's love), *A Valediction: of the booke* (an analysis, with much metaphor and hyperbole, of the nature of a mutual love), *Communitie* (a demonstration that women, being neither good nor bad, may be treated like fruit or nuts), *Loves growth* (an analysis of his love and analogical demonstration that the fact of its growth in springtime is not inconsistent with its purity, constancy and permanence), *A Valediction: forbidding mourning* (an analytical demonstration that true love is unchanged by absence), *The Extasie* (a demonstration, often supported by analogy, that lovers must break out of that initial entrancement which comes over them when their souls first unite), *Lovers infiniteness* (an elaborate demonstration that the only way in which he can be sure of possessing all her present and all her future love will be for them to join hearts and become one another's all), *Negative love* (a discovery, as the result of analysis, that his love can only be defined by negatives), *The Prohibition* (metaphorical arguments against loving him, against hating him, and in favour of doing both), *The Expiration* (a series of ingenious metaphorical variations on the metaphor of parting as a kind of death, which might be regarded as an analysis of the nature of parting), *The Computation* (a hyperbolically analytical description, in numerical terms, of the state of being parted), *The Paradox* (that love is a death, that one who has loved has died, and that any appearance of his being still alive is an illusion).

There remain a few poems which have an affinity, sometimes essential, sometimes more or less incidental, with contemporary emblem and epigram, and which for that reason stand out rather exceptionally. Those where the affinity is not essential are those where the poet himself is (or, what amounts to the same thing, gives the impression of being) least involved, least concerned with his own actual or imaginary moods, feelings, attitudes, relationships, situations, experiences and discoveries. One of the most detached, least self-involved, of these poems is *A Feaver*, the only one of the *Songs and Sonets*, except for *Womans constancy*, that satirical attribution to an imaginary female listener of arguments in favour of inconstancy, and *Breake of day*, an aubade spoken by a woman, where a figure other than the poet himself occupies, so to speak, the centre of the stage. It is a poem distinguishable only by the extreme brilliance, intellectuality, avoidance of conventional allusions, and comparative length (seven stanzas) from

such examples of hyperbolical eulogy as Milton's three epigrams on
Leonora Baroni. It begins:

> Oh doe not die, for I shall hate
>   All women so, when thou art gone,
> That thee I shall not celebrate,
>   When I remember, thou wast one.
>
> But yet thou canst not die, I know;
>   To leave this world behinde, is death,
> But when thou from this world wilt goe,
>   The whole world vapors with thy breath.
>
> Or if, when thou, the worlds soule, goest,
>   It stay, tis but thy carkasse then,
> The fairest woman, but thy ghost,
>   But corrupt wormes, the worthyest men.
>
> O wrangling schooles, that search what fire
>   Shall burne this world, had none the wit
> Unto this knowledge to aspire,
>   That this her feaver might be it?

Then, after declaring that there is not enough corruption in her to
fuel such a fever for long, Donne concludes:

> Yet t'was of my minde, seising thee,
>   Though it in thee cannot persever.
> For I had rather owner bee
>   Of thee one houre, then all else ever.

The poem is indeed a continuous discourse, and the stanzas are connected by such phrases as 'But yet', 'Or if', 'And yet'; nevertheless,
the fourth stanza ('O wrangling schooles') could well stand alone, as a
complete and self-sufficient epigram, with the title 'On his Mistress's
Fever'; and, with a slight alteration in its first two lines,

> T'was of my own minde, seising thee,
>   Though it in thee could not persever,

the last stanza could stand as a self-sufficient epigram 'On his Mistress's
Recovery from a Fever'. Both the subject and the hyperbolically
eulogistic comparisons and metaphors are quite in the tradition of
Renaissance epigram. What is characteristic of Donne is not so much

the reconditeness of his comparisons and metaphors (he was to use that of a woman as the world's soul in the first of his two *Anniversaries* 'On the Religious Death of Mistris Elizabeth Drury') as their unexpectedness in such a context and the way in which, instead of producing them with that excited flourish, that obvious intention of hitting for six, that appearance of flung bouquets, to which readers of eulogistic epigram were accustomed, he introduces them into a discourse that is at once grave and familiar, as though they were established and obvious truths. In other words, he has discovered a new way of being hyperbolical—hyperbolical in an essentially unhyperbolical style, a style that has the appearance of being concerned only with the precise expression of carefully ascertained fact. This particular brand of discourse (and, although at least two of this poem's stanzas could stand alone as self-sufficient epigrams, the weaving of them into a continuous discourse introduces almost a difference in kind) could be more or less successfully imitated by other poets, and Marvell has caught something of its manner in *Mourning* and elsewhere. The poem also has affinity with emblem and allegory as well as with epigram, for the comparison of the fever with various kinds of fire is pursued throughout the entire poem; this is commonly supposed to be what Donne is always doing, and it has often been exhibited as one of the chief characteristics of so-called metaphysical poetry, but it is really abnormal to Donne's usual procedure in the *Songs and Sonets*. The most famous example of it is *The Flea*, and it is not difficult to understand why that poem should have been so enormously popular in the age of the emblem and the epigram. Other essentially emblematical poems are *The Primrose; A Valediction: of my name, in the window*, where, through eleven stanzas, Donne performs a series of ingenious and highly intellectualised variations on the possible significance of his 'scratch'd name'; *A Ieat Ring sent*, which in the Westmoreland manuscript was included in the small section of epigrams; and that very ingenious but rather trivial poem *Witchcraft by a picture*, where he imagines his picture as burning in her eye and drowned in her tear, considers the dangerous possibility that she may possess the art of killing by making pictures and then destroying them, and declares that he has insured himself against this by drinking all her tears, so that the only picture of him he has left her is that in her heart, and there she cannot harm it without harming herself.

There remain a few poems which still have some affinity with epigram or emblem, but where that affinity is often very incidental,

and where, to a greater or lesser degree, Donne's more characteristic
and less imitable qualities appear. The first two stanzas of *A Valediction: of weeping* might be described as a hyperbolical emblematisation
of tears and sighs, nearer than Donne's poetry commonly is to the
kind of thing Crashaw and his Jesuit masters wrote about tears and
to the numerous poems and passages in poems about seas of tears
and tempests of sighs; but in the last stanza, beginning

> O more then Moone,
> Draw not up seas to drowne me in thy spheare,

'the whole thing', as Professor Crofts remarked, 'explodes with a
passionate outcry and a familiar image'.[1] *The broken heart* begins with
a reflection,

> He is starke mad, who ever sayes,
> That he hath beene in love an houre,

and, despite the element of emblem and allegory that runs through it,
the poem is essentially one of Donne's characteristic analyses of the
nature of love. *A Lecture upon the Shadow* is a discourse upon morning
shadows as an emblem of growing and upon evening shadows as an
emblem of declining love, which is perfect only at noon. Like *The
Flea*, it is one of the most completely and consistently emblematical
of Donne's poems, and one of the very few in which a single comparison is developed throughout; nevertheless, unlike *The Flea*, it is a
serious piece of analysis, expressing the profound psychological truth
that love's 'first minute, after noone, is night'. *The Funerall* might
conceivably have been included by some seventeenth-century mis-
cellanist in a collection of epigrams, with the title 'On a Bracelet of
Hair', followed, as 'Another on the Same', by *The Relique*, but how
different they would have seemed to us from anything else in the
collection!—especially *The Relique*, where the initial or ostensible
subject expands and flowers into a brilliantly imagined situation: the
opening of his grave in a time of idolatry by persons who may assume
that the 'bracelet of bright haire' and the bone it encircles are relics of
some loving couple, whose love-miracles Donne proceeds, for the
benefit of such idolatrous discoverers, to describe in one of his characteristic 'proclamations'. More conventionally and continuously
emblematical is *The Blossome*, although there too there is something of

1. 'John Donne', in *Essays and Studies by Members of the English Association*, 1936,
p. 143.

the rhythmic tenderness which distinguishes *The Funerall* and *The Relique*, and there too, though far less brilliantly and dramatically than in *The Relique*, a situation gradually emerges. The confident flower apostrophised in the first stanza is regarded as a kind of emblem of the heart apostrophised in the second, a heart which does not know that tomorrow it must take a journey with its owner. The poet then attributes objections to the heart and replies to them, and from this dialogue emerges his situation, that of loving a woman who does not love him in return.

Whether the degree of seriousness in them, the presence or absence of what I have called 'self-involvement', be maximal or minimal, one thing is common to all these poems of Donne's which have some affinity with epigram or emblem: their unpicturesqueness, the almost complete absence from them of visual details and visual descriptions. The 'bracelet of bright haire about the bone' in *The Relique* is perhaps the only really striking and memorable piece of purely visual detail in the whole group. One might add (although it is rather an evocation than a description) the use of the word 'busie' in that poem: when at last his grave is reopened, will not these 'relics' lead the digger to

> thinke that there a loving couple lies,
> Who thought that this device might be some way
> To make their soules, at the last busie day,
> Meet at this grave, and make a little stay?

If Donne can here be said to be visualising the Last Judgment, it is by a process of analogies and abstraction that he has reached and communicated the essence of the scene—its 'business', with souls everywhere seeking and re-entering their resurrected bodies. More often than not in the *Songs and Sonets*, where Donne may seem to be describing he is really analysing, and, if he evokes scenes and situations, it is nearly always in and through a descriptive analysis, or analytical description, of his emotional and psychological responses to scenes and situations which he does not objectively describe. None of his poems evokes a particular situation, one might almost say, a particular scene, more vividly than *The Dreame*, and yet it does so entirely in and through a description of the poet's emotional and psychological responses to his beloved's coming and going, and entirely without that scene-setting and scene-painting which, from Ovid's *Amores* until Donne's own day, we find, with more or less of elaboration, in every treatment of that well-established poetic subject the love-dream.[1] There is, as I have said, considerable intellection in Crashaw's *Epigrammata Sacra*, in his English poems, and, indeed, in almost all those various kinds of seventeenth-century poetry which have been loosely described as 'metaphysical'; nevertheless, while Crashaw thinks in pictures and is usually trying to make pictures more pictorial and thoughts more seeable and feelable, Donne's feeling, one might almost say, is a kind of thinking, and he is concerned primarily with relationships and their analogies and barely at all with appearances and their description. When Mr Eliot said that for Donne a thought was a sensation his emphasis was surely wrong, for his remark suggests that Donne began with thoughts and ended with sensations, which would be a truer description of Crashaw's poetry than of Donne's. While most of what we find in Crashaw's poetry might be appropriately described as a sensationalising of thought, most of what we find in Donne's might be more appropriately described as an intellectualising of sensation. The fact that a poem so intellectual and, in a sense, so abstract as *The Dreame* should yet seem so vivid and so immediate may perhaps be regarded as at least partial confirmation of what Rilke, at the conclusion of one of his later poems, proclaimed as a general truth: 'Denn auch der Leib ist leibhaft erst im Geiste', which may be roughly rendered: 'For even the body is only full-bodied in the mind.'[2] If some of the *Songs and Sonets* are in some sort emblematical, there is nothing really pictorial or picturesque in them, nothing like those picturesque allegorisations, which compel us to visualise them, in Marvell's *Unfortunate Lover* and *The Gallery*; and if some of them are in some sort epigrammatic, what they are *epi*, 'on', is nearly always something intimately Donne's: his name in a window, his picture in a tear, his reopened grave, his (and her) shadow. In fact, they are ultimately all 'on' himself and on the meaning of various relationships to himself. Even in *A Feaver*, the only one of these poems which is predominantly 'on' someone other than himself, it is, at least professedly, if not very seriously, with the meaning of that person, not with her appearance, that he is concerned. In a word, although some of Donne's poems may be regarded as epigrammatic, they have no real affinity with the descriptive epigram. There is indeed, as I have said,

1. See Mario Praz, 'Donne's Relation to the Poetry of his Time', in *The Flaming Heart*, 1958, pp. 186–90.
2. 'O wenn ein Herz, längst wohnend im Entwöhnen', *Sämtliche Werke*, II 237–8; *Poems 1906 to 1926*, translated by J. B. Leishman, pp. 239–40.

something of Donne's analysis and intellectualisation in Marvell's
Fair Singer, and it is true that in that poem Marvell does not describe
the singer's appearance; nevertheless, his relation with the singer is
quite impersonal, and he is concerned not with her meaning to him
but with the effect upon him of her singing. It is quite impossible to
imagine Donne writing an elaborate poem on such a subject, or, for
that matter, as Marvell has done in *Mourning*, 'On a Fair Widow',
although this last is a subject he might conceivably have treated in
one of his short and presumably juvenile epigrams, which do not
significantly differ from hundreds of similar witticisms by dozens of
other poets. Obviously, poems on such impersonal subjects could
have found no place in *Songs and Sonets*; but is it even possible to imagine
there, as distinct from poems proclaiming or analysing Donne's own
discoveries about love, poems chiefly, or largely, consisting of more or
less objective descriptions, however wittily hyperbolical, of the
appearance and actions of an actual or imaginary mistress in various
situations? Poems 'On his Mistress singing and playing on the Vir-
ginals', 'On his Mistress bathing in the River', 'On his Mistress in a
Prospect of Flowers', 'On his Mistress complaining for the Death of
her Fawn'? Or, to crown and dismiss these impossibilities, a poem
'On his Mistress dandling their Child', beginning in some such
strain as

> Say, pretty infant, whence arose
> That twinkle in thine Eye?

There is no prettiness in the *Songs and Sonets* and almost no archness;
in most of Marvell's poems there is much of the former and not a
little of the latter. Many of the *Songs and Sonets* achieve perfection in
their kind, and in respect of this might be called 'beautiful', although
it would seem, as it were, more idiomatic to call them 'fine' or 'splendid'
or 'superb'. It seems somehow more natural, more idiomatic, to cal
many of Marvell's best poems beautiful, because their beauty is so
often a kind of sublimated prettiness. Marvell, like some of his contemporaries, though with a more triumphant success, gave prettiness
a kind of face-lift or shot-in-the-arm, and applied to all manner of
external appearances something of that analysis, intellectualisation,
and close-knit but essentially colloquial discourse which Donne
had applied to relationships and emotional and psychological
discoveries.

Is Marvell ever more than superficially like Donne? His *Definition of*

Love,[1] although its last stanza, almost certainly the germ from which
the whole poem sprang, was suggested by the third stanza of a not very
good poem in Cowley's *The Mistress* entitled *Impossibilities*—his *Definition of Love* is, as many readers must have felt, more like Donne's *A
Valediction: forbidding mourning* than perhaps any other single seventeenth-century poem is like any one of Donne's *Songs and Sonets*: 'like',
but not as a deliberate and inferior imitation, as are so many of the
poems in Cowley's *Mistress*, but like with the likeness of a peer.
Certainly, without the example of Donne's *Valediction* I doubt whether
Marvell's poem could have been what it is. In what might be called
(although I do not much like the phrase) its concrete intellectuality,
the way in which it intellectualises feelings or sensations into conceptions, into more or less abstract ideas, which will retain the vivid-
ness of perceptions, the style of Marvell's poem strikingly resembles
Donne's. It begins (unlike the *Valediction*) with one of those excited
and exciting proclamations, or announcements, as I have called them,
which are so characteristic of the *Songs and Sonets*:

> My Love is of a birth as rare
> As 'tis for object strange and high:
> It was begotten by despair
> Upon Impossibility.

Is this, though, as Donne's usually are, the announcement of a personal discovery? Is there not, below the surface resemblance between
the stanzas that follow and Donne's *Valediction*, a fundamental difference? Let us place three stanzas from each poem side by side:

> Dull sublunary lovers love
>   (Whose soule is sense) cannot admit
> Absence, because it doth remove
>   Those things which elemented it.
>
> But we by a love, so much refin'd,
>   That our selves know not what it is,
> Inter-assured of the mind,
>   Care lesse, eyes, lips, and hands to misse.

---

1. In what I have to say about this poem I am greatly indebted to some remarks
by Professor R. Ellrodt, *Les Poètes métaphysiques anglais*, première partie, II (1960),
123 and 148.

> Our two soules therefore, which are one,
>   Though I must goe, endure not yet
> A breach, but an expansion,
>   Like gold to ayery thinnesse beate.

Donne, as in nearly all the more serious of the *Songs and Sonets*, is here analysing his immediate experience of a particular situation, actual or imagined, and developing the paradox that for true lovers absence is not incompatible with presence. Is this really the sort of thing that Marvell is doing in the following stanzas?

> For Fate with jealous Eye does see
> Two perfect Loves; nor lets them close:
> Their union would her ruine be,
> And her Tyrannick pow'r depose.

> And therefore her Decrees of Steel
> Us as the distant Poles have plac'd,
> (Though Loves whole World on us doth wheel)
> Not by themselves to be embrac'd.

> Unless the giddy Heaven fall,
> And Earth some new Convulsion tear;
> And, us to joyn, the World should all
> Be cramp'd into a *Planisphere*.[1]

Is not this a brilliant imitation by an essentially extrovert poet of a manner and technique developed by an essentially introspective one? Marvell is not starting from the immediate experience of a particular situation, is not really being analytic and psychological and paradoxical, like Donne, but is simply performing, with characteristically seventeenth-century intellectuality, ingenuity, hyperbole and antithesis, an elaborate series of variations on the ancient theme of star-crossed lovers. While Donne, not merely in the stanzas I quoted but throughout his poem, is developing an argument ('Even though physically parted, we can remain spiritually united'), Marvell is simply saying over and over again, in various ingenious ways, 'We can never meet'. He is not really, like Donne, being paradoxical: what at first sight

---

1. A map or chart formed by the projection of a sphere, or part of one, on a plane. *OED* quotes from Thomas Blundeville's *Exercises*, 1594: 'Astrolabe . . . is called of some a planispheare, because it is both flat and round, representing the Globe or Spheare, having both his Poles clapt flat together.'

looks like paradox appears, when we examine it more closely, to be merely antithesis:

> Their union would her ruine be
> And her Tyrannick pow'r depose.

And that characteristically exhilarating piece of semi-burlesque hyperbole, that the poles-apart lovers could only be joined if the world were 'cramp'd into a *Planisphere*'—what is it but our old friend the catalogue of impossibilities, ἀδύνατα ('till oaks sweat honey', 'till fish scale the mountains' etc), so familiar in Greek and Roman poetry, brought up to date? This is one of the great differences between Donne and Marvell: while Donne, one might say, devised entirely new ways of saying entirely new things, Marvell assimilated, re-combined and perfected from his contemporaries various new ways of saying old ones.

In what, after the *Horatian Ode*, is perhaps Marvell's finest single poem, *To his Coy Mistress*, it can be shown that throughout he is doing very old and traditional things in a new way, and that he is only being very superficially like Donne. The poem is indeed, like many of Donne's and unlike *The Definition of Love*, a continuous argument, and even a more rigidly syllogistic argument than I think we shall find in any of the more serious of the *Songs and Sonets*, where Donne is usually concerned with analogies rather than with demonstration: 'If we had infinite time, I should be happy to court you at leisure; But our life lasts only for a moment: Therefore, in order to live, we must seize the moment as it flies.' It is only in such fundamentally unserious poems as *The Will* that we shall find Donne being as neatly syllogistic as this. Where this poem most resembles Donne, and is perhaps more fundamentally indebted to his example than any other of Marvell's poems, is in its essentially dramatic tone (more dramatic than anywhere else in Marvell), in the way in which it makes us feel that we are overhearing one of the speakers in a dialogue. But, before proceeding, let us make sure that we have the poem vividly in our minds:

> Had we but World enough, and Time,
> This coyness Lady were no crime.
> We could sit down, and think which way
> To walk, and pass our long Loves Day.
> Thou by the *Indian Ganges* side
> Should'st Rubies find: I by the Tide

Of *Humber* would complain. I would
Love you ten years before the Flood:
And you should if you please refuse
Till the Conversion of the *Jews*.
My vegetable Love should grow
Vaster then Empires, and more slow.
An hundred years should go to praise
Thine Eyes, and on thy Forehead Gaze.
Two hundred to adore each Breast:
But thirty thousand to the rest.
An Age at least to every part,
And the last Age should show your Heart.
For Lady you deserve this State;
Nor would I love at lower rate.
    But at my back I alwaies hear
Times winged Charriot hurrying near:
And yonder all before us lye
Desarts of vast Eternity.
Thy Beauty shall no more be found;
Nor, in thy marble Vault, shall sound
My ecchoing Song: then Worms shall try
That long preserv'd Virginity:
And your quaint Honour turn to dust;
And into ashes all my Lust.
The Grave's a fine and private place,
But none I think do there embrace.
    Now therefore,—

and Marvell reaches the conclusion of his semi-syllogistic argument
and, after some lines which are poetically rather below the general level
of his poem, magnificently concludes:

Let us roll all our Strength, and all
Our sweetness, up into one Ball:
And tear our Pleasures with rough strife,
Thorough the Iron gates of Life.
Thus, though we cannot make our Sun
Stand still, yet we will make him run.

The tempo, *allegro molto* at least, is much faster than that of any of the
more serious of Donne's *Songs and Sonets*, and, both in its speed, its

mock-serious argument and its witty hyperbole, the poem might
seem to have some affinity with Donne's tone and manner in some of
his more exuberant Elegies. The hyperbole, though—often, like that
in *A Definition of Love*, approaching burlesque—is not, as I shall try
to show later, really like Donne's, and the argument, although I have
called it 'mock-serious', is really more serious, less paradoxical, than
the sort of argument Donne conducts in the Elegies. It is also, I think,
an argument which Donne would have regarded as too traditional
and literary—the argument of Catullus's

> Vivamus, mea Lesbia, atque amemus . . .
> Soles occidere et redire possunt:
> nobis cum semel occidit brevis lux,
> nox est perpetua una dormienda,

which Ben Jonson so delightfully paraphrased as:

> Come my CELIA, let vs proue,
> While we may, the sports of loue;
> Time will not be ours, for euer:
> He, at length, our good will seuer.
> Spend not then his guifts in vaine.
> Sunnes, that set, may rise againe:
> But if once we loose this light,
> 'Tis, with vs, perpetuall night.

On this ancient theme Marvell has executed a series of brilliant seventeenth-century variations, which were partly suggested to him by the
last stanza of a poem in Cowley's *The Mistress* entitled *My Dyet*, a
stanza from which Marvell has borrowed and made unforgettable
the phrase 'vast Eternity':[1]

---

1. Cowley, too, evidently thought the phrase a good one, for he used it again
in the penultimate line of his ode *Sitting and Drinking in the Chair made out of the
Reliques of Sir* Francis Drake's *Ship*, first printed in *Verses lately written upon Several
Occasions*, 1663:

> The streits of time too narrow are for thee,
> Launch forth into an indiscovered Sea,
> And steer the endless course of vast Eternity,
> Take for thy Sail this Verse, and for thy Pilot Me.

It should be noted that the phrase also occurs in Herrick's *Eternitie* (*Hesperides*,
1648), as well as in a scene which Davenant added to his play *The Unfortunate Lovers*
after the Restoration.

> On 'a *Sigh* of Pity I a year can live,
>   One *Tear* will keep me twenty' at least,
>   Fifty a gentle *Look* will give:
> An hundred years on one *kind word* I'll feast:
>   A thousand more will added be,
> If you an *Inclination* have for me;
> And all beyond is vast *Eternitie*.

Cowley was by no means the first to introduce arithmetic into love-poetry, but he has here exploited its possibilities in a way that seems to be original.[1] The earliest of these arithmetical amorists, so far as I know, was an anonymous Alexandrian imitator of Anacreon, who, anticipating Leporello's catalogue of his master's conquests in Mozart's *Don Giovanni*, wrote a poem which begins: 'If you can count the leaves of all trees and the waves of the whole ocean, then I will make you sole reckoner of my loves. First set down twenty from Athens and add to them fifteen. Then set down whole chains of loves from Corinth, for it is in Achaea, where women are beautiful.'[2] Catullus, at the conclusion of *Vivamus mea Lesbia*, seems to have been the first poet to write arithmetically of kisses:

> Da mi basia mille, deinde centum,
>   dein mille altera, dein secunda centum—

In Ben Jonson's paraphrase:

> Kisse againe: no creature comes.
> Kisse, and score vp wealthy summes
> On my lips, thus hardly sundred,
> While you breath. First giue a hundred,
> Then a thousand, then another
> Hundred, then vnto the tother

---

1. Still more original, more remote from classical precedent, and more essentially intellectual and psychological had been Donne's use of arithmetic in *The Computation*, a poem which begins

> For the first twenty yeares, since yesterday,
>   I scarce beleev'd, thou could'st be gone away,

and which might be called a hyperbolically analytical description of the state of being parted. Donne there divides the time (as experienced and measured by a lover) since their yesterday's parting into periods ranging from twenty to a thousand years.

2. *Anacreontea* 14, Εἰ φύλλα πάντα δένδρων.

> Adde a thousand, and so more:
> Till you equall with the store,
> All the grasse that *Rumney* yeelds,
> Or the sands in *Chelsey* fields,
> Or the drops in siluer *Thames*,
> Or the starres, that guild his streames.

Like Johannes Secundus before him,[1] the French Renaissance Latin poet Étienne Pasquier, whom I have already quoted on the subject of a lovely widow, combined, in a poem *Ad Sabinam*, this osculatory arithmetic, or arithmetical osculation, with one of the most popular themes of classical and Renaissance love-poetry, the catalogue of a mistress's charms, declaring that he would print a thousand kisses on every part of Sabina's body:

> Quid renitteris? obstinatiora
> Carpo basia mille singulatim.
> Labris millia, millia en ocellis,
> Genis millia, millia en papillis,
> Obsignabo, licet puella nolit.[2]

('Why do you resist? I snatch my kisses all the more resolutely, a thousand at a time. Thousands on lips, thousands on eyes, thousands on cheeks, thousands on breasts I will implant—unwilling though the girl may be.')

Throughout the first twenty lines of his poem Marvell is making a brilliantly original use of the time-measuring arithmetic in that stanza of Cowley's from which he borrowed the phrase 'vast Eternity'. In the passage beginning

> An hundred years should go to praise
> Thine Eyes, and on thy Forehead Gaze,

he has applied it to that traditional and popular topic, the catalogue of a mistress's charms—a novel combination, I think, although it may have been suggested to him by Pasquier's combination of that traditional catalogue with the osculatory arithmetic of Catullus. In the exuberant hyperbole and antithesis of his opening lines, declaring that, had they but world enough and time, he would be willing to court

---

1. *Basia*, vii.
2. *Deliciae C. C. Poetarum Gallorum*, ed. R. Gherus (i.e. Janus Gruterus), 1609, i 10100.

her and be refused by her from ten years before the Flood until the Conversion of the Jews, Marvell is not only being original, but writing in a manner in which no poets except some English seventeenth-century ones ever wrote. When ancient poets handled the topics of *carpe diem* and *carpe florem*, when they pointed, like the author of the *Epitaphium Bionos*, to the contrast between the returning anise and parsley, or, like Horace in *Diffugere nives*, to the contrast between the returning seasons, the returning sun and moon, and the unreturning lives of men, or when they exhorted some unresponsive girl or boy to learn a lesson from the withering and neglected rose, they nearly always wrote with an undiluted pathos and seriousness and even solemnity; or, if any trace of a smile was there, it was a sad one. And the Renaissance Italian and French poets, when they handled these topics, nearly always preserved a similar tone. It was only certain English poets of the earlier seventeenth century who expanded and varied these and other traditional topics with the witty, elaborate, and sometimes positively hilarious ingenuity of Marvell in this poem.

This does not mean that Marvell's poem is, in comparison, slight or unserious or superficial, for in its central section it sounds notes as deep as those of any ancient poetry on the topics of *carpe diem* and *carpe florem*:

> But at my back I alwaies hear
> Times winged Charriot hurrying near:
> And yonder all before us lye
> Desarts of vast Eternity.
> Thy Beauty shall no more be found;
> Nor, in thy marble Vault, shall sound
> My ecchoing Song: then Worms shall try
> That long preserv'd Virginity:
> And your quaint Honour turn to dust;
> And into ashes all my Lust.
> The Grave's a fine and private place,
> But none I think do there embrace.

'Your quaint Honour': that indeed is a characteristically post-classical conception, with a faint echo of the *Roman de la Rose* and a much stronger one of a famous chorus in Tasso's pastoral drama *Aminta*, celebrating that *bel età del oro* when *il gigante Onor* was unknown. But behind the rest of this passage lies, I feel almost sure, either directly or indirectly (for it was imitated by several Renaissance poets, both Latin

and vernacular), something much more ancient: an epigram of Asclepiades in the Greek Anthology (V 85):

> Φείδη παρθενίης· καὶ τὶ πλέον; οὐ γὰρ ἐς "Ἀδην
> ἐλθοῦσ' εὑρήσεις τὸν φιλέοντα, κόρη.
> ἐν ξωοῖσι τὰ τερπνὰ τὰ Κύπριδος· ἐν δ' Ἀχέροντι
> ὀστέα καὶ σποδιή, παρθένε, κεισόμεθα.

('Hoarding your maidenhood—and why? For not when to Hades
   You've gone down shall you find, maiden, the lover you lack.
Only among the alive are the joys of Cypris, and only,
   Maiden, as bones and dust shall we in Acheron lie.')

Here, as so often, out of something old Marvell has made something
entirely new—or, what amounts to the same thing, something that
gives the impression of being entirely new.

> ἐν δ' Ἀχέροντι
> ὀστέα καὶ σποδιή, παρθένε, κεισόμεθα.

> The Grave's a fine and private place,
> But none I think do there embrace.

Had he not known that epigram of Asclepiades, I doubt whether
Marvell would, or perhaps could, have written those lines; and yet
their irony, their concentration, their colloquial vigour are absolutely
Marvellian and absolutely seventeenth-century: they could have been
written at no other period and probably by no other poet. How pale
and thin and unmemorable in comparison (to mention two of the most
famous poets of the preceding century) are Johannes Secundus's imitation of this epigram in one of his Elegies (I v) and Ronsard's imitation of Secundus's imitation in his Ode à sa Maîtresse![1] While Marvell
remains absolutely contemporary, Ronsard brings in Pluto and
Charon's skiff:

> Pour qui gardes-tu tes yeux,
> Et ton sein délicieux,
> Ta joue et ta bouche belle?
> En veux-tu baiser Pluton,
> Là-bas, après que Caron
> T'aura mise en sa nacelle?

1. In his Poèmes of 1569 Ronsard published an undistinguished translation of
this epigram of Asclepiades, beginning Dame au gros cœur, pourquoy t'espargnes-tu, and
a not much more distinguished expansion of it into a sonnet, beginning Douce
beauté, meurdrière de ma vie.

While Ronsard's lines are no more than an agreeable example of neo-classic imitation, such as any other member of the Pléiade could have produced, what Marvell has given us is not so much an imitation as a transmutation. And, indeed, his whole poem is a superb example of the fact that his poetry, although in the highest degree original, would have been impossible without the numerous literary sources from which he derived inspiration, stimulation and suggestion. A stanza of Cowley's, a poem by Catullus, a Greek epigram, possibly a neo-Latin one—we can see how they all played an essential part in the genesis of Marvell's poem, and yet, at the same time, we can also see that he has transmuted them into something unmistakably his own. This is indeed originality, but it is a different kind of originality from that which Donne wanted to achieve. Marvell, here and elsewhere, though nowhere more notably than here, has given a dose of reanimating and renovating intellectuality, or intellection, to all manner of traditional topics and traditional procedures which Donne would probably have disdained and which, at any rate, would have been incompatible with that predominantly analytical and inward-looking kind of poetry he was writing in the *Songs and Sonets*. For, while Donne is there primarily concerned with love as an experienced fact, Marvell, in this brilliant poem, is primarily concerned with it as a topic. Both Donne and Marvell were amateur, not professional, poets, and their motives for writing, apart from the incidental one of pleasing and exciting admiration among friends, was the sheer desire to exercise an exceptional gift for making something with words. No doubt with both the desire to exercise this gift only became irresistible when they felt they had something, or had found something, which they particularly wanted to write *about*; but, while with Donne this something would seem normally to have emerged from an examination of his own actual or imagined experience, with Marvell it would seem normally to have emerged from his reading and from reflection upon his reading: from a sudden perception of the possibility of performing new and exciting variations on old themes. The main theme of *To his Coy Mistress* is the very ancient one of *carpe florem*, the invitation, sometimes mainly pleading, sometimes mainly admonitory, to 'gather the Rose of love whilest yet is time'. It is (I use the word unpejoratively) an essentially rhetorical theme, a theme in which there is no proper place for that self-analysis which is so characteristic of Donne's *Songs and Sonets*. There are indeed a few poems in that collection, presumably written during his middle years and perhaps in order to please some of his noble patronesses, where Donne, uncharacteristically, one is inclined to say, and not very seriously, represents himself as languishing in hopeless adoration for a woman, sometimes older than himself, who does not return his affection, or who cares only for his mind; but it is surely significant that the only two poems where courtship or invitation predominates should be *The Baite*, that parody, or semi-parody, of Marlowe's 'Come live with me and be my love', and the wholly unserious *Flea*. It was partly, perhaps, this almost complete absence of pleading and courtship from the *Songs and Sonets*, together with the fact that in so many of those poems Donne writes either as one who has disgustedly had, or ecstatically has, or only on his own contemptuous and humiliating terms will have, love, which led Professor Crofts to declare, not quite fairly, that Donne wrote 'not of love, but of himself loving'.[1] I should prefer to say that both Donne in his way, and the Shakespeare of the Sonnets in his, write of love experienced, whereas Marvell writes of (or rather, perhaps, on) love as a topic. Nevertheless, unlike Cowley, who too often wrote on love as a topic in clever but unconvincing imitations of the manner in which Donne wrote of it as an experience, Marvell has demonstrated that even on love as a topic it is possible to write incomparable poetry. We tend to forget that, despite the Horatian variety of subject-matter to which Ben Jonson, in this respect an innovator, gave lyrical expression, love, whether as a topic or as an experience, whether considered seriously, playfully, or satirically, still remained the most natural, the most expected, the most obvious subject for a seventeenth-century lyrical poet to write about. It too often deflected Cowley from that semi-Horatian reflective and moral poetry where his true bent lay and where we can still hear what Pope called 'the language of his heart'. In the rest of Marvell's poetry it often makes incidental appearances, but seldom predominates; it is as though in these two poems he had resolved to show what he could do with this favourite subject, and they are two poems that would have to be included in any representative anthology of seventeenth-century poetry.

It is not only in what, comparatively speaking, may be called its literariness and traditionality that Marvell's manner in *To his Coy Mistress* differs from Donne's.

1. 'John Donne', in *Essays and Studies by Members of the English Association*, 1936, p. 134.

                                    I would
                    Love you ten years before the Flood:
                    And you should if you please refuse
                    Till the Conversion of the *Jews*.
                    My vegetable Love should grow
                    Vaster then Empires, and more slow.

Here we have not merely what seems to be an entirely original use of
the well-established topic, or trope, of amatory arithmetic; we have
also, as in *The Definition of Love*, our old classical friend, the catalogue
of improbabilities, ἀδύνατα, brought up to date.[1] But the manner in
which it is brought up to date is not, I think, a manner which Marvell
learnt from Donne. Donne, it is true, excelled in witty hyperbole,
but these lines are not merely hyperbolical, they are almost burlesque
—or, at any rate, they have a touch of that burlesque extravagance
and hilarity which Marvell, I am convinced, learnt from that enormously popular contemporary poet John Cleveland and practised extensively
in the Bilborough and Appleton House poems and even, to some
extent, in *The Garden* and the *Dialogue between the Soul and Body*. Consider, for example, the third stanza of Cleveland's *To the State of Love;
or, The Senses' Festival*, first printed in the 1651 edition of his poems:

                    My sight took say,[2] but (thank my charms!)
                    I now impale her in my arms;
                    (Love's compasses confining you,
                    Good angels, to a circle too.)
                    Is not the universe strait-laced

1. Contrast the way in which, both here and in *The Definition of Love*, Marvell has
modernised the catalogue of ἀδύνατα with the traditional and unoriginal manner in
which Carew has used it in *The Protestation* (*Poems*, ed. Dunlap, p. 109), a poem of
four stanzas, of which this, the second, is typical:

                    The fish shall in the Ocean burne,
                    And fountaines sweet shall bitter turne,
                    The humble oake no flood shall know,
                    When floods shall highest hills ore-flow;
                    Blacke *Læthe* shall oblivion leave,
                    If ere my *Celia* I deceive.

The editor remarks that the style of this poem was old-fashioned by Carew's day,
and quotes two very similar stanzas from a poem in *The Paradyse of daynty deuises*,
1576.

2. Made trial: see *OED*, *say*, sb. (an aphetic form of *assay*), sense 6, 'a trial of
food by taste or smell'. *OED* quotes Cooper, *Thesaurus*, 1565: 'Degusto, . . . to taste:
to take a little saye.'

When I can clasp it in the waist?
My amorous folds about thee hurled,
Like Drake I girdle in the world;[1]
I hoop the firmament, and make
This, my embrace, the zodiac.
   How would thy centre take my sense
   When admiration doth commence
   At the extreme circumference?

It was Cleveland too, who, in his poem *Upon Phillis walking in a morning before sun-rising*, consummated, in a manner which inspired many passages in Marvell's *Appleton House*, a characteristic seventeenth-century development of what, since it occurs in pastorals by Theocritus and Virgil, I have been accustomed to call the 'pastoral hyperbole', and which in those two poets amounted to little more than saying that all things flourished in the presence of the beloved and withered at her (or his) departure. It seems likely that the attention of our seventeenth-century poets was first directed to the possibilities of witty elaboration on this topic by that popular poem of Strode's *On Chloris walking in the Snow*, itself inspired by a poem of Tasso's,[2] in whose *Rime* there are many elegant variations on this topic, most of them rather pale and anaemic in comparison with those of our own poets.[3] Even after the topic had been so often handled as to excite Suckling to something like parody,[4] Waller seems to have given a new lease of

1. In Geoffrey Whitney's *A Choice of Emblemes and other Devises*, 1586, there is an emblem (reproduced in Rosemary Freeman's *English Emblem Books*, 1948, p. 56) representing a freely suspended globe, on the top of which is poised Drake's ship. In the top left-hand corner the hand of Providence, outstretched from a cloud, grasps one end of a girdle which hangs in a loop around the suspended globe, its other end being attached to Drake's ship.

2. *Ritorno di Madonna in tempo di neve* ('La terra si copria d'orrido velo'), *Rime*, ed. Solerti, II 61. Tasso also has a similar poem entitled *Vista impedita della Neve* ('Negro era intorno, e' in bianche falde il cielo'), *op. cit.*, 331, together with many less specialised developments of the 'pastoral hyperbole', among the more notable of which are 'Or che riede Madonna al bel soggiorno' (p. 232) and 'Or che l'aura mia dolce altrove spira' (p. 258). See also pp. 216, 222, 224 etc.

3. Strode's poem was first printed in 1632, in W. Porter's *Madrigals and Airs*. Among the 'Excellent Poems . . . by other Gentlemen' in Benson's edition of Shakespeare's *Poems*, 1640, are *Lavinia walking in a frosty Morning* (L6ᵛ) and *Vpon a Gentlewoman walking on the Grasse* (M2ᵛ). In the same year appeared as no. 126 in the first edition of *Wits Recreations* (Camden Hotten reprint of *Musarum Deliciae* etc., II 17) a poem, perhaps more obviously inspired by Strode's, beginning 'I saw faire *Flora* take the aire'.

4. In the dialogue-poem between himself ('J.S.') and Carew ('T.C.') *Vpon my Lady Carliles walking in Hampton-Court garden*, which must have been written before Carew's death in 1640 and Suckling's in 1642.

life to it with one of his Sacharissa poems, *At Penshurst*,[1] first printed in the 1645 edition of his *Poems*, a poem from which I think it can be shown that both Cleveland and Marvell took hints.[2] But while Waller and his predecessors, though bolder and more vigorous than Tasso, had still kept their personifications within more or less decorous and classical bounds, Cleveland in this poem, printed in his first volume of 1647, lets himself go with a riotous and hilarious extravagance that approaches burlesque.

> The sluggish morn as yet undressed,
> My Phillis brake from out her East,
> As if she'd made a match to run
> With Venus, usher to the Sun.
> The trees, like yeomen of her guard,
> Serving more for pomp than ward,
> Ranked on each side, with loyal duty
> Weave branches to enclose her beauty.
> The plants, whose luxury was lopped,
> Or age with crutches underpropped,
> Whose wooden carcasses are grown
> To be but coffins of their own,
> Revive, and at her general dole
> Each receives his ancient soul.
> The winged choiristers began
> To chirp their mattins, and the fan
> Of whistling winds like organs played,
> Until their voluntaries made
> The wakened East in odours rise
> To be her morning sacrifice.

In a later chapter I shall examine in some detail how Marvell, in the

1. 'Had Sacharissa (1645: 'Dorothea') lived when mortals made', *Poems*, ed. Thorn Drury, I 46. Waller seems to have begun paying his addresses to Lady Dorothy Sidney ('Sacharissa') towards the end of 1635, and presumably ceased to address poems to her after her marriage in 1639.

2. In a later chapter (pp. 233, ff.) I shall show that Waller, 'betwixt two ages cast' and in whom there is so much that is both old and new, has one or two other poems whose semi-humorous, semi-burlesque hyperbole to some extent anticipates both Cleveland and Marvell, and that there is an enormous contrast between these occasional experiments in a new manner and the old-fashioned eulogy and panegyric, the pompous and inane hyperboles, in so many of his poems to the King and Queen and on public events. One of the great differences, not only between Marvell and Waller but also between Marvell and Dryden, is that Marvell's hyperbolical compliments are nearly always intended to cause amusement as well as gratification.

Bilborough and Appleton House poems, has combined what may be
called Clevelandish hyperbole and burlesque, or near burlesque, with
more permanent sources of poetic pleasure: here, in order to demonstrate that this way of writing, which we have come to regard as so
characteristic of Marvell, was suggested to him by Cleveland, it should
be sufficient to place side by side with the passage I have just quoted
a few lines from that passage towards the end of *Appleton House* where
Nature pays her respects to the 'young Maria'.

> See how loose Nature, in respect
> To her, it self doth recollect;
> And every thing so whisht and fine,
> Starts forth with to its *Bonne Mine*.
> The *Sun* himself, of *Her* aware,
> Seems to descend with greater Care;
> And lest *She* see him go to Bed;
> In blushing Clouds conceales his Head.
>
> (st. LXXXIII)

> 'Tis *She* that to these Gardens gave
> That wondrous Beauty which they have;
>
> (st. LXXXVII)

> Therefore what first *She* on them spent,
> They gratefully again present.
> The Meadow Carpets where to tread;
> The Garden Flow'rs to Crown *Her* Head;
> And for a Glass the limpid Brook,
> Where *She* may all *her* Beautyes look;
> But, since *She* would not have them seen,
> The Wood about *her* draws a Skreen.
>
> (st. LXXXVIII)

Nowhere is the essential unlikeness of Marvell's poetry to Donne's
more apparent than in his happy acquiescence in various characteristic
seventeenth-century developments of the pastoral tradition and of
what, including therein both Marlowe's *Passionate Shepherd* and Milton's
L'Allegro and *Il Penseroso*, may be called 'the catalogue of delights'.
Much of Marvell's best poetry is pastoral or semi-pastoral, and in most
of it description, however wittily intellectualised, of things obviously
beautiful or attractive plays a very great part. There is nothing of this
in Donne: his only approach to pastoral is his parody of Marlowe's

Passionate Shepherd in *The Baite*; in the *Songs and Sonets* static or exterior description, as distinct from the analysis or evocation of moods, relationships and situations, is almost completely absent; and elsewhere in his poetry any vivid visual description is usually satirical. There are indeed a few exceptions to this last remark, the most notable being *The Storme* and *The Calme*, written during the Islands Voyage of 1597, but nothing could be more remote from pastoral and prettiness than the description in those two poems. Donne is sometimes fascinated, stimulated or irritated into visual description, but we never feel that he is in love with what he is describing in the way that Marvell almost always is. There is, as I have said, no prettiness in Donne's poetry. Was his rejection of it deliberate and contemptuous, or was it simply instinctive? Something of both, perhaps. He was presumably well aware that he was attempting to do something the like of which no English poet had done before. Was he, at the same time, scornfully rejecting anything that might seem to give him, as it were, a poetical advantage, anything that might stimulate what modern critics call the stock response? Was he resolved that no readers should admire him for the wrong reasons, or imagine that they were enjoying his poetry when they were really enjoying allusions to classical mythology, shepherds and shepherdesses, singing birds, silver streams, enamelled meads, new-blown roses, and so on? Or was it simply that he was not deeply interested in such things, and that they were not really compatible with the only kinds of poetry he cared to write? Marvell's originality was of a much more tolerant and unambitious kind. He was ready, one might almost say, to accept, to exploit, and to recombine, to Marvellise and seventeenth-centurify, anything that had ever made poetry enjoyable.

There is a memorable passage in *The Compleat Angler* where Izaak Walton describes the milkmaid and her ditty:

'twas that smooth Song which was made by *Kit Marlow*, now at least fifty years ago; and the Milkmaids mother sung an answer to it, which was made by Sir *Walter Raleigh* in his younger dayes.

They were old fashioned Poetry, but choicely good, I think much better than the strong lines[1] that are now in fashion in this Critical age.

1. See an article by G. Williamson, 'Strong lines', in *English Studies*, 1936, pp. 152 ff.; reprinted in *Seventeenth-Century Contexts*, 1960. (1) The term was presumably first used as one of commendation, but it is hard to find any surviving example of its use that is not more or less pejorative or sarcastic. There is here some analogy

There were many seventeenth-century readers who could enjoy both
the old-fashioned Elizabethan pastoral poetry and the more intellectual, more 'strong-lined' poetry of Donne and Ben Jonson, and there
were many seventeenth-century poets, of whom Marvell was the most
notable, who saw the possibility of combining something of both.
Besides his three pastoral dialogues, many of Marvell's best poems
are at least formally pastorals, and others have at least a strong
affinity with the pastoral tradition. I shall consider them and some
of their precursors in detail in a following chapter: here it is sufficient
to mention them as evidence of that eclecticism, traditionality, recep-
tiveness and predominance of description over analysis which distinguishes Marvell's poetry from Donne's.

And yet, despite what, in comparison, might almost be called its
'literariness', Marvell's best poetry is as original, or, what amounts
to the same thing, as irreplaceable, as Donne's, even though Donne's
conforms so much more closely to the characteristically modern,
post-Romantic, conception of originality. It is true that not even
Donne had sprung, as Homer would say, from an oak or a rock, and
that we can point to this and that as having suggested to him various
possibilities and poetic procedures: to Wyatt's Songs; to the dramatic
element, especially the sudden turns and the frequency of dialogue, in
Horace's Satires; to Ovid's *Amores* and *Ars amatoria*; to the Italian
writers of paradoxes, epigrams and *capitoli*—even, in *Twicknam Garden*,
to the Petrarchan situation of a lover surrounded by beautiful sights
and sounds which are no compensation for the absence or unrespon-
siveness of his beloved. Nevertheless, Donne is not, in the sense in
which Ben Jonson and Milton and Marvell are, a 'literary' poet: in
general, he has taken no more than hints and suggestions from literary
sources and has developed them in quite unprecedented ways; it is
only occasionally, and seldom very confidently, that we can point to
particular passages which he has imitated, and it would be hard to

---

with the use of the word 'sensitive' in modern journalistic criticism: one would
probably have to go back many years to find unambiguously eulogistic applications
of it to lady-novelists and chroniclers of childhood. (2) There are a few passages
which suggest that the term may have been first used, not as one of general commendation, but, as it were, technically, to describe the kind of heroic couplet which
seems first to have been used by Donne, in his Satires, as an English equivalent of
the 'harsh' satirical hexameter of Horace: Henry Reynolds, *Mythomystes* (?1633),
in *Critical Essays of the Seventeenth Century*, ed. J. E. Spingarn, I 143, ll. 9–12; Thomas
Pestell, *Poems*, ed. Hannah Buchan, 1940, p. 6; Dudley North, *A Forest of Varieties*,
1645, pp. 216 ff.

find a single example of that deliberate imitation or adaptation of another poet's phrases which is not infrequent in Marvell and which
occurs continually in the earlier poems of Milton. Had there been no
Spenser, no Sidney, no Shakespeare, and even no Jonson, Donne's
poetry would still, one feels, have been very much what it is. If he
was inspired at all by contemporary English poetry, he was inspired
in the way that Hopkins said he was by masterpieces—inspired to do
something different. More so, perhaps, than any other notable English poet except Hopkins, Donne wrote his poetry, as children say,
out of his own head. In recent times there has been some tendency
to set an excessive value upon this kind of originality: Marvell's poetry
may serve to remind us that there are other kinds of originality not
less valuable; that (to make a rough and ready distinction) originality
of combination can be as triumphantly successful as originality
of invention, and that the value of a poet's achievement is not necessarily diminished by the fact that he could not have written his poetry
if his immediate predecessors had not already written theirs.

I have several times remarked that in his various combinations of
old and new Marvell was doing more successfully and memorably
the sort of thing that many of his predecessors had been doing.
Nevertheless, the difference between the impression produced upon
us by a reading of his non-political poetry in its entirety and that produced upon us by a reading of the poetry of almost any other secular
poet of the earlier seventeenth century, except Milton, in its entirety is
so great as to amount almost to a difference of kind. In most of the
other poets a few triumphant successes stand out from a mass of more
or less tedious and mediocre verse, but in almost all Marvell's poems
and in most of his stanzas, despite the too frequent inversions and expletives, there is something individual and memorable. From what
other seventeenth-century poet is it possible to recall so many phrases?
—'That unfathomable Grass', 'the brotherless *Heliades*', 'Musick, the
Mosaique of the Air', a 'green Thought in a green Shade': one could
prolong the list indefinitely, including in it something from almost
every stanza of the *Horatian Ode*. For, although Marvell occasionally
appropriates or adapts the phrases of other poets, what in the main he
imitates is not verbal details but poetic effects, and he often seems to
be exploiting possibilities which he has not actually found in other
poets but which, nevertheless, their poems have suggested to him.
It seems probable, for example, that *L'Allegro* and *Il Penseroso* both
increased his awareness of the possibilities of the octosyllabic couplet

and largely inspired those two quite different 'catalogues of delights', *The Garden* and *Appleton House*. And, when I speak of his originality of combination, I am thinking chiefly of that sheer poetic energy and poetic tact which have so often enabled him to fuse into new compounds elements which in other poets we usually find either separate or merely mixed. As I shall attempt to demonstrate in a later chapter, he has combined in the descriptive passages of *Appleton House* much Clevelandish hyperbole and burlesque with more permanent sources of poetic pleasure, and even in what may be called his Sylvestrian descriptions of nature in terms of art he has contrived to achieve a just balance between the surprising and the permanently delightful. The permanently delightful: there are very few of Marvell's non-political poems where this is not present, whereas in the collected works of most other secular poets of the earlier seventeenth century there are only a few poems where it is. This is especially true of those in whose poetry intellection predominates: Carew's finest poems are, I think, finer than any of Herrick's, but in Herrick's collected poems, despite much that is quite negligible, there are far more poems that are permanently delightful.

It is illuminating to compare Marvell with that once enormously popular Cambridge poet Thomas Randolph, whose poems were published posthumously in 1638 and 1640 and who was regarded by many of his contemporaries as the legitimate successor of Ben Jonson. How many of Randolph's poems have remained 'permanently delightful'? Certainly, what is probably his best poem, *An Ode to Mr* Anthony Stafford *to hasten him into the Country*,[1] where Randolph appears as a not unworthy 'Son of Ben', writing in a manner reminiscent of some of Jonson's best 'Horatian' poems, such as the *Ode to Himself* and the *Epistle to Sir Robert Wroth*; certainly, too, *Upon his Picture*,[2] a little poem with a touch of the Greek Anthology about it; then perhaps only certain passages in his pastorals or semi-pastorals, including *Upon Love fondly refus'd for Conscience Sake*,[3] whose metre Marvell seems to have imitated and one of whose arguments he seems to have taken as his starting-point in *The Mower against Gardens*. It is the most consistently successful of Randolph's pastoral or semi-pastoral poems, and comes nearest to achieving that special combination of intellection and prettiness which Marvell has achieved in so many poems. Elsewhere in Randolph's pastoral or semi-pastoral poems, and to some extent even

1. *The Poems of Thomas Randolph*, ed. G. Thorn Drury, 1929, p. 79.
2. *op cit.*, p. 79.   3. *op. cit.*, p. 128.

here, the kind of thing Marvell achieved is present to us only in a
sense approaching that in which Michelangelo declared that the statue
was present to him in the block of marble—present only as a poten-
tiality which it required a Marvell to actualise. In most of Randolph's
other poems there appears, either separately or incongruously juxtaposed, not fused, on the one hand, an abundance of the tritest sort of
allusion to classical legend and mythology, and, on the other hand,
as in so much of the academic verse of the time, a kind of abstractness
which is quite unlike that in many of Donne's *Songs and Sonets*, and
which might be more accurately described as cerebral than as intellectual, since it is concerned not with significant and permanent relationships and experiences but with a rather trivial exploitation of the possibilities of antithesis and epigram offered by any subject that comes to
hand. To consider first the trite classicism, Randolph's editor has
justly remarked:

> There is scarcely a proper name familiar to the Classical Dictionary
> that he has failed to introduce . . . To Randolph the sea is 'Neptune's
> watry plaine';[1] he cannot write an elegy on Lady Digby[2] without
> introducing Mars and Venus, Paris and Helen, Troy and the Greeks
> and all the Spices of Arabia; if the idea of wealth occurs to him . . .
> it is always accompanied by the Indies, Tagus and Pactolus, each
> with its constant epithet; if he fails to fall in love[3] he fears it may be
> because, like Tethys with Achilles and the Styx, his parents may
> have tried to render him invulnerable.[4]

Thorn Drury declares that the Indies, Tagus and Pactolus appear at
least three times; in fact, they appear at least five, and, in order to point the
contrast with Marvell, it seems worth while to exhibit the passages
where they occur. Towards the end of his poem *On the inestimable
Content he injoyes in the Muses*, he exclaims:

> O humane blindnesse! had we eyes to see,
> There is no wealth to valiant poetry!
> And yet what want I Heaven or Earth can yeeld?
> Me thinkes I now possess the *Elisian* field.
> Into my chest the yellow *Tagus* flowes,
> While my plate fleete in bright *Pactolus* rowes.

1. *On the inestimable Content he injoyes in the Muses, op. cit.*, p. 24.
2. *op. cit.*, p. 52.
3. *A Complaint against* Cupid *that he never made him in Love, op. cit.*, p. 36.
4. *op. cit.*, p. xxiv.

Th' *Hesperian* Orchard's mine; mine, mine is all:
Thus am I rich in wealth poëticall.[1]

In *A gratulatory to Mr Ben Johnson for his adopting of him to be his Son*, he thus acknowledges, in a passage of considerable literary historical interest, the poetical indebtedness of himself and others to the master:

Have I a sparke of that cœlestiall flame
Within me, I confesse I stole the same
Prometheus like, from thee; and may I feed
His vulture, when I dare deny the deed.
Many more moones thou hast, that shine by night,
All Bankrups, wer't not for a borrow'd light;
Yet can forsweare it; I the debt confesse,
And thinke my reputation ne're the lesse.
For Father let me be resolv'd by you;
Is't a disparagement from rich *Peru*
To ravish gold; or theft, for wealthy Ore
To ransack *Tagus*, or *Pactolus* shore?
Or does he wrong *Alcinous*, that for want
Doth take from him a sprig or two, to plant
A lesser Orchard? sure it cannot bee:
Nor is it theft to steale some flames from thee.[2]

He has only written five lines of his poem *In Lesbiam, & Histrionem*, on a wealthy woman who lavishes her money on a young player, before this stock simile appears:

The play-boy spends secure; he shall have more;
As if both *Indies* did supply his store.
As if he did in bright *Pactolus* swim,
Or *Tagus* yellow waves did water him.[3]

An Epithalamium to Mr F. H. was written in 1628, while Randolph was still at Cambridge, and is filled with what Dr Johnson contemptuously and, with respect to *Lycidas*, unjustly described as 'a long train of mythological imagery, such as a College easily supplies'. Towards the middle of his poem Randolph observes that the bridegroom, though his name is Ward, has nothing in common with his namesake, the notorious Jacobean pirate, but he immediately proceeds to smother this original and contemporary witticism in schoolboyish recollections

1. *op. cit.*, p. 28.   2. *op. cit.*, p. 41.   3. *op. cit.*, p. 42.

of the classics, and mention of the pirate's ill-gotten gains produces
Tagus and Pactolus as inevitably as the repeated stimulus produced
saliva from Pavlov's dogs: this Ward, he declares, only sails, like
Leander, the Hellespont of love and steals only what is within the
breast:

> Yet let that other *Ward* his thefts compare,
> And ransack all his treasures, let him beare
> The wealth of worlds, the bowels of the *West*
> And all the richest treasures of the *East*,
> The sands of *Tagus*, all *Pactolus* ore,
> With both the *Indies*; yet this one gets more
> At once by Love then he by force could get
> Or ravish from the Marchants; let him set
> His Ores together; let him vainely boast
> Of spices snatch'd from the *Canary* coast;
> The Gummes of *Ægypt*, or the *Tyrian* fleece
> Dyed in his Native purple, with what *Greece*,
> *Colchos*, *Arabia*, or proud *China* yeilds,
> With all the Metals in *Guiana* feilds.
> When this has set all forth to boast his pride
> In various pompe; this other brings his Bride,
> And I'le be judg'd by all judicious eyes,
> If shee alone prove not the richer prize.[1]

Even in *A parley with his empty Purse*, one of his (in its kind) better
poems and one especially admired by his contemporaries, Tagus and
Pactolus make their all too expected appearance, although it might be
pleaded that here his allusion to them, like the immediately following
one to Orpheus, is essentially burlesque:

> Can meeter cancell bonds? is here a time
> Ever to hope to wipe out chalke with rime?
> Or if I now were hurrying to the jaile
> Are the nine *Muses* held sufficient baile?
> Would they to any composition come
> If we should morgage our *Elisium*,
> *Tempe*, *Parnassus*, and the golden streames
> Of *Tagus*, and *Pactolus*, those rich dreames
> Of active fancy? Can our *Orpheus* move
> Those rocks, and stones with his best straines of love?[2]

1. *op. cit.*, pp. 73–4.   2. *op. cit.*, pp. 127–8.

How enormous is the difference between these simple, automatic and merely line-filling enumerations from the classical dictionary and the witty, individual transmutation in Marvell's occasional allusions to classical mythology!

> She courts her self in am'rous Rain;
> Her self both *Danae* and the Showr
>
> *(Mourning,* ll. 19–20)

> The brotherless *Heliades*
> Melt in such Amber Tears as these
>
> *(The Nymph complaining,* ll. 99–100)

> The *Gods,* that mortal Beauty chase,
> Still in a Tree did end their race.
> *Apollo* hunted *Daphne* so,
> Only that She might Laurel grow.
> And *Pan* did after *Syrinx* speed,
> Not as a Nymph, but for a Reed
>
> *(The Garden,* ll. 27–32)

And there is, of course, nothing in Randolph's poetry comparable with that complete digestion and contemporising of the classics which we have already observed in Marvell's *To his Coy Mistress.* 'The grand old fortifying curriculum' did not, in fact, exert an equally beneficent influence on all seventeenth-century poets. Randolph remained until the end very much of a Westminster schoolboy, filling out and 'beautifying' his English verses from dictionary and *Gradus* in much the same way as he had done with his Latin verses at school. And in this respect he was no true son of Ben Jonson, who, despite occasional lapses into pedantry, was at his best able to transmute and contemporise what he admired in the classics. Indeed, the contrast between such verse as I have been exhibiting and the Jonsonian Horatianism of the *Ode to Mr Anthony Stafford* confirms the truth of Dr Leavis's admirable remark that

> The indebtedness to Jonson's models is of a kind that it took Jonson's genius in the first place to incur; if the later poets learnt from those models, they had learnt from Jonson how to do so.[1]

---

1. *Revaluation,* 1936, p. 20.

It is not here necessary to mention more than one or two examples of that more sheerly cerebral kind of verse of which Randolph, like other academic poets, wrote so much. In *Upon a very deformed Gentlewoman, but of a voice incomparably sweet* he extracts from his subject all the antitheses he can think of, and the result is a string of antitheses that might be indefinitely extended rather than an organised poem. Sufficiently representative are the concluding lines, which are by far the best:

> Turne only Voice, an *Eccho* prove,
> Here, here, by heav'n, I find my Love:
> If not, you Gods, to ease my mind,
> Or make her dumbe, or strike me blind;
> For griefe, and anger in me rise
> Whil'st shee hath tongue, or I have eyes.[1]

In the famous short poem *On the losse of his Finger*[2] he declares that he is tempted to envy trees, whose lopped boughs will grow again. Then he reminds himself that at the Resurrection his finger will be revived from dust and reunited to his hand as quickly as those which he retained till the end of his life. Let the lost finger stand, then, as in a margin to point his thoughts to the Resurrection. The ideas, here and elsewhere, are ingenious and often brilliant: one can admire these poems in a detached sort of way, but one feels no need whatever to return to them, and the reason is that there is scarcely ever anything distinguished or memorable about their expression. Dozens of other poets, one feels, could have 'worded' Randolph's ideas equally well. This is the great difference between Randolph's poems, and indeed between hundreds of clever and even brilliant poems in the miscellanies and manuscript commonplace-books of the time, and Marvell's: no other poet could have made out of Marvell's ideas what Marvell has made out of them. One might be tempted to regard the fact that, with one or two exceptions, it is only Randolph's pastoral or semi-pastoral poems, or certain passages in them, than can still give pleasure to a modern reader as proof that a poet (or, at any rate, a seventeenth-century one) can only successfully dispense with 'prettiness' when he is deeply concerned either with the serious examination and analysis of his own experience, like Donne and the religious poets, or with large moral ideas, like Ben Jonson. Nevertheless, although our pleasure in

1. *Poems*, ed. Thorn Drury, p. 117.   2. *op. cit.*, p. 135.

much of Marvell's poetry arises from the new visual experiences he gives us, this pleasure is probably inseparable from our simultaneous pleasure in the new linguistic experiences with which it is combined. Randolph's *A Maske for Lydia* is almost a limiting case. Both the subject and the treatment are more traditional and less time-limited, more 'courtly' and less 'academic', than the two poems I have just mentioned. It begins:

> Sweet *Lydia* take this maske, and shroud
> Thy face within the silken cloud,
>   And veile those powerfull Skies:
> For he whose gazing dares so high aspire,
>   Makes burning glasses of his eyes,
> And sets his heart on fire.

In each of the six following stanzas Randolph develops a new hyperbole, declaring in the penultimate one:

> Where's *Lydia* now? where shall I seeke
> Her charming lip, her tempting cheeke
>   That my affections bow'd?
> So dark a sable hath ecclipst my faire,
>   That I can gaze upon the cloud,
> That durst not see the Star.[1]

It is an accomplished and even brilliant poem, but, like so many other poems of its kind, an entirely unmemorable one: not merely because it communicates no new or exciting visual experience, but because it does not contain a single unforgettable line or phrase: nothing (to take two epigrammatically descriptive poems with which it may not unjustly be compared) like the

> Whose subtile Art invisibly can wreath
> My Fetters of the very Air I breath

of Marvell's *Fair Singer*; nothing like 'The floor lay paved with broken hearts' in Lovelace's unequal poem on *Gratiana Dancing and Singing*.

More comparable than anything of Randolph's with some of Marvell's combinations of old and new, of the surprising with the permanently delightful, is Cowley's *Clad all in White*, one of the most successful and memorable poems in *The Mistress* (1647). Too many of the

---

1. *op. cit.*, pp. 126–7.

poems in this book are no more than talented but, as it were, simplified and conventionalised imitations of Donne's characteristic themes,
manners and attitudes by a poet who was quite unlike Donne, but
in this poem Cowley has successfully synthesised a great variety of
more objectively descriptive manners and traditions in a way that is
truly original, or (it amounts to the same thing) which produces an
impression of true originality. It might well be one of those occasional
and memorable successes of minor or unknown poets which are to be
found in the miscellanies and manuscript commonplace-books of the
time; and it is surely not without significance that A. H. Bullen, when
he came upon it in *The New Academy of Complements* (1671), should
have failed to recognise it as Cowley's and should have printed it in
his *Speculum Amantis* as an anonymous poem. I will admit that it was
in this anthology of Bullen's that I first became really aware of it
myself, and it may well be that there are other poems in *The Mistress*
that might arrest our attention if we encountered them elsewhere.
Clad all in White is far below the best of Marvell, but it is a good example of the sort of thing that he was continually doing, even though
his sheer poetic genius and verbal energy were far greater than
Cowley's, so that his various combinations of old and new are more
of transmutations and less easily resolvable into their component
elements. It produces a somewhat similar impression of what may be
called original traditionality, and is a fine poem that would never have
been written without the examples and stimulations provided, directly
or indirectly, by numerous earlier poets, Latin, French and English.

I

Fairest thing that shines below,
Why in this Robe dost thou appear?
Wouldst thou a *white* most perfect show,
Thou must at all *no garment wear*:
Thou wilt seem much whiter so,
Than *Winter* when 'tis *clad* with snow.

II

'Tis not the *Linnen* shews so fair:
Her skin shines through, and makes it bright;
So *Clouds* themselves like *Suns* appear,
When the *Sun* pierces them with Light:
So *Lilies* in a Glass enclose,
The *Glass* will seem as white as those.

III

Thou now *one heap* of *beauty* art;
Nought outwards, or within is foul:
Condensed beams make every part;
Thy *Body's Cloathed* like thy *Soul*.
Thy *Soul*, which does it self display,
Like a *Star* plac'd i' th' *Milkie* way.

IV

Such Robes the Saints departed wear,
Woven all with *Light* Divine;
Such their exalted *Bodies* are,
And with such full Glory shine.
But they regard not Mortals pain;
Men *pray*, I fear, to *both* in vain.

V

Yet seeing thee so gently pure,
My hopes will needs continue still;
Thou wouldst not take this Garment sure,
When thou hadst an intent to *kill*.
Of *Peace* and *yielding* who would doubt,
When the white *Flag* he sees hung out?

One might be tempted to say that here Cowley's initial inspiration, as his first stanza suggests, was the delightful anonymous lyric 'My love in her attire doth shew her Wit', which first appeared in Davison's *Poetical Rhapsody* (1602), and that Cowley has proceeded to execute a series of elaborate and sophisticated seventeenth-century variations on that simple Elizabethan theme. That theme, though, was at least as old as Propertius, and had been treated by many Renaissance poets before the unknown Elizabethan played with it so perfectly: the second elegy of Propertius's First Book begins

> Quid iuvat ornato procedere, vita, capillo
> et tenues Coa veste movere sinus?
> . . .
> nec sinere in propriis membra nitere bonis?
> crede mihi, non ulla tua est medicina figurae:
> nudus Amor formae non amat artificem.

('What is the point, life of my life, of sallying out with an elaborate hair-do and rustling in slender folde of Coan silk . . . instead of allowing your limbs to shine in their own glory? Believe me, no art of yours can add beauty to your form. Love, naked himself, loves not beauty's artificer.')

Marot was only one of many Renaissance poets whom this theme had attracted when he wrote

> Qui cuyderoit desguiser Ysabeau
> D'un simple habit, ce seroit grand' simplesse,

and, after declaring that she remained beautiful whatever she wore, concluded

> Mais il me semble (ou je suis bien trompé),
> Qu'elle seroit plus belle toute nue.

And Herrick, as might be expected, performs many variations on the theme.[1]

The charming image of lilies in a glass at the end of the second stanza was one of several similar comparisons much used by Renaissance poets, all of whom, it would seem, had been either directly or indirectly inspired by a passage in Ovid's *Metamorphoses* and by two of Martial's epigrams. The Ovidian passage (IV 354–5) occurs in the much-translated and imitated story of the naiad Salmacis and the youth Hermaphroditus (son of Hermes and Aphrodite): Hermaphroditus, watched from her hiding-place by the inflamed Salmacis, plunges into a pool:

> In liquidis translucet aquis, ut eburnea si quis
> signa tegat claro vel candida lilia vitro

('He shines through the limpid water as when one covers ivory statuettes or white lilies with transparent glass.')

The image, to a modern reader, seems so oddly and unexpectedly Victorian that he is almost inclined to wonder whether Ovid had waxen lilies in mind. Martial, in the first of his two epigrams (IV

---

1. e.g. *Clothes do but cheat and cousen us* ('Away with silks, away with Lawn'), *Poetical Works*, ed. L. C. Martin, 1956, p. 154; *To* Anthea *lying in bed* ('So looks *Anthea*, when in bed she lyes'), *ibid.*, p. 34.

xxii), may well be imitating this Ovidian comparison: Cleopatra, to escape her newly wedded husband's embraces, plunged in a gleaming pool:

> sed prodidit unda latentem;
> lucebat, totis cum tegeretur aquis.
> condita sic puro numerantur lilia vitro,
> sic prohibet tenues gemma latere rosas

('But the wave betrayed her as she lurked there; she shone while all covered by the waters. So enclosed in pure glass lilies may be counted, so crystal forbids tender roses to escape the eye.')

Here Martial seems to be alluding to the same kind of ornament, or toy, as Ovid; but in the second of these two epigrams (VIII lxviii), complimenting a friend on his ingenuity in cultivating grapes in some kind of conservatory throughout the winter, he declares:

> condita perspicua vivit vindemia gemma
> et tegitur felix nec tamen uva latet:
> femineum lucet sic per bombycina corpus,
> calculus in nitida sic numeratur aqua

('The blooms enclosed in transparent glass, your vineyard, and the happy grape is roofed yet does not escape the eye: so shines through silks a woman's body, so countable are pebbles in gleaming water.')

Here Martial is applying the words *vitrum* and *gemma* to the *specularia*, the panes of glass or mica, within or under which, in greenhouses or frames, flowers and fruit were cultivated, and which, it would seem (cf. VIII xiv), were also set up in the open, like shields, to protect orchard trees from the wind, while admitting the sun. Flowers or fruits seen through the far from perfectly transparent glass or mica of the Romans was indeed a very exact comparison for the appearance of a woman's limbs through silk, just as in Martial's other epigram and in the Ovidian passage ivory statuettes or lilies seen through *Roman* glass was an exact comparison for the appearance of a human body through water. Seventeenth-century English poets were probably unaware of the difference between Roman glass, or mica, and English crystal; neither do they seem to be imitating, even if they understood it, Martial's horticultural comparison. What they are imitating is the comparison with glass-enclosed lilies in Martial's earlier epigram and in Ovid, although they seem to have supposed that Ovid and Martial were alluding to an attractive kind of toy that has survived until the present day, namely, the crystal globe in which flowers are preserved under water; for, like Cowley, they often write of 'lilies in *a* glass', 'in *a* crystal', phrases which they would hardly have used had they been thinking of glass domes such as enclosed rococo clocks and Victoria wax flowers. It is significant that even George Sandys seems to have been baffled by the Ovidian comparison and quite unable to imagine how 'statues' (Ovid almost certainly meant statuettes) could be enclosed in the kind of crystal globe with which he was himself familiar, for he translates:

> And, with his rowing armes, supports his lims:
> Which, through the pure waves, glister as he swims:
> Like Ivory statues, which the life surpasse;
> Or like a Lilly, in a chrystall glasse.[1]

In this popular English comparison of limbs seen through water or lawn or silk to 'lilies in a glass' prettiness has perhaps been allowed to prevail over exactness. It is also possible that the poets may have been influenced by their delight, attested by numerous imitators, in those epigrams in the Greek Anthology and in Martial upon bees, flies or other insects preserved in amber. The earliest English example I have found is in Sylvester's translation of Du Bartas, where Bersabe (Bathsheba) bathing is 'Like to a Lilly sunk into a glasse'.[2] With no poet (as might have been expected) were comparisons of this kind such favourites as with Herrick, whose *Hesperides* were published in 1648, a year after Cowley's *The Mistress*: in three of his poems he compares the silk-clad or lawn-clad woman (or some part of her) to roses under lawn,[3]

1. Ed. 1640, p. 68, col. 2.
2. Second Week, Fourth Day, *The Trophies*, ed. 1621, p. 434. The French original (*Works*, ed. Holmes, III 363) has 'Telle qu'un lis qui tombe au creux d'une phiole'.
3. *To* Anthea *lying in bed* ('So looks *Anthea*, when in bed she lyes'), *Poetical Works*, ed. Martin, p. 34. A slightly different form of the lawn-over-roses comparison had been used (as Mr L. C. Martin, to whose commentary I am much indebted, has observed) by Shakespeare in *Venus and Adonis*, ll. 589–91:

> 'The boar!' quoth she; whereat a sudden pale,
> Like lawn being spread upon the blushing rose,
> Usurps her cheek.

to cherries under lawn,[1] and to strawberries under cream;[2] and in three other poems he uses, together with other comparisons, that of lilies in a glass or crystal. Of these the longest (fifty-six lines) and most elaborate is actually entitled *The Lilly in a Christal*,[3] its argument being 'as lilies, grapes or cherries are more beautiful when we see them through glass, and amber when we see it through a stream, even so nakedness is more enticing when seen through lawns and silks.' *To* Julia, *in her Dawn, or Day-breake*[4] concludes:

> As Lillies shrin'd in Christall, so
>   Do thou to me appeare;
> Or Damask Roses, when they grow
>   To sweet acquaintance there;

and in another poem[5] we find:

> So *Lillies* thorough Christall look:
> So purest pebbles in the brook:
> As in the River *Julia* did,
> Halfe with a Lawne of water hid.

While, though, in his first two stanzas Cowley is writing in a manner somewere between that of Herrick and that (as one might say) of a kind of secularised Crashaw, in the rest of his poem he becomes much more conceptual, dialectical, or 'metaphysical', using theological comparisons in the witty and slightly irreverent manner of the pre-ordained Donne. Indeed, his last stanza, with its ingenious conceit of the 'white flag', coming as it does immediately after a comparison of his white-robed mistress to the white-robed saints, may perhaps be regarded as a profane reappropriation of the consecrated profanity at the conclusion of the thirteenth of Donne's *Holy Sonnets*:

> And can that tongue adjudge thee unto hell,
>   Which pray'd forgivenesse for his foes fierce spight?

---

1. *The Lawne* ('Wo'd I see Lawn, clear as the Heaven, and thin?'), *op. cit.*, p. 158.
2. *Upon the Nipples of* Julia's *Breast* ('Have ye beheld (with much delight)'), *op. cit.*, p. 164.
3. 'You have beheld a smiling *Rose*', *op. cit.*, p. 75.
4. 'By the next kindling of the day', *op. cit.*, p. 271.
5. *Upon* Julia's *washing her self in the river* ('How fierce was I, when I did see') *op. cit.*, p. 294.

No, no; but as in my idolatrie
I said to all my profane mistresses,[1]
Beauty, of pitty, foulnesse onely is
A signe of rigour: so I say to thee,
To wicked spirits are horrid shapes assign'd,
This beauteous forme assures a pitious minde.

One could spend much time producing parallels and possible sources for most of the images and conceits in this poem, but it will be sufficient to observe that Cowley, like Marvell, has here applied that continuous, witty, hyperbolical argument, which seems to have been Donne's most profitable and learnable lesson to so many seventeenth-century poets, to a kind of subject and a kind of imagery which Donne would probably have regarded as too conventional, too merely pretty, too unoriginal. There is, in fact, a balance between the dialectical and the pictorial similar to that in much of Marvell's poetry. Cowley also resembles Marvell in the way in which he keeps his eye steadily upon his object, and, although he uses simile where Marvell would probably have used metaphor or personification, he surprises and delights, like Marvell, rather by what he is able to get out of his subject than by what he is able to bring into it. Nevertheless, although in his eclecticism Cowley here resembles Marvell, and although he has produced something charming and, in a sense, original out of materials provided by others, his combination of old and new is less individual, less of a transmutation, than that in most of Marvell's poems. What is important, however, is to recognise that this is the *sort of thing* that Marvell is continually doing, and not to search in his poems, as has too often been done in recent times, for all manner of ambiguities and profundities which are not really there. There is, for example, every reason to suppose that the 'meaning' of Marvell's poem on *The Nymph complaining for the death of her Faun* is as much on the surface as is the 'meaning' of Cowley's *Clad all in White*, and that the image of the white fawn reclining among white lilies and pasturing on red roses gave essentially the same kind of pleasure to Marvell, and was intended to give essentially the same kind of pleasure to his readers, as did the image of lilies under glass or crystal or of women's bodies seen through lawn or water to Ovid, Martial, Herrick, Cowley and other poets; true though it be that Marvell, by sharpening and, in a

1. A strange remark, perhaps, for in none of his surviving love-poems does Donne address a woman in this pseudo-Petrarchan fashion, and it is hard to imagine that he ever did so.

sense, intellectualising the possibilities of antithesis, has been able to communicate this agreeable visual experience in and through a more exciting linguistic one than Cowley has achieved in his poem, so that we remember not merely the image but its expression:

> Had it liv'd long, it would have been
> Lillies without, Roses within.

3

PASTORAL AND SEMI-PASTORAL

In the course of the preceding general survey I have several times insisted on the essential unlikeness of Marvell's poetry to Donne's. Nowhere is this more apparent than in the comparatively large number of his poems which are either within, or have affinities with, the pastoral tradition: *Clorinda and Damon, A Dialogue between Thyrsis and Dorinda, The Nymph complaining for the death of her Faun, Daphnis and Chloe, The Mower against Gardens, Damon the Mower, The Mower to the Glo-Worms, The Mower's Song, Ametas and Thestylis making Hay-Ropes*—is it possible to imagine Donne writing poems with these or similar titles at any period of his poetic career?

Generalisations about seventeenth-century poetry, and in particular about the characteristic differences between the typical Elizabethan and the typical earlier seventeenth-century lyric, tend to be based almost exclusively upon the poems, too often the selected poems, of only a few seventeenth-century poets. Since so many of the Elizabethan lyrics are anonymous, it is clearly impossible to form any opinion at all without consulting at least a selection from the song-books and miscellanies. On the other hand, since so many seventeenth-century lyrics are by well-known poets, who have left a considerable body of poetry, most writers on the subject have been content to base their generalisations about the seventeenth-century lyric upon the work of only a few poets, and, consequently, both to form an insufficiently comprehensive view of seventeenth-century poetry as a whole and to suppose that the gulf between the Elizabethan period and the earlier seventeenth-century was greater than it really was. If, however, one studies, not merely a few well-known seventeenth-century poets, but the various seventeenth-century printed miscellanies and manuscript collections, one becomes far more aware of continuity and of all manner of interesting meetings and minglings of old and new.

One learns that, in spite of the admiration for Donne and Ben Jonson, and in spite of the great influence they exerted, many even of those comparatively sophisticated readers who made their own manuscript collections continued to admire typically Elizabethan poems. In many of the miscellanies printed shortly before and shortly after the Restoration, and which may be taken to reflect tastes formed during the reign of Charles I, the Elizabethans are well represented. In, for example, that delightful collection *The Marow of Complements*, published in 1655, not only are there many of Shakespeare's and Fletcher's songs but many Elizabethan madrigals and lute-songs, and many poems which, although I have been unable to identify them, are very much in that manner. For it was quite possible to apply something of Jonsonian epigram or Donneian dialectic to material and 'keepings' in many respects typically Elizabethan.

It is, above all, in the persistence of the pastoral tradition that this continuity and these interesting minglings of old and new are most apparent. I have already quoted[1] that passage in the *Compleat Angler* about the milkmaid and her ditty, where Walton, the admirer and friend of Donne (of the later Donne, it is true) and his first and best biographer, was not ashamed to confess his taste for 'old-fashioned poetry' such as Marlowe's *Come live with me and be my love* and his preference of it to the 'strong lines' which Donne and Ben Jonson had made fashionable. There were others, however—Marvell is the most notable example—who saw the possibility of combining something of the more artless charm of this old-fashioned pastoral poetry with something of what may be called the 'strong-line tradition'. Indeed, we occasionally find in the Elizabethan song-books and miscellanies certain poems which are already very near to that tradition, especially certain poems which not so long ago would have been deemed unsuitable for family reading. There is, for example, the wittily epigrammatic 'My love in her attire doth show her wit' in Davison's *Poetical Rhapsody*, 1602, and in John Dowland's *Third Book of Songs or Airs*, 1603, there is a wittily indecent poem in pastoral vein which so hit the taste of many seventeenth-century readers that in *Wits Interpreter*, 1655, and other miscellanies it appears with the addition of a third stanza:

> When Phoebus first did Daphne love,
> And no means might her favour move,
> He craved the cause: 'The cause,' quoth she,

1. p. 83.

> 'Is I have vowed virginity.'
> Then in a rage he sware and said,
> Past fifteen years that none should live a maid.

> If maidens then shall chance be sped
> Ere they can scarcely dress their head,
> Yet pardon them, for they be loth
> To make God Phoebus break his oath:
> And better 'twere a child were born
> Than that a God should be foresworn.

To which some later poet added:

> Yet silly they, when all is done,
> Complain our wits their hearts have won,
> When 'tis for fear that they should be
> With Daphne turn'd into a tree:
> And who would so herself abuse
> To be a tree, if she could chuse?[1]

Much more innocent pastorals often achieved a surprising popularity. In *Choyce Drollery*, 1656, there appeared a poem in six stanzas by Dr Henry Hughes *On a Shepherd that died for Love*, which begins:

> *Cloris*, now thou art fled away,
> Amintas' sheep are gone astray,
> And all the joyes he took to see
> His pretty Lamb run after thee.
> *She's gone, she's gone, and he alway*
> *Sings nothing now but Welladay.*[2]

It is an artless little poem, remarkable neither for wit nor distinction of phrase, and yet it seems to have been very popular, for in the same year it appeared, with variations, in *Sportive Wit*, together with an 'Answer' in which Cloris complains that it was Amyntas who fled away after he had had his will of her. It was set to music by Henry Lawes and published by him, together with settings of thirty-five other poems by Dr Hughes, many of them of a more or less pastoral kind, in the Third Book of his *Ayres and Dialogues*, 1658. Much nearer

---

1. I quote the poem from Bullen's *Speculum Amantis*, p. 55. The third stanza also appears in *The Academy of Complements*, 1646, pp. 167–8, and in the collection of poems published in 1660 by the younger Donne and attributed by him to the third Earl of Pembroke and Benjamin Ruddier, p. 115.

2. p. 63.

to the 'witty delicacy' (to borrow Lamb's phrase) of Marvell's pastorals is the poem *On a Shepherd losing his Mistris*, which, although it may well have been written much earlier, first appeared in the First Part of the *Westminster Drollery*, 1671.

1. Stay Shepherd, prethee Shepherd stay:
   Didst thou not see her run this way?
   Where may she be, canst thou not guess?
   Alas! I've lost my Shepherdess.

2. I fear some Satyr has betray'd
   My pretty Lamb unto the shade:
   Then wo is me, for I'm undone,
   For in the shade she was my Sun.

3. In Summer heat were she not seen,
   No solitary Vale was green:
   The blooming Hills, the downy Meads,
   Bear not a Flower but where she treads.

4. Hush'd were the senseless Trees when she
   Sate but to keep them company:
   The silver streams were swell'd with pride,
   When she sate singing by their side.

5. The Pink, the Cowslip, and the Rose,
   Strive to salute her where she goes;
   And then contend to kiss her Shoo,
   The Pancy and the Daizy too.

6. But now I wander on the Plains,
   Forsake my home, and Fellow-Swains,
   And must for want of her, I see,
   Resolve to die in misery.

7. For when I think to find my Love
   Within the bosom of a Grove,
   Methinks the Grove bids me forbear,
   And sighing says, She is not here.

8. Next do I fly unto the Woods,
   Where *Flora* pranks her self with Buds,
   Thinking to find her there: But lo!
   The Myrtles and the Shrubs say, No.

9. Then what shall I unhappy do,
   Or whom shall I complain unto?
   No, no, here I'm resolv'd to die,
   Welcome sweet Death and Destiny.[1]

This poem was eventually set to music by Henry Bowman and published by him in his Songs, 1677, but in the *Westminster Drollery* it is
described as to be sung to the tune of 'Amongst the Myrtles as I
walk'd': this is Herrick's poem in the *Hesperides* on *Mrs Eliz. Wheeler,
under the Name of the lost Shepherdess*, which had appeared in Playford's
Select Musicall Ayres and Dialogues, 1652, with music by Henry Lawes.

Nowhere is the persistence of the pastoral tradition in seventeenth-
century poetry more apparent than in the numerous collections of
songs by the chief composers of the day put out by that pioneer and
almost monopolist of music publishing, John Playford, between 1651
and 1655. The titles of most of these collections indicate that they
contain 'Ayres and Dialogues', and in the text these dialogues or duets
are almost invariably described as 'Pastoral Dialogues', a form which
seems to have been especially fashionable. Marvell himself has three
poems which may be properly so described: *Clorinda and Damon*, *A
Dialogue between Thyrsis and Dorinda*, and *Ametas and Thestylis making
Hay-Ropes*; and it is an interesting and significant fact that the *Dialogue
Between Thyrsis and Dorinda*, besides being one of the only three of his
non-political poems that have survived in manuscript as well as in
print, is one of the few that during his lifetime found its way into print.
There is a setting of it by John Gamble in his Second Book of *Ayres
and Dialogues*, 1659, another by Matthew Locke in Playford's *Choice
Ayres*, 1675, and yet a third in an unpublished autograph manuscript
of some sixty songs by William Lawes, brother of the more famous
Henry, a manuscript which he must have completed before he was
killed at the siege of Chester in 1645;[2] it also appears among the 'Ingenious Poems of Wit and Drollery' appended to the very late reprint,
1663, of Samuel Rowlands's *A Crew of Kind London Gossips* (first published in 1609), where (p. 92) it is entitled *A Pastoral Dialogue between
Thirsis and his Dorinda*, and in R.V.'s *New Court-Songs and Poems*, 1673
(p. 132). It so happens that there is a very interesting and, so far as I
can see, quite direct link between this poem of Marvell's and Elizabethan pastoral. Enraptured by Thyrsis's description of Elysium, he

---

1. *Westminster Drollery*, pt. I, ed. Ebsworth, p. 56.
2. The manuscript was described and the text of Marvell's poem given in a
letter to *TLS*, 8 August 1952, from Mr John P. Cutts.

and Dorinda resolve to drink poppy-juice and 'smoothly pass away in sleep', and the four concluding lines, which they sing together, begin—or, rather, should begin, for in no existing text or manuscript is the proper name correct:

> Then let us give *Carillo* charge o'th Sheep.

The folio of 1681 has 'Corellia', the Bodleian manuscript (Rawlinson Poetical 81) 'Corella', Gamble (1659) and *New Court-Songs* (1672) 'Corilla', the British Museum Manuscript (Addit. 29921) and Locke (1675) 'Clorillo', and the version in the 1663 edition of *A Crew of Kind London Gossips* has 'Corillo'. Where did Marvell find the name 'Carillo', a name with which the various transcribers, composers and printers were evidently unfamiliar? It seems to me almost certain that he found it in the only passage in English poetry where I have been able to find it myself, in one of the songs in Bartholomew Yonge's translation (1598) of Montemayor's *Diana*. This song was printed in *Englands Helicon* (1600) with the title '*The Sheepheard* Carillo *his Song*', and begins

> I pre-thee keepe my Kine for me
> *Carillo*, wilt thou? Tell.

A somewhat altered version of it, beginning 'I prethee keep my sheep for me', was set by Nicholas Lanier as a 'pastoral dialogue' and printed in Playford's *Select Musicall Ayres and Dialogues*: in the first edition (1652) the unfamiliar name is corrupted to 'Corillo' and in the second edition (1653) to 'Clorillo'. Nothing could better illustrate both the continuity of the pastoral tradition and a variety of seventeenth-century poetic taste which we tend rather to overlook than this link between Marvell, Lanier, and *Englands Helicon*. It is even possible that the name 'Carillo' came to Marvell not directly from a reading either of *Englands Helicon* or of Yonge's complete translation of the *Diana*, but from a hearing of Lanier's song.

Apart altogether from the publishing and more or less professional poets, even the amateur or society poets of the seventeenth century had their Elizabethan affinities and did not owe an exclusive allegiance to the examples of Jonson and Donne. Jonson's professed dislike for Spenser, together with his general practice in his non-dramatic poetry, tends to make us overlook the very considerable Spenserian and pastoral elements in his Masques; and Carew's praise, in his celebrated elegy, of Donne's originality, tends to make us assume, without any careful examination of their surviving poems, that Carew and his Court friends had turned their backs for ever upon pastoralism and mythology. And as for Herrick, I suppose we are too preoccupied with the task of picking out the more distinctively Jonsonian poems in the volume of that greatest of the Sons of Ben to notice the very large number that are related in one way or another to the pastoral tradition. That the pastoral dialogue was such a favourite form with Court musicians such as Henry Lawes seems to indicate that it was also appreciated in those courtly and aristocratic circles for which Lawes and his fellow-musicians composed.

The pastoral dialogue as practised by Renaissance poets may be regarded as a lyrical offshoot, for which, except perhaps for Horace's dialogue between himself and Lydia, there was no real classical precedent, from the pastoral proper, for which, of course, the great classical precedent was Virgil's Eclogues. Of these, at least five (i, iii, v, vii, ix) are true dialogues and one (viii) gives the two songs sung by two shepherds in a contest. So far as I have been able to discover, the earliest English poem actually so described was Ben Jonson's *The Musicall Strife; In a Pastorall Dialogue*, the third poem in *The Underwood* and one which Jonson repeated to Drummond of Hawthornden when he visited him in 1619. Apart from what may perhaps be regarded as certain approximations to the form in Spenser's *Shepheardes Calender* (1579), the earliest printed examples would seem to be the duet between Paris and Œnone in Peele's *Arraignment of Paris* (1584) and at least four of the Songs in Bartholomew Yonge's translation of Montemayor's *Diana* (1598), which reappeared in *Englands Helicon* (1600).[1] The popularity of the form may well have been increased by the many translations and imitations, from that in Davison's *Poetical Rhapsody* (1602) onwards, of the ninth ode of Horace's Third Book, the *Dialogue of Horace and Lydia*, as Ben Jonson entitled his own version,[2] a

1. Ed. Hugh Macdonald, p. 120 (*A Song betweene* Syrenus *and* Sylvanus), p. 130 (Faustus *and* Firmius *sing to their Nimph by turnes*), p. 133 (*A Song betweene* Taurisius *and* Diana, *aunswering verse for verse*), p. 141 (*A Dialogue Song betweene* Sylvanus *and* Arsilius). There is also in *Englands Helicon* (p. 171) *A Pastorall Song betweene* Phillis *and* Amarillis, *two Nimphes, each aunswering other line for line*, by 'H.C.', and a stichomythic question-and-answer dialogue, entitled Coridon *and* Melampus *Song* (p. 32), from Peele's lost play *The Huntinge of Cupid* (see Macdonald's note, p. 232).

2. In *The Underwood*, no. LXXXVII. For a list of other seventeenth-century versions, see the commentary on this poem in the Oxford *Jonson*, XI 109. The version in the *Poetical Rhapsody* was included in the 1640 edition of *The Academy of Complements*, p. 156.

poem of which, without presuming to compete with the seventeenth-century translators, I will here impartially offer an isometric version of my own:

> 'While I still was the one you loved,
>   while no happier young rival had yet with his
> arms encircled your gleaming neck,
>   I was living in more bliss than the Persian King.'

> 'While no other had more inflamed
>   you, and Lydia still occupied Chloe's place,
> I, your Lydia, lived in such
>   high renown as surpassed Ilia's Roman fame.'

> 'Thracian Chloe commands me now,
>   skilled in ravishing song, wise in the lyre's strings,
> she for whom I would gladly die,
>   would Fate leave her, the dear soul of my soul, behind.'

> 'Son of Thurian Ornytus,
>   now it's Calaïs burns me with a mutual flame,
> he for whom I would doubly die,
>   would Fate only allow him to remain behind.'

> 'What if former desire returned,
>   joining us the estranged up with a yoke of bronze?
> Fair-haired Chloe were shaken off,
>   long-closed doors were again opened to Lydia?'

> 'Though his beauty excels the stars,
>   though you're lighter than cork, proner to angriness
> than our horrible eastern sea,
>   I'd choose living with you, gladly with you would die.'

In this dialogue there is nothing that could have seemed either to Horace or to his contemporaries in any sense pastoral; nevertheless, a Caroline poet might well have described his version of it as a 'pastoral dialogue' and for Henry Lawes and his fellow-musicians it would have fulfilled all the requirements of the form: it is a dialogue between a 'nymph' and a 'swain' about love, and it contains what for a Renaissance poet (though not for Horace) were the specifically pastoral names of Lydia and Chloe. All that a Caroline composer would seem to have required in the text of a dialogue, or duet, which he wished to describe

as 'pastoral' was that it should be between a 'nymph and a 'swain',
normally about love, occasionally (in elegiac dialogues) about death,
these subjects being treated in any way the poet chose. Indeed, in
Jonson's *The Musicall Strife*, which, as I have remarked, is the earliest
poem I have been able to discover which is actually described as a
'pastoral dialogue', the only specifically pastoral element is the song-
contest itself, and the intellectuality, precision and unpicturesqueness
of the poem are remote from that characteristic anthology of Elizabethan pastoralism, *Englands Helicon*:

SHEE

Come, with our Voyces, let us warre,
    And challenge all the Spheares,
Till each of us be made a Starre,
    And all the world turne Eares.

HEE

At such a Call, what beast or fowle,
    Of reason emptie is?
What Tree or stone doth want a soule?
    What man but must lose his?

SHEE

Mixe then your Notes, that we may prove
    To stay the running floods,
To make the Mountaine Quarries move,
    And call the walking woods.

HEE

What need of mee? doe you but sing,
    Sleepe, and the Grave will wake.
No tunes are sweet, nor words have sting,
    But what those lips doe make.

SHEE

They say the Angells marke each Deed,
    And exercise below,
And out of inward pleasure feed
    On what they viewing know.

HEE

O sing not you then, lest the best
Of Angels should be driven
To fall againe; at such a feast,
Mistaking earth for heaven.

SHEE

Nay, rather both our soules be strayn'd
To meet their high desire;
So they in state of Grace retain'd,
May wish us of their Quire.[1]

So many dialogue poems, pastoral and other, were written by seventeenth-century poets, and so many of them were set to music by contemporary composers, that it is difficult not to suppose that most of them were written at the request of composers, or at least in the hope that a composer would eventually set them. It is surprising to discover how many highly intellectual, abstract, and, as one might be inclined to say, essentially unlyrical poems were actually set to music. The two of his poems which Carew specifically described as 'pastoral dialogues', the pastoral courtship (as one might call it, borrowing a title of Randolph's) 'As *Celia* rested in the shade'[2] and the aubade 'This mossie bank they prest',[3] both of which were set to music by Henry Lawes, are indeed, even for the least sophisticated readers, sufficiently pastoral and sufficiently simple. On the other hand, Carew's much more abstract dialogue, *A Lover upon an Accident necessitating his departure, consults with Reason*,[4] was also set by Henry Lawes, and perhaps still more surprising to a modern reader are his *Foure Songs by way of Chorus to a play*.[5] The first of these is a question-and-answer dialogue on the origin of jealousy, and Thomas Killigrew, who later included it in a play of his own, declared that it had been sung at a Whitehall masque in 1633, and that Carew had written it at his request, on the occasion of a dispute between himself and his future wife, Cicilia Crofts.[6] There follow two (as it might seem to a modern reader) equally unlyrical solo songs, and then yet another question-and-answer dialogue, this time in triplets, entitled *Incommunicabilitie of Love*, where the argument is as

1. Oxford *Jonson*, VIII 143.   2. *Poems*, ed. Dunlap, p. 42.
3. *op. cit.*, p. 45.   4. *op. cit.*, p. 48.
5. *op. cit.*, p. 59 ff.   6. *op. cit.*, p. 244.

intellectual and undecorated as the title might lead one to expect. It is remarkable that all four of these poems should have been sung in a masque. I have mentioned them partly in order to suggest that, despite Dryden's famous objection to Donne's love-poetry, the minds of the Caroline 'fair sex' (the mind, for example, of Cicilia Crofts, the Maid of Honour, and even, it may well be, of her mistress, Queen Henrietta Maria) were by no means unwilling to be perplexed with 'nice speculations of philosophy'; partly as evidence that the comparative abstractness and unpicturesqueness of some of Marvell's pastorals and semi-pastorals were quite as much within an established (even though less widely accepted) fashion as was (if one may use the word in an unpejorative sense) the prettiness and the comparatively unstrenuous argumentation of the majority.

Pastoral dialogues, whether or no described as such by their authors, were written by many seventeenth-century poets, and it would be easy to compile a long list. I will content myself with remarking that Herrick wrote at least seven.[1] Carew's considerably older friend Aurelian Townshend (he was born in 1583) has a charming *Dialogue betwixt Time and a Pilgrim* ('Aged man, that mowes these fields'), which was set by Henry Lawes, and which, in its fainter kind, has considerable affinities with Marvell's pastoral and garden poems. If, though, I were to choose one pastoral dialogue for comparison with Marvell's *Thyrsis and Dorinda* and *Clorinda and Damon*, I do not know whether I could produce anything more obviously similar than a little dialogue by James Shirley ('the last Elizabethan', as he has sometimes been called) in his play *The Cardinal* (licensed 1641), which was set by William Lawes:[2]

---

1. *Poetical Works*, ed. L. C. Martin, p. 70, *A Dialogue betwixt* Horace *and* Lydia, *Translated* Anno 1627. *and set by Mr.* Ro: Ramsey; p. 130, *The Kisse. A Dialogue;* p. 183, *An Eclogue, or Pastorall between* Endimion Porter *and* Lycidas Herrick, *set and sung;* p. 280, *The Sacrifice, by way of Discourse betwixt himselfe and* Julia; p. 305, *A Bucolick betwixt Two:* Lacon *and* Thyrsis; p. 309, *Upon Love, by way of question and answer;* p. 323, *A Dialogue betwixt himselfe and Mistresse* Eliza: Wheeler, *under the name of* Amarillis.

2. At some time before he was killed at the siege of Chester in 1645. His setting of the poem, in which he changed the name of 'Strephon' to that of 'Damon' and made a few other alterations, appeared in Playford's *Select Musicall Ayres and Dialogues*, 1652 and 1653. In this song-book there are two other (anonymous) pastoral dialogues which, though inferior, are very similar in style to Shirley's 'Dear *Silvia*, let thy *Thirsis* know', set by Charles Colman, and (among the additional dialogues in the 1653 edition) '*Thyrsis*, kind Swain, come near, & lend', set by 'Mr William Caesar, alias Smegergill'.

Strephon	Come, my Daphne, come away,
	We do waste the crystal day;
	'Tis Strephon calls.
Daphne	What would my love?
Strephon	Come, follow to the myrtle grove,
	Where Venus shall prepare
	New chaplets for thy hair.
Daphne	Were I shut up within a tree,
	I'd rend my bark to follow thee.
Strephon	My shepherdess, make haste,
	The minutes fly too fast.
Daphne	In these cooler shades will I,
	Blind as Cupid, kiss thine eye.
Strephon	In thy perfumed bosom then I'll stray;
	In such warm snow who would not lose his way?
Chorus	We'll laugh and leave the world behind;
	And Gods themselves that see
	Shall envy thee and me,
	But never find
	Such joys when they embrace a deity.

To those who, having assumed that pastoralism had been banished by Jonson and Donne, and, finding only what they have been taught to look for, have failed to notice its flourishing persistence during the Caroline period, the really unoverlookable pastoralism in the songs, both occasional and dramatic, of the Restoration, the ever-recurring Chloes and Celias and Strephons, has probably appeared as some kind of artificial revival, somehow connected with those French romances which partly formed the taste for the Heroic Play. Nowhere, however, can the continuity of the pastoral tradition (with, of course, various characteristic changes and developments) be more clearly perceived than in the song-books. Even the pastoral elegy is there. Among the 'pastoral dialogues' in Playford's *Select Musicall Ayres and Dialogues*, 1652, we find, set by William Lawes, *A Dialogue. Charon & Eucosmia. Occasion'd by the death of the Young Lord Hastings.* This is Herrick's 'Charon, O Charon, draw the boat to the shore',[1] his contribution to

1. Herrick also has a dialogue between Charon and Philomel (the nightingale), beginning 'Charon, O gentle *Charon*, let me wooe thee' (*Poetical Works*, ed. Martin, p. 248), which appeared with music by William Lawes in Playford's *Select Musical Ayres and Dialogues*, 1652 and 1653. In the Harflet MS, presented to the Bodleian Library by Sir Charles Firth, there is a charming dialogue between Hobson the

Lacrimae Musarum, 1649, that collection in which the youthful Dryden's Clevelandish elegy had also appeared—a juxtaposition which, like that of Milton's *Lycidas* and the other effusions on the death of Edward King, may serve to remind us that the poets of the Caroline period were not all sitting compulsorily in two 'schools' founded respectively by Jonson and by Donne (or even in a single academy where some graduated into the Jonsonian, and some into the Donneian Sixth). In Playford's *Choice Ayres, Songs, & Dialogues*, 1675, there appeared, with music by Matthew Locke, *A Dialogue between Apollo and Neptune: Occasioned by the unfortunate Death of the Right Honourable Edward, Earl of Sandwich*. In the Third Book (1681) of this collection there are two pastoral elegies by Thomas Flatman, one on the musician Pelham Humphrey and the other on the Earl of Rochester, which begins:

> As on his Death-bed gasping *Strephon* lay,
> *Strephon* the wonder of the Plains,
> The noblest of the *Arcadian* Swains,
> Strephon the bold, the witty, and the gay.

And in the Fifth Book (1684) there is Flatman's elegy on the death of his son Thomas, entitled *A Pastoral Elegy on the Death of a lovely Boy*. It is also, perhaps, worth noticing, as a further example of that continuity on which I have been insisting, that in the *Poems* of Mrs Anne Killigrew, 1686 (the poetess whom Dryden commemorated), the title 'pastoral dialogue', so firmly established by the co-operation of poets and musicians, is given to each of three poems[2] of considerable length in the heroic couplet, which a little later would have been described simply as 'pastorals'. Indeed, it is this persistence of the pastoral tradition until long after the Restoration which makes it unwise to assume as a matter of course that Marvell must have written all his pastoral or semi-pastoral poems at an earlier period. His best editor, the late H. M. Margoliouth, perhaps too readily supposed that Marvell's political preoccupations deprived him of the inclination, or even of the ability, to write anything but satirical verse. It is true that none of his poems is in an unmistakably Restoration manner, with phrases

---

Carrier and Charon, very unlike the facetious commemorations by Milton and others. It was printed by G. C. Moore Smith in his Warton Lecture on *Thomas Randolph*, 1927, pp. 20-1, and ascribed by him, with not wholly convincing arguments, to Randolph. Dialogues between Charon and either a mourner or the soul of the departed would seem to have become common enough to invite parody, for Lovelace has *A Mock Charon*, satirising a Parliamentary sequestrator.

2. On pp. 11, 57, 63.

such as 'the *Arcadian* Swains', but he may well, for all we know, have retained both the ability and the inclination to write occasionally, even after the Restoration, poems in an earlier and better manner.[1]

In some of the examples I have quoted and in many others we can perceive how the framework, properties, and 'keepings' of the more unsophisticated Elizabethan pastoral could be combined to a greater or lesser degree with characteristic seventeenth-century dialectic, point, epigram, ingenuity and 'wit'. No other poet achieved this particular combination of old and new so delightfully and memorably as Marvell, but there can be no doubt that he was stimulated by the example of many contemporary poets, and that he was neither the first nor the last to whom this particular kind of poetic beauty, this blend of naïveté and sophistication, naturalness and artifice, presented itself as an exquisitely piquant and attractive possibility. I have already remarked that in reading him we are often reminded not only of earlier but of later poets. Consider the following poem, *On his Mistris that lov'd Hunting*, which I have only met with in the Second Part of the *Westminster Drollery* (1672):[2] I think (although I am by no means certain) that it is probably post-Restoration, but is it not unmistakably in the tradition of Marvell's pastorals?

1. Leave *Cælia*, leave the woods to chase,
   'Tis not a sport, nor yet a place
   For one that has so sweet a face.

2. Nets in thy hand, Nets in thy brow,
   In every limb a snare, and thou
   Dost lavish them thou car'st not how.

3. Fond Girle these wild haunts are not best
   To hunt: nor is a Savage beast
   A fit prey for so sweet a breast.

4. O do but cast thine eyes behind,
   I'le carry thee where thou shalt find
   A tame heart of a better kind.

5. One that hath set soft snares for thee,
   Snares where if once thou fettered be,
   Thou't never covet to be free.

1. See Chapter 2, p. 31, note (arguments for and against an early date for *A Dialogue Between the Resolved Soul, and Created Pleasure*).
2. Ed. Ebsworth, Pt. II, p. 125.

6. The Dews of *April*, Winds[1] of *May*
   That flowr[2] the Meads, and glad[3] the Day
   Are not more soft, more sweet than they.

7. And when thou chancest for to kill,
   Thou needst not fear no other ill
   Than Turtles suffer when they Bill.

Although to persons unfamiliar with them a list of their titles might suggest that all Marvell's pastorals were very similar, there are in fact considerable differences between them. Some are as colourful and detailedly pastoral as any Elizabethan poem in that kind, while others (quite in accordance, as I have shown, with much contemporary practice) have nothing that to a modern reader seems distinctively pastoral except the pastoral names. In every one of them there is a wittily conducted argument, sometimes grave, sometimes light-hearted, but the balance between the abstract and the concrete, the conceptual and the pictorial, varies considerably from poem to poem. The simplest, the most conventional, the nearest, so far as we can judge from the miscellanies and song-books, to average contemporary taste in pastoral, is the *Dialogue between Thyrsis and Dorinda*, and that perhaps is why it found its way into print. Thyrsis's description of the delights of Elysium so enraptures Dorinda that she longs to die:

> *Dorinda*   Oh sweet! oh sweet! How I my future state
> By silent thinking, Antidate:
> I prethee let us spend our time to come
> In talking of *Elizium*.
> *Thyrsis*   Then I'le go on: There, sheep are full
> Of sweetest grass, and softest wooll;
> There, birds sing Consorts, garlands grow,
> Cool[4] winds do whisper, springs do flow.
> There, always is, a rising Sun,
> And day is ever, but begun.
> Shepheards there, bear equal sway,
> And every Nimph's a Queen of *May*.

1. *W.D.* 'the Winds'.   2. *W.D.* 'That flowr's'.
3. *W.D.* 'glads'.
4. The reading of 1681 is 'cold'; but 'cool', the reading of the texts in *A Crew of Kind London Gossips*, etc., 1663, *New Court-Songs*, 1672, and Playford's *Choice Ayres*, etc., 1675, is, as Margoliouth agreed with me, certainly correct. For his remarks on this and various other discoveries and suggestions of mine about this poem, see his letter to *TLS*, 19 May 1950.

Dorinda   Ah me, ah me. (*Thyrsis*.) *Dorinda*, why do'st Cry?
Dorinda   I'm sick, I'm sick, and fain would dye:
             Convince me now, that this is true;
             By bidding, with mee, all adieu.
Thyrsis   I cannot live, without thee, I
             Will for thee, much more with thee dye.
Chorus   Then let us give *Carillo*[1] charge o'th Sheep,
             And thou and I'le pick poppies and them steep
             In wine, and drink on't even till we weep,
             So shall we smoothly pass away in sleep.

One would like to think that in the text of this poem in *A Crew of Kind London Gossips*, 1663, the clumsy and quite unnecesary inversion in the 1681 folio and all other texts, 'pick poppies and them steep', had been corrected by Marvell himself to 'pick poppies which wee'l steep'; and, indeed, so many of the alterations in that text are obvious improvements that they may well all be authentic. Nevertheless, the fact remains that, while almost every poem of Marvell's is, as a whole and in its total effect, such as only he could have written, almost every one contains lines which scores of contemporary readers could have improved and which, no doubt, many of us could improve with very little trouble. It would seem that he wrote rapidly and that his indisputable poetic genius did not include that 'infinite capacity for taking pains' which Carlyle thought essential. If, like Shakespeare, 'he never blotted a line', I am tempted to exclaim with Ben Jonson, adjusting his figure to Marvell's less voluminous production, 'Would he had blotted a hundred!'

In style and 'keepings' *Thyrsis and Dorinda* is close to Elizabethan pastoral. It is true that it would be hard to find an Elizabethan pastoral dialogue in which, as distinct from the reiteration by two speakers of opposing points of view, or alternate variations by two speakers on a single theme, there was, as here, a real discussion, one speaker's arguments gradually breaking down the resistance or incredulity of his companion. And even in those seventeenth-century pastoral dialogues by other poets, of which I have quoted or referred to so many examples, although there is more true dialogue, more of a definite beginning, middle and end, than in the Elizabethan ones, I must admit that I have never found anything like so much real discussion and real argument

1. 1681 '*Clorillo*': see p. 106 for a list of the various other perversions of his name.

as in *Thyrsis and Dorinda*. The nearest approach to it, in this respect, is that brilliant dialogue of Horace's, of which there were so many seventeenth-century versions, in which Horace and Lydia concurrently persuade themselves that each still loves the other more than Chloe and Calaïs. Randolph's *A Pastorall Courtship* does indeed contain a long and elaborately illustrated argument in favour of 'fruition', but it is not really a dialogue; for, while the shepherd's argument occupies (in Thorn Drury's edition) more than five pages, the regretful exclamation of the persuaded and betrayed shepherdess occupies only twelve lines. In fact, it is not in the dialogues but in the many deliberately amoral and paradoxical poems 'For Fruition', of which Randolph's *Upon Love fondly refus'd for Conscience sake* is one of the best examples, that real argument is to be found. Marvell, as I shall show later, was undoubtedly familiar with this poem of Randolph's, and it may well be that to this and similar poems *Thyrsis and Dorinda* and *Clorinda and Damon* were written, in some sort, as replies—partly suggested, perhaps, by those attempts to Christianise Cupid which we find in the enormously popular *Pia Desideria* (1624) of the Jesuit Herman Hugo and in many other collections of sacred epigrams and emblems published, usually by members of religious orders, during the seventeenth century. I doubt, however, whether it was in any spirit of strong moral or religious revulsion against Randolph and his fellows that Marvell wrote these two dialogues, for their religiosity is striking only in its context, and is otherwise as conventional as the libertinism to which it may perhaps be regarded as a reply. All one can say with certainty is that, in making the shepherd in a pastoral dialogue persuade his shepherdess to desire God's (or 'Pan's') Heaven, instead of Cupid's 'heaven' and to die with him literally instead of 'dying' with him metaphorically, Marvell, here as so often elsewere, was executing an original variation on a familiar theme. It was no doubt this combination of an (at least for England, and in a pastoral dialogue) entirely original argument with simplicity and even conventionality of form and expression which made *Thyrsis and Dorinda* popular, and led to its appearance in so many song-books and miscellanies not conspicuous for piety or high seriousness.

The same combination of originality of argument and traditionality of expression occurs in that neater and more satisfying dialogue *Clorinda and Damon*, in which there is perhaps something Spenserian in spirit, as there is certainly something Spenserian in style:

C. *Damon* come drive thy flocks this way.

D. No: 'tis too late they went astray.

C. I have a grassy Scutcheon spy'd,
Where *Flora* blazons all her pride.
The Grass I aim to feast thy Sheep:
The Flow'rs I for thy Temples keep.

D. Grass withers; and the Flow'rs too fade.

C. Seize the short Joyes then, ere they vade.[1]
Seest thou that unfrequented Cave?

D. That den? C. Loves Shrine. D. But Virtue's Grave.

C. In whose cool bosome we may lye
Safe from the Sun. D. not Heaven's Eye.

C. Near this, a Fountaines liquid Bell
Tinkles within the concave Shell.

D. Might a Soul bath there and be clean,
Or slake its Drought? C. What is't you mean?

D. These once had been enticing things,
Clorinda, Pastures, Caves, and Springs.

C. And what late change? D. The other day
Pan met me. C. What did great *Pan* say?

D. Words that transcend poor Shepherds skill,
But He ere since my Songs does fill:
And his Name swells my slender Oate.

C. Sweet must *Pan* sound in *Damons* Note.

D. *Clorinda's* voice might make it sweet.

C. Who would not in *Pan's* Praises meet?

Chorus

Of Pan *the flowry Pastures sing,*
Caves eccho, and the Fountains ring.
Sing then while he doth us inspire;
For all the World is our Pan's *Quire.*

Not only is the Christianisation of Pan, or representation of Christ, the
Good Shepherd, under the name of Pan, together with much in the
phraseology, reminiscent of Spenser's *Shepheardes Calender*; Clorinda's
lines

---

1. *Vade* seems etymologically to be a variant of *fade*, and is often used by
Elizabethan poets, although they sometimes seem to have associated it with Latin
vadere, to go, and to have used it in the sense of 'pass away', 'vanish'.

> I have a grassy Scutcheon spy'd,
> Where *Flora* blazons all her pride

were pretty clearly written with a passage in the *Faerie Queene* in mind: that where Guyon, on entering the Bower of Bliss, beholds a plain interspersed with flower-beds:

> whose fayre grassy ground
> Mantled with greene, and goodly beautifide
> With all the ornaments of *Floraes* pride.
>
> (II xii 50)

Was Spenser Marvell's, as he was also (according to Dryden) Milton's, 'original', and did Marvell too regard him as 'a better teacher than Scotus or Aquinas'? Even here, though, in this predominantly Spenserian poem and in this passage so clearly suggested by Spenser, Marvell has introduced a characteristic piece of seventeenth-century particularity and wit; for his 'Scutcheon' and 'blazons' recall Gervase Markham's information (in *The English Husbandman*, 1637) that in the gardens of noblemen their coats-of-arms were often delineated. This metaphorical description of a piece of flowery meadow in terms of what might be called an armorial flower-bed is reminiscent of those many descriptions of Nature in terms of art which we find in *Appleton House*. Since the passage under consideration makes it clear that Marvell had Spenser's Bower of Bliss canto in mind when he wrote this poem, it seems likely that when he made Clorinda exclaim 'Seize the short Joyes then, ere they vade' he was recalling those two stanzas (74-5), culminating in the exhortation to 'Gather the Rose of Love whilest yet is time', which Spenser imitated from Tasso, and which contain one of the most memorable of all variations on that favourite topic of pagan love-poetry, *carpe florem*.

The neat and charming dialogue *Ametas and Thestylis making Hay-Ropes* may seem at first sight as artless and unperplexed as anything in the Elizabethan song-books; yet when one looks into it more closely, one becomes aware of a continuousness, an intellectuality, and a subtlety of distinction that is more characteristic of seventeenth-century poetry. Both partners perceive an analogy between Love's binding of them and their binding of hay, but each sees it differently, Ametas finding in it an argument for identity of response (We are both binding), Thestylis one for contrariety (We are twisting in opposite directions): until Ametas, seeing that this argument from analogy is getting him

nowhere, is ready to abandon both it and the occupation which suggested it.

I
AMETAS

Think'st Thou that this Love can stand,
Whilst Thou still dost say me nay?
Love unpaid does soon disband:
Love binds Love as Hay binds Hay.

II
THESTYLIS

Think'st thou that this Rope would twine
If we both should turn one way?
Where both parties so combine,
Neither Love will twist nor Hay.

III
AMETAS

Thus you vain Excuses find,
Which your selve and us delay:
And Love tyes a Womans Mind
Looser then with Ropes of Hay.

IV
THESTYLIS

What you cannot constant hope
Must be taken as you may.

V
AMETAS

Then let's both lay by our Rope,
And go kiss within the Hay.

Nothing could well be more remote from the Elizabethan or Spenserian simplicity of *Thyrsis and Dorinda* and *Clorinda and Damon*, or even
from the more sophisticated but still comparatively simple *Ametas
and Thestylis*, than that elaborately intellectualised description of an
encounter and an emotional situation, *Daphnis and Chloe*. It is not,
strictly speaking, a dialogue, for although, after the situation of the

pair has been described, Daphnis addresses Chloe, she herself does
not reply. There is no description of external surroundings, and
nothing distinctively pastoral except the pastoral names. Daphnis,
grieved by Chloe's unyielding coldness, resolved to leave her, and
when at the moment of parting, she suddenly relented, he was too
full of sadness and painfully achieved resignation to be able suddenly, as
it were, to unwind himself; suddenly to exchange his laboriously
prepared part of a lover accepting his dismissal for the part of a lover
joyfully welcoming his acceptance. It is almost as though Marvell,
as a kind of wager with himself or with some friend, had deliberately
set himself the task of intellectually elaborating and paradoxicalising
to the highest possible degree a situation which poets of almost any
earlier period could only have treated simply, making Daphnis either
joyfully surrender (*Amantium irae amoris redintegratio est*) or depart in a
mood of injured pride, with a warning to other coy women to learn a
lesson from the fate of Chloe. The impulse to write original variations
often seems to have come to Marvell from his reading. I have suggested[1]
that *The Definition of Love* and even, perhaps, *To his Coy Mistress* seem to
have crystallised around stanzas from poems in Cowley's *The Mistress*:
it seems more than likely that the germ of this poem was implanted in
Marvell by a passage in Suckling's play *Aglaura* (printed in 1638). In a
stanza which I shall quote again in its context Daphnis says to Chloe:

> Gentler times for Love are ment;
> Who for parting pleasure strain
> Gather Roses in the rain,
> Wet themselves and spoil their Scent.

This (as my friend Mrs E. E. Duncan-Jones, to whom I owe so much,
has pointed out to me) was almost certainly suggested by a passage
(Act III, scene i) where Aglaura begs Thersames not to consummate
their marriage while his life is in peril:

> Gather not roses in a wet and frowning hour,
> They'll lose their sweets then, trust me they will, Sir.
> What pleasure can Love take to play his game out,
> When death must keep the stakes?

Pliny,[2] it is true, had said that roses were best gathered in clear weather,
but Suckling's metaphor is striking and seems to be original, and it is

1. Chapter 2, pp. 68, 72.
2. *Naturall Historie*, transl. Philemon Holland, 1635, II 87 (Book XXI, ch. vii).

Marvell's use of it in a similar context and situation that makes his indebtedness almost certain: Daphnis will not accept Chloe's offer of herself when his departure, which (like Donne in several of the *Songs and Sonets*) he often likens to death, is imminent. Marvell, it would seem, was fascinated by the paradox in Aglaura's speech, the paradox that consummation, however passionately desired, can become undesirable; and this fascination led him, first to devise a situation of far greater complexity, and then to probe, disintricate and display with the utmost possible explicitness its various psychological and emotional implications and to exploit all its possibilities of antithesis. The paradox in Aglaura's speech may also have fascinated him as a particularly striking example of that more general paradox which had been expressed both by Hamlet in the words 'for there is nothing either good or bad, but thinking makes it so',[1] and by Donne at the conclusion of a poem (*The Progresse of the Soule*) almost exactly contemporary with Hamlet:

> Ther's nothing simply good, nor ill alone,
> Of every quality comparison,
> The onely measure is, and judge, opinion;

and it seems possible that the contrast between the almost brutal simplicity of the last two stanzas and the preceding complexities and hyperboles was deliberately intended as a contrast between reality and appearance, and that, accordingly, we should, at least to some extent, regard the whole poem as a satire on that 'hyperbolical joy and outrageous sorrow' which Dr Johnson commended Shakespeare's plays for being free from.[2] But it is time that we had before us some representative portion of this remarkable poem, so here, with the omission of two stanzas, is the whole of Daphnis's speech, together with the three concluding stanzas of the poem:

> Are my Hell and Heaven Joyn'd
> More to torture him that dies?
> Could departure not suffice,
> But that you must then grow kind?
>
> Ah my *Chloe* how have I
> Such a wretched minute found,
> When thy Favours should me wound
> More than all thy Cruelty?

1. II ii 255–7.
2. *Johnson on Shakespeare*, ed. Walter Raleigh, 1925, p. 13.

So to the condemned Wight
The delicious Cup we fill;
And allow him all he will,
For his last and short Delight.

But I will not now begin
Such a Debt unto my Foe;
Nor to my Departure owe
What my Presence could not win.

Absence is too much alone:
Better 'tis to go in peace,
Than my Losses to increase
By a late Fruition.

Why should I enrich my Fate?
'Tis a Vanity to wear,
For my Executioner,
Jewels of so high a rate.

Rather I away will pine
In a manly stubborness
Than be fatted up express
For the *Canibal* to dine.

Whilst this grief does thee disarm,
All th' Enjoyment of our Love
But the ravishment would prove
Of a Body dead while warm. . . .

Gentler times for Love are ment
Who for parting pleasure strain
Gather Roses in the rain,
Wet themselves and spoil their Sent.

Farewel therefore all the fruit
Which I could from Love receive:
Joy will not with Sorrow weave,
Nor will I this Grief pollute.

Fate I come, as dark, as sad,
As thy Malice could desire;
Yet bring with me all the Fire
That Love in his Torches had.

At these words away he broke;
As who long has praying ly'n,
To his Heads-man makes the Sign,
And receives the parting stroke.

But hence Virgins all beware.
Last night he with *Phlogis* slept;
This night for *Dorinda* kept;
And but rid to take the Air.

Yet he does himself excuse;
Nor indeed without a Cause.
For, according to the Lawes,
Why did *Chloe* once refuse?

I will begin my consideration of possible precedents and analogies by remarking that, of the stanza which Marvell has here used, trochaic heptasyllabics rhyming *abba*, I know of only two previous examples: in the poem beginning 'Let the bird of loudest lay', which Shakespeare contributed to those 'Poeticall Essaies on the former Subject; viz.: the *Turtle* and Phoenix' appended to Robert Chester's *Loves Martyr* (1601), and in a poem of Carew's, the third of *Foure Songs by way of Chorus to a play*, entitled *Separation of Lovers*.[1] I have somewhere either read or heard it remarked that this poem of Shakespeare's has some title to be regarded as the first truly 'metaphysical' English poem to have appeared in print; certainly, I can think of nothing earlier that is so exclusively and concentratedly intellectual and 'difficult' as are the first three of its four concluding stanzas:

Propertie was thus appalled,
That the selfe was not the same:
Single Natures double name
Neither two nor one was called.

Reason, in it selfe confounded,
Saw Division grow together,
To themselves yet either neither,[2]
Simple were so well compounded.

---

1. *Poems*, ed. Dunlap, p. 61.
2. 'Yet in such a way that to itself each was neither itself nor the other.' I have slightly modified the original punctuation of these stanzas.

That it cried, how true a twaine
Seemeth this concordant one;
Love hath Reason, Reason none,
If what parts can so remaine.

Carew's short poem is far simpler than either Shakespeare's or
Marvell's in both subject and expression; nevertheless, in intellectualising and raising, as it were, to the plane of philosophic meditation
the simple theme that love is at first sharpened but later extinguished
by absence, he is doing, though with exceptional success, the sort of
thing that many of his Caroline contemporaries were continually trying to do. One recalls Thomas Killigrew's mention of that dispute
between himself and Cicilia Crofts, the Maid of Honour,[1] which led
him to request Carew to write the first of these *Foure Songs*, a question-
and-answer dialogue on the origin of jealousy. No doubt many of
these predominantly analytical and intellectual love-poems of the time,
often graceful and accomplished, though seldom 'difficult' and profound, may be regarded as, at least in part, a reflection of such dis-
cussions between men and women at Court or in country houses. They
are neither serious and self-involved analyses of particular moods,
situations and relationships, as are most of Donne's *Songs and Sonets*, nor,
on the other hand, are they poems of courtship and what Dr Johnson
called 'fondness', like Waller's to Sacharissa—those poems which,
from the Restoration until almost the end of the eighteenth century,
were regarded as patterns to which all love-poems ought more or
less to approximate.

SEPARATION OF LOVERS

Stop the chafed Bore, or play
    With the Lyons paw, yet feare
    From the Lovers side to teare
Th' Idoll of his soule away.

Though Love enter by the sight
    To the heart, it doth not flye
    From the mind, when from the eye
The fair objects take their flight.

But since want provokes desire,
    When we lose what wee before

>   Have enjoy'd, as we want more,
>   So is Love more set on fire.
>
>   Love doth with an hungrie eye
>   Glut on Beautie, and you may
>   Safer snatch the Tygers prey
>   Then his vitall food deny.
>
>   Yet though absence for a space
>   Sharpen the keene Appetite,
>   Long continuance doth quite
>   All Loves characters efface.
>
>   For the sense not fed, denies
>   Nourishment unto the minde,
>   Which with expectation pinde,
>   Love of a consumption dyes.

Not very profound, perhaps, but with a sufficient appearance of profundity and intellectuality to make Miss Crofts and her friends feel that they were reading, and enjoying, 'philosophy'.

If, then, we are to compare Marvell's poem with what seem to be its only two predecessors in the same metre, we may say that it resembles both Shakespeare's and Carew's in its detachment, but that it is far nearer to Shakespeare's than to Carew's in complexity and ambitiousness. A poet of an earlier generation than Carew's (he was born in 1583), who wrote love-poems that were both detached and often far more intellectually ambitious than those of Carew and his contemporaries, was Lord Herbert of Cherbury. It is true that he did not collect and publish his poems until 1665, but they seem to have had a considerable circulation in manuscript. His most famous, longest, and most ambitiously philosophic love-poem, *An Ode upon a Question moved, Whether Love should Continue for ever*, is a kind of pastoral dialogue within a descriptive framework. It begins with a description of the vernal landscape in which Melander and Celinda were walking and in which they finally laid themselves down, and then reports their very philosophic discourse, Celinda's six stanzas being introduced with the words 'She first brake silence' and Melander's seventeen stanzas, which contain the substance of what Lord Herbert has to say on this subject, with the words 'he thus repli'd'. To Celinda's fear that love will end with terrestrial life Melander replies in stanzas which, individually, are often of considerable poetic merit; nevertheless, although it is superficially impressive and full of high-mindedness and of what is popularly regarded as 'Platonism', when one looks into it more closely its argument seems to be so riddled with inconsistencies, contradictions and *non sequiturs* that it is hard to disentangle even its bare outlines. It seems to be that God is best known through his creatures, and that through our senses and our bodies we can come to know Him and acquire virtuous habits which must necessarily endure as long as the soul endures. It is not clear whether the soul is being regarded as naturally and absolutely, or only as potentially and conditionally, immortal—as endowed, that is to say, with a capacity, which it either may or may not use, to make itself immortal; it does, however, seem to be declared that it is through the senses that it begins the process of immortalisation, and that, in immortalising itself, it somehow immortalises the senses. The following four stanzas (ll. 109–24) will serve as a specimen:

> These eyes again then, eyes shall see,
> And hands again these hands enfold,
> And all chast pleasure can be told
> Shall with us everlasting be.
>
> For if no use of sense remain
> When bodies once this life forsake,
> Or they could no delight partake,
> Why should they ever rise again?
>
> And if every imperfect mind
> Make love the end of knowledge here,
> How perfect will our love be, where
> All imperfection is refin'd?
>
> Let then no doubt, *Celinda*, touch,
> Much less your fairest mind invade,
> Were not our Souls immortal made,
> Our equal loves can make them such.

Although Lord Herbert was more than ten years younger than his friend Donne and can hardly, one supposes, have written this poem before he reached the age of twenty in 1603, I have often wondered whether it may not have provided a kind of model for Donne's

Extasie, for although the argument of Donne's poem, obscure as it may be, is very different from the vague, high-minded twaddle of Lord Herbert's, the essentially undramatic style of *The Extasie* and its rather prosaic and plodding argumentation distinguish it sharply from every other poem in the *Songs and Sonets* and make it more like the *Ode upon a Question moved* and other productions of Lord Herbert's solemn and often rather pompous, prosy and stiff-jointed muse. After all, did not Ben Jonson tell Drummond of Hawthornden 'That Done said to him, he wrott that Epitaph on Prince Henry, *Look to me, Faith*, to match Sir Ed: Herbert[1] in obscurenesse'?

Both as an argumentative poem in short-lined quatrains and as a kind of semi-pastoral semi-dialogue, *Daphnis and Chloe* has some affinity with Lord Herbert's *Ode* and with Donne's *Extasie*. Nevertheless, it differs from them, not only in its continuous use of personification, metaphor and simile, but in the fact that, although I have called it an argumentative poem, Daphnis is not, in his long address to Chloe, attempting, like Lord Herbert's Melander and Donne's pair of lovers, to expound any doctrine or to demonstrate any truth, but is simply performing a series of elaborate variations on the theme, suggested to Marvell by that passage from Suckling's *Aglaura*, that the moment of parting is not the right moment for consummation. In the previous chapter[2] I have remarked that even *The Definition of Love*, which at first sight seems to be so very much in the manner of Donne, reveals itself, on closer examination, to be only superficially like him, and that in it Marvell is 'simply performing, with characteristically seventeenth-century intellectuality, ingenuity, hyperbole and antithesis, an elaborate series of variations on the ancient theme of star-crossed lovers'. *Daphnis and Chloe* certainly is, or has the appearance of being, more abstract and intellectual than most of Marvell's poems, but even here this predominantly descriptive and extrovert poet is really performing a series of hyperbolical, metaphorical, semi-picturesque, semi-epigrammatic variations in a manner which is fundamentally nearer to that of Crashaw than to that of Donne. There is, too, about *Daphnis and Chloe*, as there is about some others of Marvell's poems, a certain ambiguousness, a certain suggestion of solemn parody and near-burlesque, which differentiates it from those various examples of detached and intellectual love-poetry with which I have been com-

---

1. Edward Herbert was knighted in 1603, created a peer of Ireland in 1624 and a peer of England, as Lord Herbert of Cherbury, in 1629.
2. pp. 68–9.

paring it. I have called it an 'elaborately intellectualised description'.[1] Sometimes this description, which, unlike that in many of Marvell's other poems, can never be called more than 'semi-picturesque', has in it something of allegory and emblem, recalling the far more toppling and extravagant descriptions in that unparalleled poem *The Unfortunate Lover*:

> As the Soul of one scarce dead,
> With the shrieks of Friends aghast,
> Looks distracted back in hast,
> And then streight again is fled.
>
> So did wretched *Daphnis* look,
> Frighting her he loved most.
> At the last, this Lovers Ghost
> Thus his Leave resolved took.
>
> (st. X–XI)

But in most of the stanzas of Daphnis's reply it is epigrammatic antithesis that predominates:

> Are my Hell and Heaven Joyn'd
> More to torture him that dies?
> Could departure not suffice,
> But that you must then grow kind?
>
> (st. XII)
>
> Absence is too much alone:
> Better 'tis to go in peace,
> Than my Losses to increase
> By a late Fruition.
>
> (st. XVI)

The chain, the 'rosary', of variations recalls the Crashaw of *The Weeper* and of *Wishes. To his (supposed) Mistresse*; at the same time, stanzas such as those I have just quoted, not merely in their metrical form but in what might be called the concretely abstract, or abstractly concrete, manner of their epigrammatic exploitation of antithesis and paradox, recall, more than anything in any other seventeenth-century poet, certain stanzas in Shakespeare's poem on the Phoenix and Turtle:

1. p. 120.

> Propertie was thus appalled
> That the selfe was not the same:
> Single Natures double name
> Neither two nor one was called.

It was, one may suppose, in very similar moods of emotional detachment and intellectual fascination that Shakespeare and Marvell wrote these two poems. But while Shakespeare only once indulged in this particular kind of game, just as he only once contributed to the kind of symposium in which his poem appeared, it would seem to have been the kind of game which Marvell most enjoyed and out of which many, perhaps most, of his best poems emerged.

Perhaps the most wholly characteristic of Marvell's pastorals, those, at any rate, in which his own inimitable blending of the conceptual and the pictorial, of intellectual excitement and visual delight, is most apparent, are the four Mower poems. We may begin with *The Mower against Gardens*, that witty elaboration of the antithesis between Nature and Art. The subject is in some sense an abstract idea, but Marvell does not treat it abstractly, and his poem, though full of intellect and argument, does not leave with us an impression of something predominantly intellectual, but rather of a witty and affectionate presentation of particular visible things. His wit and hyperbole, his argument and intellection, here as so often elsewhere, are playing above and around a substratum of description, or evocation, of simple natural beauty, such as had long given, and would long continue to give, unsophisticated readers an unsophisticated pleasure. Had Donne written a poem about Nature and Art, and, in the course of it, had incidentally referred to gardens and orchards, flowers and fruit-trees, he would not have conveyed the impression that he had any particular affection for them, and we should not remember his poem as being *about* them; most readers, however, probably remember Marvell's poem even more as an evocation of gardens and orchards than as an argument about Nature and Art. Almost all his best poems are as much descriptions and evocations of things he finds it delightful to contemplate as they are wittily constructed arguments. He has none of those purely cerebral poems, those witty discourses on a Broomstick, as one might call them, of which there are so many in that characteristic anthology of academic wit, *Parnassus Biceps*.

The Mower against Gardens

Luxurious Man, to bring his Vice in use,
  Did after him the World seduce:
And from the fields the Flow'rs and Plants allure,
  Where Nature was most plain and pure.
He first enclos'd within the Gardens square
  A dead and standing pool of Air:
And a more luscious Earth for them did knead,
  Which stupifi'd them while it fed.
The Pink grew then as double as his Mind;
  The nutriment did change the kind.
With strange perfumes he did the Roses taint,
  And Flow'rs themselves were taught to paint.
The Tulip, white, did for complexion seek;
  And learn'd to interline its cheek:
Its Onion root they then so high did hold,
  That one was for a Meadow sold.
Another World was search'd, through Oceans new,
  To find the *Marvel of Peru.*[1]
And yet these Rarities might be allow'd,
  To Man, that sov'raign thing and proud;
Had he not dealt between the Bark and Tree,
  Forbidden mixtures there to see.
No Plant now knew the Stock from which it came;
  He grafts upon the Wild the Tame:
That the uncertain and adult'rate fruit
  Might put the Palate in dispute.
His green *Seraglio* has its Eunuchs too;
  Lest any Tyrant him out-doe.
And in the Cherry he does Nature vex,
  To procreate without a Sex.[2]
'Tis all enforc'd; the Fountain and the Grot;
  While the sweet Fields do lye forgot:

1. *Mirabilis Jalapa,* 'native of tropical America, with handsome funnel-shaped flowers of various colours which expand towards night'. (OED)

2. Hugh Macdonald, in his *Muses' Library* ed., remarks: 'Mr John Gilmour tells me that these lines (which previous editors have been unable to explain) only refer to the practice of vegetative or asexual propagation of cherries and other fruits by budding and grafting, which has, of course, been extensively practised for many hundreds of years.'

Where willing Nature does to all dispence
  A wild and fragrant Innocence:
And *Fauns* and *Faryes* do the Meadows till,
  More by their presence then their skill.
Their Statues polish'd by some ancient hand,
  May to adorn the Gardens stand:
But howso'ere the Figures do excel,
  The *Gods* themselves with us do dwell.

This charming poem is an example both of the way in which Marvell performs original variations upon familiar themes and of the way in which possibilities, new and amusing things to do, were suggested to him by various contemporary poets whom he had been, one cannot but suppose, recently reading. From Montaigne onwards the antithesis between Nature and Custom, Nature and Art, had been a favourite topic with sixteenth- and seventeenth-century writers and poets. One need only recall the arguments of Donne and other witty defenders of paradox against 'unnatural' constancy in love, or, in more serious vein, such famous passages as the amicable dispute between Perdita and Polixenes about 'streak'd gillyvores' in *The Winter's Tale* and Gonzalo's description of his ideal commonwealth in *The Tempest*. It is impossible to suppose that Marvell, that great reader of contemporary verse, was not familiar with that most highly esteemed Caroline poet Thomas Randolph, whose poems had been posthumously published in 1638, 1640, 1643 and 1652; and I think Professor Kermode was certainly right when he suggested[1] that there was a connexion between *The Mower against Gardens* and one of Randolph's poems. Professor Kermode would regard Marvell's poem as a reply to Randolph's, or rather, as a reply to one of its arguments; I myself should prefer to say that Randolph's argument (original, so far as I am aware), regarded simply as a piece of witty and charming dialectic with whose ethical implications neither poet is seriously concerned, was the inspiration of Marvell's poem. Marvell has inverted it, expanded it, and made a whole poem out of it; and the fact that his own poem is not only in the same metre as Randolph's (couplets consisting of alternate decasyllabic and octosyllabic lines), but is his only poem in that metre, increases the likelihood that Randolph's poem was fresh in his memory. In this poem, *Upon Love fondly refus'd for Conscience sake*,[2] Randolph tries to

1. In a talk on Marvell's poetry on the Third Programme, 3 January 1953.
2. *Poems*, ed. Thorn Drury, 1929, p. 128. G. C. Moore Smith, a fine scholar, but one whose taste and judgment were sometimes erratic, declared in his Warton

persuade another man's wife (or mistress), with arguments similar to those which had been used by Donne, that monogamy and constancy, like other human 'inclosures', are opposed to the liberality and diffusiveness of nature. Randolph's general argument, like his appeal to the unfettered loves of birds and animals, is far from original, but he nevertheless contrives to execute several original variations on the old theme—in particular, by professing to deduce from the practice of the Gardener that it is as 'lawful' or 'natural' to 'inoculate' (commit adultery) as to 'plant' (produce children within the bonds of wedlock):

> If the fresh Trunke have sap enough to give
>> That each insertive branch may live;
> The Gardner grafts not only Apples there,
>> But addes the Warden and the Peare,
> The Peach, and Apricock together grow,
>> The Cherry, and the Damson too.
> Till he hath made by skilfull husbandry
>> An intire Orchard of one Tree.
> So least our Paradise perfection want,
>> We may as well inoculate as plant.

It was, I am sure, this passage in a poem whose garden setting and garden imagery were so congenial to him that suggested to Marvell the whole plan and idea of *The Mower against Gardens*, of which perhaps the Mower's argument against grafting and 'adult'rate fruit' (the neat inversion of Randolph's argument in favour of adultery), as the supreme example of man's 'unnaturalness', may be regarded as the core and the beginning:

> And yet these Rarities might be allow'd,
>> To Man, that sov'raign thing and proud;
> Had he not dealt between the Bark and Tree,
>> Forbidden mixtures there to see.

Lecture on *Thomas Randolph*, 1927, p. 52, that Randolph's *Upon Love fondly refus'd* 'was an answer to another poem', *Love refused for Conscience Sake*, in the same metre, which he found without ascription of authorship in a British Museum MS, he inclined to attribute to Randolph himself, and which he printed on p. 45 of his published lecture. It is a poor performance, with a few imitations of passages in other poems by Randolph, and may well be by that butt of the Oxford wits Samuel Austin, who, when he published in 1661 a *Panegyrick* on the Restoration of Charles II, declared that, if it were well received, he would include in a larger book of poems 'The Author's Answer to Mr Randolph's Poem styled, *Love fondly refus'd for Conscience sake*'. See Thorn Drury's edition of Randolph, p. 208.

> No Plant now knew the Stock from which it came;
>   He grafts upon the Wild the Tame:
> That the uncertain and adult'rate fruit
>   Might put the Palate in dispute.

But if the initial impulse to write this poem came from Randolph, there can, I think, be no doubt that there also entered into it many recollections of a favourite book to which, in various passages in other poems, Marvell has quite unmistakably revealed his indebtedness. Both at Nunappleton and at the other country houses where he stayed there would almost certainly be found a copy of what few seventeenth-century country gentlemen's libraries would be without, Philemon Holland's translation of Pliny's *Natural History*. It is, as Mrs E. E. Duncan Jones has said,[1] 'the sort of compendium which a writer of Marvell's day would have always at his elbow; and in Holland's English it offers not only information but delight'. Pliny speaks of the invention of gardens by Epicurus in much the same tone as Marvell, in his opening lines, speaks of their invention by 'Luxurious Man':

> The inuention to haue gardens within a citie, came vp first by *Epicurus* the doctor and master of all voluptuous idlenesse, who deuised such gardens of pleasance in Athens: for before his time, the manner was not in any citie, to dwell (as it were) in the countrey, and so to make citie and countrey al one, but all their gardens were in the villages without.[2]

> The Pink grew then as double as his Mind;
>   The nutriment did change the kind.
> With strange perfumes he did the Roses taint,
>   And Flow'rs themselves were taught to paint.

Pliny, too, had spoken reprovingly of devices used to improve the natural flower:

> Yet are not such Roses of the sweetest kind, that are so double and double againe . . . All the said Roses . . . haue no smell with

---

1. In an unpublished article which she has generously allowed me to make use of. It is to this scholar, to whom all students of Marvell owe so much, that I am almost exclusively indebted for what I have to say on this subject.

2. *The Historie of the World: Commonly called, the Naturall Historie of C. Plinius Secundus*, 1635 (reissue of the 2nd ed. of 1634; the first was 1601), II 10 (Bk. XIX, ch. iv. Holland's chapter-division differs from that of the more generally accepted Latin text.)

them in the whole world naturally, but are brought to it by many deuises & sophistications;[1]

and had objected to the 'excessiue ryot and prodigall superfluitie of men' in 'surmounting the natural sauor of simple floures, by their artificial odors and compound perfumes'[2] and, still more strongly, to 'the monstrous deuises of some fantastical spirits, that they inuented forsooth a new kind of artificiall coloring and dying of Lillies'.[3]

> No Plant now knew the Stock from which it came;
> He grafts upon the Wild the Tame:
> That the uncertain and adult'rate fruit
> Might put the Palate in dispute.

Pliny, too, after treating of the Olive, had declared:

As for all other fruits of trees, they are hardly to be numbred and reckoned by their forme and figure; much lesse by their sundry tasts and diuers juices that they yeeld, so intermingled they are together by varietie of graffing one into another.[4]

He had indeed admitted that 'Generally all trees that are tame and gentle may wel be graffed into stocks and roots of the wild',[5] but he was inclined to think that the possibilities of legitimate grafting had now been more than exhausted—had, indeed, been carried so far that he too, though in a more impartial and scientific spirit, had found it necessary to deliver a warning against what Marvell's Mower calls 'forbidden mixtures':

So as in this point verily the world is growne alreadie to the highest pitch, insomuch, as there is not a fruit, but men haue made trial and many experiments, for euen in *Virgils* daies the deuise of graffing strange fruits, was very rife: considering that he speakes of the Arbute tree graffed on Nut-trees, the Plane vpon Apple-trees, and the Elme vpon Cherrie stockes. In such sort, as I see not how men can deuise to proceed farther. And certes for this long time, there hath not beene a new kind of Apple or other fruit heard of.

And yet as industrious as men haue been that way, they are not

1. 1635, II 83 (Bk. XXI, ch. iv).   2. II 88 (Bk. XXI, ch. viii).
3. II 85 (Bk. XXI, ch. v).   4. I 435 (Bk. XV, ch. ix).
5. I 519 (Bk. XVII, ch. xv).

permitted to graffe all manner of trees indifferently one in another, no more than it is lawfull to graffe vpon bushes and thornes: seeing that it is not so easie a matter to appease lightenings: for looke how many sorts of trees are thus engraffed contrarie to nature, so many kinds of lightenings and thunderbolts, by report, are flashed and shot at once.[1]

Although in this poem it can scarcely be shown, as it can in others, that Marvell is indebted to the actual language of Holland's Pliny, there is here at least one striking example of the fact that he, like Ben Jonson, was as ready to borrow or adapt phrases from prose writers as from poets.

> He first enclos'd within the Gardens square
> A dead and standing pool of Air:

there can be no doubt that Marvell borrowed what to most readers must have seemed the brilliantly original phrase and metaphor in the second line from a passage in Sir Henry Wotton's little treatise *The Elements of Architecture*, which was first published in 1624, but which Marvell may well have read for the first time in the *Reliquiae Wottonianae* (1651), which Izaak Walton had recently published. At the very beginning of his treatise Wotton declares that in choosing a site for your house it is most important to ensure that it is surrounded by the right kind of air.

> That it be not too *gross*, nor too *penetrative*; Not subject to any foggy noisomness, from *Fens* or *Marshes* neer adjoyning; nor to *Mineral* Exhalations from the Soil it self. Not indigested, for want of *Sun*: Not unexercised, for want of *Wind*: which were to live, as it were, in a *Lake*, or standing *Pool* of *Aire*, as *Alberti*[2] the *Florentine Architect* doth ingeniously compare it.[3]

To any readers who, with modern notions of literary property and propriety, may object that Marvell 'stole' the phrase from Wotton, it may be replied that, if it had remained in Wotton's book it would have remained forgotten, and that Marvell has given to it what Milton,

1. I 439 (Bk. XV, ch. xv).
2. Leon Baptista Alberti, *De Re Aedificatoria*, 1485.
3. *Reliquae Wottonianae*, 3rd ed., 1672, p. 7 (in 1651, p. 203). See Marcia E. Allentuck, 'Marvell's Pool of Air', *Modern Language Notes*, lxxiv 587-9.

in his earlier poems, has given to so many borrowed phrases, a context that makes it memorable. Indeed, I might well apply to Marvell's best poems what, some years ago, I wrote about *L'Allegro* and *Il Penseroso*: that in those two poems 'every detail receives the maximum emphasis and produces the maximum effect', that 'everything stands out clearly, nothing gets lost in the crowd', and that

> Poets who had used such phrases before him did not, one might say, know what to do with them; they fumbled, they dropped their catches. Milton picked them up, and phrases which might otherwise have quietly disappeared from the language are now among the most memorable in these two poems.[1]

Although I have remarked that most readers probably remember *The Mower against Gardens* rather as an evocation of gardens and orchards than as an argument in favour of the superiority of Nature to Art, it would seem that the idea (which, after all, though it is here playfully and paradoxically treated, is in some sort a 'philosophical' one) came first, and, as it were, attracted the imagery. What, on the other hand, gives that equally charming, though less tightly constructed, poem *Damon the Mower* such unity and coherence as it possesses is not, properly speaking, an idea, but two very ancient poetic topics, which Marvell characteristically elaborates. Damon's insistence that the 'unusual Heats' are caused not by the sun but by '*Juliana*'s scorching beams' may be regarded as a form of what I have called the 'pastoral hyperbole', a topic to which I have briefly alluded in the preceding chapter[2] and to which I shall return in my chapter on *Appleton House*; and his description of the gifts he can offer his Shepherdess and his praise both of the life he leads and even of his own appearance are characteristically original variations on that 'catalogue of delights' which seems to have begun with Polyphemus's wooing of Galataea in Theocritus's eleventh Idyll, a passage partly imitated by Virgil in his presentation of the wooing of Alexis by Corydon in the second Eclogue, and exuberantly and, at times, grotesquely elaborated by Ovid in his own Polyphemus's wooing of Galataea in the thirteenth book of the *Metamorphoses* (ll. 798 ff.). Marlowe, in that most famous of Elizabethan lyrics, *The Passionate Shepherd to his Love*, had treated this second

1. '*L'Allegro* and *Il Penseroso* in their Relation to Seventeenth-century Poetry', *Essays and Studies 1951*, pp. 31–2.
2. See p. 80.

topic with charming artificiality and without the least attempt at
realism, but Marvell, although there is no definite evidence, here or
elsewhere, that he had read Theocritus, has achieved, here and elsewhere, a blend of the idyllic and the realistic that might almost be
called Theocritean, and his poem is full of detailed evocations of the
English rural scene.

I have called Damon's insistence that the 'unusual Heats' are caused
not by the sun but by Juliana a form of the 'pastoral hyperbole'. It
seems possible, however, that this particular elaboration may have
been suggested to Marvell by a poem of Randolph's, and that it was
Randolph who provided the initial impulse for the writing of this
poem, just as he seems to have done for *Damon the Mower*. His *A Dialogue. Thirsis. Lalage*[1] is a neat and ingenious piece of argumentation,
and contains the most elaborate development I have met with of that
conceit about heat and cold, fire and snow, the beloved's burning cold,
the lover's freezing fire, which is as old as the Greek Anthology.[2]
Why, exclaims Thyrsis, does Lalage, who herself remains so cold,
make him so hot?

> *Th.* My *Lalage* when I behold
>   So great a cold,
> And not a spark of heat in thy desire,
> I wonder what strange power of thine
>   Kindles in mine
> So bright a flame, and such a burning fire.
>
> *La.* Can *Thirsis* in Philosophy
>   A truant bee,
> And not have learn'd the power of the Sun?
> How he to sublunary things
>   A fervour brings,
> Yet in himselfe is subject unto none?
>
> *Th.* But why within thy eyes appeare
>   Never a teare,
> That cause from mine perpetuall showres to fall?
>
> *La.* Foole 'tis the power of the fire you know
>   To melt the snow,
> Yet has no moisture in it selfe at all.

1. *Poems*, ed. Thorn Drury, p. 84.
2. e.g. V 209, by Poseidippus or Asclepiades: 'Cleander saw Nico swimming in
the blue sea, and, burning with love, took to his heart dry coals from the wet maid.'

Th. How can I be, deare Virgin show,
     Both fire and snow?
   Doe you that are the cause, the reason tell;
   More then miracle to me
     It seems to be,
   That so much heate with so much cold should dwell.

La. The reason I will render thee
     Why both should bee:
   Audacious *Thirsis*, in thy love too bold,
   'Cause thy sawcinesse durst aspire
     To such a fire,
   Thy love is hot; but 'tis thy hope is cold.

And so the poem continues to its concluding chorus:

> Ah cruell Love how great a power is thine?
> Under the Poles although we lye
>   Thou mak'st us frye:
> And thou canst make us freeze beneath the line.

Good as this is of its kind, it is thin, cerebral stuff in comparison with the glow and colour of the poem for which it may well have provided the initial impulse. While Randolph confines himself to the possibilities of logical, or pseudo-logical, antithesis that he can extract from the contrast between the warmth of Thyrsis and the coldness of Lalage, for Marvell the contrast between the warmth of the Mower and the coldness of Juliana is no more than a kind of unifying principle within which vibrates a brilliant pattern of sensuous images. His poem might almost be said to begin where Randolph's ends, for, here as elsewhere, he has combined with more permanent sources of poetic pleasure what to a modern reader seem the too monotonous and indigestible ingredients out of which his contemporaries and immediate predecessors so often composed whole poems.

Before quoting Marvell's poem as a whole, I will permit myself a comment upon its eighth stanza, the only one in which I have been able to detect anything like direct imitation:

> Nor am I so deform'd to sight,
> If in my Sithe I looked right;
> In which I see my Picture done,
> As in a crescent Moon the Sun.

> The deathless Fairyes take me oft
> To lead them in their Danses soft;
> And, when I tune my self to sing,
> About me they contract their Ring.

Marvell's 'deform'd' seems pretty clearly to be a rendering of *informis* in Corydon's speech, partly imitated from that of Theocritus's Polyphemus, in Virgil's second Eclogue (ll. 25-7):

> Nec sum adeo informis: nuper me in litore vidi,
> cum placidum ventis staret mare; non ego Daphnim
> iudice te metuam, si numquam fallit imago

(Nor am I so unsightly; on the shore the other day I looked at myself when the sea lay becalmed by the winds. Even with you for judge, I should not fear Daphnis, if [it be true that] a reflection never deceives);

but his 'Sun' may perhaps have been suggested by one of the many passages (*Metamorphoses*, xiii, 840-1, 851-3) in which Ovid transformed the simple and rather pathetic figure of Theocritus's Polyphemus into a monstrous grotesque:

> Certe ego me novi liquidaeque in imagine vidi
> nuper aquae placuitque mihi mea forma videnti . . .
> unum est in media lumen mihi fronte, sed instar
> ingentis clipei. quid? non haec omnia magnus
> sol videt e caelo? soli tamen unicus orbis

(I know myself very well; I lately beheld myself in a limpid water's reflection, and my appearance pleased me as I beheld it . . . I have only one eye, in the middle of my forehead, but it is like a vast shield. What of that? Does not the great sun behold from heaven this whole universe? And yet the sun has but a single eye.)[1]

---

1. In his brief self-description (31-3) in Theocritus's eleventh Idyll Polyphemus does not speak of his reflection in the water, although he does so in Damoetas's impersonation of him in the sixth Idyll (35-8). The young Shakespeare, not very happily, imitated the Ovidian passage in Talbot's speech over the slain Salisbury in *I Henry VI*, I iv 82-4:

> Yet liv'st thou, Salisbury? Though thy speech doth fail,
> One eye thou hast, to look to heaven for grace;
> The sun with one eye vieweth all the world.

The Mower's contemplation of his reflection in his scythe, though it may well have been suggested by Virgil and Ovid, is an excellent example of that thorough adaptation and, as it were, localisation of ancient pastoral, and of that almost Swiftian particularity and concreteness, which Marvell achieves throughout his poem; and even in this stanza the transformed classical reminiscences are immediately followed by the introduction of English fairies. Why, incidentally, should Virgil's Corydon happen to be on the sea-shore? For we are not told that he was an island-dweller, like Polyphemus, and he is not in love with a sea-nymph. Was it simply because a sea-shore seemed to Virgil a 'poetic' sort of place to be on? Marvell could more 'poetically', idyllically and traditionally have made his Mower contemplate his reflection in a pool; instead, with a characteristic blend of the realistic, the fanciful and the emblematic, with a touch of humour that approached, but remains on this side of, the whole poem's side of, the burlesque and the grotesque, and with a wit that is both surprising and 'natural', he makes him contemplate it on his scythe.

Damon *the Mower*

I

Heark how the Mower *Damon* Sung,
With love of *Juliana* stung!
While ev'ry thing did seem to paint
The Scene more fit for his complaint.
Like her fair Eyes the day was fair;
But scorching like his am'rous Care.
Sharp like his Sythe his Sorrow was,
And wither'd like his Hopes the Grass.

II

O what unusual Heats are here,
Which thus our Sun-burn'd Meadows sear!
The Grass-hopper its pipe gives ore;
And hamstring'd Frogs can dance no more.
But in the brook the green Frog wades;
And Grass-hoppers seek out the shades.
Only the Snake, that kept within,
Now glitters in its second skin.

III

This heat the Sun could never raise,
Nor Dog-star so inflame[1] the dayes.
It from an higher Beauty grow'th,
Which burns the Fields and Mower both:
Which mads[2] the Dog, and makes the Sun
Hotter then his own *Phaeton*.
Not *July* causeth these Extremes,
But *Juliana*'s scorching beams.

IV

Tell me where I may pass the Fires
Of the hot day, or hot desires.
To what cool Cave shall I descend,
Or to what gelid Fountain bend?
Alas! I look for Ease in vain,
When Remedies themselves complain.
No moisture but my Tears do rest,
Nor Cold but in her Icy Breast.

V

How long wilt Thou, fair Shepheardess,
Esteem me, and my Presents less?
To Thee the harmless Snake I bring,
Disarmed of its teeth and sting.
To Thee *Chameleons* changing-hue,
And Oak leaves tipt with hony-dew.[3]
Yet Thou ungrateful hast not sought
Nor what they are, nor who them brought.

---

1. 1681 'inflame's'.

2. 1681 'made'. The clearly correct 'mads' is the reading in 'Thompson's second MS book', a copy of the 1681 folio with MS emendations, now in the Bodleian Library, which reached Captain Edward Thompson after the edition of Marvell which he published in 1776 was already in the press, and which I shall henceforth refer to as 'T2'. It has been described by Hugh Macdonald, *TLS*, 13 July 1951, and, more briefly, by Margoliouth in the Additional Notes (pp. xiv–xv) prefixed to the first volume of the second edition of his *Marvell*, 1952. The 'Dog' is, of course, the Dog-star, which Juliana's beams have maddened in the way that the star itself was supposed to madden dogs.

3. T2; 1681 'hony due'.

VI

I am the Mower *Damon*, known
Through all the Meadows I have mown.
On me the Morn her dew distills
Before her darling Daffadils.
And, if at Noon my toil me heat,
The Sun himself licks off my Sweat.
While, going home, the Ev'ning sweet
In cowslip-water bathes my feet.

VII

What, though the piping Shepherd stock
The plains with an unnumbred[1] Flock,
This Sithe of mine discovers wide
More ground then all his Sheep do hide.
With this the golden fleece I shear
Of all these Closes ev'ry Year.
And though in Wooll more poor then they,
Yet am I richer far in Hay.

VIII

Nor am I so deform'd to sight,
If in my Sithe I looked right;
In which I see my Picture done,
As in a crescent Moon the Sun.
The deathless Fairyes take me oft
To lead them in their Danses soft;
And, when I tune my self to sing,
About me they contract their Ring.

IX

How happy might I still have mow'd,
Had not Love here his Thistles sow'd!
But now I all the day complain,
Joyning my Labour to my Pain;
And with my Sythe cut down the Grass,
Yet still my Grief is where it was:
But, when the Iron blunter grows,
Sighing I whet my Sythe and Woes.

1. T2; 1681 'unnum'red'.

X

While thus he threw his Elbow round,
Depopulating all the Ground,
And, with his whistling Sythe, does cut
Each stroke between the Earth and Root,
The edged Stele by careless chance
Did into his own Ankle glance;
And there among the Grass fell down,
By his own Sythe, the Mower mown.

XI

Alas! said He, these hurts are slight
To those that dye by Loves despight.
With Shepherds-purse, and Clowns-all-heal,
The Blood I stanch, and Wound I seal.
Only for him no Cure is found,
Whom *Julianas* Eyes do wound.
'Tis death alone that this must do:
For Death thou art a Mower too.

Next, in the 1681 edition, comes *The Mower to the Glo-Worms*, a shorter but more concentrated poem, and an especially notable example of Marvell's capacity to make small things great, or at least memorable. His 'meditating' nightingale and his glow-worms as 'Country Comets' were undoubtedly, as I shall show, suggested to him by Holland's *Pliny*, but I will begin by insisting that the beauty and memorability of this poem largely depends on the fact that it consists of a single elaborate sentence, whose main verb does not appear until the beginning of the fourth and last stanza, and that the three preceding stanzas, apostrophising the glow-worms, consist of balanced relative clauses whose pattern is almost exactly repeated in each stanza. It is largely the repetition of such a syntactical and rhythmical pattern through three stanzas which culminates in a clinching and concluding fourth that makes Wotton's famous poem on Queen Elizabeth of Bohemia so memorable:

You meaner beauties of the night,
That . . .
What are you when the moon shall rise?

You curious chanters of the wood,
That . . .
                    what's your praise
When Philomel her voice shall raise?

You violets that first appear . . .
What are you when the rose is blown?

So when my Mistress shall be seen . . .
Tell me if she were not designed
Th' eclipse and glory of her kind?

And it was no doubt its strikingly successful employment of phrase-
ological, rhythmical, and syntactical repetition that made Carew's
'Aske me no more where *Iove* bestowes' one of the most widely circulated, parodied and satirically adapted poems of the seventeenth
century.[1]

The Mower to the Glo-Worms

I

Ye living Lamps, by whose dear light
The Nightingale does sit so late,
And studying all the Summer-night,
Her matchless Songs does meditate;

II

Ye Country Comets, that portend
No War, nor Princes funeral,
Shining unto no higher end
Then to presage the Grasses fall;

III

Ye Glo-worms, whose officious Flame
To wandring Mowers shows the way,
That in the Night have lost their aim,
And after foolish Fires do stray;

IV

Your courteous Lights in vain you wast,
Since *Juliana* here is come,
For She my Mind hath so displac'd
That I shall never find my home.

1. See Dunlap's notes on pp. 263–6 of his edition of Carew's *Poems*.

What makes this brilliant little poem fall short of perfection is some-thing which mars too many passages in Marvell's poetry, including many which I have already quoted without more than briefly and occasionally commenting upon this defect: the use of the expletives 'do', 'does', 'doth' and 'did', sometimes merely in order to obtain an extra syllable, but more frequently in order to be able to use a form of the verb (the infinitive) that will rhyme with a word already chosen, and a too frequent use of inversion, not in order to obtain some special emphasis, but merely in order to obtain a rhyme. It is because the near-perfection of this short poem casts, as it were, a particularly glaring light upon the 'does sit' and 'does meditate' in the first stanza, the 'do stray' in the third, and the 'For She my Mind hath so displac'd' in the fourth that it seems appropriate to make this the place for some general comment upon these and similar imperfections. I am unable to offer any statistical presentation of their relative frequency in the poetry of Marvell and in that of other seventeenth-century poets, or to declare positively whether or no it is simply the fact that Marvell, un-like most of his contemporaries and immediate predecessors, wrote so few negligible poems that gives me so strong an impression that he is one of the worst offenders; for almost all seventeenth-century poets habitually committed these two closely related faults (the use of ex-pletives and inversions for the sake either of rhyme or of mere metrical convenience), and they do not seem to have become generally recog-nised as such until the time of Dryden. Indeed, so far as I know, Dry-den, although he does not, I think, say anything about expletives, was the first writer who both publicly and memorably condemned the use of 'unnatural' inversions, his attention having been particularly di-rected to them in the course of his attempt to defend the 'naturalness' of rhyme in drama against the advocates of blank verse, or, as it was then commonly called, 'prose'. In his *Epistle Dedicatory of The Rival Ladies* (1664), after remarking that some writers even of blank verse habitually inverted sentences because they thought it sounded more 'heroically', he continued:

I should judge him to have little command of English, whom the necessity of a rhyme should force often upon this rock; though some-times it cannot easily be avoided; and indeed this is the only in-convenience with which rhyme can be charged. This is that which makes them say, rhyme is not natural, it being only so, when the poet either makes a vicious choice of words, or places them, for rhyme sake, so unnaturally as no man would in ordinary speaking; but when 'tis so judiciously ordered, that the first word in the verse seems to beget the second, and that the next, till that becomes the last word in the line, which, in the negligence of prose, would be so; it must then be granted, rhyme has all the advantages of prose, besides its own.[1]

In the *Essay of Dramatic Poesy* (1668), Neander (Dryden), replying to the arguments of Crites (Sir Robert Howard) against rhyme, again takes 'the common way of speaking' as his criterion;

> Is there any thing in rhyme more constrained than this line in blank verse, *I heaven invoke, and strong resistance make?* where you see both the clauses are placed unnaturally, that is, contrary to the common way of speaking, and that without the excuse of a rhyme to cause it.[2]

Too often the use of inversions and expletives by Marvell and other seventeenth-century poets, including even Donne, counteracts to a greater or lesser extent that approximation to 'the common way of speaking' and that piquant contrast between the 'artificiality' and formality of the metrical pattern and the 'naturalness' and informality of diction and rhythm which is their most distinguishing characteristic and their chief glory. Dryden, as I have said, does not actually mention expletives. So far as I know, the first recorded and explicit objection to them occurs in the youthful Pope's well-known letter to William Walsh (22 October 1706), describing 'certain Niceties, which, tho' not much observed even by correct versifiers, I cannot but think, deserve to be better regarded'.

> Another nicety is in relation to Expletives, whether words or syllables, which are made use of purely to supply a vacancy: *Do* before verbs plural is absolutely such; and it is not improbable but future refiners may explode *did* and *does* in the same manner, which are almost always used for the sake of rhyme.

Pope's distinction between the use of *do* with plural subjects, which he found totally inexcusable, and *did* and *does* with singular ones, which for the time being he was willing to excuse, has been clarified by Professor Geoffrey Tillotson, in a passage where he also shows how Pope gradually came to find *did* and *does* inexcusable as well:

1. *Essays*, ed. Ker, I 6–7.   2. *op. cit.*, I 94–5.

If a poet wishes to rime the verb 'play' with 'day' and to use it as a plural of the present tense, the rime is achieved as easily without an expletive as with one. Instead of ending his line with 'the boys do play', he can as easily end it with 'the young boys play'. But if the word which has to have a rime found for it is still 'day', and the subject of the convenient rime 'play' happens to be singular, then the poet, who is prevented by grammar from 'the boy play', can be allowed to write 'the boy does play'. But Pope came to be numbered among the 'future refiners' at the latest by 1717. The many revised poems in the *Works* of this year, as well as the few new poems, mark together a great technical advance. In the edition of the *Rape of the Lock* in this volume there are several verbal changes, four of which affect passages which contain the word *did*.

> *Sol* thro' white Curtains did his Beams display, (1712)

becomes

> *Sol* thro' white curtains shot a tim'rous ray, (1717)

> Steel did the Labour of the Gods destroy,
> And strike to Dust th'aspiring Tow'rs of *Troy*; (1712)

becomes 'Steel could . . .' in 1717: ('th'aspiring' had been changed to 'th'Imperial' in 1714.)

> 'Twas this, the morning *Omens* did foretel[l];

becomes '. . . seem'd to tell;' in 1717.

> See the poor Remnants of this slighted Hair!
> My hands shall rend what ev'n thy own did spare. (1712)

becomes

> See the poor remnants of these slighted hairs!
> My hands shall rend what ev'n thy rapine spares; (1717)[1]

Although Pope, in 1706, could speak of the avoidance of these expletives as a 'nicety' which he seems to imply that few English poets (perhaps, so far as he was aware, none) either had observed or were observing, and although he himself only gradually came to 'explode' *does* and *did*, Dr Johnson, in his notices of Cowley and Waller in the *Lives of the Poets* (begun 1777, published 1779–81), speaks of them as though they were devices which, within living memory, no self-respecting poet had permitted himself to use. He says of Cowley:

> The words *do* and *did*, which so much degrade in present estimation the line that admits them, were in the time of Cowley little

1. *On the Poetry of Pope*, 1950, pp. 121–3.

censured or avoided; how often he used them and with how bad an effect, at least to our ears, will appear by a passage, in which every reader will lament to see just and noble thoughts defrauded of their praise by inelegance of language.[1]

And of Waller:

He uses the expletive *do* very frequently; and though he lived to see it almost universally ejected, was not more careful to avoid it in his last compositions than in his first. Praise had given him confidence, and, finding the world satisfied, he satisfied himself.[2]

Since in what he says about Cowley, although it is *do* and *did* that Johnson actually mentions, it is the word *does* which he six times italicises in the passage he quotes from him, it may perhaps be assumed that, in complaining of Waller's use of *do*, he was including his use of *does* and *did* as well: if so, he can hardly have been correct in declaring (or implying) that Waller, who died in 1687, lived to see all these expletives 'almost universally ejected'; for, as we have seen, it was only between 1706 and 1717 that Pope himself was gradually feeling his way towards the ejection of *does* and *did*. So far as I am aware, no statistics have been collected on this interesting and important subject, and I can offer no more than my general impression that these expletives are at least not *strikingly* frequent in Donne, George Herbert, and the rhymed verse of Milton, that they are more frequent in Carew, still more so, despite the praise of his smoothness, sweetness and easiness by Dryden and others, in Waller, and most strikingly frequent of all, perhaps because so often present in poems and passages that would otherwise be perfect, in Marvell. Were those poets in whom they are at least not strikingly frequent consciously aware of them as defects to be, if possible, avoided, or did they, as it were, unconsciously tend to avoid them in the course of their conscious attempts to realise definite ideas of style? For they were, of course, equally incompatible both with 'the Common way of Speaking', which Donne, like Dryden after him, was trying to follow, and with that classic elegance and gravity at which Milton aimed. Bradshaw's *Concordance* to Milton's poems records only those occurrences of *do* where it is an active verb, not an auxiliary, and does not record *does*, *doth* and *did* at all—presumably on the assumption that such information could be of no conceivable interest to students of literature! I have not attempted

---

1. *Lives*, ed. Birkbeck Hill, I 60.   2. *op. cit.*, I 293–4.

to supply the deficiency, but I will remark that there are three examples even in *Lycidas*:

> Whom universal Nature did lament (l. 60)
> Fame is the spur that the clear spirit doth raise (l. 70)
> Last came, and last did go (l. 108)

A fairly detailed exhibition of the comparative frequency of expletives in Dryden's poetry at various periods and in Pope's up to and including the first edition of *The Rape of the Lock* would be most interesting, and would enable us to pronounce positively upon the correctness or incorrectness of Johnson's assertion that Waller lived to see them 'almost universally ejected'. I can only say that in those couplet passages of Dryden's which are most present in my own memory I can only recall one example:

> Great Wits are sure to Madness near alli'd
> And thin Partitions do their Bounds divide[1]

There are none in *A Song for St Cecilia's Day* and only one in *Alexander's Feast* (ll. 54–6):

> *Bacchus* ever Fair and Young
> Drinking Joys did first ordain.

These are not trivial matters, for they concern the difference between perfection and imperfection. Those who require some moral as well as aesthetic justification for the study of literature ought surely to seek it precisely here; for, in so far as they attempt to obey the commandment *Estote perfecti*, 'Be ye perfect', all human endeavours, religious and moral, intellectual and aesthetic, are impelled by the motion with which man was intended to move. And to those who ask in what sense the study of literature and, in particular, of poetry, can act, or can be made to act, as a discipline, it may be replied that the serious study of poetry can provide an incomparable training in the ability to distinguish and discriminate: for we must first try to distinguish the 'thisness' of the poet we are studying, and we must then try to discriminate between his more perfect and his less perfect poems, and to decide just where and how and why some of his near-perfect poems fall short of perfection. Here I cannot do better than quote from a letter (15 December 1921) which Rilke wrote to Countess Margot Sizzo, who

1. *Absalom and Achitophel*, First Part, ll. 163–4.

had sent him the manuscript of her translation of his *Lay of the Life and Death of Cornet Christoph Rilke* into French. Just because her translation had achieved some measure of success, he must, Rilke declared, judge it all the more severely:

> For when anywhere in the realm of art a certain achievement is reached, there forthwith presents itself the demand for perfection, or at least for what we are more or less ready to call by that name. And the longer one practises this singular *métier* of artistic activity, the severer one becomes towards all who meddle with it, and has, if one finally grows relentless, only the one excuse: that one is no less so towards oneself.

The fact is that Marvell, like many other fine amateur poets of the seventeenth century (and, except for Milton and Dryden, they were all amateurs), was not sufficiently relentless towards himself. Indeed, in none of them is the contrast between almost miraculous achievement and almost incredible carelessness and clumsiness so glaring and so distressing, as from time to time in the course of this study I shall find further occasion to demonstrate. His verse is sometimes no more careful and (alas!) no more distinguished than that of his patron the Lord General, who, together with the few other friends to whom Marvell may have shown his poems, probably enjoyed and applauded his successes, but paid little or no attention to those 'innumerable minutiae' on the observance of which, as Wordsworth wrote to his young friend William (later Sir William) Hamilton, absolute success in the art of poetry depends.[1]

We may now return from the *does's* and the *do's* to the 'studying' and 'meditating' nightingale and the glow-worms as 'Country Comets', which, as I have remarked, were undoubtedly suggested to Marvell by his reading of Holland's *Pliny*. Pliny has a long and elaborate description of the nightingale and its song, which may well have suggested to Strada the famous Latin poem which Crashaw paraphrased as *Musicks Duell*. The passage in it that most concerns us is this:

> Ye shall haue the yong Nightingales studie and meditate how to sing, by themselues; ye shall haue them listen attentiuely to the old birds when they sing, and to take out lessons as it were from them, whom they would seeme to imitate staffe by staffe. The scholler when she hath giuen good eare vnto her mistresse, presently rehearseth

1. 22 November 1831, *Letters*, ed. de Selincourt, no. 995.

what she hath heard; and both of them keep silence for a time in their turns.[1]

Pliny not merely compares the glow-worms to stars, but explicitly declares that they are a sort of terrestrial stars which Nature has given to the countryman to inform him of the progress of the seasons and of the times for reaping and sowing. Chapter xxvi of his eighteenth book (in Holland's translation) concludes:

> As for the later end of this foresaid time, it must be employed in the sowing of Panicke and Millet; for it is ordinarie and vsual to sow this kind of graine after that hastie Barley is ripe, and also vpon the very same lands where it grew. Now the signe common to them both, testifying as wel the ripenes of one, as the Seednes of the other, are the glo-birds or glo-worms Cicindelae, shining in the euening ouer the corne-fields, for so the rustical paisants and country clowns cal certain flies or worms glowing and glittering star-like; and the Greeks name them Lampyrides: wherein we may see the wonderfull bounty and incredible goodnes of Nature, in teaching vs by that silly creature.[2]

And the next chapter begins:

> Nature contented not her selfe to assemble a troup of starres together in a knot . . . but she would needs giue the Husbandman other starres beneath vpon the earth, as signes to shew him the true seasons and times when and how to go to worke: as if she cried out and spake vnto him after this manner: Why shouldest thou looke vp to the heauens, thou that art to till the ground? Why keepest thou a seeking among the stars for thy countrey worke? . . . Behold I scatter and spread here and there among thy very weeds and grasse growing vpon the ground, other especiall shining stars . . . Seest thou not these flies or glo-birds aforesaid couer their bright and glittering light, resembling sparckles of fire, when they keep their wings close together, and carrie fire-light about them euen in the night?[3]

Earlier (Book XI, chapter xxviii) Pliny had declared that 'These Glow-bards neuer appeare before hay is ripe vpon the ground, ne yet after it is cut downe'[4]—a remark which, in association with the passages

1. *The Historie of the World*, ed. of 1635, I 286 (Bk. X, ch. xxix).
2. *op. cit.*, I 593.   3. *op. cit.*, I 593.   4. *op cit.*, I 326.

I have quoted, undoubtedly suggested to Marvell the idea of glow-worms, not merely as country stars, but as country comets, presaging not (as he adds, with characteristic exploitation of the possibilities of antithesis) a war or a prince's funeral, but the fall of the grass.

There could be no better example than this poem of what, contrasting Marvell with Randolph and others, I insisted on in the previous chapter:[1] his ability to combine various kinds of intellectual wit with more permanent sources of poetic pleasure, and to achieve a just balance between the surprising and the permanently delightful; for he has here combined hyperbole and exploitation of the possi-bilities of antithesis with the kind of pleasure which any unsophisti-cated seventeenth-century country gentleman or, for that matter, any modern reader, might find in many of the pages of Holland's *Pliny*.

The Mower's Song, the last of the Mower poems, is another charming, though less concentrated and memorable, exploitation of the possi-bilities of hyperbole and antithesis. Its last stanza was certainly sug-gested by yet another passage in Holland's *Pliny*, and it may well be that on this last stanza, in which the Mower declares that the mown meadows, emblem of Juliana's triumph over him,

> Shall now the Heraldry become
> With which I shall[2] adorn my Tomb,

Marvell built, as it were, the rest of the poem, containing the Mower's reproaches to ungrateful meadows for continuing to flourish while he was withering under Juliana's disdain. In a passage that Marvell was remembering when he began his poem *Hortus* with the lines

> Quisnam adeo, mortale genus, præcordia versat?
> Heu Palmæ, Laurique furor, vel simplicis Herbæ!

(What furious desire, O mortal kind, so agitates your hearts, alas, for palm, for laurel, or even for simple grass),

Pliny, in the third chapter of his twenty-second book, entitled by Hol-land *Of grasse Chaplets*, declares that:

> No Coronets verily were there euer at Rome better esteemed, either to testifie the triumphant majestie of that victorious citie (the soueraign lady of the whole world) or to giue testimony of honour

1. See pp. 86 ff.   2. T2, 'will'.

and reward for some notable seruice performed for the Common-
weale, than those which were made simply of green grasse.[1]

And in the fourth chapter:

> For in truth, the greatest signe of victory in old time, and of
> yeelding to the mercy of the enemy, was this, If the vanquished did
> take vp grasse, and tender it vnto the conqueror: for this serued
> as a confession and protestation, That they rendered vp all their
> interest which they might challenge in the earth (the mother
> that bred and fed them) yea, and the very right of sepulture in
> her.[2]

This passage certainly 'gave' Marvell his last stanza, which he may
well have written first, and then built up to it (as to the climax) the
rest of his poem. It is less tightly constructed than *The Mower to the
Glo-Worms*, for each stanza forms a complete sentence; nevertheless,
the stanzas are untransposable, and in each of the first four the syntactical pattern, if not identical, is at least very similar, for in each the
second couplet is a particularisation of the more general statement
expressed in the first. It is also the only poem where Marvell has used
a refrain, a refrain whose rhythm, as Margoliouth remarks, 'suggests
the long regular sweep of the scythe'.

The Mower's Song

I

My Mind was once the true survey
Of all these Medows fresh and gay;
And in the greenness of the Grass
Did see its Hopes as in a Glass;
When *Juliana* came, and She
What I do to the Grass, does to my Thoughts and Me.

II

But these, while I with Sorrow pine,
Grew more luxuriant still and fine;
That not one Blade of Grass you spy'd,
But had a Flower on either side;
When *Juliana* came, and She
What I do to the Grass, does to my Thoughts and Me.

---

1. Ed. 1635, II 115.   2. *op. cit.*, p. 116.

III

Unthankful Medows, could you so
A fellowship so true forego,
And in your gawdy May-games meet,
While I lay trodden under feet?
When *Juliana* came, and She
What I do to the Grass, does to my Thoughts and Me.

IV

But what you in Compassion ought,[1]
Shall now by my Revenge be wrought:
And Flow'rs, and Grass, and I and all,
Will in one common Ruine fall.
For *Juliana* comes, and She
What I do to the Grass, does to my Thoughts and Me.

V

And thus, ye Meadows, which have been
Companions of my thoughts more green,[2]
Shall now the Heraldry become
With which I shall[3] adorn my Tomb;
For *Juliana* comes, and She
What I do to the Grass, does to my Thoughts and Me.

The longest of Marvell's pastorals (122 lines) is *The Nymph complaining for the death of her Faun*. Nowhere can one perceive more clearly than here his own peculiar exquisiteness and, at the same time, that amateurishness and clumsiness with which his most exquisite lines and phrases are too often juxtaposed. It does not seem to me necessary to suppose, with Margoliouth and others, that Marvell received any suggestion from William Browne's allegorical description of Fida and her hind in the third and fourth songs of the first book of *Britannia's*

---

1. 'Owed': cf. *I Henry IV*, III iii 151: 'And said this other day you ought him a thousand pound'.

2. In the sixteenth and seventeenth centuries *green*, like Latin *viridis*, was used as frequently in various metaphorical senses as in the literal sense of green in colour. Here, as in the 'green Thought' at l. 48 of *The Garden*, the predominant sense is probably that of 'tender', 'innocent'; yet here too, although the word is not, as there, used twice, there is a kind of punning antithesis between the literal and metaphorical senses: 'a green thought in a green mead'.

3. T2, 'will'.

Pastorals—that hind which was killed by Riot and from whose body
emerged the radiant Figure of Truth. If the subject in the most general
terms, a girl's lament for her dead pet, did not occur to him spontaneously, it might well have been suggested by either or both of
two very ancient and famous laments which had been much imitated
by Renaissance poets (including Skelton in *Philip Sparrow*), Catullus's
poem on the death of Lesbia's sparrow and Ovid's (*Amores*, II vi) on
that of Corinna's parrot. Is it not likely, however, that Marvell's
untraditional particularisation of this traditional topic, the slaughter of
a child's pet by foraging (and presumably Parliamentary) troopers,
was suggested to him by the sort of thing that was going on all around
him, and had been going on all over England since the beginning of
the Civil War; and may not this contemporisation of the traditional
topic be related to what Mr Eliot has said about the contrast between
the romantic mistiness and vagueness of at any rate the latter part
of Morris's *Nymph's Song to Hylas* and the 'bright, hard precision' of
Marvell's poem?[1] Most readers, I think, remember only the description
of the nymph's garden of roses and lilies and of how the fawn, had it
lived, would have been 'Lillies without, Roses within'. Few remember
the opening lines:

> The wanton Troopers riding by
> Have shot my Faun and it will dye.

After some witty reflection on the unatonableness of the troopers'
offence, a passage where wit and hyperbole never break loose from a
befitting tenderness, or from the balanced combination of seriousness
and light-heartedness with which Marvell has chosen to treat his subject, the nymph's thoughts turn to her 'unconstant *Sylvio*', the faithless
lover who had given her the fawn, a passage which, with its artlessness
and its puns, is nearer to the typical Elizabethan manner than to the
more sophisticated, ingenious, and surprising wit of the preceding
paragraph:

> Said He, look how your Huntsman here
> Hath taught a Faun to hunt his *Dear*.
> But *Sylvio* soon had me beguil'd.
> This waxed tame, while he grew wild,
> And quite regardless of my Smart,
> Left me his Faun, but took his Heart.   (ll. 31–6)

---

1. *Selected Essays*, 1932, p. 285.

There follow some thirty lines of simple description of the unkindness of Silvio and the lovingness and beauty of the fawn, lines which do not attempt ingenuity or surprise, and which might almost have been written by an Elizabethan poet, had he been able to dispense for so long with coral clasps, amber studs, and classical mythology; lines, too, it must be admitted, which sometimes recall those many passages where Elizabethan poets even of Spenser's stature seem to write as though the height of their ambition were to produce verse that scanned and rhymed:

> Had it liv'd long, I do not know
> Whether it too might have done so
> As *Sylvio* did: his Gifts might be
> Perhaps as false or more than he.
> But I am sure, for ought that I
> Could in so short a time espie,
> Thy Love was far more better then
> The love of false and cruel men.   (ll. 47–54)

Then comes the description of the nymph's garden, for most readers the most memorable passage in the poem. What distinguishes it is, on the one hand, an intense and precise visualisation of things obviously beautiful, and, on the other hand, a presentation of these things, in a terse and almost epigrammatic way, with sudden and surprising contrasts and juxtapositions. It has been suggested[1] that the image of the white fawn reposing among white lilies may have owed something to a passage in one of the Eclogues (vi 32–45) of Calpurnius Siculus, a poet of the age of Nero, a passage where the challenger in a song-contest offers as a prize

> illum,
> candida qui medius cubat inter lilia, cervum,
>
> (that stag reclining there among white lilies.)

That stag (stag, not fawn) is not described as white, though, and the fact that the poet specifically mentions (l. 45) the snow-white crescent on its breast proves that he imagined the rest of it as being of some other colour. Whether or no Marvell is here developing a hint which he found in Calpurnius, the fact that he might well be doing so may serve

---

1. By Don Cameron Allen, *Metaphoric Traditions in Renaissance Poetry*, 1960, pp. 96–7. With most of what is there said about Marvell's poem I find it impossible to agree.

to remind us, as I remarked at the end of my second chapter,[1] that the image of the white fawn reclining among white lilies and pasturing on red roses gave him the same kind of pleasure as the image of lilies seen through glass or of women's bodies seen through lawn or water, which they found in Martial and Ovid, gave to Herrick, Cowley and other poets.

> I have a Garden of my own,
> But so with Roses over grown,
> And Lillies, that you would it guess
> To be a little Wilderness.
> And all the Spring time of the year
> It onely loved to be there.
> Among the beds of Lillyes, I
> Have sought it oft, where it should lye;
> Yet could not, till it self would rise,
> Find it, although before mine Eyes.
> For, in the flaxen Lillies shade,
> It like a bank of Lillies laid.
> Upon the Roses it would feed,
> Until its Lips ev'n seem'd to bleed:
> And then to me 'twould boldly trip,
> And print those Roses on my Lip.
> But all its chief delight was still
> On Roses thus its self to fill:
> And its pure virgin Limbs to fold
> In whitest sheets of Lillies cold.
> Had it liv'd long, it would have been
> Lillies without, Roses within.   (ll. 71–92)

This is quite different from the manner of Elizabethan pastoral, which, at its best, tends to give us a charming re-combination of stock properties rather than anything like a new visual experience. In Donne's poetry visual description for its own sake scarcely exists, and the more obviously attractive *visibilia* seem to be deliberately excluded as insipid or conventional. The descriptive element in his poetry is nearly always either satirical, or incidental to some ingenious and astonishing comparison. There are indeed some intense visualisations in Vaughan's poetry, but they are invariably illustrative and without either that own-sakeness or that piquant and inimitable blend of nature and arti-

1. See p. 100.

fice that distinguish Marvell's. Herrick's comparisons of Julia's limbs to lilies seen through crystal, of the nipples of her breasts to strawberries peeping out of cream, and other things of the kind, are much closer to those passages in the Roman and Alexandrian poets which ultimately suggested them, much closer, one might almost say, to the toy-shop, and lack what can only be called the 'naturalness' with which Marvell is somehow able to infuse his semi-Alexandrian artifice. This is probably because Marvell pursues these visual contrasts, antitheses and comparisons through much wider and more varied contexts than Herrick, and sees not just particular details but whole scenes in this way. The only other seventeenth-century poet in whom I can find anything at all strikingly similar to his witty visualisations is Crashaw, whom Marvell has occasionally imitated, and by whom it seems not unlikely that the possibilities of this kind of description were first suggested to him. And they were, I think, above all suggested to him by the wittily pictorial stanzas of *The Weeper*, the poem that opens both editions (1646 and 1648) of Crashaw's *Steps to the Temple*. To demonstrate this, it is almost sufficient to place side by side the lines immediately following the nymph's description of her garden and these two stanzas from *The Weeper*, the first of which, the original eighth, Crashaw omitted after 1646, and the second of which, the original (1646) twelfth, became in the later editions (1648 and 1652) the ninth:

> Not the soft Gold which
> Steales from the Amber-weeping Tree,
> Makes sorrow halfe so Rich,
> As the drops distil'd from thee.
> Sorrowes best Iewels lye in these
> Caskets, of which Heaven keeps the Keyes . . .

> There is no need at all
> That the Balsame-sweating bough
> So coyly should let fall
> His med'cinable Teares; for now
> Nature both learn't t' extract a dew
> More soveraigne and sweet from you.

With his 'Amber-weeping Tree' Crashaw is alluding to the transformation, described by Ovid in the second book of the *Metamorphoses*, of the Heliades, or daughters of Helios, the sun-god, while grieving for their brother Phaeton, into poplar trees:

> From these cleere dropping trees, teares yearely flow:
> They, hardned by the Sunne, to Amber grow;
> Which, on the moisture-giving River spent,
> To *Romane* Ladies, as his gift, is sent.[1]

And with his 'Balsame-sweating bough' he is alluding to one of the various balm-yielding trees, perhaps to the one mentioned by Jeremy Taylor in one of his sermons: 'Falling like the tears of the balsam of Iudea'.[2] It was pretty clearly with these two stanzas in his memory that Marvell made his Nymph exclaim:

> O help! O help! I see it faint:
> And dye as calmely as a Saint.
> See how it weeps. The Tears do come
> Sad, slowly dropping like a Gumme.
> So weeps the wounded Balsome: so
> The holy Frankincense doth flow.
> The brotherless *Heliades*
> Meet in such Amber Tears as these.   (ll. 93–100)

For can it be doubted that his 'wounded Balsome' was suggested by Crashaw's 'Balsame-sweating bough' and his 'Amber Tears' by Crashaw's 'Amber-weeping Tree'? He has made Crashaw's implicit allusion to the Heliades explicit, and, in so doing, has coined one of his most memorable phrases and written one of his most perfect octosyllabic couplets.

Marvell concludes his poem with a characteristic piece of seventeenth-century ingenuity about marble and tears. It was perhaps a line of Petrarch's,[3] declaring that the pure ivory of Laura's face transformed to marble whoever gazed upon it from anear (*Che fa di marmo chi da presso 'l guarda*), which first suggested, as topics in eulogy and funeral elegy, the marmorealising or petrifying powers of admiration or grief. Donne declared that the dead Lord Chamberlain[4] needed no marble tomb, since grief had turned his children to stone; William Browne declared that some future female reader of his epitaph

---

1. Sandys's translation (first published 1626; I quote from the second, enlarged, edition, 1640, p. 28, col. 2).
2. Quoted by *OED*, 'Balsam', sb., 8.
3. Sonnet 131, *Io canterei d'Amor si novamente*, l. 11.
4. Lord Hunsdon, the probable subject of the 'Elegie on the L.C.' (*Poems*, ed. Grierson, I 287): see John Sampson, 'A contemporary Light upon John Donne', *Essays and Studies by Members of the English Association*, 1921, pp. 95 ff.

upon the Countess of Pembroke would be transformed by grief into a marble monument and marble tomb; and Milton, going one better, declared in his lines on Shakespeare that admiration already produced that effect on each one of Shakespeare's readers. And it was, so far as I know, Milton, not usually regarded as a pioneer of these matters, who first revealed the stone-engraving property of tears. It is worth quoting the lines on the Holy Sepulchre in his ode on *The Passion*, because they produce, with their detailed working out of the conceit, an impression of oddity and quaintness which Marvell, through being far less explicit, has largely avoided:

> Mine eye hath found that sad Sepulchral rock
> That was the Casket of Heav'ns richest store,
> And here though grief my feeble hands up-lock,
> Yet on the softned Quarry would I score
> My plaining verse as lively as before;
>   For sure so well instructed are my tears,
> That they would fitly fall in order'd Characters.

One Eldred Revett, a young Cambridge and Inns of Court man, who published a volume of *Poems* in 1657, and who was a friend of the poet Lovelace, contributed to Lovelace's *Posthume Poems* (1659), which he had helped the poet's youngest brother to edit, an elegy which concludes with some lines in which Revett may well have been trying to improve upon that stanza of Milton's *Passion*:

> Why should some rude hand carve thy sacred stone,
> And there incise a cheap inscription;
> When we can shed the tribute of our tears
> So long, till the relenting marble wears?
> Which shall such order in their cadence keep,
> That they a native Epitaph shall weep;
> Untill each Letter spelt distinctly lyes,
> Cut by the mystick droppings of our eyes.[1]

Milton's, and still more Revett's, lines are very much in the manner of the more academic wit of the time, that wit of which so many examples can be found in manuscript commonplace-books, in that anthology of university wit *Parnassus Biceps*, and in the poems of Cleveland. Marvell, like Revett, may well have taken a hint from Milton's lines on the Holy Sepulchre; yet while their lines are no more

1. *The Poems of Richard Lovelace*, ed. C. H. Wilkinson, II 208.

than ingenious and dated verse, Marvell's remain highly poetical, and
this in spite of the fact that in ingenious combination he has even gone
a step further than Milton. There are numerous contemporary allusions
to the 'sweating' or 'weeping' of marble or stone as the result of con-
densation,[1] but Marvell has combined an allusion to this phenomenon
with Milton's conceit (if Milton was really its inventor) of stone-
engraving tears:

> First my unhappy Statue shall
> Be cut in Marble; and withal,
> Let it be weeping too: but there
> Th' Engraver sure his Art may spare;
> For I so truly thee bemoane,
> That I shall weep though I be Stone:
> Until my Tears, still dropping, wear
> My breast, themselves engraving there.
> There at my feet shalt thou be laid,
> Of purest Alabaster made:
> For I would have thine Image be
> White as I can, though not as Thee.   (ll. 111-22)

Marvell, while being highly ingenious, has contrived to remain
poetical (I might almost say, classical) by leaving something to the imagination, by refusing to be too detailed and explicit. 'I shall require a
sculptor to cut my statue, but no engraver to inscribe my epitaph:
that will be done by my own tears falling upon my breast'—even that
degree of antithetical explicitness Marvell has avoided, and the prevailing impression produced by his lines is one of rather charming
hyperbole. The hyperbole is indeed produced by ingenious means,
but the means are largely concealed by the effect. Suppose he had
written:

> Until my Tears, still dropping, wear
> My breast, themselves engraving there
> In order'd Characters that tell
> The fate which thee and me befell—

this would not entirely have spoilt the passage, but it would have
given it an effect of oddness and quaintness from which it is now free.
As it is, there is nothing to distract the imagination from that pre-

---

1. e.g. in G. Herbert's *The Church-floore*, l. 15, and in John Hall's *Julia Weeping*,
ll. 1-7 (*Caroline Poets*, ed. Saintsbury, II 197).

dominant impression of whiteness in which the last lines culminate. Again and again we find Marvell doing the sort of things that other seventeenth-century poets were or had been doing, but doing them with an interesting and characteristic difference. In this poem, as in several others, one might say, without excessively over-simplifying, that he is combining something of Elizabethan pastoralism and picturesqueness with something of seventeenth-century epigram, hyperbole, ingenuity and wit: the seventeenth-century qualities saving the Elizabethan ones from insipidity, and the Elizabethan qualities saving the seventeenth-century ones from that too cerebral and prosaic oddness into which they often degenerated.

In this poem Marvell's use of his favourite metre, the octosyllabic couplet, a metre in which, I cannot but think, he was confirmed, if not actually impelled to it, by his reading of Milton and Crashaw, is much looser than in that superb poem *To his Coy Mistress* and is often rather slipshod. Here, though, as in even his finest poems, he is almost exclusively iambic, and seldom makes use of that substitution of trochee for iamb in the first foot

(Ŭndĕr thĕ Hāwthŏrn īn thĕ dāle)

and that admixture of trochaic heptasyllabics

(Clēarlў rōuse thĕ slŭmbrĭng mōrn)

of which Milton frequently avails himself. His few metrical licences or variations usually stand out and are among his most memorable lines: here, the substitution of a trochee for an iamb in both the first and the third foot of

Līlliĕs wĭthōut, Rōsĕs wĭthīn—

a music which he may well have learnt from Crashaw

(Swēetnĕsse sŏ sād, sādnĕs sŏ swēet),[1]

in whose use of this metre there is, I think, more variety, more examples of substitution and compensation, than in the work of any other seventeenth-century poet. The metrical boldness of that memorable line in *The Garden*,

Tŏ ă grēen Thōught ĭn ă grēen shade,

where two pyrrhics (˘˘) and two spondees (¯¯) are substituted for iambs (˘¯), may possibly have been suggested by the 'music' of Crashaw's

Whŷ tŏ shōw lŏve shĕe shŏuld shēd blōod.[2]

There can, I think, be no doubt that the octosyllabic couplet is most

---

1. *The Weeper*, st. 10 in 1646, st. 6 in 1648 and 1652.
2. *Hymn to St Teresa*, l. 22.

successful and most satisfying when it is comparatively closed, when, that is to say, the first line ends with a syllable which one can, to some extent, hold on to:

> The brotherless *Heliades*
> Melt in such Amber Tears as these.

It would indeed be almost impossibly difficult to give each first line the degree of self-sufficiency possessed by 'The brotherless *Heliades*'; nevertheless, such a couplet as this should, I think, represent the desirable, the ever-present, the continually attempted ideal. Milton, in *L'Allegro* and *Il Penseroso*, seldom falls much below it, but Marvell, here and elsewhere, is often far too easily satisfied. He will rhyme on a word that will not really bear the weight of a rhyme, such as 'in' or 'then' (=than) or 'to' or 'will' (verb), and, by dividing a phrase between two lines, will produce an awkward jolt between the end of the first line and the beginning of the second.

> Their Stain
> Is dy'd in such a Purple Grain.
> There is not such another *in*
> The World, to offer for their Sin.
>
> (ll. 21-4, of the murderous troopers)

Similarly in lines 53-4 where, moreover, 'expletives their feeble aid do join':

> Thy Love was *far more better then*
> The love of false and cruel men;

and in lines 105-6:

> Now my Sweet Faun is vanish'd *to*
> Whether the Swans and Turtles go.

The clumsiness of the following lines (101-3) is almost unbelievable in a poet of Marvell's talent: how, one wonders, could he possibly have remained satisfied with them?—

> I in a golden Vial will
> Keep these two crystal Tears; and fill
> It till it do o'reflow with mine.

If he had to use 'will' and 'fill' as rhymes he ought to have avoided an awkward *hiatus* by making the lines that follow them begin with unaccented syllables: something like (I offer it only *metri gratia*)

> In sacramental gold I will
> Preserve these crystal tears, and fill
> The vial, till it o'erflow, with mine.

But even so there is something profoundly unsatisfying about these two consecutive run-overs. Such verse tends to give the impression of a piece of material being unwound from one roller on to another, while the rhymes, like the jumping finger of a dial, indicate the passage of each successive length. In fact, it does not sufficiently contain within itself the reason for its being verse. And this metrical insufficiency is too often combined, as in some of Wordsworth's 'experimental' ballads, with an enfeebling use of inversion:

> With sweetest milk, and sugar, first
> *I it* at mine own fingers nurst

(ll. 55–6)

> But so with Roses over grown,
> And Lillies, that you *would it guess*
> To be a little Wilderness.

(ll. 72–4)

Byron once spoke of the 'fatal facility' of the octosyllabic couplet.[1] When used as a vehicle for narrative poetry, that has usually been its predominant characteristic; but certain late Elizabethan and seventeenth-century poets discovered and revealed that its real virtue, the thing, as Aristotle would say, that it was intended to be, was not narrative, but—using that word in a rather wide sense—epigrammatic. It requires, in fact, if its true potentialities are to be realised, an exceptional choiceness, precision, and unsuperfluousness of diction and the greatest economy and restraint in the use of *enjambement*. Even in the hands of so accomplished a practitioner as Marvell we can sometimes see it relapsing towards that medieval babel from which it had been redeemed.

If those two charming poems, *Young Love* and *The Picture of Little T.C. in a Prospect of Flowers*, are to be classified at all, they may most appropriately be classified as semi-pastorals, although the *Little T.C.* poem, with its floral background, is perhaps nearer to pastoral than its

1. In the dedication of *The Corsair* to Thomas Moore.

companion. Either or both would provide an admirable text for a discourse on the relation between Tradition and the Individual Talent and on the stimulating and fertilising (as distinct from the often constricting and conventionalising) influence of 'the classics' on seventeenth-century poets. For it was a single Greek epigram (or possibly two epigrams) and a single ode of Horace that suggested, directly or indirectly, the possibilities of the topic therein handled first to some of Marvell's contemporaries and then to Marvell himself. Stated as concisely as possible, the argument of *Young Love* is as follows: 'Child, love me now, instead of waiting until you reach what is commonly regarded as an age ripe for love; for this will enable us either to steal from Fate a happiness which, by cutting you off in your childhood, she intends to deny us, or to anticipate a happiness which she intends to bestow upon us later.' This, regarded simply as a piece of argumentation, is far more elaborately intellectual than we should be likely to find in any lyric poem by a Greek or Roman poet, and a good deal more elaborate than anything in the poems on the subject by Marvell's English predecessors; for the moment, though, we are concerned only with outlines. The argument of the *Little T.C.* poem, a poem in which there is much more fine description, is less complex: 'Let me make my peace with this now harmless beauty before her power becomes dangerous, even though it is possible that Fate may never allow her to reach that destructive age.' Before examining the treatment of this topic, or of these related topics, by earlier poets, I will observe, wise after the event, that the general subject, the address to a beautiful female child, or beautiful young girl still almost a child, implicitly contained, as it were, fine possibilities of rhetorical or dialectical elaboration, the link between them being (to borrow the opening word of Horace's contribution) *nondum*, 'not yet': (1) Her beauty is not yet dangerous; (2) She is not yet ripe for love; (3) She is supposed to be not yet ripe for love, though in fact she is so; (4) She has not yet been, though she may be, cut off by a cruel Fate before outgrowing her childhood. (2) and (3) are, of course, mutually exclusive, and (1) and (3), if, as I have never found them, used together, would tend to counteract each other. In *Young Love* Marvell has combined (3) and (4) and in the *Little T.C.* poem (1) and (4). Let us now turn to his Greek, Roman and English predecessors.

Preserved in the Greek Anthology (V 124) is the following epigram by Philodemus, a poet of the first century B.C.:

Οὔπω σοι καλύκων γυμνὸν θέρος, οὐδὲ μελαίνει
βότρυς ὁ παρθενίους πρωτοβολῶν χάριτας·
ἀλλ' ἤδη θοὰ τόξα νέοι θήγουσιν Ἔρωτες,
Λυσιδίκη, καὶ πῦρ τύφεται ἐγκρύφιον.
φεύγωμεν, δυσέρωτες, ἕως βέλος οὐκ ἐπὶ νευρῇ·
μάντις ἐγὼ μεγάλης αὐτίκα πυρκαϊῆς.

(Your summer is not yet bare of its sheathes, nor darkening is the grape-cluster now first out-shooting maiden graces; but already young Loves are sharpening swift arrows, Lysidice, and fire is smouldering concealed. Let us fly, we wretched lovers, while as yet the shaft is not upon the string: I prophesy a mighty conflagration soon.)

The particular theme of Philodemus's epigram, which, in order to show the relationship to other possible treatments of the more general theme of 'Young Beauty', I classified negatively as 'Her beauty is not yet dangerous', might, when looked at in isolation, be more satisfactorily described as 'Young beauty's power foretold'. Philodemus (like Marvell in the *Little T.C.* poem) prays that he himself may not be one of the victims of his prophecy's fulfilment. A later poet, Antiphilus of Byzantium, who flourished in the first century of our era, declared, in an epigram (V 111) also preserved in the Greek Anthology, that he himself was suffering from what he had foretold. Here we may dispense with the Greek and content ourselves with Paton's translation:

I said even formerly, when Tereina's charms were yet infantile, 'She will consume us all when she grows up'. They laughed at my prophecy: but lo! the time I once foretold is come, and for long I suffer myself from the wound. What am I to do? To look on her is pure fire, and to look away is trouble of heart, and if I pay my suit to her, it is 'I am a maid'. All is over with me.[1]

1. For sixteenth- and seventeenth-century readers who did not know Greek, or did not read it easily, an enormous number of epigrams from the Greek Anthology were available in Latin translations. Three different Latin versions of Philodemus's epigram had appeared (*Nondum folliculis*, by Fausto Sabeo, in his *Epigrammatum . . . Libri Quinque*, 1556, p. 655; *Flos tuus nondum*, by Baïf, in his *Carmina*, 1577, f. 29ʳ; *Virgineae nec*, by the Younger (J. J.) Scaliger, among the translations appended to his father's *Poemata Omnia*, 1600, p. 61), and two of Antiphilus's (*Predixi quum parva*, by Sabeo, *op. cit.*, p. 663; *Dicebam infantes*, by Florent Chrestien, in his *Epigrammata ex libris Anthologiae, etc.*, 1608, f. 102ʳ). Filippo Alberti, a friend and literary adviser of Tasso, had expanded Philodemus's epigram into an Italian madrigal in his *Rime*, 1602, p. 206. This is quoted in full by James Hutton on pp. 335–6 of his *The Greek Anthology in Italy*, a book to which, and to the same author's *The Greek Anthology in France*, I am indebted for the information I have given about Latin versions.

We may now turn to that remarkable piece of eclecticism, the fifth ode of Horace's second book, which begins:

> Nondum subacta ferre iugum valet
> cervice, nondum munia comparis
>   aequare, nec tauri ruentis
> in venerem tolerare pondus.

Addressing either himself or an imaginary friend (it is not clear which and perhaps it does not matter), and in metaphors suggested to him by Anacreon, by Theocritus, and perhaps by that epigram of Philodemus we have been considering, Horace develops during the greater part of his ode the theme (so far as I am aware, an original one) that Lalage is not yet ripe for love; and then, declaring that one day she will be more beloved than Pholoë, Chloris or Gyges, seems to conclude with a variation on Philodemus's theme of 'Young beauty's power foretold'. Since a text of Horace is presumably possessed by any reader who may wish to consult the original, I will offer a translation as near as I can get to Horace's alcaics, his rhythms, and his phrases:

> She cannot yet, with bending submissiveness,
> support the yoke, match labouring fellowship,
>   or tolerate some bull's torrential
> rise and descent in the rites of Venus.
>
> Among the verdant meadows your heifer's mind
> finds full contentment: now in the cooling stream
>   assuaging heat, now all-intent on
> innocent sport with her calf-companions
>
> among the river sallows. Restrain the lust
> for grapes unmellowed. Colourful Autumn soon
>   will deck for you those now already
> darkening clusters in deepest purple.
>
> She'll soon pursue you (Time, irrestrainably
> careering, adds those years he deprives you of
>   to hers), and soon with wanton boldness
> Lalage also will seek a consort:
>
> She more belov'd than fugitive Pholoë,
> than Chloris even, gleaming with shoulders white
>   as cloudless moon in still nocturnal
> ocean reflected, or Cnidian Gyges,

whose gender, should you place him among the girls,
would baffle guests of sharpest sagacity,
    obscured so well by loosely flowing
locks and a face that were fit for either.

I have called this poem a remarkable piece of eclecticism, and indeed we
can here see Horace accepting, modifying and re-combining things
that had pleased him in other poets in a manner essentially similar
to that of which we have already noticed so many examples in Marvell.
The image, or metaphor, of Lalage as a young heifer, grazing and playing with her calf-companions, may be regarded as an adaptation, with
the substitution of 'heifer' for 'filly', of the following six lines of
Anacreon:

Thracian filly, why do you eye me askance and pitilessly flee?
Do you think I know nothing worth knowing? Be sure, I could
finely fling the bridle upon you and hold the reins, and drive you
round the posts of the course. Now you graze the meadows and
play there nimbly leaping; for you have no dexterous horseman
to mount you.[1]

With this Horace seems to have combined recollections both of a
passage in Theocritus (xi 20-1), where Polyphemus declares that his
Galataea is 'whiter than pressed-cheese, tenderer than a lamb, wilder
than a heifer, plumper than unripe grapes', and of Philodemus's declaration that the grape-cluster of Lysidice's maiden graces is not yet
darkening into ripeness.

We may now consider some treatments of these topics by seven-
teenth-century poets: first, two poems, the one certainly, the other
probably, deriving from Horace's ode and leading us to Marvell's
Young Love; these two poems deriving, either directly or through
Latin versions, from Philodemus's epigram and leading us to Marvell's
Little T.C. poem.

What may be regarded as a free paraphrase of Horace's ode, considerably abbreviated and genteelised, was made by some anonymous
seventeenth-century poet, and, no doubt because of the novelty of
the idea and feeling it so neatly expressed, became very popular, for it
is found in several printed miscellanies and manuscript commonplace-

1. Diehl, *Anthologia Lyrica Graeca*, I 470, fragment 88; *Oxford Book of Greek
Verse*, no. 177.

books.[1] In some of Horace's diction (*tolle cupidinem inmitis uvae*, 'Restrain the lust for grapes unmellowed'), in his detailed comparison of Lalage to a heifer, and in the way in which he lingers, with, as it were, watering mouth, over the metaphor of the ripening grapes, there is, as in several ancient love-poems, a strong whiff of the ancient world, of the slave-market, or, one might almost say, of the flesh-market: something, in comparison with the love-poetry of the Troubadours, of Dante and Petrarch and their successors, almost crassly realistic and unideal. The seventeenth-century paraphraser has omitted the heifer, and his treatment of the grape-metaphor could hardly have been more delicate, more calculated not to 'bring a blush to the cheek of modesty'· He has also confined himself to the one topic and has omitted Horace's concluding variation on Philodemus's theme of 'Young Beauty's power foretold'.

> Why should passion lead thee blind
> 'Cause thy mistress is unkind?
> She's yet too young to shew delight
> And is not plumed for Cupid's flight;
> She cannot yet in height of pleasure
> Pay her lover equal measure,
> But like the rose new blown doth feed
> The eye alone but bears no seed.
>
> She is yet but in her spring,
> Cold in love till Cupid bring
> A hotter season with his fire,
> Which soon will ripen her desire.
> Autumn will shortly come and greet her,
> Making her taste and colour sweeter:
> Her ripeness then will soon be such
> As she will fall even with a touch.

It may well have been this popular paraphrase which suggested the remarkable little poem *Ad Amicam*, a poem found in only one manuscript, where it is attributed to Randolph, but which, with the omission of four lines and with some variants, was quoted, evidently as being well known, in a dialogue in Thomas May's comedy *The Old Couple*. May's comedy was first printed in 1658, but was probably first acted

1. The earliest printed version I have found is in the 1646 edition of *The Academy of Complements*, p. 202. I quote it in the version, taken from a manuscript in the British Museum, given by A. H. Bullen in his *Speculum Amantis*, p. 56.

long before Randolph's death in 1635.[1] The poet, whoever he was, anticipating Marvell in *Young Love*, has neatly inverted Horace's argument, and, instead of saying 'She is still too young for love', addresses the young person directly and says 'You think you are too young although in fact you are not.' He has also anticipated Marvell and departed from Horace by introducing in his final couplet that so favourite topic of ancient love-poetry, *carpe florem*, that topic in which ancient love-poets performed so many variations, exhorting coy mistresses to gather the rose of love before it withered, to respond to a lover's advances while youth and beauty still made them desirable and before age and wrinkles began to make them repulsive.

> Sweet, doe not thy beauty wrong
> By thinking still thou art too young,
> The rose & lilly in each cheeke
> Flourish, & noe more ripenesse seeke.
> Those flaming beames, shott from thine eye,
> Doe shew Loves Midsomer is nigh.
> Thy cherry cheekes red, soft & sweet
> Proclaim such fruit for use is meet.
> Love's still young, & a buxome boy,
> And young things be allowed to toy,
> Then lose no time, for love hath wings,
> And flies away from aged things.[2]

Horace's Lalage, although a very young girl, is no longer an infant; in the poem of his seventeenth-century paraphraser, though still 'unripe', she is already described as a 'mistress', and the girl addressed by the poet of *Ad Amicam*, though still ripening, is told that she is already ripe enough. Here it is worth recalling that Carew, in *The second Rapture*, declared that there was no happiness in life to be compared with

> a wench about thirteene,
> Already voted to the Queene
> Of lust and lovers.[3]

Marvell, though, in *Young Love*, not merely, like the author of *Ad*

---

1. For a discussion of these problems, see Thorn Drury's edition of Randolph's *Poems*, pp. 188 and 214-15.
2. *The Poems of Thomas Randolph*, ed. G. Thorn Drury, 1929, p. 168.
3. *Poems*, ed. Dunlap, p. 103.

Amicam, inverts the Horatian topic of 'not yet ripe' into 'already ripe enough', but goes still deeper into paradox (or rather, as his manner is, into antithesis which has the appearance of paradox), and makes his addressee, like Lysidice and Tereina in the epigrams of Philodemus and Antiphilus on 'Young Beauty's power foretold', and like 'Little T.C.' in his other poem, an 'infant'. Fundamental to his whole treatment of the subject is the distinction, or antithesis (disregarded by Carew in the lines just quoted), between love and lust, which he introduces in his third and fourth stanzas, declaring that the 'infant', though unripe for lust, is ripe enough for love. It is a distinction that would perhaps have been scarcely comprehensible (or, at most, just fleetingly apprehensible) to Horace and other ancient poets: nevertheless, I think it must be admitted that Marvell's metaphors, especially in the fourth stanza, where Love is a pagan deity accepting pagan sacrifices, have been more influenced than he perhaps recognised by the Horatian *ethos*, and that his almost casual mention of love and lust as things for each of which there is an appropriate season and a time, is, in its context, somewhat incongruous and disconcerting: for is not the distinction between lust and love, made at the end of the third stanza, almost obliterated by the personification, in the fourth, of Love as a deity who accepts with equal pleasure either the loving sacrifice of a snowy lamb or the lustful sacrifice of a wanton kid, lusty bull, or lusty ram? In fact, these essentially pagan metaphors do not really blend with the general texture of Marvell's poem, the rest of which, with its strenuously intellectual though only half-serious dialectic, its conscious extravagance and semi-humorous hyperbole, is utterly remote from the thinking, feeling and writing of Horace or any other ancient love-poet. In what an almost unrecognisably intellectual form the old pagan argument of *carpe florem* appears in the fifth and sixth stanzas! Despite what Mr Eliot once wrote about Donne, Marvell, like Donne and many other so-called 'metaphysical poets', is more often to be found intellectualising sensation than sensationalising thought.

Young Love

I

Come little Infant, Love me now,
While thine unsuspected years
Clear thine aged Fathers brow
From cold Jealousie and Fears.

II

Pretty surely 'twere to see
　　By young Love old Time beguil'd:
While our Sportings are as free
　　As the Nurses with the Child.

III

Common Beauties stay fifteen;[1]
　　Such as yours should swifter move;
Whose fair Blossoms are too green
　　Yet for Lust, but not for Love.

IV

Love as much the snowy Lamb
　　Or the wanton Kid does prize,
As the lusty Bull or Ram,
　　For his morning Sacrifice.

V

Now then love me: time may take
　　Thee before thy time away:
Of this Need wee'l Virtue make,
　　And learn Love before we may.

VI

So we win of doubtful Fate;
　　And, if good she to us meant,
We that Good shall antedate,
　　Or, if ill, that Ill prevent.[2]

VII

Thus as Kingdomes, frustrating
　　Other Titles to their Crown,
In the craddle crown their King,
　　So all Forraign Claims to drown,

1. Wait until they are fifteen before loving and being loved.
2. Anticipate, forestall: enjoy a good measure of mutual love before Fate, if she
intends to do so, snatches you untimely away.

VIII

> So, to make all Rivals vain,
>   Now I crown thee with my Love:
> Crown me with thy Love again,
>   And we both shall Monarchs prove.

The last stanza recalls, and may have been partly suggested by, the last stanza of Donne's *The Anniversarie*, where the poet declares that, while in Heaven the bliss of himself and his beloved, though perfect, will be no greater than that of the other spirits:

> Here upon earth, we'are Kings, and none but wee
> Can be such Kings, nor of such subjects bee.
> Who is so safe as wee? Where none can doe
> Treason to us, except one of us two.

But while, with its continuous and strenuously intellectual argumentation, Marvell's poem, like so many other seventeenth-century poems, could probably not have been what it is without the example of Donne, in several other respects it is quite unlike him: in its use of classical topics ('unripe for love', *carpe florem*), in its perpetual striving, both in thought and expression, for antithesis, and in what might be called, not depreciatingly, but simply in order to point the contrast with Donne, its whimsicality. In the *Songs and Sonets*, even in the most 'serious' of them, there is often something semi-humorous, something of conscious extravagance, about Donne's hyperboles, but they are nearly always used to express some deeply experienced mood, whether of affection or disgust. It is true that the comparative value of different poems cannot be assessed entirely according to the degree of 'real' experience which they communicate, or seem to communicate; and that the poet's arrangement of his words must have been raised to the level of literature before it becomes worth our while to attend to them: nevertheless, it is not nonsensical to say that such a poem as *Young Love* is more 'literary' or more 'purely literary' than almost any of Donne's *Songs and Sonets*.

On what a modern reader might perhaps have expected to present itself to seventeenth-century poets as a more obviously imitable and attractive theme, that of 'Young Beauty's power foretold', the theme of Philodemus's epigram, I have found only two variations before Marvell's *Little T.C.* poem, neither of them of much distinction, and one of them which Marvell is unlikely to have seen, since it remained in manuscript. Waller's poem *To a very young lady*, or, as it was originally entitled in the 1645 edition of his poems, *To my Young Lady Lucy Sidney*, the sister of 'Sacharissa', is a graceful but rather flimsy expansion of the simple argument: 'Although I was born too early to be your lover, don't disdain maturity, for what wonders you will perform when you reach it yourself!'

> Why came I so untimely forth
> Into a world which, wanting thee,
> Could entertain us with no worth
> Or shadow of felicity,
> That time should me so far remove
> From that which I was born to love?
>
> Yet, fairest blossom! do not slight
> That age which you may know so soon;
> The rosy morn resigns her light,
> And milder glory, to the noon;
> And then what wonders shall you do,
> Whose dawning beauty warms us so?[1]
>
> Hope waits upon the flowery prime;
> And summer, though it be less gay,
> Yet is not looked on as a time
> Of declination or decay;
> For with a full hand that does bring
> All that was promised by the spring.[2]

In the Cambridge University Library there is now a manuscript volume of *Poems and Translations* by Thomas Stanley, dated 1646, from which the poet seems to have prepared the printer's copy for the edition he published in 1647. In this manuscript there are six poems which Stanley never printed, and one of these is entitled *The Bud. To a Young Gentlewoman*. It can scarcely, although as such I have mentioned it, be regarded as a variation of the theme of 'Young Beauty's power foretold', for it is simply a graceful and rather wordy expansion of the twin-hyperbole that the child's budding beauty surpasses the full-blown

1. Such execrable rhymes as *do–so* are more frequent in this 'reformer of our numbers' than in almost any of the better seventeenth-century poets: e.g. *allow–too* (*Poems*, ed. Thorn Drury, II 35, ll. 27–8), *though–do* (p. 35, ll. 3–4), *should–mould* (p. 64, ll. 9–10), *stock–took* (p. 63, ll. 13–14, in an epitaph to be incised in marble!)
2. *Poems*, ed. Thorn Drury, I 57.

beauty of others and her dawning beauty that which is setting. It looks almost as though the idea of addressing a poem to a beautiful child had been suggested to Stanley by Waller, and as though Waller's apostrophe of the child, at the beginning of his second stanza, as 'fairest blossom' gave Stanley the metaphor which he has, more or less, expanded into a whole poem, developing the paradoxical hyperbole that 'Nature has here done more in doing lesse'.

> See how this infant bud, so lately borne,
> Swelld with the Springs warme breath and dew o' th' morne,
> Contracted in its folded leaves doth beare
> The richest treasure of the teeming yeare,
> By whose young growing beauties conquerd yield
> The full-blowne glories of the painted field,
> And, thus surpast, do jointly all confesse
> Nature hath here done more in doing lesse.
>
> Such is thy early beauty, such appeares
> That blooming Sweetnes which thy soft cheek weares;
> To this new Deity our vowes we pay,
> And on thy virgin shrine our offerings lay;
> Whilst blind Idolaters, who did before
> The reliques of some vulgar Saint adore,
> Or some decaying beauty learnt t'admire,
> Shall here renew their now[1] expiring fire,
> And, in the change, confesse thou dost outshine
> Their setting beauties by the dawne of thine.[2]

These, as I have said, are the only two poems addressed to beautiful female children which I have been able to discover before Marvell's *Little T.C.* poem. There remains, indeed, a third poem of which both the date and the authorship are uncertain, and which Marvell is unlikely to have seen, since it seems to have been first printed in *The New Academy of Complements*, 1671. Oldys, in the *Biographia Britannica* (1730), ascribed it to Etherege, but, although this ascription was apparently accepted by Norman Ault,[3] the poem seems to me more likely to have been written before than after the

---

1. The reading of the MS (a scribal copy, not an autograph) is 'new', which cannot possibly be right. Perhaps 'near'.

2. *The Poems and Translations of Thomas Stanley*, ed. G. M. Crump, 1962, p. 327.

3. In his *Seventeenth-Century Lyrics*, 1928, p. 357, from which I quote the poem.

Restoration. It is entitled, like Waller's, *To a very young Lady*, and is obviously based on Waller's second stanza, of which it may be regarded partly as an expansion (Waller's 'fairest blossom' having suggested the prayer, developed in the first eight lines, that the 'sweetest bud' may not be destroyed by frost before it has unfolded into an incomparable rose) and partly as a concentration (Waller's antithesis between morning and noontide beauty being greatly sharpened in the concluding lines). The opening prayer against untimely frost anticipates (if, as seems likely, this poem was earlier than his) Marvell's prayer at the conclusion of his *Little T.C.* poem. It is a much neater, tighter and more epigrammatic poem than Waller's, and seems to have been very congenial to post-Restoration taste, for between 1671, when it was first printed, and 1713 it reappeared in four other miscellanies.[1]

> Sweetest bud of beauty, may
> No untimely frost decay
> The early glories, which we trace
> Blooming in thy matchless face;
> But kindly opening, like the rose,
> Fresh beauties every day disclose,
> Such as by Nature are not shown
> In all the blossoms she has blown:
> And then, what conquest shall you make,
> Who hearts already daily take!
> Scorched in the morning with thy beams,
> How shall we bear those sad extremes
> Which must attend thy threatening eyes
> When thou shalt to thy noon arise?

Am I being merely fanciful and wise after the event in seeming to perceive a certain appropriateness in the fact that the first seventeenth-century poet who addressed a poem to an infant, or near-infant, and performed a variation on the theme of 'Young Beauty's power foretold' should apparently have been Waller, in whose poetry there are so many anticipations of a style and sensibility far more characteristic of various Augustan and even Victorian poets than of those who may be regarded as typical of the earlier seventeenth century? It is, of course, impossible to imagine Donne, and almost impossible to imagine Ben Jonson, writing poems on either of the two themes we are considering, but can one not feel that, while the element of rather crass and pagan

1. See Ault's note on the poem, *op. cit.*, p. 488.

realism in the themes of 'not yet ripe' or 'nearly ripe' or 'ripe enough' for love belong to the world of Carew and his nymphets ('Give me a wench about thirteene'), the element of archness, or whimsicality, or both, which seems not only unavoidable but requisite in any success- ful treatment of 'Young Beauty's power foretold', belongs to a kind of sensibility more readily associated with Addison and *The Spectator*? I say deliberately 'a kind of sensibility', for the change of *mores* in the sense of manners, which we are here concerned with, does not always co-exist with a change of *mores* in the sense of morals. When Dryden, as he so often does, writes of the tremendous improvement in 'man- ners', 'refinement', 'conversation' and 'politeness' since the Restora- tion, he is not writing primarily as a moralist. Many of his own songs are as licentious as any of the poems of Charles I's time, but their 'wit' is of a kind that seemed to him far more 'gentlemanly'. He seems, indeed (like some old-fashioned college servants I have known), to have regarded a certain licentiousness as an indispensable part of the character of a gentleman: comparing Beaumont and Fletcher with Shakespeare, he declared that they 'understood and imitated the con- versation of gentlemen much better; whose wild debaucheries, and quickness of wit in repartees, no poet can ever paint as they have done'.[1] Waller, it is true, who, although he in so many ways anticipated post- Restoration conceptions of gallantry, is reported to have said, quite Addisonianly, that 'he would blot from his works any line that did not contain some motive to virtue',[2] was no doubt a man of stricter morals than Carew; it may be doubted, though, whether Sedley was, and Sedley, in his play *The Mulberry Garden*, 1668, has a song which, although it might just conceivably have been written by Waller, could not possibly, one feels, have been written by Carew or Randolph. I will quote the first five stanzas, in which he has ingeniously transposed the theme of 'Young Beauty's power foretold' from the future into the past, making the lover look back to the harmless infancy of the woman whose beauty has now enthralled him.[3]

> Ah, Chloris! that I now could sit
> As unconcerned as when
> Your infant beauty could beget
> No pleasure, nor no pain.

1. *Essays*, ed. Ker, I 81.
2. Johnson, *Lives of the Poets*, ed. Birkbeck Hill, I 283.
3. It is possible that the transposition may have been suggested to Sedley, directly or indirectly, by that epigram of Antiphilus quoted on p. 167.

When I the dawn used to admire,
    And praised the coming day,
I little thought the growing fire
    Must take my rest away.

Your charms in harmless childhood lay
    Like metals in the mine:
Age from no face took more away
    Than youth concealed in thine.

But as your charms insensibly
    To their perfection pressed,
Fond Love, as unperceived, did fly,
    And in my bosom rest.

My passion with your beauty grew,
    And Cupid at my heart,
Still as his mother favoured you,
    Threw a new flaming dart.[1]

Archness (I use the word not pejoratively but factually) seems first to appear in seventeenth-century poetry with Waller. It sometimes reappears in Marvell; but, before turning to Marvell's *Little T.C.* poem, I will pass from Sedley to Prior's charming poem *To a Child of Quality of Five Years Old, the Author suppos'd Forty*,[2] where one can see in, as it were, its pure and unadulterated form, that kind of archness, or whimsicality, or facetiousness which seems to have begun with Waller and which Marvell, in poems where we breathe 'an ampler ether, a diviner air', has combined with other moods, other attitudes, and other traditions.

Lords, knights, and squires, the num'rous Band
    That wear the Fair Miss *Mary*'s Fetters,
Were summon'd, by her high Command,
    To show their Passion by their Letters.

My Pen amongst the rest I took,
    Least those bright Eyes that cannot read
Shou'd dart their kindling Fires, and look
    The Pow'r they have to be obey'd.

---

1. I quote from *Seventeenth-Century Lyrics*, ed. Norman Ault, 1928, p. 35c.
2. *Literary Works*, ed. Wright and Spears, I 190.

Nor Quality, nor Reputation,
  Forbid me yet my Flame to tell,
Dear Five Years old befriends my Passion,
  And I may Write, till she can Spell.

For while she makes her Silk-worms Beds
  With all the tender things I swear,
Whilst all the House my Passion reads,
  In Papers round her Baby's Hair.

She may receive and own my Flame,
  For tho' the strictest *Prudes* shou'd know it,
She'll pass for a most virtuous Dame,
  And I for an unhappy Poet.

Then too, alas, when she shall tear
  The Lines some younger Rival sends,
She'll give me leave to Write, I fear,
  And we shall still continue Friends.

For as our diff'rent Ages move,
  'Tis so ordain'd, wou'd Fate but mend it,
That I shall be past making Love,
  When she begins to comprehend it.

In Prior's poem mythology, what may be called organic or consti-
tuted metaphor (as distinct from metaphorical phrases such as 'wear
fetters' or 'eyes that dart kindling fire'), and hyperbole of the classical
and traditional kind (as distinct from the somewhat arch and facetious
image of the 'summoning' child) have completely disappeared. All
three are present in Philodemus's epigram. Waller has no mythology
(Philodemus, it is true, only has 'young Loves' sharpening their
arrows), but his second and third stanzas consist almost entirely of
metaphors (dawn and noontide, spring and summer flowers); so does
Stanley's whole poem, which was probably suggested by Waller's;
and so does the poem doubtfully ascribed to Etherege, where Waller's
influence is certain. Even in Sedley's poem, with its quite Augustan
striving for antithesis, metaphor and simile (dawn and day, metals
in the mine) play an important part, and mythology (if only in beautifying Venus and dart-throwing Cupid) still persists. Marvell's poem,
on the other hand, in strong contrast with Prior's, is not only drenched
in metaphor, hyperbole and mythology (or mythological personifica-

tion), but the personal relationship between himself and the child, which is the main (one might almost say, the sole) theme of Prior's and Sedley's poems, as also, though perhaps less explicitly, of Waller's, is only incidental. To make this clear, I will offer, before eventually quoting it in full, a more elaborate analysis of Marvell's poem than the very compressed one I gave at the beginning of this discussion:

> How harmlessly she begins her career, playing with flowers! (1st stanza). Yet one day she will cause terrible destruction (2nd stanza). Let me make my peace with her before that day comes! (3rd stanza). Meanwhile, let her reform the errors of the Spring by adding fragrance to the tulip, depriving roses of their thorns, and making violets longer-lasting (4th stanza). Let her, though, while gathering the flowers, spare the buds, lest angry Flora nip her too in the bud and with her all our hopes (5th stanza).

Only in the second and third stanzas does Marvell handle the topic of 'Young Beauty's power foretold', generally in the second, personally in the third; and in each of these stanzas the archness, which, as I have remarked, seems not only unavoidable but requisite in any successful treatment of this topic, is, as it were, insinuated into passages of such splendid and expansive hyperbole that we experience it only as an ingredient, a piquant element of contrast, modifying and modified by its more traditional context. Then, in his last two stanzas, Marvell returns to the 'Prospect of Flowers' with which he had begun, and treats the relationship between the child and these 'natural objects' (as Wordsworth would have called them) in a manner quite different from that of his predecessors. In the poems of Philodemus, Waller and Stanley, and in the poem doubtfully ascribed to Etherege, these things are only introduced metaphorically: the child is a budding flower, or ripening fruit, or dawning day. Marvell, though, remembering, no doubt, as he could scarcely avoid doing, those many passages where ancient poets and their modern imitators had exhorted coy mistresses to gather the rose of love before it faded, uses his recollection of them to develop what, so far as I know, is the original even if fairly obvious theme, introduced, as we have seen, at the beginning of the poem doubtfully ascribed to Etherege, of 'Young Beauty's flowering prayed for' or 'Young Beauty's frost fore-feared'. This, indeed, rather than 'Young Beauty's power foretold', with which he has so exquisitely combined it, may perhaps be regarded as the main theme of his poem. There is reason to believe that Marvell himself so regarded it, for, as

Margoliouth convincingly suggested,[1] 'Little T.C.' may well have been Theophila Cornewall, whose mother, also called Theophila, was the sister of that Cyriack Skinner to whom Milton addressed a sonnet and whom Marvell later came to know. Humphry Cornewall and his wife seem to have spent part of their married life with the wife's mother, Mrs Bridget Skinner, at Thornton College in Lincolnshire, for it was there that their first Theophila was baptised on 23 August 1643 and died two days later. A second Theophila was baptised on 26 September 1644, and this child may well have been Marvell's 'Little T.C.'—not only because girls' names beginning with T are rare, but because, as Margoliouth expressed it, 'the premature death of the first Theophila would give point and poignancy to the last stanza, which otherwise seems almost gratuitously ill-omened'. It has also been suggested[2] that the phrase 'Darling of the Gods' at the beginning of the second stanza,

> Who can foretel for what high cause
> This Darling of the Gods was born!

occurred to Marvell, although he was not the first to use it,[3] simply as a more or less literal translation of the child's Christian name, Theophila, 'dear to the gods'.

For the floral background of the poem and for what I have described as being, so far as I know, the original theme of 'Young Beauty's frost fore-feared' it does not seem necessary to seek any literary source of inspiration, especially since the scene, like the child herself, may well have been actual, not just imaginary. Nevertheless, remembering how 'literary' Marvell was and how often hints and suggestions came to him from his reading, I am inclined to wonder whether his recollection of the 'Picture' he had actually seen did not perhaps combine with recollections of two passages in Ovid's *Metamorphoses*: the description, in the fifth book (390 ff.), of the Rape of Proserpina—how, beside a woodland-encinctured lake in the Vale of Enna, where reigned perpetual Spring, she was trying to outvie her companions in gathering

1. In 'Andrew Marvell: some biographical Points', *Modern Language Review*, October, 1922.

2. By Mrs E. E. Duncan-Jones in a letter to *TLS*, 30 October 1953.

3. It had been used by Carew in his poem *Vpon the Kings sicknesse* (*Poems*, ed. Dunlap, p. 35), l. 37, 'That Darling of the Gods and men'; and later (presumably) in *The Character of Holland*, l. 146, Marvell was to describe England as 'Darling of Heaven, and of Men the Care'. It seems likely that 'darling of the Gods' may have been a familiar and current rendering of some Latin phrase such as *cura deum*. Suetonius describes Titus as *amor ac deliciae generis humani*.

violets and lilies when she was seen, desired and captured by 'gloomy Dis'; and a passage in the fourteenth book (761–4), where the god Vertumnus, having entered, in the disguise of an old woman, the orchard of his beloved but recalcitrant Pomona and told her the cautionary tale of Anaxarete, metamorphosed into stone because her hardness of heart had caused the suicide of her lover Iphis, says to the hamadryad:

> Quorum memor, O mea, lentos
> Pone, precor, fastus et amanti iungere, nympha.
> sic tibi nec vernum nascentia frigus adurat
> poma, nec excutiant rapidi florentia venti.

(Remembering which things, O my nymph, lay aside, I beseech you, obstinate disdain and be united with your love. Then may no vernal frost consume your budding fruit, nor ravaging winds scatter them in their flower.)

In the second of these passages Vertumnus's argument is not, like that of those many passages in ancient poets on the theme of *carpe florem*, 'Yield to love before you become like a faded and unwanted flower', but 'Yield before the gods punish your cruelty'. If, which is by no means certain, the buds and blossoms are to be understood metaphorically as well as literally, and if Vertumnus is not merely threatening Pomona with the destruction of her orchard by frost and wind but with the destruction of herself by an early death, or (since she was at least a semi-divinity) with some petrifying metamorphosis, this must be almost the only passage in ancient poetry (certainly, I can recall no other) where this argument and this metaphor occur together, and Marvell may well have so understood and remembered it. He wanted to conclude his poem with an evocation of that 'prospect of flowers' with which it had begun, with a prayer that his prophecies of the child's future triumphs might not be nullified, and with a warning to the child herself similar in style, though not in content, to those which ancient love-poets had delivered. As Wordsworth said in his famous account of the planning of *The Ancient Mariner*, 'Some crime was to be committed'—or, rather, the child was to be warned not to commit some crime. Into this pictorial, mythological and metaphorical context it is hard to see how Marvell could have introduced any other ruling divinity than Flora, or any 'crime' other than the destruction of her buds. If, however, he did not immediately perceive that this was the only possible solution, it may be that recollection of the vernal frost and budding fruits in Vertumnus's warning to Pomona finally enabled him to do so.

The elaborate eight-line stanza Marvell has chosen permits a far greater subtlety and variety of rhythm and inflection than does the simple heptasyllabic quatrain of *Young Love*. Except for the two-line exclamations at the beginning of the first, second and third stanzas and at the conclusion of the third, each stanza consists of a single complex and (except for some of the usual clumsy inversions and expletives for the sake of rhyme) beautifully articulated sentence. Throughout these five stanzas the argument is as close and continuous as in the finest of Donne's *Songs and Sonets*, and there is an exquisite balance, not only, as in many of Donne's poems, between seriousness and light-heartedness, but also, as almost never in Donne, between the dialectical and the pictorial, between things thought and things seen. For the poem is, as its title proclaims, a 'Picture', and the child in her prospect of flowers is present from the first line to the last and seems immediately, naturally and spontaneously to suggest every reflexion, metaphor and hyperbole. How wonderfully a certain intellectual and verbal energy has lifted mere prettiness to the level of beauty, and how, in the second and third stanzas, the familiar topic of The Triumph of Cupid (here inverted into The Triumph *over* Cupid) is deprived of triteness by an injection of something approaching mock-heroic!

The Picture of little T.C. in a Prospect of Flowers

I

See with what simplicity
This Nimph begins her golden daies!
In the green Grass she loves to lie,
And there with her fair Aspect tames
The Wilder flow'rs, and gives them names:
But only with the Roses playes;
   And them does tell
What Colour best becomes them, and what Smell.

II

Who can foretel for what high cause
This Darling of the Gods was born!
Yet this is She whose chaster Laws

The Wanton Love shall one day fear,
And, under her command severe,
See his Bow broke and Ensigns torn.
    Happy, who can
Appease this virtuous Enemy of Man!

III

O then let me in time compound,
And parly with those conquering Eyes![1]
Ere they have try'd their force to wound,
Ere, with their glancing wheels, they drive
In Triumph over Hearts that strive,
And them that yield but more despise.[2]
    Let me be laid[3]
Where I may see thy Glories from some shade![4]

IV

Mean time, whilst every verdant thing
It self does at thy Beauty charm,
Reform the errours of the Spring;
Make that the Tulips may have share
Of sweetness, seeing they are fair;
And Roses of their thorns disarm:
    But most procure
That Violets may a longer Age endure.

V

But O young beauty of the Woods,
Whom Nature courts with fruits and flow'rs,
Gather the Flow'rs, but spare the Buds;
Lest *Flora* angry at thy crime,
To kill her Infants in their prime,
Do quickly make th' Example Yours;
    And, ere we see,
Nip in the blossome all our hopes and Thee.

How unmemorable and insipid seems the diction not only of Stanley's

---

1. 'Eyes!', 1681 'Eyes;'.   2. 'despise.', 1681 'despise,'.
3. 'laid', 1681 'laid,'.   4. 'shade!', 1681 'shade.'.

rather trivial but even of Waller's quite graceful poem in comparison with that of Marvell's, most of whose lines consist not merely of words but of phrases! In four out of his five stanzas the splendidly hyperbolical beginnings announce the style and tone and attitude that are to be preserved throughout:

> See with what simplicity
> This Nimph begins her golden daies!

> Who can foretel for what high cause
> This Darling of the Gods was born!

> O then let me in time compound,
> And parly with those conquering Eyes!

> But O young beauty of the Woods,
> Whom Nature courts with fruits and flow'rs:

just as (to mention one of the finest poems by another seventeenth-century poet)

> Know *Celia*, (since thou art so proud,)
> 'Twas I that gave thee thy renowne

announces the style and tone and attitude which Carew will preserve throughout *Ingratefull beauty threatned*. In these lines of Carew's there is a combination of what might be described as Roman insolence (utterly remote from love-poetry in the Dantesque or Petrarchan tradition), Roman elegance, and Roman marmoreality, and Carew has preserved this tone and attitude and this level and quality of style throughout his poem. Marvell's tone and attitude, conveyed (except for a few of the usual clumsinesses) in a style not less distinguished than Carew's, are more complex and more difficult to define: mock-heroic with just a trace of 'mock'; splendid hyperbole with a slightly and, as it were, gravely humorous recognition that it *is* hyperbole; tenderness; archness raised almost to the sublime in

> Happy, who can
> Appease this virtuous Enemy of Man!

and

> Let me be laid
> Where I may see thy Glories from some shade!

and all this sophistication combined with an almost naïve and unsophisticated delight in the picture of the child in her 'prospect of
flowers'. How unsatisfactory the result would seem if I tried to describe this extraordinary synthesis in terms such as I have used (not
unsatisfactorily, I think) to describe the characteristic qualities of
Carew's poem, and spoke of a combination of Roman *gravitas* and
marmoreality, Alexandrian and Wallerian archness, Clevelandish
hyperbole, Crashavian tenderness and witty visualisation, Ovidian
and Elizabethan pastoralism, Donneian dialectic, and so on. For, although one can see (or think one sees) that Marvell could not have
written this poem had he not read hundreds of poems by preceding
poets, scarcely one of the qualities I have been trying to indicate exists
in quite the same way in any poem by any other poet, since each has
been so modified by the qualities with which it has been combined.
Partly, perhaps, because it immediately suggests a comparison with
Prior's, this poem, written probably in the very middle of the seventeenth century, seems to me, looked at from the literary-historical
point of view, one of the most central, by which I mean at once most
recapitulatory and anticipatory, of all Marvell's poems. Waller's poems,
as I have remarked, often seem to anticipate the work of much
later poets, but they do so with a loss of many of those qualities
we regard and prize as characteristically seventeenth-century; Marvell's
poems, however, often seem to anticipate various Augustan tones and
attitudes without losing any of the more valuable seventeenth-century
ones. Prior's variation on the theme of 'Young Beauty's power foretold' seems to me a charming poem (although I can think of many
modern critics who would probably affect to despise it), but it is far
less complex and far more limited than Marvell's. Its diction, though
precise and elegant and with most of the qualities of good prose, has
no touch of splendour. It is *vers de société*, with no vistas or perspectives
beyond the time and place in which it was written; whereas Marvell's
poem has a kind of extra dimension, and seems to inherit and renew
whole centuries of poetic tradition and achievement. Nevertheless,
Prior's poem is one of the most memorable examples of that plain,
familiar style so successfully practised by Swift, and by Pope in some
of his shorter poems, and readers who do not sufficiently appreciate
how difficult it was, on such a topic, to preserve exactly the right tone
throughout, without a single slip into sentimentality or absurdity,
may be recommended to compare it with those lamentable poems which
Ambrose ('Namby Pamby') Philips, some twenty years later, wrote for

the Pulteney and Carteret children. In 1727 he addressed *To Miss Margaret Pulteney . . . in the Nursery* a poem beginning (in all seriousness)

>Dimply damsel, sweetly smiling,

and concluding with the following lines on our topic of 'Young Beauty's power foretold'

>Ten years hence, when I leave chiming,
>Beardless poets, fondly rhyming,
>(Fescu'd now, perhaps, in spelling,)[1]
>On thy riper beauties dwelling,
>Shall accuse each killing feature
>Of the cruel, charming, creature,
>Whom I knew complying, willing,
>Tender, and averse to killing.[2]

But while Prior's poem is a unique achievement within the limits of that kind of familiar style practised by some of the best poets of his time, Marvell, like other seventeenth-century poets, like Horace in some of his Odes, and perhaps unlike any post-seventeenth-century poet before Yeats, has been able to combine a kind of familiarity with a kind of splendour.

With perfection so often within his grasp, it is distressing to find Marvell twice resorting to his clumsy and all too habitual inversions for the sake of rhyme, and admitting the enfeebling auxiliary 'does' into contexts where every other word is really working its passage:

>And them does tell
>What Colour best becomes them, and what Smell
>>>(end of first stanza)

and

>Mean time, whilst every verdant thing
>It self does at thy Beauty charm
>>>(beginning of fourth stanza)

which is immediately followed by the exquisite line:

>Reform the errours of the Spring.

In the next two lines, although there is no inversion, the syntax is

1. Now perhaps learning to spell with the aid of a fescue, a small stick or pin used for pointing out the letters.
2. *Poems*, ed. M. G. Segar, 1937, p. 122.

clumsy and stilted, and it looks as though, after hitting upon the idea
of adding scent to tulips and choosing the rhyme 'share-fair', Marvell
has been content to fill-out with something approaching verbiage:

> Make that the Tulips may have share
> Of sweetness, seeing they are fair.

I am aware that his expletives and inversions (though not, I think,
such lines as I have just quoted) may to some extent be defended on
historical grounds (although, as I have remarked, my impression is
that in this respect he is a far worse offender than any other seventeenth-
century poet of anything like his quality), and that it may be pleaded
that even Pope only gradually felt his way towards complete 'correctness' in this matter; nevertheless, except when departure from it is
justified by the achievement of some otherwise unattainable emphasis,
the principle, the law, of good rhymed verse is that, as Dryden expressed it in a passage already quoted,[1] it should be so written 'that the
first word in the verse seems to beget the second, and that the next, till
that becomes the last word in the line, which, in the negligence of
prose, would be so'. Although this law seems to have been first
explicitly stated by Dryden and Pope, and although they may have
been the first poets to become fully conscious of it, its validity, when
once stated, is so immediately apparent that it is impossible for us, in
judging earlier poetry, to pretend that we are unaware of it. The laws
of poetry, like those of the gods in Greek tragedy, are immutable,
and pleas of ignorance cannot be entertained.

Of the pastorals and semi-pastorals we have been considering,
only the *Little T.C.* poem and, just possibly, *The Nymph complaining
for the death of her Faun* were in any sense occasional poems. But while
those two poems have survived and transcended their occasions, the
same can scarcely be said of the pair of pastoral dialogues entitled
Two Songs at the Marriage of the Lord Fauconberg *and the Lady* Mary
Cromwell, which were presumably set by some composer and sung,
on 19 November 1657, at the marriage of Cromwell's third daughter
Mary to the second Viscount Fauconberg. They are neat and pretty
enough, but scarcely, one feels, beyond the reach of several contemporary poets, and perhaps even less distinctively Marvellian than
Thyrsis and Dorinda and *Clorinda and Damon*. They may remind us for
how long, in various kinds of poetic eulogy, including epithalamia,
as well as in funeral elegy, the taste for mythological allegory, or

1. See p. 147.

allegorical mythology, still persisted. In the first of them Endymion
(Fauconberg), encouraged and finally congratulated by the chorus,
pursues his courtship of Cynthia (Mary Cromwell) to a successful
conclusion; and in the second, a trio with a concluding chorus, two
shepherds, Hobbinol and Tomalin, and Phillis, a shepherdess, having
heard the news, hasten to the scene and sing a 'carol' in praise of the
happy pair, here pastoralised into Damon and Marina. There is hyperbole, even witty hyperbole, but (for obvious reasons) without that
touch of burlesque or mock-heroic with which we have so often seen
Marvell transforming the older kind of hyperbole into something new.
When Endymion's entreaties meet only with the response

> I have enough for me to do,
> Ruling the Waves that Ebb and flow,

and he replies

> Since thou disdain'st not then to share
> On Sublunary things thy care;
> Rather restrain these double Seas,
> Mine Eyes uncessant deluges,

one may indeed fancy one can perceive a characteristically Marvellian
variation on the well-worn topic of seas and tears, terser, more epigrammatic, more antithetical than, for example, the sort of thing that
recurs so often in that volume of elegies on Edward King to which
Milton contributed *Lycidas*. When, however, in the following stanza,
the encouraging chorus thus allegorically alludes to the fact that a
week earlier Cromwell's youngest daughter Frances had married
Robert Rich ('Anchises'), grandson and heir of the Earl of Warwick,
most readers will feel that Marvell's muse has had to be very much
subdued to what she is working in, and that here, as distinct from those
touches of conscious humour or semi-burlesque which have delighted
them in earlier poems, there is at least something of that unconscious
absurdity into which, as it seems to us, seventeenth-century eulogists
so often fall:

> Courage, *Endymion*, boldly Woo,
> *Anchises*[1] was a *Shepheard* too;

---

1. Anchises, though related to the royal house of Troy, was (at least according
to Theocritus, I 106) a neat-herd on Mount Ida, where Aphrodite (Venus) fell in
love with him, descended in the form of a nymph, and bore him a son, Aeneas. By
allegorising Robert Rich as Anchises, Marvell, as Professor Legouis has remarked,
is implicitly allegorising Frances Cromwell, 'Cynthia's' younger sister, as Venus.

> Yet is *her younger Sister* laid
> Sporting with him in *Ida's shade*:
> And *Cynthia*, though the strongest,
> Seeks but the honour to have held out longest.

And the concluding chorus of this first song, praising Jove-Cromwell for condescending to marry his two remaining unmarried daughters to a mere viscount and a mere heir to an earldom, instead of (presumably) to European royalties, is the sort of thing of which Dr Johnson might have said, as he did of Dryden's dedication of *The State of Innocence* to Mary of Modena, that it was written 'in a strain of flattery which disgraces genius, and which it was wonderful that any man that knew the meaning of his own words could use without self-detestation':[1]

> Joy to *Endymion*,
> For he has *Cynthia's* favour won.
> And *Jove* himself approves
> With his serenest influence their Loves.
> For he did never love to pair
> His Progeny above the Air;
> But to be honest, valiant, wise,
> Makes *Mortals* matches fit for *Deityes*.

Here, certainly, the eulogistic and complimentary style of the 'poète puritain', as Professor Pierre Legouis has called him, is not noticeably either more restrained or more pious than that of his unpuritanical predecessors and successors.

In the second song there is a rather charming allusion to the time of year (November):

> *Phillis*
> Stay till I some flow'rs ha' ty'd
> In a Garland for the bride.

> *Tomalin*
> If thou would'st a Garland bring,
> *Phillis* you may wait the Spring:
> They ha' chosen such an hour
> When *She* is the only flow'r.

1. *Lives of the Poets*, ed. Birkbeck Hill, I 359.

Still, the best that can be said of these two poems is that it is hard to see how Marvell could have done better within the limitations imposed upon him by the occasion. With a few rare exceptions, of which the most notable is Marvell's *Horatian Ode* (which, incidentally, he never published), seventeenth-century poets never seem so remote both from ourselves and from what we have come to regard as their peculiar excellencies as when they are engaged in public celebration or public lament.

4

'RELIGIOUS' POEMS

The six poems which may be classified as 'religious' are: *The Coronet*, *On a Drop of Dew*, *A Dialogue Between the Resolved Soul, and Created Pleasure*, *A Dialogue between the Soul and Body*, *Musicks Empire* (which I include for no better reason than its compliment to Fairfax and his religion in the final stanza), and *Bermudas* (which, for various reasons, I shall not examine in detail until my next chapter). I have placed the word 'religious' in inverted commas because most of these poems, for all their scriptural language, are far from what we have in mind when we speak of the religious poetry of the seventeenth century. Only *The Coronet* and *Bermudas* contain specifically Christian allusions, and only *Bermudas*, where the colonists express their gratitude to God for having brought them to a place 'Safe from the Storms, and Prelat's rage', can be in any sense regarded as the characteristic utterance of a 'poète puritain', or, at least, of a poet who sympathised with those whom we rather loosely call 'Puritans', including in that term all, from Presbyterians to Independents, who were dissatisfied with the Anglican Establishment. In the other four poems there is indeed nothing incompatible with Christianity, but neither, on the other hand (unless exceptions are to be made in favour of the Old Testament allusion to manna at the end of *A Drop of Dew* and the conventional allusion to 'Heaven's Hallelujahs' at the end of *Musicks Empire*), is there anything that would not be compatible with a kind of Platonic Deism. Leaving aside *Musicks Empire*, which perhaps does not really belong here, and leaving aside *Bermudas*, which is perhaps as much a descriptive as a religious poem, it may be said that what the remaining four have in common is a more serious and consistent concern with 'man's chief end' than appears in Marvell's other poems. They are all essentially 'moral', and, if they are not all equally 'religious', they are all expressions of what may perhaps best be described as 'religiousness'.

If it be asked why I have not here included those two 'religious pastorals', *Thyrsis and Dorinda* and *Clorinda and Damon*, I can only reply, because they seem to me essentially less serious, their religiosity being, as I have said,[1] of the most conventional kind, striking only in its pastoral context and as an original variation on a familiar theme. Nevertheless, I must admit that there is a certain affinity between those two rather slight poems and that much more serious religious pastoral *The Coronet*. While, however, the two (presumably) earlier poems are, with the addition of various characteristic seventeenth-century touches, close to Elizabethan pastoral and to Spenser, *The Coronet*, although it contains a phrase ('speckled breast') borrowed from Spenser, is quite unlike anything in Spenser's pastorals, and the manner of it may well have been partly suggested to Marvell by a curious, if unarresting, poem of Randolph's to which I shall refer. *The Coronet* is both curious and arresting. It might be described either as an emblematical pastoral or as a pastoral emblem, and it is, so far as I know, quite unlike any other seventeenth-century religious poem. It is not, indeed, one of Marvell's most memorable poems, and, although compressed and closely argued, is perhaps a little over-ingenious. Proposing to crown his Saviour's too-long thorn-crowned head with the flowers that once garlanded his mistress, he finds that the serpent has coiled itself into this re-woven coronet. Let his Saviour disentangle it, or, if that be impossible, let him trample upon both serpent and coronet and allow his feet to be crowned by those flowers that could not crown his head. This, I think, is many times more ingenious than anything in Herbert, or Vaughan, or even in Crashaw; indeed, although more serious and more beautiful and less merely surprising, it is, in respect of sheer ingenuity, comparable with such a poem of Donne's as *The Flea*. But while the ingenuity is comparable with Donne's, the pastoral and pictorial imagery is quite alien to Donne, who would probably have disdained it, and more like what we are accustomed to find in Crashaw.

The Coronet

When for the Thorns with which I long, too long,
    With many a piercing wound,
    My Saviours head have crown'd,
I seek with Garlands to redress that Wrong:
    Through every Garden, every Mead,

1. Chapter 3, pp. 117.

I gather flow'rs (my fruits are only flow'rs)
    Dismantling all the fragrant Tow'rs[1]
That once adorn'd my Shepherdesses head.
And now when I have summ'd up all my store,
    Thinking (so I my self deceive)
    So rich a Chaplet thence to weave
As never yet the king of Glory wore:
    Alas I find the Serpent old
    That, twining in his speckled breast,[2]
    About the flow'rs disguis'd does fold,
    With wreaths of Fame and Interest.
Ah, foolish Man, that would'st debase with them
And mortal Glory, Heavens Diadem!
But thou who only could'st the Serpent tame,
Either his slipp'ry knots at once untie,
And disintangle all his winding Snare:
Or shatter too with him my curious frame:[3]
And let these[4] wither, so that he may die,
Though set with Skill and chosen out with Care.
That they, while Thou on both their Spoils dost tread,
May crown thy Feet, that could not crown thy Head.

Mainly, it would seem, because of the necessity of finding rhymes for 'untie' (l.20) and 'Snare' (l.21), Marvell's syntax in the last four lines has got rather tangled and obscure, which is probably why what ought to have been, and partly is, a single sentence has been interrupted (for the sake of clarity?) by a full-stop. Surely a little effort could have improved this syntax; I even think (although I do not claim that my altered phrasing is also an improvement) that I can do so myself:

1. T2; 1681 'Towers'. Not, as a modern reader might suppose, an original metaphor suggested by the need to find a rhyme for 'flow'rs', but a word in common use to denote a very full head-dress worn by women. (*OED*, *Tower*, sb[1], sense 6b). Sylvester, in his poem on the death of Prince Henry in *Lacrymae Musarum*, 1612–13, has

                  Stript, from Top to Toe,
    Of giddiegauds, Top-gallant Tires and Towers.

2. Borrowed from Spenser's description of the dragon in *FQ*, I xi 15.

        Forelifting vp aloft his speckled brest.

3. My elaborate chaplet (or coronet).
4. The flowers, subject of 'set' in the next line.

And let them wither, so that he may die,
These flow'rs, though set with Skill and culled with Care,
That they, while Thou on him and them dost tread,
May crown thy Feet, that could not crown thy Head.

Marvell, who took hints from so many of his immediate predecessors,
seems occasionally, as we have seen, to have taken hints from Randolph,
and it may well be that the manner of this quite un-Spenserian religious
pastoral was partly suggested to him by a curious poem of Randolph's
entitled *An Eglogue occasion'd by two Doctors disputing upon predestination*.
The poem begins with Tityrus asking Alexis why one of the two lambs
to which a ewe of his has given birth should be black. It could not,
before its birth, have committed any sin. Was not this a piece of divine
injustice? Alexis rebukes him for questioning God's providence, and
then they are interrupted by Thyrsis, who declares that, instead of
disputing in this unprofitable way, they ought to celebrate Love,
the son of Heaven's King, who descended to earth and performed
many miracles.

More wonders did he, for all which suppose
How he was crown'd, with Lilly, or with Rose?
The winding Ivy, or the glorious Bay,
Or mirtle, with the which *Venus*, they say,
Girts her proud Temples? Shepheards, none of them,
But wore (poore head) a thorny Diadem.[1]

It seems to me more than likely that it was the simple contrast between
the crown of flowers and the crown of thorns in Randolph's comparatively artless pastoral that provided Marvell with the theme on which
he has performed his own ingenious and elaborate variation.

What, for want of a better word, may be described as a far more
classical working out of an elaborate analogy is the beautiful poem
On a Drop of Dew. One might be inclined to suppose that the idea of it
was suggested to Marvell by Vaughan's *The Water-fall*, were it not
for the fact that that poem first appeared in the enlarged re-issue of
Silex Scintillans in 1655. There is not, indeed, anything obviously
impossible in the hypothesis that Marvell wrote his poem as late as
1655; nevertheless, the fact that on the subject both of this poem and of
The Garden he also wrote Latin poems strongly suggests that the two
poems were written about the same time, and *The Garden* must surely

1. *Poems*, ed. Thorn Drury, 1929, p. 103.

be contemporary with *Appleton House* and Marvell's residence with Fairfax between 1651 and 1653. The fact none the less remains that *The Water-fall* is the only other seventeenth-century poem between which and Marvell's *On a Drop of Dew* there is a really striking resemblance; and some, perhaps, taking into account Marvell's imitativeness and eclecticism and his readiness to experiment on pre-established manners and to perform original variations on unoriginal themes, may be inclined to regard this resemblance as sufficient proof that he wrote his poem after he had read Vaughan's, and as providing stronger evidence for a later date of composition than the existence of the Latin version does for contemporaneity with *The Garden*. Familiar though it is, it will be as well, for purposes of comparison and contrast, to have Vaughan's poem before us.

The Water-fall

With what deep murmurs through times silent stealth
Doth thy transparent, cool and watry wealth
Here flowing fall,
And chide, and call,
As if his liquid, loose Retinue staid
Lingring, and were of this steep place afraid,
The common pass
Where, clear as glass,
All must descend
Not to an end:
But quickned by this deep and rocky grave,
Rise to a longer course more bright and brave.

Dear stream! dear bank, where often I
Have sate, and pleas'd my pensive eye,
Why, since each drop of thy quick store
Runs thither, whence it flow'd before,[1]
Should poor souls fear a shade or night,
Who came (sure) from a sea of light?
Or since those drops are all sent back
So sure to thee, that none doth lack,

1. Runs back into the stream where it was flowing before the fall interrupted it. Throughout Vaughan is regarding the stream and the 'steep place' as two distinct things, the single stream being momentarily disintegrated by the fall into a multitude of 'drops', which almost immediately reunite into the same stream they composed before.

Why should frail flesh doubt any more
That what God takes, hee'l not restore?
O useful Element and clear!
My sacred wash and cleanser here,
My first consigner[1] unto those
Fountains of life, where the Lamb goes!
What sublime truths, and wholesome themes,
Lodge in thy mystical, deep streams!
Such as dull man can never finde
Unless that Spirit lead his minde,
Which first upon thy face did move,
And hatch'd all with his quickning love.[2]
As this loud brooks incessant fall
In streaming rings restagnates[3] all
Which reach by course the bank, and then
Are no more seen, just so pass men.
O my invisible estate,
My glorious liberty, still late![4]
Thou art the Channel my soul seeks,
Not this with Cataracts and Creeks.

Between this poem and Marvell's there are great and characteristic differences. In the first place, the purely descriptive part of it is small in proportion to the expository, didactic and doctrinal. After devoting a kind of twelve-line stanza, consisting of mingled decasyllabic and quatrosyllabic couplets, to a description of the waterfall, Vaughan adds thirty-eight lines of octosyllabic couplets, in which the application of his analogy is mingled with much exclamation and apostrophe, beautiful in its way, but quite different from Marvell's cool detachment; and in his last four lines he seems, like the Platonic philosopher, to kick away that sensory and phenomenal ladder by which he has climbed to an insight now independent of the senses. In the second place, he has not attempted to elaborate his analogy (which probably could not have yielded so many points of resemblance) with anything

1. The water of baptism, which signed the cross upon his forehead and consigned him to the fellowship of Christ.
2. *Genesis* i, 2, 'And darkness was upon the face of the deep. And the Spirit of God moved upon the face of the waters'.
3. Restagnifies, recomposes into stagnant in the sense of voluminous and quiet water.
4. Recent.

like Marvell's ingenuity; yet even so it cannot, perhaps, survive quite such minute inspection as can Marvell's. For, while the water, hesitating and murmuring on the brink of the fall, is indeed, for a believing Christian, an apt symbol of man approaching death, it may be doubted whether Vaughan, although, like all Christians, he regarded souls as being in some sort portions of a single spirit, regarded them as being so essentially unindividual as the drops which compose a stream. In other words, the stream's continuance after the fall which caused it to hesitate and murmur is a more lively and exact symbol (or emblem) of the preservation of the trembling individual soul than the relation between the unlost drops and the stream is of the relation between the totality of Christian souls and their Creator.

Marvell's analogy between the dew-drop and the soul (and this, no doubt, was why he chose it) provided far more points of correspondence than did Vaughan's analogy between the stream approaching the fall and the soul approaching death, and he has worked it out with far greater subtlety and minuteness. His poem is also far more of a unity than Vaughan's, and does not, like his, fall into two distinct parts, one mainly descriptive and the other mainly expository, but is essentially descriptive throughout. After devoting eighteen lines to a description of the dew-drop as though it were a soul, he devotes another eighteen—without, it is true, preserving any exact correspondence in the distribution of long and short lines and in the placing of rhymes—to a description of the soul as though it were a dew-drop. He declares, of the drop of morning-dew on the rose: (1) that it scarcely touches, seems to be withdrawing itself as much as possible from, its new home, as though it were trying to create of itself and within itself the closest possible resemblance to that celestial sphere whence it came: (2) that it is, as it were, its own tear, grieving for its separation from the skies, to which it looks back sadly; (3) that it seems to tremble lest some contact should soil its purity; (4) that it is waiting for the sun to take pity on it and 'exhale it back again'. He then turns to the soul: it, too, shrinks from the leaves and blossoms of the human flower and tries to remember and recover the celestial light of its first home; it is as loosely attached to the body as is the dew-drop to the rose, and

> Moving but on a point below,
> It all about does upwards bend.

And Marvell concludes his poem with a four-line comparison of (presumably) both the dew-drop and the rose to that manna which the Israelites gathered at dawn and which melted when the sun became hot.

On a Drop of Dew

See how the Orient Dew,
Shed from the Bosom of the Morn
   Into the blowing Roses,
Yet careless of its Mansion new;
For the clear Region where 'twas born,
   Round in its self incloses,
   And in its little Globes Extent,
Frames as it can, its native Element.[1]
   How it the purple flow'r does slight,
      Scarce touching where it lyes,
      But gazing back upon the Skies,
      Shines with a mournful Light;
        Like its own Tear,
Because so long divided from the Sphear.
   Restless it roules and unsecure,
      Trembling lest it grow impure:
   Till the warm Sun pitty it's Pain,
And to the Skies exhale it back again.
   So the Soul, that Drop, that Ray
Of the clear Fountain of Eternal Day,
Could it within the humane flow'r be seen,
      Remembring still its former height,
      Shuns the sweet[2] leaves and blossoms green;
      And, recollecting[3] its own Light,
Does, in its pure and circling thoughts, express
The greater Heaven in an Heaven less.

1. I have made what seem to me necessary changes in the punctuation of ll. 4–8, which I take to mean: 'Still careless of its new dwelling in favour of ('for') that clear region where it was born, roundly encloses within itself, and, so far as it can, reconstitutes within the extent of its own little globe, that native element from which it has descended'.

2. T2; 1681 'sweat'.

3. Probably both 'gathering together again', 're-collecting', and (in the Platonic sense) 'remembering'. Here, as sometimes elsewhere, Marvell seems to be using a word both in its original and literal and in its later and metaphorical sense—a use of language that might more appropriately be described as 'concentrated' than as 'ambiguous'.

In how coy a Figure wound,
Every way it turns away:
So the World excluding round,[1]
Yet receiving in the Day.
Dark beneath, but bright above:
Here disdaining, there in Love.
How loose and easie hence to go:
How girt and ready to ascend.
Moving but on a point below,
It all about does upwards bend.
Such did the Manna's sacred Dew destil;
White, and intire, though congeal'd and chill.
Congeal'd on Earth: but does, dissolving, run
Into the Glories of th'Almighty Sun.

Marvell has developed his analogy with an ingenuity, a symmetry and a detachment which it was not Vaughan's purpose to achieve. To describe Vaughan, as many have done, as a 'Nature-poet', and to compare him with Wordsworth, is wide of the mark. It is true that the starting-point of several of his most memorable poems is some natural sight which he has observed during a solitary walk, but such sights are significant to him only as more or less imperfect emblems of spiritual truths, and the poems they inspire are essentially expository and didactic and only incidentally descriptive. It might almost be said that, while Vaughan is only accidentally and incidentally concerned with the waterfall, Marvell is exclusively concerned with the drop of dew and with the ingenious and consistent working-out of the analogy between it and the soul, and that, while Vaughan is primarily concerned with the communication of a truth or lesson, Marvell is primarily concerned with the making of a poem. He never for a moment takes his eye off the dew-drop, and, without a trace of didacticism or devotional fervour, describes the soul in relation to its celestial and terrestrial dwellings entirely and exclusively in language that might be applied without alteration to the drop of dew. While Vaughan, throughout the application of his analogy, writes with specifically Christian fervour and in specifically Christian terms, in Marvell's poem Christian doctrine is never more than implicit—indeed, except for the manna-simile in the last lines, there is nothing that might not have been written by a kind of Platonising deist. Some writers on Marvell have tended to

1. Excluding the surrounding world.

take his 'religious' poems far too seriously and to regard them as evidence for some kind of spiritual progress or development. It seems to me, though, that in these poems he is being neither more nor less serious than in *The Garden* or *To his Coy Mistress* or *The Picture of Little T.C.* Inveterate imitator and experimenter that he was, trying his hand at almost every kind of poetry that his contemporaries and immediate predecessors had been writing, it was only to be expected that sooner or later he would attempt religious poetry too, applying that eclectic technique he so delighted to exercise to a more or less 'religious' subject-matter.

If *On a Drop of Dew* has affinities with Vaughan's *The Waterfall*, it also, like so many of Marvell's poems, has affinities with Crashaw.

> Trembling lest it grow impure:
> Till the warm Sun pitty it's Pain,
> And to the Skies exhale it back again:

this, though not, so far as I know, imitated from any particular passage in Crashaw, is nevertheless, in its limpid precision and tremulous tenderness, indistinguishable from the manner of Crashaw at his very best and most characteristic, and, but for his example, would probably have remained beyond Marvell's reach. And the following lines contain a phrase and a conceit ('its own Tear') which Marvell has almost certainly borrowed from Crashaw:

> But gazing back upon the Skies,
> Shines with a mournful Light;
> Like its own Tear,
> Because so long divided from the Sphear.

Here Marvell almost certainly had in mind a passage in Crashaw's *Wishes. To his (supposed) Mistresse* (ll. 52–4):

> Each Ruby there,
> Or Pearle that dare appeare,
> Bee its owne blush, bee its owne Teare.

But while Crashaw, though he often achieves an exquisite economy and precision within single stanzas or short passages, generally tends in whole poems towards diffuseness, the far more intellectual and unecstatic Marvell writes throughout this poem with a compression that sometimes borders on obscurity, as in lines 4 to 8, where the meaning, which I have thought it necessary to elucidate in a footnote, only becomes clear after several readings.

It is this extreme compression which makes all the more noticeable and (I am almost inclined to say, despite whatever historical excuse may be adduced) inexplicable the usual clumsy inversion and expletives (there are not less than five of them) to which Marvell has resorted in order to obtain a too easy rhyme.

> How it the purple flow'r does slight
>
> (l. 9)
>
> Does, in its pure and circling thoughts, express
>
> (l. 25: why not 'would'?)
>
> It all about does upwards bend
>
> (l. 36)
>
> . Such did the Manna's sacred Dew distil
>
> (l. 37)
>
> Congeal'd on Earth: but does, dissolving, run
>
> (l. 39)

I make no apology for my continual insistence on this defect. Pope's cultivation of 'correctness' was not, as those brought up on the Romantics and on the notion of poetry as 'self-expression' are inclined to suppose, a trivial preoccupation, the mere fad of a nasty, niggling little creature who conceived his poetry, not in his soul, but in his wits, and scribbled it on the backs of letters. Perfection is perfection, and that which, however good of its kind, is less than perfect remains imperfect. It is too often forgotten that, in the reading of poetry, one of the great sources of pleasure is a perpetual awareness, or, at least, undersense, of the difficulties that have been overcome. Even in his best poems Marvell has too many lines which we feel that, with a little trouble, we could improve ourselves.

A Dialogue Between the Resolved Soul, and Created Pleasure and *A Dialogue between the Soul and Body* may be regarded, partly at least, as further and more elaborate experiments in that very popular dialogue or duet form, of which (if we include the two songs for the Cromwell-Fauconberg marriage) Marvell has three pastoral examples, one of them, *Thyrsis and Dorinda*, a poem that was thrice set to music. But while the *Dialogue between the Soul and Body* is an essentially unlyrical and unsingable poem, the *Dialogue Between the Resolved Soul, and Created Pleasure*,[1]

---

1. In a footnote towards the beginning of my second chapter (p. 31), where I was considering available evidence for the chronology of some of Marvell's poems, I suggested that two passages in this poem may have been inspired by passages in *Paradise Lost* and that, accordingly, Marvell may have written it after the publication of Milton's poem in 1667.

perhaps in somewhat abbreviated form, might well have appeared in some collection of 'Ayres and Dialogues': indeed, the comparative simplicity of its style, the well-marked metrical differentiation between Pleasure's trochaic and heptasyllabic temptations and the Soul's iambic and octosyllabic replies, and the two choruses, almost suggest that Marvell conceived and wrote it with at least the possibility in mind of its being set to music. Besides the continuously preserved trochaic and iambic contrast between Pleasure and the Soul there are some broad and well-spaced changes in verse-pattern that would have provided considerable opportunity to a composer. The Soul begins by expressing its resolution in a kind of prologue of ten lines of octosyllabic couplets, and then, in a six-line heptasyllabic stanza (a b a b c c), Pleasure greets the Soul and proceeds to tempt the sense of taste. The Soul replies with a single couplet, and Pleasure then proceeds to tempt the other four senses (Touch, ll. 19–22; Smell, ll. 25–8; Sight, ll. 31–4; Hearing, ll. 37–40), each temptation being expressed in four lines of heptasyllabic couplets, to the first three of which the Soul replies with a single couplet and to the last with two. Then comes the first chorus, consisting of an octosyllabic quatrain (a b b a) followed by a decasyllabic couplet. In what might be called the second part of the poem Pleasure, still trochaically but with a change of verse-pattern, tempts the Soul, in four quatrains of alternate seven-syllable and six-syllable lines (a b a b), with Beauty, Wealth, Glory and Knowledge, to each of which the Soul replies with a single couplet. The final chorus is an octosyllabic quatrain (a b a b).

A Dialogue Between the Resolved Soul, and Created Pleasure

> Courage my Soul, now learn to wield
> The weight of thine immortal Shield.
> Close on thy Head thy Helmet bright.
> Ballance thy Sword against the Fight.
> See where an Army, strong as fair,
> With silken Banners spreads the air.
> Now, if thou bee'st that thing Divine,
> In this day's Combat let it[1] shine:
> And shew that Nature wants an Art
> To conquer one resolved Heart.

1. The fact that you are 'that thing Divine'.

PLEASURE

Welcome the Creations Guest,
Lord of Earth and Heavens Heir.
Lay aside that Warlike Crest,
And of Nature's banquet share:
Where the Souls of fruits and flow'rs
Stand prepar'd to heighten yours.

SOUL

I sup above, and cannot stay
To bait so long upon the way.

PLEASURE

On these downy Pillows lye,
Whose soft Plumes will thither fly:
On these Roses strow'd so plain
Lest one Leaf thy Side should strain.

SOUL

My gentler Rest is on a Thought,
Conscious of doing what I ought.

PLEASURE

If thou bee'st with Perfumes pleas'd,
Such as oft the Gods appeas'd,
Thou in fragrant Clouds shalt show
Like another God below.

SOUL

A Soul that knowes not to presume
Is Heaven's and its own perfume.

PLEASURE

Every thing does seem to vie
Which should first attract thine Eye:
But since none deserves that grace,
In this Crystal view *thy* face.

SOUL

When the Creator's skill is priz'd,
The rest is all but Earth disguis'd.

PLEASURE

Heark how Musick then prepares
For thy Stay these charming Aires;
Which the posting Winds recall,[1]
And suspend the Rivers Fall.

SOUL

Had I but any time to lose,
On this I would it all dispose.
Cease Tempter. None can chain a mind
Whom this sweet Chordage cannot bind.

CHORUS

Earth cannot shew so brave a Sight
As when a single Soul does fence
The Batteries of alluring Sense,
And Heaven views it with delight.
  Then persevere: for still new Charges sound:
  And if thou overcom'st thou shalt be crown'd.[2]

PLEASURE

All this fair, and soft,[3] and sweet,
  Which scatteringly doth shine,
Shall within one Beauty meet,
  And she be only thine.

SOUL

If things of Sight such Heavens be,
What Heavens are those we cannot see?

PLEASURE

Where so e're thy Foot shall go
  The minted Gold shall lie;
Till thou purchase all below,
  And want new Worlds to buy.

---

1. Which recall the posting winds.
2. cf. *Revelation* ii 10, 'Be thou faithful unto death, and I will give thee a crown of life', and, in *Rev.* ii 7, 11, 17, 26; iii 5, 12, 21; xxi 7, the phrases 'to him that overcometh' and 'he that overcometh'.
3. T2 and Margoliouth; 1681 'coft'.

SOUL

Wer't not a price who'ld value Gold?
And that's worth nought that can be sold.

PLEASURE

Wilt thou all the Glory have
    That War or Peace commend?
Half the World shall be thy Slave
    The other half thy Friend.

SOUL

What Friends, if to my self untrue?
What Slaves, unless I captive you?

PLEASURE

Thou shalt know each hidden Cause;
    And see the future Time:
Try what depth the Centre draws;
    And then to Heaven climb.

SOUL

None thither mounts by the degree[1]
Of Knowledge, but Humility.

CHORUS

Triumph, triumph,[2] victorious Soul;
The World has not one Pleasure more:
The rest does lie beyond the Pole,
And is thine everlasting Store.

Like the *Horatian Ode* (which it does not otherwise resemble), this poem is nearer to Ben Jonson's manner than is usual with Marvell, although I cannot point to any particular poem of Jonson's for comparison. There is little in it that is conspicuously ingenious or surprising, and it is classical in a sense in which scarcely anything of Donne's is and in which several of Marvell's own more memorable poems are

1. Used primarily in the original sense of the word (Late Latin *de-gradus*), 'a step in an ascent or descent', but also, probably, with some suggestion of the later sense of 'amount'.
2. The accent, as was normal, is on the second syllable.

not. Margoliouth, indeed, has called it 'a rather thin poem'.[1] It is true
that it lacks the hyperbole, the dialectical ingenuity, and the exquisite
pictorialism which in other poems Marvell has so inimitably combined;
nevertheless, its energetic and soaring progression, its solidity of
structure, its epigrammatic terseness and its effective metrical contrasts
and changes are surely admirable. It is difficult not to suppose that
Marvell intended it to be set to music and that he therefore deliberately
imposed certain limitations upon himself and exerted himself to supply
such, and only such, material as a musician could most rewardingly
exploit. If so, he produced something admirably adapted to his purpose, something, too, which represents, in respect of the qualities I have
just mentioned, an enormous advance on that rather slight pastoral
dialogue, *Thyrsis and Dorinda*, which, in comparison, might not un-
fairly be described as 'rather thin'. I have already remarked that in its
high-spirited exaggeration *To his Coy Mistress* was reminiscent not only
of Donne but of Dryden: the present poem, in its metrical contrasts
and changes, has some affinity with Dryden's *Song for St Cecilia's Day*,
Alexander's Feast and *Secular Masque*.

The only striking piece of ingenuity or, as one might say, of un-
Jonsonian wit, is the double meaning of 'Chordage' in the Soul's
reply to Pleasure's temptation of the sense of hearing with music:

> Cease Tempter. None can chain a mind
> Whom this sweet Chordage cannot bind.
>
> (ll. 43–4)

Otherwise the 'wit' of the poem may be described as 'Jonsonian', and
consists in terseness, epigram, antithesis, together with great naturalness and propriety of diction. For its perfect success, however, this
kind of writing seems to require, as a principle of compensation, a
more sparing use of inversion, a more careful and consistent observance of natural word-order, than Marvell has here achieved. The general impression I have formed from his poetry as a whole is that he
was aware of such naturalness (or 'correctness') as a desirable ideal,
but that he was too ready to use an inversion as a short cut to a rhyme.
This tends to give to much of his work, in spite of its beauty and its
frequent perfection, a touch of amateurishness and even, at times, of
slovenliness. In the first ten lines, although there are three inversions,
two of them ('that thing Divine', 'In this day's Combat let it shine')
are entirely justifiable on grounds of emphasis, and one ('thy Helmet

1. *RES*, April 1941, p. 220.

bright') is perhaps defensible on the ground of its frequency in contemporary practice:

> Courage my Soul, now learn to wield
> The weight of thine immortal Shield.
> Close on thy Head thy Helmet bright.
> Ballance thy Sword against the Fight.
> See where an Army, strong as fair,
> With silken Banners spreads the air.
> Now, if thou bee'st that thing Divine,
> In this day's Combat let it shine:
> And shew that Nature wants an Art
> To conquer one resolved Heart.

In addition to this splendid (I might even say, this perfect) use of the octosyllabic couplet, which may be compared to that in certain passages which I criticised in *The Nymph complaining for the death of her Faun*—in addition to this, I think it will be agreed that the naturalness of the word-order is an important element in the impression of grace and strength which these lines convey. In the rest of the poem inversions (not all of them, it is true, equally reprehensible) are rather too frequent, and their cumulative effect tends to weaken the general impression of grace and strength and to cause a fine poem to fall somewhat short of perfection:

And of Nature's banquet share	(l. 14)
Lest one Leafe thy Side should strain	(l. 22)
Such as oft the Gods appeas'd	(l. 26)
Every thing *does* seem to vie	(l. 31)
these charming Aires;	
Which the posting Winds recall	(ll. 38–9)
On this I would it all dispose	(l. 42)
As when a single Soul *does* fence	(l. 46)
Which scatteringly *doth* shine	(l. 52)
If things of Sight such Heavens be	(l. 55)
Wilt thou all the Glory have	(l. 63)
The rest *does* lie beyond the Pole	(l. 77)

None of these inversions and expletives seems to me defensible. On the other hand, I am not inclined to object to 'Shall within one Beauty meet' (l. 53) and 'And then to Heaven climb' (l. 72).

In contrast to the poem we have been considering, *A Dialogue between the Soul and Body* is remote from Music and Song, and Marvell has here adopted a much less serious, a much more non-committal, attitude, and indulges much more in the pleasures of ingenuity and surprise. It is, though, not merely one more essay in the popular dialogue form, but an example of a particular kind of dialogue, that between Body and Soul, which seems to have originated in England during the Middle Ages, to have disappeared from European literature, after enjoying a brief popularity with writers of medieval Latin, and then, suddenly and inexplicably, to have reappeared in the country of its origin at the beginning of the seventeenth century. I shall, therefore, before considering Marvell's poem, say a word or two about this phenomenon.

An investigation of the medieval poetic debates on this subject[1] has been able to discover only two passages in the Bible that may possibly have suggested it: I *Peter* ii 11, 'Dearly beloved, I beseech you as strangers and pilgrims, abstain from fleshly lusts, which war against the soul'; and *Galatians* v 16–25, where St Paul begins 'This I say then, Walk in the Spirit, and ye shall not fulfil the lust of the flesh. For the flesh lusteth against the Spirit, and the Spirit against the flesh: and these are contrary the one to the other: so that ye cannot do the things that ye would', and then proceeds to give a long list of the works of the flesh. The earliest surviving example, not a true dialogue, since it is only towards the end of it that Caro attempts to rebut Anima's accusations, is a late twelfth-century Latin poem of 2,544 short rhymed lines, probably written in England and commonly known, since it is preserved in the Royal Manuscript Collection in the British Museum, as *The Royal Debate*. It purports to record a dream in which a Soul, standing beside a coffin, is heard accusing the body it has just left of responsibility for their joint damnation. Towards the end of the poem the body tries to reply, and the Soul, after a brief lament, is carried off to Hell by demons. A shorter and much more effective Latin poem of 312 lines, apparently based on the *Royal Debate* and variously entitled *Dialogus inter Corpus et Animam*, *Conflictus Corporis et Animae* and *Visio Philiberti*, was written in England during the early thirteenth century and seems to have enjoyed enormous popularity, since it has survived in no less than 132 manuscripts. It is a genuine dialogue, for it assigns four separate speeches to Anima and three to Caro, and it seems to have influenced all later medieval debates on this subject.

1. H. Walther, *Das Streitgedicht in den lateinischen Literatur des Mittelalters*, Munich 1920, p. 64.

Among these was a late thirteenth-century Middle English poem of 608 lines, entitled *Desputisoun bitwen the Bodi and the Soule*, which has survived in several manuscripts and versions. Unless, which seems unlikely, the reappearance of the topic in seventeenth-century English poetry was a piece of spontaneous regeneration, the suggestion for it must have come from one or more of the medieval Latin poems, since our earlier Middle English poetry was then almost completely unknown. A very possible source of inspiration would seem to be the *Altercacio Carnis et Spiritus*,[1] which, like the seventeenth-century poems, is comparatively short and nearer to what we commonly classify as lyric than to the normally much longer medieval debate. It is preserved in an early thirteenth-century manuscript in the library of Corpus Christi College, Cambridge, and consists of ten nine-line rhymed stanzas, spoken alternately by Spiritus and Caro. I quote the first two stanzas, which are sufficiently representative:

> *Spiritus* O Caro, cara vilitas,
> cauens carere carie,
> celer ad sordes vetitas,
> procliua immundicie,
> tue memor miserie
> ad semitas iusticie
> gressus torpentes applica,
> linque post tergum lubrica,
> vt sis ouis dominica!

> *Caro* Stultum est visibilibus
> nondum uisa preponere
> et pro spiritualibus
> carnalia contempnere
> et solita relinquere;
> trita curruntur libere,
> non trita in periculum;
> ergo complectar seculum,
> quod cernitur ad oculum.

(*Spirit:* O flesh, dear cheapness, anxious to escape decay, but swift to make for forbidden filth and prone to uncleanness; be mindful of your wretchedness and apply your sluggish steps to the paths of

---

1. Printed by Walther, *op. cit.*, p. 215.

righteousness; leave wantonness behind you, so that you may be one of the Lord's sheep!

Flesh: It is foolish to set above things visible things not yet seen and to despise carnal for spiritual things, and to forsake things that are customary; trodden ways are sped along freely, untrodden at one's peril; I will therefore embrace the world, since it shows itself to the eye.)

This uniquely medieval English topic, which, so far as I have been able to discover, does not occur at all in the Renaissance poetry, Latin or vernacular, of other European countries, makes its first sudden reappearance (no very distinguished one) in the following short poem in Davison's *Poetical Rhapsody*, 1602.[1] It consists (although this is not, perhaps, immediately clear) of two six-line stanzas, rhyming a b a b c c.

Dialogue betweene the Soule and the Body

Soule	Ay me, poore Soule, whom bound in sinful chaines
	This wretched body keepes against my will!
Body	Aye mee poore Body, whom for all my paines,
	This froward soule causlesse condemneth stil.
Soule	Causles? whenas thou striu'st to sin each day?
Body	Causles: whenas I striue thee to obay.
Soule	Thou art the meanes, by which I fall to sin,
Body	Thou art the cause that set'st this means awork.
Soule	No part of thee that hath not faultie bin:
Body	I shew the poyson that in thee doth lurke.
Soule	I shall be pure when so I part from thee:
	So were I now, but that thou stainest mee.

The topic next appears in Quarles's *Emblemes*, 1635, book III, no. xiv, a dialogue, in heroic couplets, between Flesh and Spirit. It is significant that the plate for this was one of the very few which had to be specially made by an English engraver and which did not imitate, either exactly or with slight modifications, the plates in two enormously popular continental collections, the *Typus Mundi*, published by the Jesuits of Antwerp in 1627, which was the main source for the plates in Quarles's first two books, and the *Pia Desideria* of the Jesuit Hermann Hugo, published in 1624, which was the main source for those in his last three. Flesh (naked) and Spirit (clothed) are sitting

1. Ed. Rollins, I 197.

together at one end of a garden alley, and Spirit is looking through an 'optic glass' towards the other end, where stands Death the skeleton, holding in one hand a naked sword and in the other a palm branch, the flames of Hell ascending from below him, and above him the enthroned Christ, flanked by two trumpeting angels. Flesh, however, prefers to look through a triangular glass which presents all things in attractive colours. Vaughan, in the first edition of *Silex Scintillans*, 1650, has three dialogues between Body and Soul which are almost exclusively doctrinal and almost entirely undramatic. They are not, like the medieval poems, like those we have been considering, and like Marvell's, concerned with the various points of conflict between Body and Soul and with the opportunities offered for the exploitation of antithesis, but only with the nature of immortality and resurrection. *Death. A Dialogue*[1] is, like many of Vaughan's poems, quite unmemorable. *Resurrection and Immortality*[2] is a much finer poem, though scarcely a true dialogue. The Body, in an irregular stanza of eighteen lines, professes to find in the apparently miraculous revival of a silk-worm some grounds for hoping that it too may be revived; whereupon the Soul, in two stanzas of fifty-one lines, rebukes the Body for its ignorant and superficial conception of death, of which it proceeds to expound the true doctrine: that nothing is destroyed, that spirits, after their brief incarnation, return to the Spirit whence they came, and that the 'passive Cottage' will eventually re-arise to receive its 'more noble *Essence*':

> So shalt thou then with me
> (Both wing'd, and free,)
> Rove in that mighty, and eternall light
> Where no rude shade, or night
> Shall dare approach us; we shall there no more
> Watch stars, or pore
> Through melancholly clouds, and say
> *Would it were Day!*
> One everlasting *Saboth* there shall runne
> Without *Succession*, and without a *Sunne*.

The Evening-watch,[3] a poem short enough to be here quoted in full, bears the sub-title *A Dialogue*, although in it the Body merely plays the part of what actors used to call a 'feeder', and the two couplets

1. *Works*, ed. L. C. Martin, p. 399.   2. *op. cit.*, p. 400.
3. *op. cit.*, p. 425.

it utters might be slightly altered and transferred to the Soul without fundamentally changing the poem. It may indeed be doubted whether the essentially contemplative, single-minded and consistently serious author of *Silex Scintillans* would have been capable of writing a genuinely dialectical, dramatic and two-sided dialogue: would not the attempt to devise lively and ingenious arguments in defence of 'sinful' attitudes have seemed to him too nearly related to those 'willingly-studied and wilfully-published vanities' he had left behind him?

Farewell! I goe to sleep; but when	*Body*
The day-star springs, I'le wake agen.	
Goe, sleep in peace; and when thou lyest	*Soul*
Unnumber'd in thy dust, when all this frame	
Is but one dramme, and what thou now descriest	
In sev'rall parts shall want a name,	
Then may his peace be with thee, and each dust	
Writ in his book, who ne'r betray'd mans trust!	
Amen! but hark, e'r we two stray,	*Body*
How many hours do'st think 'till day?	
Ah! go; th'art weak, and sleepie. Heav'n	*Soul*
Is a plain watch, and without figures winds	
All ages up; who drew this Circle even	
He fils it; Dayes, and hours are *Blinds*.	
Yet, this take with thee; The last gasp of time	
Is thy first breath, and mans *eternall Prime*.	

Nothing could be more remote from Vaughan's three pseudo-dialogues than Marvell's lively and utterly undoctrinal poem, which, though not irreligious, can only in the most superficial sense be classified as 'religious'. Even to that Latin *Altercatio*, from which I have quoted two stanzas, its only resemblance is that it is truly dialectical and two-sided. It is as sheerly witty, as exclusively concerned with the pleasures of ingenuity and surprise, as the most light-hearted effusions of Donne or Cleveland, and yet there is not, even for a modern reader, any incongruity between treatment and subject, as there sometimes is in poems where Donne or Cleveland treat a 'serious' subject wittily —in Donne's *Autumnall*, for example, or in Cleveland's elegy on Edward King. Here, no less than in his so different *Dialogue Between the Resolved Soul, and Created Pleasure*, Marvell has achieved precisely the effect he intended and has preserved the proper *decorum*. While so much of the once fashionable and applauded wit of his contemporaries and immediate predecessors has failed to stand the test of time, Marvell has here revealed once again his instinct for what I have called the permanently delightful, so that his poem can please most modern readers as much as it presumably pleased those who first heard or read it. What distinguishes his wit in this poem, as also in his poem *Upon the Hill and Grove at Bill-borow* and in many passages in *Appleton House*, is that he prefers metaphor to simile, comparison or analogy, and achieves his effects, not, as Donne so often does, by contriving to relate his subject (or his professed subject) to the most unlikely and astonishing kinds of 'otherness', but by a sort of hyperbolical, semi-burlesque personification of what is immediately before him, and by a continuous exploitation of its possibilities of antithesis. Donne often astonishes us by bringing so much in, Marvell by getting so much out. There is some analogy between this kind of wit and the logical, detailed, realistic, and yet at the same time fantastically extravagant exploitation and piling-up in certain passages in Ben Jonson's comic dialogue—above all, in Sir Epicure Mammon's dreams of what he will do with the philosopher's stone, a speech from which Marvell actually quotes in *The Rehearsal Transpros'd*.[1] There is also, in the touch of burlesque, an affinity (more apparent in the Bilborough and Appleton House poems) with Cleveland.

I have often dwelt upon Marvell's love of epigrammatic antithesis. One of the most striking examples of it is a passage in this poem where he has, as it were, extracted and sharpened the antithesis latent in the last two lines of Crashaw's paradoxical epigram on the Pool of Bethes-da:[2]

> Unde hoc naufragium felix? medicaeque procellae?
> Vitaque, tempestas quam pretiosa dedit?

(Whence this fortunate shipwreck? these medicinal storms?
And life, which a precious tempest has conferred?)

When Marvell makes the Soul complain that it is

> Constrain'd not only to indure
> Diseases, but, whats worse, the Cure:
> And ready oft the Port to gain,
> Am Shipwrackt into Health again,

1. 'Though the greatest Divines should be his flatterers' (1672), p. 110.
2. See Chapter 2. p. 49.

we feel that (despite the inversion in the third line) metre, syntax and diction have achieved between them a maximum of pointedness and concentrated surprise.

The poem as we have it is almost certainly incomplete. In several of his octosyllabic poems Marvell has divided his lines into stanzas of equal length; while, however, each of the first three stanzas of this poem contains ten lines, the fourth contains fourteen and seems rather to stop than to conclude. Suspicions appear to be confirmed by the anonymous corrector of 'Thompson's second manuscript book', to which, as 'T2', I have been occasionally referring in footnotes. This is an imperfect copy of the 1681 folio, now in the Bodleian Library (MS Eng. poet. d. 49), with manuscript additions, including a considerable appendage of satires, in a late seventeenth- or early eighteenth-century hand, and with a few corrections of the text of the printed portion in a hand imitating print. It reached Captain Edward Thompson when the edition of Marvell's *Works* which he published in 1776 was already in the press, and he seems to have been erroneously led to suppose that it was in the hand of Marvell's nephew William Popple. Whoever the corrector was, he has drawn his pen through the last four lines of this fourth stanza and has written below: '*Desunt multa*'. It looks as though the debate had originally continued through several more ten-line stanzas, and as though the last four lines of the present fourth had somehow survived from one of these. Lovers of speculation may, if they like, try to decide whether Marvell deleted them or simply lost them. He certainly seems to have lost several lines of his Latin poem *Hortus*, for after line 48 the words *Desunt multa* are printed between two blanks and were presumably in his manuscript.

A Dialogue Between the Soul and Body

SOUL

O who shall, from this Dungeon, raise
A Soul inslav'd so many wayes?
With bolts of Bones, that fetter'd stands
In Feet; and manacled in Hands.
Here blinded with an Eye; and there
Deaf with the drumming of an Ear.
A Soul hung up, as 'twere, in Chains
Of Nerves, and Arteries, and Veins.
Tortur'd, besides each other part,
In a vain Head, and double Heart.

BODY

O who shall me deliver whole,
From bonds of this Tyrannic Soul?
Which, stretcht upright, impales me so,
That mine own Precipice[1] I go;
And warms and moves this needless[2] Frame:
(A Fever could but do the same.)
And, wanting where its spight to try,
Has made me live to let me dye.
A Body that could never rest,
Since this ill Spirit it possest.

SOUL

What Magick could me thus confine
Within anothers Grief to pine?
Where whatsoever it complain,
I feel, that cannot feel, the pain.
And all my Care its self employes,
That to preserve, which me destroys:
Constrain'd not only to indure
Diseases, but, whats worse, the Cure:
And ready oft the Port to gain,
Am Shipwrackt into Health again.

BODY

But Physick yet could never reach
The Maladies Thou me dost teach;
Whom first the Cramp of Hope does Tear:
And then the Palsie Shakes of Fear.
The Pestilence of Love does heat:
Or Hatred's hidden Ulcer eat.
Joy's chearful Madness does perplex:
Or Sorrow's other Madness vex.
Which Knowledge forces me to know;
And Memory will not foregoe.

---

1. Margoliouth quotes from Marvell's *Rehearsal Transpros'd*: 'After he was stretch'd to such an height in his own fancy, that he could not look down from top to toe but his Eyes dazled at the Precipice of his Stature.'

2. 'This frame in need of nothing, but that repose which the Soul will not allow it.'

> What but a Soul could have the wit
> To build me up for Sin so fit?
> So Architects do square and hew,
> Green Trees that in the Forest grew.

The brilliant virtuosity of this poem is to some extent counteracted by the usual complement of clumsy inversions, just as in Wordsworth's *Lyrical Ballads* the colloquial simplicity at which he was aiming is similarly counteracted by lines such as (from *The Last of the Flock*)

> Sturdy he seemed, though he was sad;
> And in his arms a lamb he had;

or

> My pride was tamed, and in our grief
> I of the parish ask'd relief.

For, while Marvell's poem as a whole is such as no other poet has written, or perhaps could have written, almost any of us would be capable of shaking and shuffling some half-dozen words until one of them supplied the rhyme he wanted:

> O who shall me deliver whole   (l. 11)
> What Magick could me thus confine   (l. 21)
> The Maladies Thou me dost teach   (l. 32)

Sometimes, moreover, the result is a clumsy (not subtle or intentional) ambiguity of expression:

> Whom first the Cramp of Hope does Tear:
> And then the Palsie Shakes of Fear.   (ll. 33–4)

Since 'Shakes', printed with a capital, may be intended as a noun, it is almost impossible to decide whether Marvell means 'And then the palsy-Shakes of fear tear' or 'And then the palsy of fear shakes'.

If *Musicks Empire* is to be grouped or classified, it seems to belong with these 'religious' poems, if only because of the graceful compliment to Fairfax on his religion and humility with which it concludes:

> Victorious sounds! yet here your Homage do
> Unto a gentler Conqueror then you;
> Who though He flies the Musick of his praise,
> Would with you Heavens Hallelujahs raise.

Marvell sets out to describe, in a kind of ingenious allegory or 'extended metaphor', the origin and development of music. At first there were only the harsh and jarring sounds of winds and waters. Jubal (described in *Genesis* iv 21 as 'the father of all such as handle the harp and organ') assembled their echoes and built for them 'the Organs City'. Here each found a note, and their progeny went out and founded colonies, some going to stringed or wired, others to wind, instruments. From all these Music prepared a 'solemn noise' with which she gained the empire of the ear.

Musicks Empire

I

First was the World as one great Cymbal made,
Where Jarring Windes to infant Nature plaid.
All Musick was a solitary sound,
To hollow Rocks and murm'ring Fountains bound.

II

Jubal first made the wilder Notes agree;
And *Jubal* tuned Musicks *Jubilee*:[1]
He call'd the *Ecchoes* from their sullen Cell,
And built the Organs City where they dwell.

III

Each sought a consort in that lovely place;
And Virgin Trebles wed the manly Base.
From whence the Progeny of numbers new
Into harmonious Colonies withdrew.

IV

Some to the Lute, some to the Viol went,
And others chose the Cornet eloquent.
These practising the Wind, and those the Wire,
To sing Mens Triumphs, or in Heavens quire.

V

Then Musick, the Mosaique of the Air,
Did of all these a solemn noise prepare:
With which She gain'd the Empire of the Ear,
Including all between the Earth and Sphear.

1 T2; 'And *Jubal* tun'd Musick's first *Jubilee*'.

VI

> Victorious sounds! yet here your Homage do
> Unto a gentler Conqueror then you;
> Who though He flies the Musick of his praise,
> Would with you Heavens Hallelujahs raise.

At first sight, and even perhaps after several readings, this seems a peculiarly delightful and athletic poem, and certainly the beautiful and original phrase 'Musick, the Mosaique of the Air,' a phrase of which I have already remarked that one might have expected to find it rather in Rilke than in Marvell, will never be forgotten. Nevertheless, the more carefully one considers the poem as a whole, the less satisfactory it appears. The 'allegory' will not bear close inspection: the correspondence between literal and metaphorical (so exquisitely preserved in *On a Drop of Dew*) is continually breaking down, and, in fact, there is a careless-ness or inattentiveness in its working out which may be regarded as having some affinity with that carelessness and slovenliness Marvell so often displays in his use of inversion. (It is possible indeed that here the preservation of an exact correspondence, as elsewhere the preser-vation of a natural word-order, was forgotten in the search for rhymes.) What Marvell seems to have *meant* to say was something like this: (1) At first there were mere natural 'noises'. (2) Jubal assembled and noted their echoes. (3) Their progeny colonised instruments of various tone-colours. (4) These colonised instruments united in a 'consort' or orchestra and produced music, 'the Mosaique of the Air'. (5) Music gained sovereign power over the sense of hearing. Even here, though, there are several breakdowns: Jubal with his harp and organ had already produced 'music', and so had the performers (unmentioned but unexorcisable) of the other instruments. Marvell, in fact, does not seem to have perceived that it was not possible to describe the origin and progress of music, even allegorically, except in terms of an in-separable triad—sounds, instruments, and instrumentalists. The result is that his poem as a whole is both intellectually and imaginatively confused.

5

THE BILBOROUGH
AND APPLETON HOUSE POEMS

(i) *Semi-burlesque hyperbole in Marvell and his seventeenth-century predecessors*

In examining the *Dialogue between the Soul and Body* I remarked that in the touch of burlesque there was an affinity with Cleveland, although this affinity was more perceptible in the Bilborough and Appleton House poems, poems in which Marvell has so often flavoured his own peculiar blend of the dialectical and the pictorial with a certain burlesque extravagance of which the possibilities were, I cannot but think, suggested to him by his reading of Cleveland.

Cleveland's poems were first printed in 1647 and 1651, and that Marvell had read them is proved beyond doubt by his description of the salmon-fishers at the conclusion of *Appleton House*:

> But now the *Salmon-Fishers* moist
> Their *Leathern Boats* begin to hoist;
> And, like *Antipodes* in Shoes,
> Have shod their *Heads* in their *Canoos*.

The ingenious comparison here was partly suggested by Cleveland's *Square-Cap*, that poem in which the author's

> Cambridge lass, Venus-like, born of the froth
> Of an old half-filled jug of barley-broth

rejects all otherwise-capped suitors in favour of the square-capped undergraduate, or sophister. The lawyer, in his coif, calot, or skull-cap, presents himself:

Then Calot Leather-cap strongly pleads,
   And fain would derive the pedigree of fashion.
The antipodes wear their shoes on their heads,
   And why may not we in their imitation?

I have already quoted in my second chapter[1] the third stanza of that
very Marvellian poem of Cleveland's, *To the State of Love, or, The Senses'
Festival*, first printed in the 1651 edition of his poems. It was undoubtedly, I think, the epigrammatic, hyperbolical, semi-burlesque wit

(Is not the universe strait-laced
When I can clasp it in the waist?)

in this and some other of Cleveland's poems that suggested to Marvell
yet further possibilities of experiment, and provided the hint for such
things as his description of the grazing cattle in *Appleton House* (stanza
LVIII):

They seem within the polisht Grass
A Landskip drawen in Looking-Glass.
And shrunk in the huge Pasture show
As Spots, so shap'd, on Faces do.
Such Fleas, ere they approach the Eye,
In Multiplying Glasses[2] lye.
They feed so wide, so slowly move,
As *Constellations* do above.

Here, however, Marvell, that remarkable combiner of old and new,
while taking a hint from Cleveland, may also have been taking a hint
from Theocritus (or—since the ascription seems doubtful—from
pseudo-Theocritus), for it seems to me by no means unlikely that the
concluding comparison of the feeding cattle to constellations may
have been suggested by one in the twenty-fifth Idyll, where Herakles,
approaching one of the great farms of King Augeas at evening, beholds
the cattle returning from the pastures to their stalls:

1. p. 79.
2. This comparison seems to have been suggested by one in the 1650 edition of
James Howell's *Epistolae Ho-Elianae* (letter dated 15 August 1646, Temple Classics
ed., II 162–3): 'You look upon me through the wrong end of the prospective, or
rather through a multiplying glass, which makes the object appear far bigger than
it is in real dimension; such glasses as anatomists use in the dissection of bodies,
which can make a flea look like a cow, or a fly as big as a vulture.' Marvell reverses
the comparison, saying that the cows look like fleas in an unoperated multiplying
glass, which, when we operate it, makes them look like cows.

Next cows in countless thousands, advancing herd on herd, showed like rain-charged clouds that roll onward across the sky driven by the force of the south wind, or of the north from Thrace. Without number, without end, they pass across the heavens, so many does the violence of the wind roll up to join the vanguard, crest following crest. Numberless like them came ever herds of kine behind, and all the plain was filled with the homing cattle, and all the paths, and the lush pastures were straitened with their bellowing.[1]

The chief difference between Marvell's simile and that of Theocritus (or his imitator) consists not in its matter but in its extreme compression. The preceding three similes not merely allude to matters unknown to the ancients, but are also (despite their triumphant success) of an ingenuity beyond both the reach and the ambition of any ancient poet. As with many other similes in *Appleton House*, one feels that they have reached, but not passed, the point where a new and exciting kind of beauty begins to turn into the merely grotesque.

To return to Cleveland, it is hard not to suppose that both the rhyme and the substance of the following couplet from his *Fuscara, or the Bee Errant* (first printed in the 1651 volume), about the bee feasting upon Fuscara's arm and

> Tuning his draughts with drowsy hums
> As Danes carouse by kettle-drums,[2]

did not suggest both the rhyme and, to some extent, the substance of a famous couplet in stanza XXXVII of *Appleton House*:

> The Bee through these known Allies hums,
> Beating the *Dian* with its *Drumms*;

although it is true that for Marvell's drumming bee in this stanza as also for his sentinel bee in stanza XL—

> Then in some Flow'rs beloved Hut
> Each Bee as Sentinel is shut;
> And sleeps so too: but, if once stir'd,
> She runs you through, or askes *the Word*—

there was plenty of Renaissance precedent, for the warrior bee was a subject often treated by poets both in Latin and in the vernacular.

---

1. ll. 88–95, A. S. Gow's translation.
2. ll. 51–2, *Caroline Poets*, ed. Saintsbury, III 80.

Tasso, for example, has a madrigal which was thus translated by
Drummond of Hawthornden:

> As an audacious Knight
> Come with some Foe to fight,
> His Sword doth brandish, makes his Armour ring:
> So this prowde Bee (at home (perhaps) a King)
> Did buzzing flie about,
> And (Tyrant) often thy faire Lip did sting:
> O Champion strange as stout!
> Who hast by *Nature* found,
> Sharpe Armes, and Trumpet shrill, to sound, and wound.[1]

And it seems probable that the ultimate inspiration of all these descriptions of the warrior-bee was a passage in Pliny's *Natural History*,
of which, as we have seen, Philemon Holland's translation was one
of Marvell's favourite books:

> The manner of their businesse is this. All the day time they haue
> a standing watch & ward at their gates, much like to the *corps de
> guard* in a campe. In the night they rest vntill the morning: by which
> time, one of them awaketh and raiseth all the rest with two or three
> big hums or buzzes that it giues, to warn them as it were with sound
> of trumpet. At which signall giuen, the whole troupe prepares to
> flie forth . . . Toward euening, their noise beginneth to slacke and
> grow lesse and lesse: vntill such time as one of them flieth about
> with the same loud humming, wherewith she waked them in the
> morning, and thereby giueth a signal (as it were) and commande-
> ment for to go to rest: much after the order in a camp. And then of
> a sudden they are all husht and silent.[2]

It was, however, not so much for particular metaphors and conceits as for what may be called a way of writing that Marvell was
chiefly indebted to Cleveland; and perhaps as an example, as a kind
of formula, no single passage in Cleveland exerted a greater influence
both upon Marvell and upon some other seventeenth-century poets
than did Cleveland's characteristic development of what I may call
the 'pastoral hyperbole' in the opening lines of his poem *Upon Phillis
walking in a morning before sun-rising*, which first appeared in the 1647

1. *Poetical Works*, ed. Kastner, I 112.
2. *Naturall Historie*, transl. Philemon Holland, ed. 1635, I 314 (Book XI,
ch. x).

edition of his *Poems*. Although I have already quoted this passage in my second chapter and compared it with those concluding stanzas of *Appleton House* where Nature pays her respects to the 'Young Maria',[1] I will here quote it again, together with various earlier examples of the 'pastoral hyperbole' which I there merely referred to, and with a few later ones which, like Marvell's, seem to have been largely inspired by Cleveland.

> The sluggish morn as yet undressed,
> My Phillis brake from out her East,
> As if she'd made a match to run
> With Venus, usher to the sun.
> The trees, like yeomen of her guard,
> Serving more from pomp than ward,
> Ranked on each side, with loyal duty
> Weave branches to enclose her beauty.
> The plants, whose luxury was lopped,
> Or age with crutches underpropped,
> Whose wooden carcasses are grown
> To be but coffins of their own,
> Revive, and at her general dole
> Each receives his ancient soul.
> The winged choiristers began
> To chirp their mattins, and the fan
> Of whistling winds like organs played,
> Until their voluntaries made
> The wakened Earth in odours rise
> To be her morning sacrifice.[2]

This so influential and, in a sense, original piece of hyperbole may be regarded as a characteristic seventeenth-century development of, or variation upon, a very ancient topic, which (although it does not occur only in pastoral) I have for long been accustomed to call the 'pastoral hyperbole'. The earliest example I can recall occurs not in pastoral but in Hesiod's *Theogony* (194–5), where, in a passage which ought perhaps to be regarded rather as a piece of folklore than as conscious hyperbole, he declares that at the birth of Aphrodite 'grass sprang up around beneath her shapely feet'; and Lucretius, in the great invocation to Venus at the beginning of his poem, declares that 'for thee the

1. See pp. 81–2.
2. *Caroline Poets*, ed. Saintsbury, III 35.

wonder-working earth puts forth sweet flowers, for thee the wide stretches of ocean laugh, and heaven grown peaceful glows with out-poured light':[1]

> tibi suavis daedala tellus
> summittit flores, tibi rident aequora ponti
> placatumque nitet diffuso lumine caelum.

In Theocritus's eighth Idyll[2] one of the topics elaborated alternately by Daphnis and Menalcas in the course of their song-contest is that all things flourish at the approach and wither on the departure of the boy Milon and the girl Naïs:

Menalcas

There sheep, there goats bear twins, there bees fill hives, and oaks are loftier where lovely Milon comes a-walking; if, though, he depart, both shepherd and pastures are lean.

Daphnis

Everywhere is Spring, everywhere meadows, everywhere udders teem with milk and young things grow where lovely Naïs wanders; if, though, she depart, both cow-herd and kine are dryer.[3]

Virgil, in his imitation of this Idyll in the seventh Eclogue, makes his song-contenders develop the same topic (ll. 53–60):

Corydon

Here stand junipers and shaggy chestnuts; strewn about under the trees lie their own divers fruits; now all nature smiles; but if fair Alexis should quit these hills you would see the very rivers dry.

Thyrsis

The field is parched; the grass is athirst, dying in the tainted air; Bacchus has grudged the hills the shade of his vines: but at the coming of my Phyllis all the woodland will be green, and Jupiter, in his fullness, shall descend in gladsome showers.[4]

It was thus with classical precedent and quite in the classical tradition that Petrarch wrote of Laura, at the beginning of his 165th sonnet:

1. Loeb translation, *De Rerum Natura*, I 7–9.
2. The arguments advanced by modern scholars against its authenticity do not seem to me very convincing.
3. ll. 45 ff. in most modern editions.
4. Loeb translation.

> Come 'l candido piè per l'erba fresca
> I dolci passi onestamente move,
> Vertú che 'ntorno i fiori apra'e rinove
> De le tenere piante sue par ch'esca

(When the white foot through the fresh grass its sweet paces mod-estly moves, virtue, that around her the flowers opens and renews, from her tender soles seems to issue.)

What distinguishes Cleveland's variation on this theme from its classical exemplars is that, by means of ingenious metaphors and similes, he personifies, humanises and, in a sense, allegorises all the elements of the natural scene. Such detailed personifications of natural phenomena are frequent in seventeenth-century poetry, and although, like so much else, they are commonly labelled 'metaphysical', they are quite un-characteristic of Donne, a supposed affinity with whose poetry the term 'metaphysical' has been traditionally used to describe. When, unlike Cleveland's personifications in these lines, they are apparently written in all seriousness and without any suggestion of conscious humour or semi-burlesque, they are among those things which some-times make seventeenth-century poetry seem 'quaint' to us. When, for example, Milton, in the Nativity Ode, wrote

> So when the Sun in bed,
> Curtain'd with cloudy red,
>   Pillows his chin upon an Orient wave,

he was certainly not trying to be funny. There is a somewhat analogous contrast between the seriously extended (if seldom seriously intended) hyperbolical compliments in seventeenth-century eulogy and funeral elegy and the semi-humorous, semi-burlesque hyperbole in Cleve-land's compliment to Phillis and in Marvell's compliments to the 'Young Maria' and the Lord General. But to return to the difference between Cleveland's use of the 'pastoral hyperbole' and that of his classical exemplars: instead of being content to say that trees crowd into a shade as Pope later did[1] (and even that was further than

1. Pope, in this passage in his *Pastorals* ('Summer', ll. 73 ff.), was probably recalling the third stanza of *The Spring*, one of the poems in Cowley's *The Mistress*, a stanza beginning:

> Where e'r you walk'd, Trees were as reverent made,
> As when of old *Gods* dwelt in every shade.

In 'Spring', ll. 69 ff. Pope had already imitated the passage in Virgil's *Eclogues*.

Theocritus or Virgil or Petrarch would probably have cared to venture),
he says that they are drawn up in ranks like loyal yeomen of the guard;
instead of being content to say that the pruned and supported shrubs
revive at Phillis's approach, he represents them as ancient and im-
poverished cripples to whom she distributes alms; and instead of being
content to say that the birds burst into song, he makes them 'choiristers'
singing 'mattins', and develops the image of a divine service, with
organing winds playing voluntaries and Earth celebrating the Eucharist:

> The winged choiristers began
> To chirp their mattins, and the fan
> Of whistling winds like organs played,
> Until their voluntaries made
> The wakened Earth in odours rise
> To be her morning sacrifice.

It seems likely that this 'extended metaphor' (to quote the medieval
definition of allegory) suggested to Edward Benlowes at least the
concluding lines of the short poem in Latin elegiacs which he prefixed as an argument to the twelfth canto of his *Theophila* (1652), a canto
entitled 'The Sweetness of Retirement, or the Happiness of a Private
Life':

> Voce Deum celebro; Concordes sponte Choristae,
>   Sunt Praecentores, dum modulantur, Aves.
> Amen subjicio; dat Amen, quasi Clericus, Echo.

(With my voice I celebrate God; willingly concordant choiristers,
precentors too, in their tuning, are the birds. 'Amen' I subjoin;
'Amen' gives out Echo, like a clerk.)

Earlier in these elegiacs Benlowes had written:

> Hoc Nemus est Templum, patuli Laquearia Rami;
>   Fit sacrae Truncus quisque Columna Domûs.

(This grove is my temple, the spreading branches are the roof; each
trunk forms a pillar of the sacred house.)[1]

It is almost certain, I think, that Marvell[2] had both Benlowes and Cleveland in mind when, in stanza LXIV of *Appleton House*, he wrote:

---

1. *Caroline Poets*, ed. Saintsbury, I 445.
2. The resemblances between Marvell and Benlowes, though not those between
both of them and Cleveland, have been noticed by Maren-Sophie Røstvig, *The
Happy Man*, 1954, pp. 247–8.

> The arching Boughs unite between
> The Columnes of the Temple green;
> And underneath the winged Quires
> Echo about their tuned Fires.

His 'winged Quires' and 'tuned Fires' are (I think I am right in saying) the only pieces of similar 'poetic diction' in *Appleton House*. 'Winged Quires' was pretty clearly suggested by Cleveland's 'winged choiristers', a piece of 'elegance' which, although perhaps rather unexpected from such a poet and in such a context, is not merely decorative, since it initiates (and may even have suggested) the sustained metaphor of a morning service: choiristers—matins—organs—incense. 'Tuned Fires', one of the most extreme examples I have encountered of such elegant periphrasis, and which, had it occurred in some minor Augustan poet, might well have been exhibited as a kind of *reductio ad absurdum* of attempts to avoid calling a spade a spade, was probably suggested by Benlowes's birds who first give out the tune like precentors (*modulantur*) and then sing as a choir. This is the Marvell who amused himself by composing Latin as well as English verses and who, despite his affinities with so many other seventeenth-century poets, is so seldom like Donne and so often and so surprisingly seems to anticipate kinds of poetry still to be written.

It would no doubt be possible to discover in Italian poetry of the sixteenth and seventeenth centuries some developments of this classical topic in a manner at least approaching Cleveland's. It was certainly, I think, a particular variation upon it by Tasso, in a short epigram or 'madrigal',[1] that inspired Strode's *On Chloris walking in the Snow*, first printed in 1632,[2] a poem which became enormously popular, for it appears in numerous miscellanies and manuscript commonplace books, and which may well have done much to attract the attention of other English poets to less specialised varieties of the pastoral hyperbole as fruitful topics for wit:

> I saw fair Chloris walk alone,
> Whilst feathered rain came softly down,
> And Jove descended from his tower
> To court her in a silver shower.

1. *Ritorno di Madonna in tempo di neve* ('La terra si copria d'orrido velo'). Tasso also has a similar poem entitled *Vista impedita della Neve* ('Negro era intorno, e in bianche falde il cielo'): *Rime*, ed. Solerti, II 61, 331.

2. In W. Porter's *Madrigals and Airs*. I quote from Ault's *Seventeenth-Century Lyrics*, 1928, p. 81.

The wanton snow flew on her breast
Like little birds unto their nest;
But overcome with whiteness there,
For grief it thawed into a tear;
Thence falling on her garment's hem,
To deck her, froze into a gem.

This famous poem seems in its turn to have inspired the anonymous
variation, *Lavinia walking in a frosty Morning*, first printed among the
'Excellent poems . . . by other Gentlemen' in Benson's edition of
Shakespeare's *Poems*, 1640:[1]

I'th nonnage of a Winters day,
Lavinia glorious as May,
To give the morne an earlier birth,
Paced a mile of crusted earth,
When each place by which she came,
From her veines conceived flame.
The amorous plant[s] began to strive,
Which should first be sinsitive,
Every hoary headed twigge
Drop'd his Snowy Periwigge,
And each bough his Icy beard.
On either side her walkes[2] was heard
Whispers of decreped wood,
Calling to their rootes for blood:
The gentle Soyle did mildely greete
The welcome kisses of her feete,
And to retaine such a Treasure,
Like waxe dissolving tooke her measure.
Lavinia stood amaz'd to see
Things of yearely certaintie
Thus to rebell against their Season,
And though a stranger to the Reason,
Backe retiring quench'd their heate,
And Winter tooke his former Seate.

---

1. L6ᵛ. In Henry Lawes's *Second Book of Ayres*, 1655, the poem is signed 'I.M.'
2. 1640 'his walkes'. I have also found it necessary to correct in places the
impossible punctuation.

A few pages later in Benson's edition of Shakespeare's *Poems*[1] there is another, very similar, variation, entitled *Vpon a Gentlewoman walking on the Grasse*:

> Sure 'twas the Spring went by, for th'earth did waste
> Her long hid sweets at her approach, and plac'd
> Quicke pregnant flowers upon the verdant grasse,
> To breath new freshnesse where she will'd to passe.
> The tender blade vail'd as she trod and kist
> The foote that covered it, but when it mist
> Her gentle pressure (like a wife whose bed
> Is scorn'd) it droopt, and since hung downe its head:
> Till by a strength Love gave, to entertaine
> Her wish'd returne, it rear'd it selfe againe:
> And now stands tall in pride; but had it seene
> Her face (that court of beauty where the Queene
> Of Love is alwayes resident) it would,
> When the Sunne dallies with it, weepe in cold
> And pearled dew at noone, greev'd that her face
> Might not as did her feete daigne equall grace
> In moving neerer to it . . .

Yet another variation, perhaps more obviously inspired by Strode's poem, was printed in the same year (1640) in the first edition of *Wits Recreations*,[2] where Strode's snow melting for grief has been replaced by the conceit of a contention between sun and wind for the privilege of kissing Flora:

> I saw faire *Flora* take the aire,
> When *Phoebus* shin'd and it was faire;
> The heavens, to allay the heat,
> Sent drops of raine, which gently beat;
> The sun retires, asham'd to see
> That he was barr'd from kissing thee.
> Then *Boreas* took such high disdaine,
> That soon he dri'd those drops again:
> Ah cunning plot and most divine!
> Thus to mix his breath with thine.

1. M2ᵛ.
2. No. 126; Camden Hotten reprint of *Musarum Deliciae*, etc., II 17, *On his Mistris*. According to a MS note by Thorn Drury in his copy of this reprint, the poem is ascribed in a British Museum MS to 'Humphrey Hide'.

Before Carew's death in 1640 and Suckling's death in 1642 versions of the pastoral hyperbole, whether special (the mistress causing snow to melt for grief, sun and wind to contend for the privilege of kissing her, a winter landscape to thaw as at the approach of spring) or general (the mistress causing all things where she moves to flourish or to pay her homage), had evidently become so frequent as to excite satire and parody; for there was printed in Suckling's *Fragmenta Aurea* (1646) the following impudent 'Dialogue' between Carew ('T.C.') and himself ('J.S.') *Vpon my Lady Carlile's walking in Hampton-Court Garden*:

THOM

> Didst thou not find the place inspir'd,
> And flow'rs as if they had desir'd
> No other Sun, start from their beds,
> And for a sight steal out their heads?
> Heardst thou not musick when she talk't?
> And didst not find that as she walkt
> She threw rare perfumes all about
> Such as bean-blossoms newly out,
> Or chafed spices give?—

J.S.

> I must confesse those perfumes (*Tom*)
> I did not smell; nor found that from
> Her passing by, ought sprung up new,
> The flow'rs had all their birth from you;
> For I pass't o're the self same walk,
> And did not find one single stalk
> Of any thing that was to bring
> This unknown after after spring.

THOM

> Dull and insensible, could'st see
> A thing so near a Deity
> Move up and down, and feel no change?

J.S.

> None, and so great, were alike strange,[1]

---

1. i.e. 'To have felt either no change at all, or so great a one as you did, would have been equally strange'.

I had my Thoughts, but not your way,
All are not born (Sir) to the Bay;
Alas! *Tom*, I am flesh and blood,
And was consulting how I could
In spite of masks and hoods descry
The parts deni'd unto the eye;
I was undoing all she wore,
And had she walkt but one turn more,
Eve in her first state had not been
More naked, or more plainly seen.

THOM

'Twas well for thee she left the place,
There is great danger in that face;
But had'st thou view'd her legg and thigh,
And upon that discovery
Search't after parts that are more dear
(As Fancy seldom stops so near)
No time or age had ever seen
So lost a thing as thou hadst been.[1]

Nevertheless, even at a time when the theme had already been so often repeated as to excite Suckling to something like parody, Waller was still able to treat it with a new and almost indefinable combination of qualities in one of his poems to 'Sacharissa', Lady Dorothy Sidney, to whom, it would seem, he first began to pay his addresses towards the end of 1635 and to whom he presumably ceased to address poems after her marriage to Lord Spencer of Wormleighton (later Earl of Sunderland) in July 1639.[2] His poem *At Penshurst*, which was first printed in the 1645 edition of his poems, would seem to have given a new lease of life to the pastoral hyperbole, and some close resemblances, which I shall indicate in footnotes, seem to me to make it almost certain that both Cleveland and Marvell took hints from this poem. Nor is this by any means the only place where Waller, together with that 'easy, sweet and flowing' strain which Dryden and his successors admired, seems to have been the first seventeenth-century poet to practise that particular kind of witty hyperbole which Cleveland and

1. *Fragmenta Aurea*, 1646, p. 27; *Poems of Thomas Carew*, ed. Dunlap, 1949, pp. 227–8.
2. See *The Poems of Edmund Waller*, ed. G. Thorn Drury, I xxiv–vii.

Marvell so delightedly exploited. Consider, for example, *Of her Passing through a Crowd of People*, which also appeared in his 1645 volume:

> As in old chaos (heaven with earth confused,
> And stars with rocks together crushed and bruised)
> The sun his light no further could extend
> Than the next hill, which on his shoulders leaned;
> So in this throng bright Sacharissa fared,
> Oppressed by those who strove to be her guard;
> As ships, though never so obsequious, fall
> Foul in a tempest on their admiral.
> A greater favour this disorder brought
> Unto her servants than their awful thought
> Durst entertain, when thus compelled they pressed
> The yielding marble of her snowy breast.
> While love insults, disguised in the cloud,
> And welcome force, of that unruly crowd.
> So the amorous tree, while yet the air is calm,
> Just distance keeps from his desired palm;
> But when the wind her ravished branches throws
> Into his arms, and mingles all their boughs,
> Though loath he seems her tender leaves to press,
> More loath he is that friendly storm should cease,
> From whose rude bounty he the double use
> At once receives, of pleasure and excuse.[1]

This, admittedly, is stiffer and heavier, less hilarious, aerated and 'high-fantastical' than Cleveland and Marvell, and one can still, as it were, see peeping through it traces of that pompous and inane hyperbole which appears so often in Waller's poems to the King and Queen. Partly, perhaps, because the octosyllabic couplet was more favourable to this kind of writing than the decasyllabic, there is a lighter touch about *The Fall*, a descriptive epigram (for as such almost all the poems we have been considering may be regarded) on a woman who slipped and fell because, apparently, the youth on whom she was leaning was not properly supporting her:

> See! how the willing earth gave way,
> To take the impression where she lay.

1. *Poems*, ed. Thorn Drury, I 51.

See! how the mould, as loth to leave
So sweet a burden, still doth cleave
Close to the nymph's stained garment. Here
The coming spring would first appear,
And all this place with roses strow,
If busy feet would let them grow.
Here Venus smiled to see blind chance
Itself before her son advance,
And a fair image to present,
Of what the boy so long had meant.
'Twas such a chance as this, made all
The world into this order fall;
Thus the first lovers on the clay,
Of which they were composed, lay;
So in their prime, with equal grace,
Met the first patterns of our race.
Then blush not, fair! or on him frown,
Or wonder how you both came down;
But touch him, and he'll tremble straight,
How could he then support your weight?
How could the youth, alas! but bend,
When his whole heaven upon him leaned?
If aught by him amiss were done,
'Twas that he let you rise so soon.[1]

But it was Waller's *At Penshurst*, of which I will here quote
the first sixteen lines, that provided hints for both Cleveland and
Marvell:

Had Sacharissa[2] lived when mortals made
Choice of their deities, this sacred shade
Had held an altar to her power, that gave
The peace and glory which these alleys have;[3]
Embroidered so with flowers where she stood,
That it became a garden of a wood.

1. *Poems*, ed. Thorn Drury, I 96.
2. 1645, 'Dorothea'. I quote from Thorn Drury's edition (I 46), where the text
is based on that of 1686, the last published during Waller's lifetime.
3. Cf. *Appleton House*, st. LXXXVII:

'Tis *She* that to these Gardens gave
That wondrous Beauty which they have.

> Her presence has such more than human grace,
> That it can civilize the rudest place;
> And beauty too, and order, can impart,
> Where nature ne'er intended it, nor art.
> The plants acknowledge this, and her admire,
> No less than those of old did Orpheus' lyre;
> If she sit down, with tops all towards her bowed,
> They round about her into arbours crowd;
> Or if she walk, in even ranks they stand,
> Like some well-marshalled and obsequious band.[1]

Nevertheless, although this may be regarded as an approach towards the manners of Cleveland and Marvell, it is, after all, no more than a rather timid and hesitant approach, and only in the last four lines of the passage quoted does the degree of personification exceed what we might expect to find in, say, Petrarch. Pope, who twice introduces this topic into his youthful pastorals, returns to the generalities of the classical tradition in the following passage (*Spring*, ll. 69–76), where he is confessedly imitating the passage in Virgil's seventh Eclogue, which I have quoted.

STREPHON

> All Nature mourns, the Skies relent in Show'rs,
> Hush'd are the Birds, and clos'd the drooping Flow'rs;
> If *Delia* smile, the Flow'rs begin to spring,
> The Skies to brighten, and the Birds to sing.

DAPHNIS

> All Nature laughs, the Groves are fresh and fair,
> The Sun's mild Lustre warms the vital Air;
> If *Sylvia* smiles, new Glories gild the Shore,
> And vanquish'd Nature seems to charm no more.[2]

And in the lines made famous by Handel (*Summer*, ll. 73–6), where the trees are at least a degree less like a human crowd than those in Waller's poem:

1. Cf. *Upon Phillis walking in a morning*:

> The trees, like yeomen of her guard . . .
> Ranked on each side, with loyal duty
> Weave branches to enclose her beauty.

2. *Poems*, ed. Butt, 1963, p. 127.

Where-e'er you walk, cool Gales shall fan the Glade,
Trees, where you sit, shall crowd into a Shade,
Where-e'er you tread, the blushing Flow'rs shall rise,
And all things flourish where you turn your Eyes.[1]

I make no apology for having treated at some length the history of
the pastoral hyperbole, for consideration of this alone is sufficient to
reveal how much of Marvell's, as of other seventeenth-century, poetry
consists of witty and ingenious elaborations of, or variations upon,
traditional themes.

Although Waller seems to have been the first, or one of the first, of
English poets to develop the classical topic in this way, ingenious
and witty elaborations of this and other classical topics had long been
practised by various Italian and French poets, and it is possible that
Marvell's elaborate compliments to the Young Maria may have been
partly suggested to him, not merely by various things in Waller and
Cleveland, but also by a poem, or series of poems, which, in its general
scheme as well as in its particular detail, has some affinity with *Appleton House*—Théophile de Viau's *La Maison de Silvie* (1624),[2] in which
the poet celebrates his patrons the Duke and Duchess of Montmorency
and their estate at Chantilly: a poem of which an abbreviated and uni-
fied version, entitled *Sylvia's Park*, had been recently (1651) published
by Thomas Stanley, to whom the Lord General's uncle William, son
of the translator of Tasso, had been tutor. Théophile, though without
the epigrammatic wit and the slightly burlesque humour of Marvell,
describes with equal hyperbole and still greater elaboration (and, it
must be admitted, diffuseness) the homage which nature—the 'method-
ised' nature of the domain—pays to its mistress. If, he declares,
Orpheus could move rocks and stones,

---

1. *ibid.*, p. 131.
2. *Oeuvres Complètes*, ed. M. Alleaume, 1885, II 193 ff. The 'poem' is divided
into ten odes, containing an irregular number (from ten to sixteen) of ten-line
octosyllabic stanzas, whose rhyme-scheme (a b a b, c c, d e e d), which Stanley has
preserved, differs considerably from that of the ten-line stanzas in Saint-Amant's
famous poem *La Solitude*. Nearly half the stanzas of Théophile's poem, stanzas
which Stanley has wisely omitted or compressed, are filled, not with witty descriptions of the domain, but with the thinnest and flattest kind of hyperbolical
compliment, with allusions to the poet's misfortunes and imprisonment (he had
been condemned to death for blasphemy, a sentence subsequently commuted to one
of banishment), and (in the concluding ode) with professions—partly hypocritical,
it would seem, and partly ironical—of religious faith.

What stranger hardness must possess
   The object by my Princess grac'd,
If quickned of that happiness,
   To voice its Joyes it do not haste?
Through this proud structures daz'ling Hight,
Through this sweet Walks secure delight,
   What Marble can so solid be,
But is transparent to her Eye?
What Trees and Fountains stealing by,
   But own her for a Deity? . . .

These floating Mirrours, on whose Brow
   Their various figures gently glide,
For love of her shall gently grow,
   In faithful Icy fetters ty'd.
This cheerful Brooks unwrinkled face
Shall smile within its Christal case,
   To see it self made permanent,
And from Times rage secur'd, the deep
Impression of my Cyphers keep,
   And my fair Princess form present.[1]

It is possible (I myself am inclined to think it is probable) that the
hyperbolical conceit in the second of the above stanzas, namely, that
the rippling brook shall be congealed into a smooth and permanent
mirror for the reflection of Sylvia's beauty, suggested to Marvell his
still more elaborate and ingenious comparison between the hyperbolically imagined and described effect of the evening halcyon upon
admiring Nature and that of the Young Maria. Just as the halcyon, he
declares (not, it must be admitted, without a certain clumsiness and
obscurity of syntax), flying between day and night, benumbs admiring
Nature and causes the stream to congeal, in the hope of being able to
fix her shadow (like, as it were, a fly in amber), even so the evening
appearance of Maria temporarily reduces the world to that crystalline
substance into which it will be permanently calcined and refined by
the fires of the Last Judgment.[2]

1. Stanley, *Poems*, ed. G. M. Crump, 1962, pp. 157–8. Théophile, *ed. cit.*, II 195,
196 (Ode I). The next passage quoted is a translation of the opening stanzas of the
second ode in Théophile's poem.

2. 'Philosophers that opinioned the worlds destruction by fire, did never dream
of annihilation, which is beyond the power of sublunary Causes; for the last action
of that element is but vitrification, or a reduction of a body into glass; and therefore

So when the Shadows laid asleep
From underneath these Banks do creep,
And on the River as it flows
With *Eben Shuts* begin to close;
The modest *Halcyon* comes in sight,
Flying betwixt the Day and Night;
And such an horror calm and dumb,
Admiring Nature does benum.

The viscous Air, wheres'ere She fly,
Follows and sucks her Azure dy;
The gellying Stream compacts below,
If it might fix her shadow so;
The stupid Fishes hang, as plain
As *Flies* in *Chrystal* overt'ane;
And Men the silent *Scene* assist,
Chàrm'd with the *Saphir-winged Mist*.

Maria such, and so doth hush
The *World*, and through the *Ev'ning* rush.
No new-born *Comet* such a Train
Draws through the Skie, nor Star new-slain.
For streight those giddy Rockets fail,
Which from the putrid Earth exhale,
But by her *Flames*, in *Heaven* try'd,
Nature is wholly *vitrifi'd*.[1]

(st. LXXXIV–VI)

In the description of '*Sylvia* angling in the Brook' there is perhaps
something more distinctively Marvellian:

---

some of our Chymicks facetiously affirm, that at the last fire all shall be christallized
and reverberated into glass, which is the utmost action of that element' (Sir Thomas
Browne, *Religio Medici*, pt. I, sect. 50, *Works*, ed. Sayle, I 72).

1. Marvell may well have had either or both of two passages in mind: that from
Browne's *Religio Medici* (1642 and 1643) quoted in the preceding footnote, and one
in the first volume (1645) of James Howell's *Epistolae Ho-Elianae*, where, in a letter
from Venice dated 1 June 1621 (Temple Classics ed., I 63), Howell describes how he
observed the process of glass-making and how 'my thoughts were raised to a
higher speculation: that if this small furnace-fire hath virtue to convert such a
small lump of dark dust and sand into such a precious clear body as crystal, surely
that grand universal fire which shall happen at the day of judgment, may by its
violent ardour vitrify and turn to one lump of crystal the whole body of the earth,
nor am I the first that fell upon this conceit'.

> There I beheld the Fishes strife,
> Which first should sacrifice its life,
>   To be the Trophey of her Hook . . .[1]

> The doubtful Sun with equal awe,
> Fear'd to approach or to withdraw:
>   The intentive Stars suspend their glowing.
> No Rage the quiet Billows swell'd,
> *Favonius* his soft breath withheld,
>   The listning Grass refrain'd from growing.[2]

Something more distinctively Marvellian: and yet, after all, is not Théophile's greater leisureliness and elaborateness precisely what is un-Marvellian, and is not the difference more important than the resemblance? It is not so much in his invention of such ingenious hyperboles as in his expression of them, which is at once terse and exuberant, that Marvell reveals his originality. He flashes them at us in such swift succession, as though he were the first person to whom they had ever occurred.

The contrast, one might say, is that between the mere graceful following of a fashion and the wearing of it with a most significant and individual difference. It fortunately happens that we are able to

---

1. The earliest example of this 'conceit' seems to be Juvenal's remark (IV 68–9) about the turbot offered to Domitian:

> Et tua servatum consume in saecula rhombum;
> ipse capi voluit.

> (Consume this turbot, which has been reserved for the age which you adorn. It positively wanted to be caught.)

Ben Jonson, in *To Penshurst*, l. 30, is probably imitating Juvenal, and Carew, in *To Saxham*, ll. 27–8, is probably imitating Jonson. The conceit also occurs in a seventeenth-century manuscript poem, *Upon a Lady's Fishing with an Angle*, ascribed (wrongly, I am inclined to think) to Waller and printed for the first time by Thorn Drury in his edition (II 116):

> See how the numerous fishes of the brook
>   (For now the armour of their scales
>   Nothing against her charms prevails)
> Willingly hang themselves upon her hook;
>   See how they crowd and thronging wait
>   Greedy to catch the proffered bait;
> In her more bright and smoother hands content
> Rather to die, than live in their own watery element

        (ll. 13–20)

One of the most elaborate developments of the conceit is in Donne's poem *The Baite*. It was used by several Italian poets, including Marino (*Rime*, Venice 1603, I 71).

2. *Poems*, ed. Crump, p. 159.

make a direct comparison between what Cleveland's original and
charming development of the pastoral hyperbole in *Phillis walking in a
morning* suggested to Marvell and what it suggested to a young Cambridge poet, seven years younger than Marvell, Nicholas Hookes
(1628–1712), who had been a contemporary of Dryden's at Westminster School and who came up to Trinity, where Dryden followed
him a year later, in 1649. Hookes's *Amanda, a Sacrifice to an unknown
Goddesse*, published in 1653, consists, first, of a number of poems to
a woman whom the poet admits, in his Epistle Dedicatory, to have
been wholly imaginary, and then of a number of miscellaneous poems
in English and Latin, which it is not here necessary to particularise,
but which include a number of funeral elegies on friends and college
dignitaries very much in the manner of those in which Milton and
others had commemorated Hobson the Carrier and in which several
Cambridge men, including Cleveland, who seems to have been the
great master, possibly the originator, of this manner, had, in the volume
to which Milton contributed *Lycidas*, commemorated Edward King.[1]
Hookes was evidently a great admirer of Cleveland, and in his poems
to the imaginary Amanda there are so many obvious attempts to imitate
Cleveland's various experiments in hyperbole and burlesque that one
may be inclined to think it was the reading of Cleveland that made
him a poet, just as Cowley, according to his own account, had been
made a poet by reading Spenser. The most consistently successful and
agreeable of these poems is *To* Amanda *walking in the Garden*, which it
is well worth while to quote in full.[2] The whole idea of it was very

---

1. This, for example, is how Hookes commemorated Dr Cumber '*late Deane of
Carlisle, and sometimes Master of* Trin. Coll. *in* Camb.':

> Who wanting but just one yeare of fourescore,
> I' th' *Colledge* of the *Trinitie* once more,
> Under the *Worlds Tutor* is gone to be
> *Admitted freshman* to Eternity;
> Would I this *Abrams* bosome-pupil were,
> Oh but they're all *Fellowes*, all *Masters* there,
> And with the glorious *Founder* of the place,
> Still richly *feasting*, yet still *saying grace*.

(p. 124)

2. It was quoted by Grosart in illustration of ll. 293 ff. (st. XXXVII–IX) of
Appleton House, as what he called 'a quaint parallel—earlier than Marvell'. It was, of
course, *printed* earlier than Marvell's poem, which, like nearly all his other non-
political poems, remained in manuscript until 1681, but it may have been written
either a year or two earlier or a year or two later than Marvell's. I am grateful to
that too copious and too hasty scholar for having directed my attention to Hookes's
poems.

obviously (perhaps too obviously) suggested to Hookes by Cleveland's
Upon Phillis walking in a morning, and the differences between the two
poems are instructive.

> And now what *Monarch* would not *Gard'ner* be,
> *My faire Amanda's* stately *gate* to see;
> How her feet tempt! how soft and light she treads,
> Fearing to wake the flowers from their beds!
> Yet from their sweet green pillowes ev'ry where,
> They start and gaze about to see *my Faire*;
> Look at yon flower yonder, how it growes
> Sensibly! how it opes its leaves and blowes,
> Puts its best *Easter clothes* on, neat and gay!
> *Amanda's* presence makes it *holy-day*:
> Look how on tip-toe that fair *lilie* stands
> To look on thee, and court thy whiter hands
> To gather it! I saw in yonder croud
> That *Tulip-bed*, of which *Dame-Flora's* proud,
> A short dwarfe flower did enlarge its stalk,
> And shoot an inch to see *Amanda* walk;
> Nay, look, my *Fairest*, look how fast they grow!
> Into a scaffold method spring! as though
> Riding to *Parl'ament* were to be seen
> In pomp and state some *royal* am'rous Queen:
> The gravel'd walks, though ev'n as a die,
> Lest some loose pebble should offensive lie,
> Quilt themselves o're with downie mosse for thee,
> The walls are hang'd with blossom'd tapestrie;
> To hide her nakednesse when look't upon,
> The maiden fig-tree puts *Eves* apron on;
> The broad-leav'd *Sycomore*, and ev'ry tree
> Shakes like the trembling *Aspe*, and bends to thee,
> And each leaf proudly strives with fresher aire,
> To fan the curled tresses of thy hair;
> Nay, and the *Bee* too, with his wealthie thigh,
> Mistakes his *hive*, and to thy lips doth flie;
> Willing to treasure up his *honey* there,
> Where *honey-combs* so sweet and plenty are:
> Look how that pretty modest *Columbine*
> Hangs down its head to view those feet of thine!

> See the fond motion of the *Strawberrie*,
> Creeping on th' earth to go along with thee!
> The lovely *violet* makes after too,
> Unwilling yet, *my Dear*, to part with you;
> The *knot-grasse* and the *dazies* catch thy toes
> To kisse *my Faire ones* feet before she goes;
> All court and wish me lay *Amanda* down,
> And give *my Dear* a new *green* flower'd *gown*.
> > Come let me kisse thee falling, kisse at rise,
> > Thou in the *Garden*, I in *Paradise*.[1]

This poem is not without a certain charm and it reveals a not inconsiderable talent, but, in comparison with Cleveland's poem and, still more, in comparison with the various things which Cleveland's poem suggested to Marvell, it is unsurprising, diluted, and rather mechanical. The kind of personification, or metaphorisation, which in Cleveland's poem was so fresh and breath-taking, has here been reduced to a kind of formula, which, one feels, dozens of other clever young minor poets could have applied equally well. I even fancy that, if I thought it worth while, I could do equally well myself—if, for example, I took some list of flowers, trees and birds from some minor Elizabethan pastoral or descriptive poem, or even, perhaps, from some medieval narrative poem, and, applying Hookes's formula, represented them as paying homage to the beloved instead of merely surrounding her. Indeed, something very like Hookes's formula had already been used by Robert Heath, a poet belonging to an older generation (he may have been the Robert Heath who was admitted at Corpus Christi College, Cambridge, in 1634), in one of the poems in his *Clarastella* (1650), a volume which had been published three years earlier than Hookes's. Heath too may well have been inspired by Cleveland's poem on Phillis, and it may well have been Heath's poem *On Clarastella, Walking in her Garden* which suggested to Hookes a manner of 'imitating' Cleveland not altogether beyond his own capacities; for this is how Heath deals with his subject:

> Here the violet bows to greet
> Her with homage to her feet;
> There the lily pales with white
> Got by her reflexed light:
> Here a rose in crimson dye
> Blushes through her modesty;

1. *Amanda*, 1653, pp. 42–4.

> There a pansy hangs his head
> 'Bout to shrink into his bed,
> 'Cause so quickly she passed by,
> Not returning suddenly;
> Here the currants red and white
> In yon green bush at her sight
> Peep through their shady leaves, and cry,
> 'Come, eat me', as she passes by;
> There a bed of camomil . . .
> Here the pinks in rows do throng . . .
> There the flexive turnsole[1] bends[2]—

and there we may leave Heath and his poem, perhaps with the reflexion that such verse is really too easy. I could myself, I think, produce a very tolerable imitation of Heath, or even of Hookes, but I certainly could not hope to imitate Cleveland or Marvell. I have spoken, as it might seem contemptuously, of 'Hookes's formula': a formula, however, is only objectionable when we become too aware of it. What I have called the 'pastoral hyperbole' is, like so many other ideas or topics of classical origin, a kind of indefinitely expandable rhetorical formula, and, in the use of such formulae, the difference between a good and an inferior poet may be expressed either by saying that the good poet knows when to stop and the inferior poet does not, or that, while the good poet makes us forget, or fail to notice, that he is applying a formula, the inferior poet soon convinces us that he is performing a kind of mechanical operation, going carefully (and, perhaps, quite cleverly) through a prescribed list or catalogue, of which he is resolved to spare us nothing. The difference is very noticeable in the successful and unsuccessful use of Senecan formulae by Elizabethan dramatists. As long ago as 1754 Lessing showed that the hint for some of the most famous lines Shakespeare ever wrote,

> Will all great Neptune's ocean wash this blood
> Clean from my hand? No, this my hand will rather
> The multitudinous seas incarnadine,
> Making the green one red,

came to him from a speech where Seneca's Hippolytus declares that neither Tanaïs nor Maeotis nor Ocean itself can cleanse him from what

---

1. The marygold, which turns towards the sun.
2. I have quoted the poem from Ault's *Seventeenth-Century Lyrics*, 1928, p. 235.

he regards as the adulterous and polluting touch of Phaedra (*Hippolytus*, 715–18), and from a speech where Seneca's Hercules, having killed his wife and children in a fit of divinely inflicted madness, declares that not Tanaïs, Nile or Tigris, not Rhine, Tagus or Maeotis, not all the waters of Ocean, could cleanse his hand (*Hercules Furens*, 323–9). Had some minor 'Senecal man' been writing a tragedy on Macbeth, or perhaps even had Shakespeare himself treated the subject at the beginning of his career, they might well have made Macbeth enumerate all, or most, of the rivers of Britain and Europe before finally reaching ocean itself.

> Not poppy nor mandragora,
> Nor all the drowsy syrups of the world
> Shall ever medicine thee to that sweet sleep
> Which thou ow'dst yesterday.

> Not that faire field
> Of *Enna*, where *Proserpin* gathring flowrs . . .
> nor that sweet Grove
> Of *Daphne* by *Orontes*, and th'inspir'd
> *Castalian* Spring, might with this Paradise
> Of *Eden* strive; nor that *Nyseian* Ile
> Girt with the River *Triton* . . .
> Nor where *Abassin* Kings thir issue Guard,
> Mount *Amara* . . .

Here are two more superb examples of the use of the same classical formula by two great poets, one of whom is not commonly considered as an exponent of the classical tradition. It is easy to perceive how in each case the mighty effect is achieved by an utter unsuperfluousness, every syllable performing the maximum amount of work, and to imagine how feebly and drearily the same formula might have been applied to the same subject by an inferior poet. While, however, a rhetorical formula such as this could be magnificently applied by great poets to a great variety of subjects (uncleansable guilt, unrestorable peace of mind, supra-terrestrial beauty), the use of the pastoral hyperbole was necessarily limited to pastoral or semi-pastoral, and successful elaboration of it in the manner suggested to Marvell by Cleveland required, in addition to sheer literary skill, a peculiar combination of qualities—wit, sense of beauty, quickness and flexibility of mind—such as even very great poets have not always possessed. Perhaps indeed Marvell was the only poet whom Cleveland inspired to write poetry that is permanently enjoyable. It was the Cleveland who declared that, with the drowning of Edward King, 'Neptune hath got an Universitie,' who could be, and was, most successfully imitated by others. The result was some truly astonishing pieces of intellectual agility, which were once immensely admired, but for which now the only appropriate place would seem to be some museum of undergraduate wit.

But, in making Nature pay her respects to the 'Young Maria' in the concluding stanzas of *Appleton House*, Marvell was taking up again a theme which he had already treated in the shorter, and presumably earlier, poem *Upon the Hill and Grove at Bill-borow*, also, like the Appleton House poem, addressed 'to the Lord Fairfax', a poem which, partly at least, may be regarded as an elaborate expansion of the idea, or conceit, in Cleveland's poem *Upon Phillis walking in a morning*. I have already remarked that in each of those two very different poems, *A Dialogue between the Resolved Soul, and Created Pleasure* and *A Dialogue between the Soul and Body*, Marvell has preserved the proper *decorum* and has done exactly what he intended to do. The same may be said of the Bilborough and Appleton House poems: their fantastic hyperboles, their toppling exaggerations, are not to be regarded as lapses of taste or failures in intention. They are essentially private poems, almost, one is tempted to say, private jokes, intended only for the eye of Marvell's friend and patron the Lord General, to whose so well-attested modesty the deliberately exaggerated and hyperbolical compliments must have caused much amusement. Marvell's first reader was also, what Mr Eliot has thought it desirable that a critic should be, a 'poetical practitioner', an industrious, though not, it must be admitted, a very distinguished, one; and no doubt he admired in these two poems a degree both of wit and of poetry which he himself could never hope to achieve.

In each of these poems (as in several others) Marvell has divided his octosyllabic couplets into stanzas of eight lines, an excellent thing in poems so largely descriptive, and in which he might otherwise have been tempted to dwell upon some favourite detail or fancy at disproportionate length. As it is, the division into stanzas has compelled him to achieve a certain neatness, economy, and precision, and to begin and complete at least one idea or conceit in each stanza.

Before quoting the poem, I will try to exhibit, by means of a brief prose analysis, the close and consecutive argument running through the ten stanzas of that delightful trifle *Upon the Hill and Grove at Bill-*

borow, the firm logical framework around which the rather Clevelandish hyperboles are woven. I, The hill is a perfect hemisphere—it might have been the model by which the world was made. II, It offers a lesson in humility to loftier and abrupter mountains. III, It rises only in an attempt to raise the plain. IV, And yet it is a landmark for sailors. V, It is crowned by a clump of trees whose sacred shade the felt presence of their awe-inspiring master has preserved from the axe. VI, The trees have been preserved too by respect for her whose name he would engrave on their bark, although it was already in their hearts. VII, For they too have a sense of love and reverence; they grow with their lord's advancement, although they never grew so straight and so green as under their present possessor. VIII, Now, though, they are content to be merely rooted, and sometimes to whisper their master's famous deeds to the breeze. IX, We know, they say, that he once thundered through groves of pikes and raised mountains of dying and that our branches cannot provide all the civic garlands he deserves. X, True, but he retreats to your shades from his own brightness, and cares for height only when it offers retirement.

Upon the Hill and Grove at Bill-borow

To the Lord Fairfax

I

See how the arched Earth does here
Rise in a perfect Hemisphere!
The stiffest Compass could not strike
A Line more circular and like;
Nor softest Pensel draw a Brow
So equal as this Hill does bow.
It seems as for a Model laid,
And that the World by it was made.

II

Here learn ye Mountains more unjust,
Which to abrupter greatness thrust,
That do with your hook-shoulder'd height
The Earth deform and Heaven fright,
For whose excrescence ill design'd,
Nature must a new Center find,
Learn here those humble steps to tread,
Which to securer Glory lead.

III

See what a soft access and wide
Lyes open to its grassy side;
Nor with the rugged path deterrs
The feet of breathless Travellers.
See then how courteous it ascends,
And all the way it rises bends;
Nor for it self the height does gain,
But only strives to raise the Plain.

IV

Yet thus it all the field commands,
And in unenvy'd Greatness stands,
Discerning further then the Cliff
Of Heaven-daring *Teneriff*.
How glad the weary Seamen hast
When they salute it from the Mast!
By Night the Northern Star their way
Directs, and this no less by Day.

V

Upon its crest this Mountain grave
A Plump of aged Trees does wave.
No hostile hand durst ere invade
With impious Steel the sacred Shade.
For something alwaies did appear
Of the *great Masters* terrour there:
And Men could hear his Armour still
Ratling through all the Grove and Hill.

VI

Fear of the *Master*, and respect
Of the great *Nymph* did it protect;
Vera the *Nymph* that him inspir'd,
To whom he often here retir'd,
And on these Okes ingrav'd her Name;
Such Wounds alone these Woods became:
But ere he well the Barks could part
'Twas writ already in their Heart.

VII

For they ('tis credible) have sense,
As We, of Love and Reverence,
And underneath the Courser Rind
The *Genius* of the house do bind.
Hence they successes seem to know,
And in their *Lord's* advancement grow;
But in no Memory were seen
As under this so streight and green.

VIII

Yet now no further strive to shoot,
Contented if they fix their Root.
Nor to the winds uncertain gust,
Their prudent Heads too far intrust.
Onely sometimes a flutt'ring Breez
Discourses with the breathing Trees;
Which in their modest Whispers name
Those Acts that swell'd the Cheek of Fame.

IX

Much other Groves, say they, then these
And other Hills him once did please.
Through Groves of Pikes he thunder'd then,
And Mountains rais'd of dying Men.
For all the *Civick Garlands* due
To him our Branches are but few.
Nor are our Trunks enow to bear
The *Trophees* of one fertile Year.

X

'Tis true, ye Trees nor ever spoke
More certain *Oracles* in Oak.
But Peace (if you his favour prize)
That Courage its own Praises flies.
Therefore to your obscurer Seats
From his own Brightness he retreats:
Nor he the Hills without the Groves,
Nor Height but with Retirement loves.

In considering the *Dialogue between the Soul and Body* I remarked that the chief difference between Marvell's descriptive wit and Donne's was that Marvell surprised and delighted, not, like Donne, by bringing so much into his subject, but by getting so much out of it; not by contriving to relate his subject to the most unlikely and astonishing kinds of otherness, but by a kind of hyperbolical personification of what was immediately before him. What distinguishes even such a comparative trifle as the Bilborough poem from anything at all like it in seventeenth-century poetry is the balance, the equivalence, between the literal and the metaphorical, the factual and the hyperbolical, the pictorial and the conceptual. The hill, or its clump of trees, or both, are visibly present in each stanza, and nothing else is brought in except their master and mistress, the sailors to whom they serve as a landmark (st. IV), and the loftier mountains to which they offer a lesson in humility (st. II: the moral emblematism, half serious, half playful, in this and in the two following stanzas is, of course, remote from all that is most characteristic in Donne's poetry). Hints and suggestions came to Marvell from many poets, and without the examples and the stimulation they provided his best poetry would never have been written: nevertheless, in his own peculiar balancing and blending, now imitating, now adapting, now almost transforming qualities and procedures that had pleased him in other poets, he reveals a most individual and unmistakable originality.

(ii) Appleton House *in general*

Upon Appleton House, to my Lord Fairfax, the longest of Marvell's poems (776 lines), is less tightly constructed than the Bilborough poem, but his descriptive wit there finds far greater scope and achieves far greater variety. Let us begin with a brief analysis of the whole poem.

This house is not an ambitious but a modest building (st. 1–4, with burlesque satire on the disproportion between man and his buildings). Future ages will wonder how such a giant as the Lord General could live in such a lowly cell, the greater in the less (st. 5–6). He, however, can endure its lowliness better than it can support his greatness (st. 7–8). It was built merely as an inn to entertain its lord for a while (st. 9). But although his other houses are fitter for their master, the glory of this house is that its surroundings belong to nature, not to art (st. 10). Its history (st. 11 ff.). Speech by a nun of the former Cistercian Priory to the heiress Isabel Thwaites, whom William Fairfax married in 1518, although her aunt the Prioress had shut her up (st. 13–25). Fairfax first tried to dissuade Isabel (st. 26–8), then got an order for her release (st. 29–34). At the dissolution he obtained the leave of the Priory (st. 35). The gardens, which the 'hero' (Sir Thomas, son of this marriage) laid out 'in the just figure of a fort' (st. 36–40). But what fate has befallen the Garden of England? (st. 41–3). The man who might have made it flourish like his own has preferred retirement (st. 44). He weeded ambition but tilled conscience (st. 45). Transition to the meadows (st. 46). The meadows and the mowers (st. 47–54). The haycocks (st. 55). The cattle in the mown meadows (st. 56–8). The flooded meadows (st. 59–60), from which the poet retires to the wood (st. 61–70), where he indulges his easy philosophy (st. 71–8). Return to the meadows and the now shrunken river, where he fishes (st. 79–81). But both he and Nature must show their respect to the Young Maria, her beauty, and her virtue (st. 82–96). The salmon-fishers now begin to hoist their boats and it grows dark (st. 97).

In the description of the house itself, with its compliments to the Master and his ancestors, with which the poem begins, and in the description of Nature's homage to the 'Young Maria', with which it concludes, the hyperbolical personification (which, as we have seen, may well have been suggested by a poem of Cleveland's) has much affinity with that in the Bilborough poem; but in the more direct, pictorial, and (as one might say) for-its-own-sake description of the garden, the meadow and the woods, which intervenes, Marvell is providing, in his own characteristic fashion, a 'catalogue of delights' which has some affinity with those of Milton in *L'Allegro* and *Il Penseroso*. And just as the passage about the salmon-fishers who,

> like *Antipodes* in Shoes,
> Have shod their *Heads* in their *Canoos*,

proves that Marvell had read Cleveland, so likewise the phrase 'gadding vines' in

> Bind me ye *Woodbines* in your 'twines,
> Curle me about ye gadding *Vines*

> (st. LXXVII)

proves that he had read Milton's *Lycidas*:[1]

> Thee Shepherd, thee the Woods, and desert Caves,
> With wilde Thyme and the gadding Vine o'regrown,
> And all their echoes mourn.
>
> (ll. 39–41)

And, since Marvell had certainly read *Lycidas*, it may be assumed (even though he has not, I think, any unmistakable verbal indebtednesses to them) that he had also read *L'Allegro* and *Il Penseroso*. It is also possible that he knew (perhaps through the Lord General) that other very popular 'catalogue of delights', which includes so many touches of what was already beginning to be called 'romantic', Saint-Amant's *La Solitude*, a poem which at some period of his life Fairfax himself translated, and which was also to be translated by Mrs Katherine Philips (the 'Matchless Orinda', 1631–64).[2]

---

1. And also (it seems almost certain) Randolph's *A Pastorall Courtship*, where, in a very un-Miltonic passage, the woodbine and its twines, as well as the vine, appears:

> Come let those thighes, those legs, those feet
> With mine in thousand windings meet,
> And woven in more subtle twines
> Then woodbine, Ivy, or the vines.

(*Poems*, ed. Thorn Drury, p. 112).

2. Fairfax's translation is in Bodleian MS Fairfax 40 (a presumably autograph collection of his poems), pp. 552 ff., and MS Fairfax 38 (a collection transcribed for him by his cousin Henry, later fourth Baron Fairfax), pp. 307 ff. The most conveniently accessible text (first printed, I think, by Clement Markham in *A Life of the Great Lord Fairfax*, 1870, pp. 419 ff.) is in M. A. Gibb's *The Lord General*, 1938, pp. 283 ff. Orinda's version is in Saintsbury's *Caroline Poets*, I 601 ff. Orinda translated all of Saint-Amant's twenty stanzas, but Fairfax omitted five. Both set out to translate the poem into stanzas of the same length (ten lines) as those of the original, but with the same alteration of the original rhyme-scheme (abab instead of abba) in the first four lines; while, though, Orinda was able to carry this through to the end, Fairfax was often stumped for a rhyme: three of his stanzas are a line short, and in others he has both departed from his original rhyme-scheme and left lines that do not rhyme. Since in MS Fairfax 40 two stanzas have been inadvertently run together, the second half of V should have been numbered VI; of what appears as IX the first half should have been numbered X and the second half XI; and the last stanza should have been numbered, not XIII, but XV. In MS Fairfax 38 Henry Fairfax has written the poem with no divisions at all, and the Lord General has placed pilcrows in the margins and written at the end of the poem: 'This mark shew's ther should be a little distance betwixt Paragraphs.'

(iii) Appleton House *as a poem celebrating a patron's estate*

Formally and externally, though scarcely, perhaps, actually and essentially, *Appleton House* may be regarded as an example of a very ancient and well-established *genre*, that of poems describing a friend's or patron's estate and praising the virtues of its owner. Actually and essentially it is rather a sequence of descriptive epigrams than a recognisable and characteristic example of this particular *genre*, and it is with the various kinds of description in it, and the ways in which they resemble and differ from earlier, contemporary and later descriptions, that I shall be primarily concerned. Nevertheless, before proceeding to a detailed examination of its more essential qualities, I will say something of the *genre* to which, with all its characteristically Marvellian departures and differences, *Appleton House* is at least formally related.

The earliest examples of the *genre* are Martial's longish epigram (III lviii, fifty-one lines) dwelling pointedly and Horatianly on the contrast between the unproductive, imitation and merely suburban country seat ('villa') of Bassus, whom he is addressing, and the modest but genuine and productive one (similar, perhaps, to Horace's Sabine Farm) of their friend Faustinus at Baiae, and Statius's much longer, most un-Horatian, and rather vulgarly panegyrical description of the villas of Manilius Vopiscus at Tibur (*Silvae*, I iii, 110 lines) and of Pollius Felix at Surrentum (Sorrento, *Silvae*, II ii, 154 lines). Martial (*c.* A.D. 42—A.D. 102) and Statius (*c.* A.D. 45—A.D. 96) were contemporaries, but the contrast between their manners and attitudes in these poems is enormous. There is much description in Martial's poem, but it is exclusively of the cheerful business of all the members of Faustinus's establishment, of the simple gifts brought by visiting neighbours, and of the homely but generous hospitality of the owner himself. It was the model (he has even imitated some of its verbal detail) for Ben Jonson's fine poem *To Penshurst*, which itself, together with Martial's, was the model for Carew's considerably inferior poem *To Saxham*[1] and much less inferior one *To my friend G. N. from Wrest.*[2] The longer and utterly different poems of Statius, describing prospects and buildings rather than activities, and full of hyperbolical panegyric, were probably in some sort the models for various poets who wrote much longer poems than those of Jonson and Carew in praise of their

1. *Poems*, ed. Dunlap, p. 27.   2. *op cit.*, p. 86.

patrons' estates: for the Polish poet Casimir Sarbiewski, who, as a
Latin poet, enjoyed a European reputation, and who celebrated in a
long Latin ode the estate of his patron the Duke of Bracciano;[1] for
Théophile, who, as we have seen,[2] celebrated the country seat of his
patrons the Duke and Duchess of Montmorency in the poem which
Stanley paraphrased as *Sylvia's Park*; and even (despite the enormous
difference in manner, spirit and attitude) for Marvell, who, as we shall
see, seems to have taken a hint from Statius in at least one passage in
Appleton House.

While Horace, in addressing even the most exalted of his friends,
always preserves an attitude of manly independence and spiritual
equality, and is not afraid of occasionally submitting Maecenas himself
to a little of what an acquaintance of mine used to call 'crural expansion',
and while Marvell's attitude to the Lord General is essentially similar,
Statius's approach to his wealthy patrons is essentially that of what
Milton contemptuously called 'a rhyming parasite'. How utterly un-
Horatian and, as it would have seemed to Horace, who died some
fifty years before Statius was born, how shockingly un-Roman, is the
gaping admiration, devoid of all irony, with which he describes their
Persicos adparatus and *divitias operosiores*! 'Shall I describe the gilded
beams, the marble, the water-nymphs [i.e. the h. and c.] running through
every bedroom, the smoking baths?' he exclaims (34–46) in his poem
on Manilius Vopiscus's villa at Tibur (Tivoli); and at the beginning of
his poem on that of Pollius Felix at Sorrento, which stood on some
coastal height between two headlands, when one is expecting a description of the bay, one gets—what? 'The first charm of the place is a
smoking bath-house with two cupolas, and a stream of fresh water
from the land meeting the salt brine' (17–19). 'Thence a colonnade
[*porticus*] climbs stairwise up the cliff, vast as a city [*urbis opus*], and its
long line of roof gains mastery over the rugged rocks' (30–1). This,
the sort of thing Horace might have described (indeed, did describe)
only to condemn,[3] Statius describes with ecstatic admiration. After a
characteristically pompous and vulgar description of Pollius's statuary,
which Statius concludes by congratulating him on his love of what is
Greek, we do indeed get what, despite its inflated beginning, is a rather
charming piece of Alexandrian romanticism:

---

1. A translation of Casimir's *Odes*, with a Latin text, was published in 1646 by
G. Hills. The ode in question is on pp. 105–21.
2. pp. 237–8.
3. In, for example, *Odes*, II xv, xviii (especially ll 17 ff.), III i 33 ff.

Why should I rehearse the wealth of the countryside, the fallows flung out into the sea and the cliffs steeped in Bacchus's nectar? Often in autumn-time, when the grapes are ripening, a Nereid climbs the rocks, and under cover of the shades of night brushes the sea-water from her eyes with a leafy vine-spray, and snatches sweet clusters from the hills. Often is the vintage sprinkled by the neighbouring foam; Satyrs plunge into the water, and Pan-gods from the mountain are fain to grasp the sea-nymph as she flies naked through the waves.[1]

Statius concludes by congratulating his patron on his wealth and on his superiority to Fortune. He does not actually say that it is Pollius's wealth that enables him to despise Fortune, but the mere fact that he should have associated the two things without a trace of irony seems to reveal the hollowness and vulgarity of his whole attitude to life. The doctrines both of the 'Gargettian author' (as he calls Epicurus) and of the Stoics are here no more than topics for rhetorical elaboration.

Long mayst thou live, enriched beyond Midas' wealth and Lydian gold, blest above the diadems of Euphrates and of Troy; whom neither fickle power nor the shifting mob, nor laws nor camps can vex, whose great heart, raised sublime over all desire, doth quell hope and fear, who are beyond the will of Fate and dost baffle the enmity of Fortune,[2] thee the last day shall find, not bewildered in the maze of things, but sated with life and ready to depart. But we, a worthless folk, slaves at the beck of transient blessings and wishes ever new, are tossed from chance to chance: thou from thy mind's high citadel dost look down upon our wanderings and laughest at human joys.[3]

1. 98–106 (Loeb translation).
2.   Qui pectore magno
     spemque metumque domas voto sublimior omni,
     exemptus fatis indignantemque refellens
     Fortunam.

If *voto* is the true reading, it would seem to mean that Pollius is raised not merely above desire but above the need for prayer. What Lucretius and Virgil thought might be achieved by philosophy, Pollius has achieved with a million sesterces!

3. 121–32 (Loeb translation). The passage reads almost like a parody and vulgarisation of that famous one at the beginning of the second book of the *De Rerum Natura*, where Lucretius declares that it is sweet to look from the land at someone contending with the stormy sea, and sweet to watch a battle without sharing its danger, but sweetest of all to look down from the ramparts of wisdom upon the errings and strayings of the generality of men: not, he concedes (in two

Nevertheless, enormous as is the difference both of Statius's description and his eulogies from those of Marvell, there can be little doubt that as what may be called estate-poems, his two poems provided, if not exactly models, at any rate precedents for Marvell as for others. And there is at least one passage (107–11) in Statius's second poem which perhaps suggested one in *Appleton House*—that where Pollius's villa at Sorrento is exhorted, with characteristically pedantic and Alexandrian periphrasis, not to let itself be outshone by his other villas at Tibur, Puteoli and Tarentum:

> Sis felix, tellus, dominis ambobus in annos
> Mygdonii Pyliique senis, nec nobile mutes
> servitium, nec te cultu Tirynthia vincat
> aula Dicarchaeique sinus, nec saepius istis
> blanda Therapnaei placeant vineta Galaesi.

(Be gracious, O domain, to your master and mistress, till they reach the years of Tithonus and of Nestor, and neither exchange this noble servitude for another nor let the Tirynthian hall [the villa at Tibur] or the Dicarchaean bay [the villa at Puteoli] outdo you in dutifulness [*cultu* is probably being used rather in this active sense than in that of 'cultivatedness' or 'elegance'], or the alluring vineyards of Therapnaean Galaesus [the villa at Tarentum] please them more often.)

Marvell may have had these lines in mind when he wrote (st. X):

> Him *Bishops-Hill*, or *Denton* may,
> Or *Bilbrough*, better hold then they:
> But Nature here hath been so free
> As if she said leave this to me.

It is true that, while Statius seems to proclaim that the villa at Sorrento

---

lines where the fundamental contrast between even the noblest paganism and Christianity becomes perhaps more strikingly apparent than anywhere else in ancient literature), that anyone's being afflicted is a delightful pleasure, but because it is sweet to look upon evils from which you yourself are exempt:

> non quia vexari quemquamst iucunda voluptas,
> sed quibus ipse malis careas quia cernere suave est.

With Lucretius contemplation of the sweetness of 'exemption' was not incompatible with nobility; with Statius it has degenerated into servile eulogies of wealth and power.

is in no respect inferior to the other three, Marvell declares that Appleton House, with its humble appurtenances, is inferior to the other three
Fairfax residences in everything but 'Nature'. It is, indeed, just possible
(though unlikely, in view of the preceding descriptions of the bath-
house, the ascending colonnade, the statuary, and other sophistications) that he may have supposed Statius to be here introducing some
sort of contrast between Nature and Art, and that he took the passage
to mean something like: 'Don't let the villas at Tibur and Puteoli,
with their cultivatedness, outdo you [in your simplicity].' This, however, is not a point I should care to press. Even if the resemblance
between the two passages is no more than superficial, it is sufficient
to indicate the *genre* to which *Appleton House* at least formally belongs.

Although it may be doubted whether it was at all widely known
by Renaissance poets, I will mention, before leaving this subject, an
estate-poem by a much later Latin poet, the Gallo-Roman nobleman
Sidonius Apollinaris (*c.* A.D. 430—*c.* 480), who lived during the
chaotic years of the first break-up of the Roman Empire in the West,
and who, after holding various high offices, was made Bishop of
Clermont Ferrand. He was a patriotic and worthy man, but, like so
many other late Latin writers, an execrable poet, for he, like them, had
been persuaded by teachers of rhetoric that poetry was essentially an
art of what several of our Elizabethan critics called 'beautification'.
His poem on the 'Burgus' (German *Burg* and—in place-names—French
bourg), or 'castle', of his friend Pontius Leontius of Bordeaux was one
of his youthful productions (*Carmina*, XXII). He introduced it with a
prose epistle and appended to it a prose epilogue, in which he defended
its length (235 lines) by appealing, as precedents, to four poems in
Statius's *Silvae*, including one of the two estate-poems I have mentioned:

> Should anyone consider that such a lengthy poem deserves censure
> for going beyond the brevity of an epigram, it is perfectly clear
> that he has not been in the habit of reading the *Baths of Etruscus* [I v],
> or the *Hercules of Surrentum* [III i], or the *Locks of Flavius Earinus*
> [III iv], or the *Tiburtine Home of Vopiscus* [I iii], or indeed anything
> from the little *Silvae* of our Statius; for that man of most assured
> reputation does not cramp any of these descriptions within the
> narrow limits of two-lined or four-lined poems, but rather does
> what the lyric poet Horace enjoins in the *Art of Poetry*: once he has
> introduced his subject, he appropriately enlarges it by the repeated use

of stock 'purple patches' (*multis isdemque purpureis locorum communium pannis semel inchoatas materias decenter extendit*).[1]

Sidonius is referring to *Ars Poetica* 14–19, which he (no doubt like his teachers) seems to have completely misunderstood. Horace begins his Epistle to the Pisos (it was not he who called it the *Ars Poetica*) by putting what is commonly understood as 'poetic licence' into its proper place, insisting, like Milton,[2] that *decorum* is 'the grand master-piece to observe'. After insisting on the absurdity of supposing that in a poem anything may be joined with anything, he proceeds:

> Inceptis gravibus plerumque et magna professis
> purpureus, late qui splendeat, unus et alter
> adsuitur pannus, cum lucus et ara Dianae
> et properantis aquae per amoenos ambitus agros
> aut flumen Rhenum aut pluvius describitur arcus.
> sed nunc non erat his locus.

(Often on to poems beginning grandly and promising great things this and that purple patch is stitched, to emit a spreading glitter when Diana's grove and altar and 'winding through pleasant fields of that swift stream', or the river Rhine, or the rainbow is being described. This, though, was not the place for them.)

Horace means that such virtuoso descriptions, though they might perhaps be appropriate in some other kind of poem, are out of keeping with the weight and dignity of epic. Sidonius, however, seems to have supposed him to be recommending the frequent use of such 'purple patches' in all poetry whatsoever—indeed, to be declaring that it is in the stitching-on of 'purple panes of topic' that the art of poetry essentially consists. Certainly, in his poem on the Castle of Pontius Leontius, Sidonius has done his best to exemplify this most un-Horatian ideal. His beginning tells us what we may expect:

May you visit the stables of the Bistonian King [i.e., Diomedes, who fed his mares on human flesh], the altars of Busiris [the Egyptian king, who sacrificed foreign visitors until he was killed by Hercules], the table of Antiphates [Homer's king of the cannibal Laestrygones], the Tauric realm of Thoas [King of Taurus, where human sacrifices were offered], and the Cyclops who was robbed of his sight

1. Loeb translation.
2. *Of Education* (*Prose Works*, Bohn's ed., III 474).

by the cunning of the man of Ithaca . . . stranger, whoever you may be, that have visited the Burg and yet propose to keep silent about it.

He then invokes the muse Erato, and requests her to reveal, in a strain accompanied by the dancing of satyrs and dryads, the origin of the house; and this leads to a long and pompous description of the triumph of Bacchus and how, as he was hastening through the air towards Thebes, he met Phoebus in a chariot drawn by gryphons and surrounded by muses; how Phoebus declared that Thebes, and its surroundings, now polluted by Pentheus and later to be polluted by Oedipus, were no fit places for their joint habitation, and that a far more suitable spot was a hill near the junction of the Garonne and the Dordogne. 'Some day, when his land shall be under Latin sway, Paulinus Pontius, the founder of the family, shall surround that hill with walls, and the towers shall soar beyond earth's atmosphere' (117–19). Phoebus then proceeds to describe the future castle, and begins, like Statius, with the baths: 'The house rises from the river's brim and gleaming baths are set within the circuit of the battlements' (127–8). A few details emerge from the sea of words. 'The house-wall is faced with slabs of cut marble up to the gilded ceiling, which is right fitly concealed by the yellow metal, for the rich prosperity of the house, brooking no secrecy, reveals its wealth when thus it hides its roof' (146–9). 'Higher up the granaries multiply with their long stretch of buildings and with produce within so abundant that even their vast space is cramped. Hither shall come as great a harvest as is reaped in,' etc., etc. (169 ff.) 'Then there is a summer portico exposed on one side to the chill north: at the other end a harmless warmth comes out from the winter baths and tempers the air of the place when the season requires' (179–81). The winter room, or hall, of the master and mistress with its log-fire, is described, and, joined to it, weaving-chambers which the founder dared to build in a style that vied with the temples of Pallas (187–93). From it a spacious colonnade leads to a lofty dining-room, with folding doors and an adjacent fish-tank (204 ff.). Bacchus accepts Phoebus's proposal that here they should make their joint home.

When we try to assess the influence on Renaissance poetry of what are commonly called 'the classics', we tend to forget that in what has survived of Latin poetry the merely rhetorical greatly predominates over what properly deserves to be called 'classical'. For example, in contrast to that 'Horatian' epigram of Martial's which inspired Jonson's poem *To Penshurst*, there is an enormous mass of verse

essentially similar to these estate-poems of Statius and Sidonius, verse
in which the 'matter' or 'subject' is inflated, 'beautified', dolled-up with
what Horace called 'purple panes' and Sidonius 'purple panes of topic':
with pompous mythological machinery, such as Sidonius's meeting
between Bacchus and Phoebus; with trite mythological comparisons
and hyperboles, whose triteness is not removed by the use of pedantic
periphrases such as 'the Bistonian king'; with endless lists of things
in which the thing or person being described excels. In other words,
there has come down to us a vast quantity of verse such as almost
anyone with a minimum of literary talent could be trained to write.
As I have already suggested, in some remarks[1] on the contrast between
Marvell and Randolph in their use of mythology, the influence of 'the
classics' on seventeenth-century poetry was very mixed, for the emptily
rhetorical strain could be more easily imitated than the truly classical.
There is almost nothing of this empty rhetoric in Marvell's poetry.
If he was familiar with Sidonius's poem, as he probably was with Statius's pair, its effect upon him was similar to what Hopkins said was
the effect upon himself of masterpieces—to make him go and do something different.

(iv) Appleton House *as 'a catalogue of delights'*

Marvell's descriptions of the garden, the meadows and the mowers,
of the wood where he meditates and of the river where he fishes, may
well be regarded as 'catalogues of delights'. What I call the 'catalogue
of delights' appears in many forms in ancient, in medieval and in
Renaissance poetry. A special, though very influential, form of it, 'The
Shepherd's Wooing', goes back to that passage in Theocritus's eleventh
Idyll (31–48) where the Cyclops Polyphemus describes what he can
offer the sea-nymph Galataea if she will 'live with him and be his love',
and to Ovid's amplification and elaboration of this passage in the
thirteenth book of the *Metamorphoses* (879 ff.). But it appears sometimes
in very simple, sometimes in quite elaborate form, in certain formulae
of comparison, which declare that A is more delightful than B or C
or D, or that A and B and C are all inferior to X, which the poet
exhibits at the end of his list, or that A and B and C, etc, are no compensation for X, which he has lost. Thus, in innumerable *reverdies*, or
spring-songs, by Provencal and early Italian poets the lover declares

1. Chapter 2, pp. 87 ff.

that, while all things around him, which he describes, are rejoicing in the return of spring, he alone is full of sadness because of the absence or loss of his lady. Petrarch, in two famous sonnets (310, *Zefiro torna, e 'l bel tempo rimena*, and 312, *Né per sereno ciel ir vaghe stelle*) written after the death of Laura, followed this example, and Ronsard imitated Petrarch.[1] Among less traditional examples of such catalogues we have the sonnet-sequence by Folgore di San Gimignano, one of the predecessors of Dante, on the delights offered by each of the twelve months.

What I have called the 'catalogue of delights', above all when, as in Milton's *L'Allegro* and *Il Penseroso* and in Saint-Amant's *La Solitude*, it is primarily a catalogue of visual delights, may be regarded as a development of that favourite topic of late Latin poetry, the *locus amoenus*, whose history has been so admirably described by Ernst Robert Curtius.[2] While in Theocritus and Virgil description of *loci amoeni* were no more than backgrounds for pastoral dialogue, they gradually came to be regarded as independent topics upon which the poet or rhetorician could display his skill. The first example of such an independent ἔκφρασις or *descriptio* which Curtius has been able to discover is by Petronius:

> Mobilis aestivas platanus diffuderat umbras
> Et bacis redimita Daphne tremulaeque cupressus
> Et circumtonsae trepidanti vertice pinus.
> Has inter ludebat aquis errantibus amnis
> Spumeus, et querulo vexabat rore lapillos.
> Dignus amore locus: testis silvestris aëdon
> Atque urbana Procne, quae circum gramina fusae
> Et molles violas cantu sua rura colebant.

(The mobile plane-tree had diffused summer shade; so too had berry-crowned Daphne, quivering cypresses, and clipped pines with swaying crowns. Among these sported with its winding waters a foaming brook that vexed the pebbles with mournful dew. A place made for love: witness the sylvan nightingale and city-haunting Procne, who, fluttering round its turf and tender violets, embellished its ruralnesses with their song.)

---

1. See the present writer's *Themes and Variations in Shakespeare's Sonnets*, 1961 and 1963, pp. 185–9.

2. *Europäische Literatur und lateinisches Mittelalter*, 1948, Kapitel X, 'Die Ideallandschaft'.

The most beautiful elaboration of the *locus amoenus* in late Latin poetry, Curtius declares, is by Tiberianus, a poet of the time of Constantine, whose description concludes with a *résumé* of the delights he has been describing:

> Sic euntem per virecta pulchra odora et musica
> Ales amnis aura lucus flos et umbra iuverat.

(Thus one going through that green domain, fair, odorous, musical,
Had found in bird, stream, air, grove, flower and shade delight.)

With this *résumé* the poet indicates that both his subject and his scheme had been prescribed, for his contemporary Libanius had declared that 'sources of delight are springs and plantations and gardens and soft breezes and flowers and the voices of birds'. Thus it was that the 'conventional' but endlessly beautifiable topic of the *locus amoenus* passed from late Latin poetry and rhetoric into the vernacular poetry of the Middle Ages and the Renaissance, into the *Roman de la Rose*, into Petrarch, Chaucer, into Ariosto, Tasso and Spenser. The finest fruit, Curtius aptly remarks, 'ripens on espaliers'.

Milton's *L'Allegro* and *Il Penseroso*, Saint-Amant's *La Solitude*, and the more directly descriptive portions of *Appleton House* have this in common, that they contain a central, a classical, case of generally acceptable and immediately recognisable *amoenitas*, although the three very characteristic seventeenth-century sensibilities of these three poets manifest themselves with differences that are more striking than their resemblances.

The two poems of Milton, that great classic and great eclectic, are far more highly organised than those of Saint-Amant and Marvell. They have indeed affinities with innumerable things in earlier English poetry: with the simple catalogue of delights in Marlowe's *Passionate Shepherd*, with the almost romantic evocation of scenes favourable to the indulgence of a luxurious melancholy in Fletcher's 'Hence, all you vaine Delights', with Shakespeare's fairy-lore and with what Wordsworth would have called his 'new images from external nature', and even, now and then, with the ingenious comparisons practised by so many of Milton's contemporaries. Nevertheless, Milton never indulges himself or spreads himself, everything is controlled by a prevailing *decorum*, a *ne quid nimis*, and all the detail is strictly subordinated to the always perceptible intention of evoking the diurnal and nocturnal pleasures appropriate to two contrasted moods.

Saint-Amant's *La Solitude* is far less complex, far more easily classifiable, than either *L'Allegro* and *Il Penseroso* or the descriptive portions of *Appleton House*. This poem, which at once became enormously popular in France, which was extensively imitated, and on which its author's reputation, both then and since, most securely rested, must surely be, if not the earliest, at any rate the earliest full-blown expression of what may be called either 'romanticism' or 'romanceyness'. Both in France and in England a new taste had been formed before a word was invented to describe it, for, according to Logan Pearsall Smith,[1] it would seem that it was not until round about 1650 that the words 'romancey' and 'romantic' began to be commonly applied to scenes which recalled those in old romances, 'old castles, mountains and forests, pastoral plains, waste and solitary places'.[2] There is something a little ironical in the fact that Saint-Amant (1594–1661), that great *bon vivant* and celebrator of *la débauche*, whose collected poems are so strongly permeated with the atmosphere of camp and tavern and with the odours of wine, women and tobacco, should be chiefly remembered as the author of this most innocuous and, one might almost say, ladylike poem, her translation of which was to be the most celebrated achievement of the Matchless Orinda. Saint-Amant wrote it sometime between 1617 and 1621, while residing, as a member of the household of the Duc de Retz, in the Château on Belle-Ile-en-Mer, an island off the coast of Brittany. It seems to have been printed separately in 1625 and appeared in the first part of Saint-Amant's *Œuvres* in 1629. Since at some indeterminable date Marvell's patron the Lord General translated this poem, and since Marvell may well have got to know it during his foreign travels, it has sometimes been assumed that they must have read it and discussed it together. Some may even like to suppose that Fairfax translated it during Marvell's residence at Nunappleton, in the course of their delightful and mutually stimulating game. Nevertheless, I do not think it possible to maintain, as has sometimes been done, that *Appleton House* has been 'influenced' by *La Solitude*, although an examination of the essentially different styles, procedures and sensibilities of the two poems may enable us to see each more clearly as in itself it really is. Towards such a perception a mere prose analysis of the twenty stanzas of *La Solitude* will take us some way. (1) How delightful and how calming is the effect of solitude, of places sacred to the night, of primeval woods, far from the world and its noise! (2) Ancient

1. *Four Romantic Words*, in *Words and Idioms*, 1928.
2. *op. cit.*, p. 79.

trees, where Pan and his demi-gods sought refuge from the Flood. (3) The nightingale singing on the flowery thorn; precipitous rocks which can tempt the unhappy to escape from a too cruel fate. (4) Savage waterfalls, which turn gradually into winding streams where naiads reign. (5) The peaceful marsh, where 'nymphs' gathering flags and rushes to make distaffs startle the leaping frogs, (6) and which is full of water-fowl. (7) No boat and no waggon ever crosses it, neither the thirsty traveller nor the goat drinks from it, and no one comes there to fish. (8) Ruined castles, haunted by owls, where witches keep their sabbaths, (9) and where from a rafter hangs the skeleton of a lover whom an unresponsive 'shepherdess' had driven to take his life. (10) Her ghost has been condemned for ever to haunt the spot. (11) Marbles with ancient emblems, initials half effaced from trees, ivy growing in the hearth. (12) A sombre grotto where Sleep in the arms of Nonchalance reclines upon sheaves of poppies. (13) Here the poet sometimes attunes his lute to the lament of Echo for her Narcissus. (14) Sometimes he gazes out from the top of a cliff, sometimes he lingers by its base which the waves have almost undermined. (15) The pleasure of being on the shore after a storm, when the Tritons are riding the waves and blowing their horns. (16) Sometimes the sea casts up wreckage and drowned men and monsters. (17) Sometimes it is like a floating mirror. (18) Bernières, accept this record of my conversations with the Muse. My most agreeable diversion, however, is my recollection of conversations with you. (19) Here you may perceive the different moods which different objects have inspired in me. (20) Solitude is the element of fine wits. It has enabled me to acquire the art of poetry without study. I love it because you love it too, but I also hate it because it deprives me of the pleasure of seeing and serving you.

Even this brief prose analysis should enable us to perceive at once that Saint-Amant's poem is, in the seventeenth-century sense, far less 'witty' than either *L'Allegro* and *Il Penseroso* or *Appleton House*, and, in the eighteenth-century sense, far more 'sentimental'. There are indeed in *L'Allegro* and *Il Penseroso* a few touches of such sentiment or romanticism, or, at any rate, a few passages which might be expanded in a thoroughly romantic way: the towers and battlements bosomed high in tufted trees; the curfew swinging slow over some wide-watered shore; the poet's lonely tower; the almost Shelleyan description of the moon:

> Like one that had bin led astray
> Through the Heav'ns wide pathless way.

Nevertheless, in the almost epigrammatic terseness, unelaborateness and uninsistence with which these 'romantic' delights are evoked there is something both 'witty', in the seventeenth-century sense, and also—just as in those few passages where Milton comes nearest to contemporary wit of the more ingenious or surprising kind, but where his ingenious comparisons are only fleetingly suggested, not quaintly elaborated—something classical, a prevailing *decorum*. Moreover, although (except in the introductions) without argument, hyperbole or strong antithesis, there is still continuously present throughout Milton's two poems the idea, the tradition, of a witty academic debate as to whether cheerfulness or pensiveness enjoys the keener or more abundant or loftier delight. Saint-Amant's poem, whose beauty and well-deserved reputation I have no desire to contest, but which I want to see as clearly as possible for what it is, is in some ways nearer to Fletcher's 'Hence, all you vaine Delights' than to either Milton or Marvell.

> A mid-night Bell, a parting groane,
> These are the sounds we feed upon.

There is nothing, as it were, kaleidoscopic about *La Solitude*: it consists of a loosely related series of leisurely and expansively described scenes and images which a mood may 'feed upon'. It is much more an indulgence, an expansion, of a mood, a taste, a sentiment than are the poems of Milton and of Marvell, and much less an exercise of 'wit'. That romanticism or romanceyness, which is only occasionally and fleetingly present in *L'Allegro* and *Il Penseroso* and not present at all in either *Appleton House* or any other poem of Marvell's, is the very substance of Saint-Amant's. We are, it is true, still very far from full-blown romanticism. Saint-Amant is far from solemn and is well aware that he is playing a kind of game. Although, for the moment, he is in love with quietness, he makes no paradoxical exaltation of solitude over society, or of the beauty of nature over the vileness of man, nor does he represent himself as fleeing from a cruel and impossible world to cry himself like a tired child to sleep upon the bosom of nature. We are still far from Rousseau, from Childe Harold exclaiming

> I live not in myself, but I become
> Portion of that around me; and to me
> High mountains are a feeling, but the hum
> Of human cities torture: I can see

> Nothing to loathe in nature, save to be
> A link reluctant in a fleshly chain,
> Class'd among creatures, when the soul can flee,
> And with the sky, the peak, the heaving plain
> Of ocean, or the stars, mingle, and not in vain;[1]

or from Berlioz's Faust apostrophising 'Nature immense', uniting his voice with that of her storms and torrents, and projecting towards the stars the desires of a heart too vast and of a soul thirsting for a happiness that eludes. Nevertheless, we are approaching a kind of sensibility which is much readier to respond to 'sentiment' or 'feeling' than to what Marvell, or even the Milton of *L'Allegro* and *Il Penseroso*, understood by 'wit'. The kind of sensibility of which Saint-Amant's poem must surely be regarded as one of the earliest complete expressions, and to which it long continued to administer congenial nourishment, is admirably revealed in a letter written in 1694 by the interesting though minor precursor of Rousseau (as in some respects we may regard him) the Marquis de Lassay, from his château of Lassay, in Maine, to Julie de Chateaubriant, natural daughter (later legitimatised) of the son of the Grand Condé, whom he married (to his swift disenchantment and discomfiture) as his second wife.

> I am in a castle, in the midst of woods and so old that the country people say it was built by the fairies. During the day I stroll under beeches like those which Saint-Amant depicts in his Solitude; and from six o'clock in the evening, when it grows dark, until midnight, which is the hour when I retire, I am quite alone in a massive tower, at more than two hundred paces from any living creature. I think you will feel afraid of ghosts merely through reading this description of the life I lead.[2]

The difference between the Marquis de Lassay, enjoying the deliciously romantic thrill of retiring to rest in an old tower 'at more than two hundred paces from any living creature', and the Lord General Fairfax, so firmly and so contentedly centred among the 'Recreations' and 'Imployments' of Nunappleton, may to some extent, perhaps, be regarded as symbolising some of the differences between those earlier seventeenth-century readers who admired the poetry of 'wit' and those

---

1. Canto III, st. lxxii.
2. *Lettres Amoureuses et Pensées diverses du Marquis de Lassay (1652–1738)*, ed. Maurice Lange, Paris 1912, pp. 120–1.

later seventeenth-century readers (and their eighteenth-century successors) who admired the poetry of 'sentiment'. It is true that Saint-
Amant was some twenty years older than Fairfax and that Fairfax
admired his poem enough to translate it, and it is also true that Saint-
Amant wrote a great many other poems, most of them as different as
possible from *La Solitude*. Nevertheless, in *La Solitude* Saint-Amant
somehow contrived to give memorable expression to a kind of sentiment that would be flourishing at a time when wit such as Marvell's
had long disappeared. It is probable that one of his impulses in writing
La Solitude was a desire to escape from boredom. It is—if I may employ
that ugly modern word—'escapist' in a sense in which Marvell's poetry
(or, for that matter, Milton's) is not. The pleasure which Marvell's
poetry offers is an exhilarating mixture of sensuous delight, intellectual
activity, and admiration for exhibited skill. The pleasure offered by
La Solitude is of a much less strenuous and intellectual kind, and the
reader's partnership is far more passive. There is already implicit
in it, or, at any rate, I think its admirers came more and more to discover and to relish in it, a distinction between a specifically 'poetic'
or 'romantic' way of regarding and feeling things and an 'ordinary'
way. It could be admired, to a degree that Marvell's poetry could not,
by readers who loved the 'poetical' but who were not deeply interested
in the art of poetry.

(v) *'Clevelandish' description in* Appleton House

The one thing that *La Solitude*, *L'Allegro* and *Il Penseroso*, and the descriptive portions of *Appleton House* have in common is that they are
catalogues of delights. Otherwise, as I have said, their differences are
more striking than their resemblances. At the same time, while Saint-
Amant and Marvell are utterly different, Milton's two poems may to
some extent be regarded as occupying a central position, and as having
affinities both with Marvell and with Saint-Amant. For, if in Milton's
poems there is still, though less obviously than in Marvell's, something
of seventeenth-century wit, there is also, occasionally and uninsis-
tently, something of that romanticism or romanceyness that predominates in Saint-Amant's—a few passages which an English M. de Lassay
might have remembered in a romantic solitude. Indeed, the Wartons,
Hurd, and other eighteenth-century romantics continually praised
what seemed to them Milton's romantic descriptions, romantic
wildness, and romantic fancy. On the other hand, in the descriptive

portions of *Appleton House*, beautiful as they are, there is not, one may say, even a foretaste of romanticism or romanceyness, nothing that could be prolonged into reverie. Everything is sharp, clear, scintillating, daylight and wide-awake. Our senses are delighted, but only with what is immediately before them, and our intellect is continuously stimulated and exercised, never lulled into a partial suspension. Nothing could be further from the world of dream; there is nothing for mere mood to 'feed upon'. On the contrary, there is nearly always present, to a greater or lesser degree, a high-spirited hyperbole and burlesque, which I have called Clevelandish, and which I think Marvell learnt from Cleveland, but in his use of which Marvell immeasurably surpasses Cleveland: by which I mean that he combines it, in a way that Cleveland almost never does, with more permanent sources of poetic pleasure, so that with Marvell such passages are not merely, as with Cleveland, astonishing, but also, as almost never with Cleveland, memorable. Too often with Cleveland such passages are either in the air, *in vacuo*, mere fireworks, or they occur in contexts where they seem to us grotesquely inappropriate. Marvell has found for them, in so far as it ever could be found for them, precisely the right place. They arise 'naturally' out of their context, and that context, the description of the estate of Nunappleton, supplies what I have called a central or classical core of generally acceptable and enjoyable *amoenitas*. Cleveland, one may say, like several other seventeenth-century poets, tended to serve up what to us seem mere ingredients; Marvell used these ingredients to season what to us seems a substantial dish. That sense of proportion, that awareness of the rest of English poetry and of its possibilities, which a powerful and popular poet like Cleveland is able for a while to suspend in his contemporaries, has now, at any rate in our estimation of the poetry of the past, returned to us, and, while it has not diminished the value of Marvell's achievement, it has greatly diminished the value of Cleveland's. We should not think it worth while to argue with anyone who told us that he thought Cleveland's poetry was better than that of Keats; if, on the other hand, someone maintained that Marvell's poetry was better than that of Keats we should, if he argued his case well, have to take him seriously, and we might find it difficult to refute him.

In these Clevelandish passages in *Appleton House* the balance between the visual and the conceptual, between sensuous delight and intellectual entertainment, varies considerably, but even the most purely conceptual passages are, so to speak, supplied by their context with a visual or sensuous core. After describing the flooding of the meadow, Marvell proceeds (st. LX):

> Let others tell the *Paradox*,
> How Eels now bellow in the Ox;
> How Horses at their Tails do kick,
> Turn'd as they hang to Leeches quick;
> How Boats can over Bridges sail,
> And Fishes do the Stables scale;
> How *Salmons* trespassing are found,
> And Pikes are taken in the Pound.

This, as a piece of description, is perhaps as 'unromantic', as remote from anything in either *L'Allegro* and *Il Penseroso* or *La Solitude*, as it would be possible to produce. It might almost have appeared in Marvell's later *Character of Holland*:

> Yet still his claim the Injur'd Ocean laid,
> And oft at Leap-frog ore their Steeples plaid:
> As if on purpose it on Land had come
> To shew them what's their *Mare Liberum*.
> A daily deluge over them does boyl;
> The Earth and Water play at *Level-coyl*;
> The Fish oft-times the Burger dispossest,
> And sat not as a Meat but as a Guest.

And yet we do not feel that it is in any way incongruous, or at all out of keeping with passages of more 'beautiful' description, passages nearer, despite their still obvious differences, to things in the poems of Milton and Saint-Amant.

> And now to the Abbyss I pass
> Of that unfathomable Grass,
> Where Men like Grashoppers appear,
> But Grashoppers are Gyants there:[1]
> They, in there squeking Laugh, contemn
> Us as we walk more low then them:

----

1. As was pointed out by Professor Pierre Legouis, this passage was certainly suggested by Numbers xiii 33 (the report brought back by those whom Moses had sent to search out the land of Canaan): 'And there we saw the giants, the sons of Anak, which come of the giants: and we were in our own sight as grasshoppers, and so were we in their sight.'

And, from the Precipices tall
Of the green spir's, to us do call.

To see Men through this Meadow Dive,
We wonder how they rise alive.
As, under Water, none does know
Whether he fall through it or go.
But, as the Marriners that sound,
And show upon their Lead the Ground,
They bring up Flow'rs so to be seen,
And prove they've at the Bottom been.

(st. XLVII–VIII)

This is as 'beautiful' as anything in *L'Allegro* and *Il Penseroso*, and yet
at the same time as 'witty' as anything in Donne's *Storme* and *Calme*.
It combines qualities and procedures which, but for this and other
examples which Marvell has given us, we should have been inclined
to regard as incompatible—or rather, perhaps I should say, the possibility of which would never have occurred to us. 'Das Unbeschrei-
bliche, hier wirds getan.' So far as I am aware, no other poet has ever
written quite like this, or communicated this particular kind of pleasure,
although there are occasional approaches to it in a few of the more
purely descriptive poems of Marvell's younger contemporary Charles
Cotton (1630–87), the friend of Izaak Walton. Cotton's *Poems on
Several Occasions* were not published until 1689, two years after his death,
and few of them can be dated; but in the rural seclusion of Beresford
Hall in Staffordshire, where he spent most of his life, he seems to have
carried well on into the Restoration period a manner of writing rooted
in the earlier seventeenth century; and there are suggestions that he
too, like Marvell, learnt something from Cleveland; for, although he
probably knew nothing of Marvell's poetry, he sometimes describes
those natural appearances which he loved in an almost Marvellian way.
The third and fourth stanzas of his *Evening Quatrains* have some affinity
with those two stanzas from *Appleton House* which I have just quoted:

The shadows now so long do grow,
That brambles like tall cedars show,
Mole-hills seem mountains, and the ant
Appears a monstrous elephant.

A very little, little flock
Shades thrice the ground that it would stock;

While the small stripling following them
Appears a mighty Polypheme.[1]

The hyperbolical description of noontide heat at the beginning of his
Noon Quatrains has some affinity with that at the beginning of Marvell's
Damon the Mower, and the following stanza (the fifth) would not have
been out of place in *Appleton House:*

> If this hold on, our fertile lands,
> Will soon be turn'd to parched sands,
> And not an onion that will grow
> Without a Nile to overflow.[2]

In his *Night Quatrains* the personifications of the Sun in his descending
and of Night in her ascending chariot are more conventional than
Marvell would have made them, but, in the third stanza, the description of the skies,

> Who bid the world's bright eye adieu
> In gelid tears of falling dew,[3]

has a touch of Marvell; and there is something of Marvellian hyperbole
and antithesis about the description of a stormy sea in the sixth and
seventh stanzas of *Winter*:

> Now fins do serve for wings, and bear
> Their scaly squadrons through the air;
> Whilst the air's inhabitants do stain
> Their gaudy plumage in the rain.

> Now stars concealed in clouds do peep
> Into the secrets of the deep;
> And lobsters spewed up from the brine,
> With Cancer's constellations shine.[4]

But while descriptions of this kind appear only in a tiny handful of
Cotton's poems, and then only intermittently, in *Appleton House* and in
many of Marvell's other poems they are the rule rather than the exception.

The 'pictorialism' in such a passage as the just-quoted description
of the meadow is more specifically literary, less paintable, more in-
dissolubly united with its own particular medium, than the pictorialism
of Spenser or of Keats. For the boundaries between poetry and painting

1. *Poems*, ed. John Beresford, 1923, p. 54.   2. *op. cit.*, p. 52.
3. *op. cit.*, p. 56.   4. *op. cit.*, p. 60.

are not, after all, so absolute as Lessing insisted. Leigh Hunt, when in *Imagination and Fancy* he amused himself by selecting various descriptive passages from Spenser and imagining the painters who could have most perfectly represented them, was not merely trifling: it is indeed possible to imagine a painting which should produce an impression and communicate an experience very similar to that which we share when we read Spenser's description of the

> hundred naked maidens lilly white,
> All raunged in a ring, and dauncing in delight

to the sound of Colin's pipe and in honour of his mistress, or to imagine four paintings representing Keats's four personifications of Autumn:

> sitting careless on a granary floor,
> Thy hair soft-lifted by the winnowing wind;
> Or on a half-reap'd furrow sound asleep,
> Drows'd with the fume of poppies, while thy hook
> Spares the next swath and all its twined flowers:
> And sometimes like a gleaner thou dost keep
> Steady thy laden head across a brook;
> Or by a cyder-press, with patient look,
> Thou watchest the last oozings hours by hours.

On the other hand, no imaginable painting could even approximately reproduce the impression made upon us by this and other descriptive passages in *Appleton House*. 'Wit' cannot be painted, and in such passages wit is not (like much of the imagery in Shakespeare's earlier plays) a mere superaddition or decoration, but integral; it does not co-exist side by side with the visual or pictorial element, but inseparably interpenetrates it.

Without wishing to set an excessive value upon Marvell's achievement, here and elsewhere, or to use it in order to disparage the achievements of less witty and more obviously pictorial poets such as Spenser and Keats, I do think it worth while to insist upon its originality, almost, I might say, its uniqueness. And I would also insist once again that this undeniable originality is essentially traditional, consisting as it does in the re-combination of hints and procedures which had been suggested to Marvell by dozens of other poets, many of them contemporary. Some poets, perhaps one might say, have invented new elements; Marvell invented new compounds. An essential part of his originality is a kind of literary tact or sense of *decorum*, an ability to perceive how various new tricks and devices which, though then much admired, could produce only a transient pleasure, might be combined with more traditional or conventional sources of poetic pleasure to form permanently satisfying wholes.

(vi) *'Sylvestrian'* and *'neo-Homeric'* description in Appleton House *and the 'Bermudas' poem*

Besides these Clevelandish passages, or these Marvellised Clevelandisms, Marvell also has various 'witty' descriptions of Nature in terms of art, which are somewhat in the manner, and which were certainly, I think, directly or indirectly suggested by the manner of numerous passages in a work which exerted an enormous influence on the diction and imagery of seventeenth-century poetry, Sylvester's translation of Du Bartas's *La Semaine*, that immense, encyclopaedic and unfinished poem which describes, with innumerable expatiations and divagations, the seven days of the Creation, the lives of Adam and Eve, of Noah and of the Patriarchs, and the story of the Jewish people until the capture of Jerusalem by Nebuchadnezzar. Sylvester's translation, which began to appear in parts from 1592, was collected in 1605 with the title *Bartas his Divine Weekes & Workes*, and was completed in 1608. When Milton, in *Arcades* (ll. 46–7), made his Genius of the Wood declare that one of his functions was to

> curl the grove
> With Ringlets quaint, and wanton windings wove;

when four times in his *Poly-Olbion* Drayton spoke of 'curled groves' or the 'curled heads' of groves; when Ben Jonson in his Epistle *To Sir Robert Wroth* spoke of 'curled woods and painted meads', and when William Browne in his *Inner Temple Masque* spoke of the 'curl'd tops' of oaks and in his *Britannia's Pastorals* made trees 'nod their curled heads', they were all repeating something they had learnt from Sylvester. In the Second Day of the First Week, among 'Divers Similes, shewing how the Rain is caused through the incounter of the Cloudes', we find:

> As after rain another rain doth drop
> In shady Forests from their shaggy top,
> When through their green boughs, whiffing Winds do whirl
> With wanton pufs their wauing locks to curl.[1]

1. ed. 1621, p. 30.

Here Sylvester, who is not infrequently more exuberant and more extravagant than his original, is being fairly literal; Du Bartas wrote:

> une aure gentille
> S'esbatant à travers les rameaux verdoyans,
> Se plaît à frisoter leurs cheveux ondoyans.

Although Du Bartas was the most extensive and the most famous (or infamous) practitioner of this kind of description, he does not seem to have invented it. The passage I have quoted was first printed in 1578, but it is an interesting fact that his contemporary Jean Passerat in his *L'Hymne de la Paix*, printed in 1562, had written:

> Zephire seul soufflait de qui la doulce haleine
> Frisoit mignardement les cheueus de la plaine,

a passage which Drummond of Hawthornden transcribed into his commonplace book as one of Passerat's striking lines and which he imitated in a sonnet on the spring: 'The *Zephyres* curle the green Lockes of the Plaine'.[1] One of the most famous passages in Sylvester occurs in the Fourth Part of the First Day of the Second Week, entitled *The Handy-Crafts*, where Adam experiences his first winter:

> But, when the Winters keener breath began
> To crystallize the *Baltike* Ocean,
> To glaze the Lakes, and bridle-vp the Floods,
> And perriwig with wooll the bald-pate Woods:[2]

Sylvester was so pleased with this periwig that he had already introduced it into an earlier passage (in the Fourth Day of the First Week) where it did not occur in his original:

> In stead of Flowrs, chill shivering Winter dresses
> With Isicles her (self-bald) borrow'd tresses:
> About her brows a Periwig of Snowe.[3]

Here Du Bartas had merely written: 'L'Hyver au lieu de fleurs se pare

1. *Works*, ed. Kastner, I 61. It is to this learned editor that I am indebted for the reference to Passerat.
2. ed. 1621, p. 223.
3. ed. 1621, p. 87. Sylvester's unauthorised introduction of the image here, which led Benlowes and Dryden to associate the later and authentic periwig with 'snow' instead of with 'wool', has been pointed out by Professor Harold Jenkins, *Edward Benlowes*, Cambridge, Mass., 1952, pp. 113–14.

de glaçons.' Edward Benlowes, who in his *Theophila* has so often imitated Sylvester and other poets, seems to have unconsciously conflated these two passages, for he wrote (xiii 54):

> When periwig'd with *Snow*'s each bald-pate Wood,
> Bound in Ice-Chains each strugling Flood.

Dryden too, evidently quoting from memory (the best evidence of familiarity), seems also to have conflated these two passages. 'I remember, when I was a boy', he wrote, in the dedication of *The Spanish Friar* (1681),

> I thought inimitable Spenser a mean poet, in comparison of Sylvester's *Dubartas*, and was rapt into an ecstasy when I read these lines:
>> *Now, when the Winter's keener breath began*
>> *To chrystallize the Baltick Ocean;*
>> *To glaze the Lakes, to bridle up the Floods,*
>> *And periwig with Snow the bald-pate Woods.*

> I am much deceived if this be not abominable fustian, that is, thoughts and words ill-sorted, and without the least relation to each other.[1]

The second song in *Arcades* begins 'O're the smooth enameld green'. It is, I suppose, just possible that Milton borrowed this phrase straight from the fourth canto of Dante's *Inferno* (ll. 118–19):

> Colà diretto, sopra il verde smalto,
>   mi fur mostrati gli spiriti magni,

'there directly, upon the green enamel, were shown to me the great spirits', a passage where Ruskin, who objected to the abuse of this metaphor by later poets, insisted that Dante was comparing, not grass in general, but, quite specifically, the grass of the *Inferno*, 'laid as a tempering and cooling substance over the dark, metallic, glossy ground', to enamel.[2] Nevertheless, it was possibly from Sylvester that Milton, like other seventeenth-century poets, learnt to enamel. Sylvester has, for example, 'th' inammeld meads',[3] 'this enammeld

1. *Essays*, ed. Ker, I 247.
2. *Modern Painters*, vol. III, part IV, ch. xiv, §47–50.
3. Second Week, First Day, Third Part ('The Furies'), ed. 1621, p. 208.

vale',[1] and—a passage where nature is very much 'trickt and frounc't'
by art—

> Th' inammell'd Vallies, where the liquid glass
> Of silver Brooks in curled streams doth pass.[2]

God chose for the first man

> A climate temperate both for cold and heat,
> Which dainty *Flora* paveth sumptuously
> With flowry VER's inameld tapistry.[3]

It may also well have been Sylvester who taught seventeenth-century
poets to 'candy' water into ice, or to candy various natural objects
with ice.

> Sometimes befals, that, when by secret powr,
> The Cloud's new-chang'd into a dropping showr,
> Th' excessive cold of the mid-Aire (anon)
> Candies-it all in bals of Icy-stone.[4]

Here Sylvester's first (or almost his first) pupil seems to have been
Shakespeare, who in *Timon of Athens* (IV iii 225–6) wrote of

> the cold brook
> Candied with ice.

Then came William Browne, in the first book of *Britannia's Pastorals*
(1613, 4th song, ll. 397–8):

> When Hyems bound the floods in silver chains,
> And hoary frosts had candied all the plains.

Drayton, in *The Quest of Cynthia* (1627, ll. 69–70), wrote of

> those Frosts that winter brings
> Which candy euery greene;

and Carew, in the opening lines of his poem *The Spring*, employs the
metaphor in one of the most Sylvesterish passages in seventeenth-
century poetry:

1. Second Week, Second Day, Second Part ('Babylon'), ed. 1621, p. 262.
2. Second Week, Second Day, Third Part ('The Colonies'), ed. 1621, p. 282.
3. Second Week, First Day, First Part ('Eden'), ed. 1621, p. 171.
4. First Week, Second Day, ed. 1621, p. 31.

> Now that the winter's gone, the earth hath lost
> Her snow-white robes, and now no more the frost
> Candies the grasse, or castes an ycie creame
> Vpon the silver Lake, or Chrystall streame.[1]

Marvell, too, sometimes writes in what may be called the Sylvester tradition, but in his 'artificial' descriptions of nature, no less than in what I have called his Clevelandisms, he contrives to preserve a certain *decorum* and to achieve a just balance between the surprising and the permanently delightful. The mown meadow, on to which the cattle will be driven, is like a canvas or 'cloth' stretched ready for Lely to paint (st. LVI):

> This *Scene* again withdrawing brings
> A new and empty Face of things;
> A levell'd space, as smooth and plain,
> As Clothes for *Lilly* strecht to stain.
> The World when first created sure
> Was such a Table rase and pure.
> Or rather such is the *Toril*
> Ere the Bulls enter at Madril.

The meadows from which the floods have receded are like new-washed silks (st. LXXIX):

> For now the Waves are fal'n and dry'd,
> And now the Meadows fresher dy'd;
> Whose Grass, with moister colour dasht,
> Seems as green Silks but newly washt.
> No *Serpent* new nor *Crocodile*
> Remains behind our little *Nile*;
> Unless it self you will mistake,
> Among these Meads the only Snake.

It seems, by the way, just possible that in the latter half of the stanza Marvell had in mind a passage in Sylvester's translation where he appropriates to England the encomium which Du Bartas has written upon France—a passage to which I shall return, because (together, no doubt with much else) it seems to lie behind Marvell's own praise of this 'dear and happy Isle':

1. *Poems*, ed. Dunlap, p. 3.

About thy borders (O Heav'n-blessed ILE)
There never crawls the noysom Crocodile;
Nor Bane-breath'd Serpent, *basking in thy sand,*
Measures an Acre of thy flowry Land.[1]

One very memorable example of such 'artificial' description of nature
occurs in that poem on the *Bermudas* which it seems reasonable to suppose that Marvell wrote during 1653 or 1654 while he was residing at
Eton, as tutor to Cromwell's ward William Dutton, in the house of
John Oxenbridge (1608–74), a Puritan divine who, after Laud had
deprived him of his Oxford tutorship in 1634, had made two voyages
to the Bermudas, and who since 1652 had been a Fellow of Eton
College.[2]

> He gave us this eternal Spring,
> Which here enamells every thing . . .
> He hangs in shades the Orange bright,
> Like golden Lamps in a green Night.
> And does in the Pomgranates close,
> Jewels more rich than *Ormus* show's.

Here, however, and indeed throughout his poem on the Bermudas,
Marvell reveals certain interesting affinities with yet another tradition
of descriptive writing, or rather, perhaps I should say, with an ancient
literary tradition which had been modified by, and which itself continued to modify, a new European experience—with, on the one hand,
Tasso's description (partly imitated from Homer) of the fruit-trees in

1. Second Week, Second Day, Third Part ('The Colonies'), ed. 1621, p. 283.
The absence of the serpent and the crocodile is still more elaborately insisted upon
in a passage in Théophile's *La Maison de Sylvie,* a poem which, as I have already
remarked (p. 237), has, at any rate in its general design, some affinity with
Appleton House. The passage (Ode III, st. iv; *Œuvres Complètes,* ed. Alleaume, 1855,
II 202) is one of the many which Thomas Stanley has omitted from his abbreviated
version of the poem:

> Là les oiseaux font leur petits,
> Et n'ont jamais veu leurs couvées
> Souler les sanglans appetits
> Du serpent qui les a trouvées;
> Là n'estend point ses plis mortels
> Ce monstre de qui tant d'autels
> Ont jadis adoré les charmes,
> Et qui, d'un gosier gemissant,
> Fait tomber l'ame du passant
> Dedans l'embuche de ses larmes.

2. See Margoliouth, I 220, 261; II 291–2.

Armida's garden and Spenser's description (partly imitated from Tasso)
of the fruit-trees in the Garden of Adonis, and, on the other hand, with
descriptions, either at first- or second-hand, of the strange climates
and *flora* of recently discovered regions. 'He gave us this eternal
Spring.' The prolific, extravagant abundance of nature in parts of the
world that were still 'new', the replacement there of the cycle of the
seasons by what, at any rate to some European visitors, seemed now
a perpetual Spring and now a perpetual Autumn, fascinated the imagi-
nations of many writers, especially poets, and seemed to some of them
to demand all their resources of paradox, antithesis, hyperbole, and
'wit', not in order to embellish the experience, but simply in order to
communicate its quality. Spenser's defence of himself, in the Proem to
the Second Book of the *Faerie Queene*, against the possible charge that
he was vouching antiquities which nobody could know, has often been
quoted:

> But let that man with better sence aduize,
>> That of the world least part to vs is red:
> And dayly how through hardy enterprize,
>> Many great Regions are discouered,
>> Which to late age were neuer mentioned.
> Who euer heard of th'Indian *Peru*?
> Or who in venturous vessell measured
> The *Amazons* huge riuer now found trew?
> Or fruitfullest *Virginia* who did euer vew?

To Spenser and his contemporaries the 'fables' of antiquity no longer
seemed quite so fabulous. In the seventh book of the *Odyssey* Homer
thus describes the trees in the orchard of King Alcinous:

> Their fruit never fails nor runs short, winter and summer alike.
> It comes at all seasons of the year, and there is never a time when the
> West Wind's breath is not assisting, here the bud, and here the
> ripening fruit; so that pear after pear, apple after apple, cluster
> on cluster of grapes, and fig upon fig are always coming to per-
> fection.[1]

> ὄγχνη ἐπ' ὄγχνῃ γηράσκει, μῆλον δ'ἐπὶ μήλῳ,
> αὐτὰρ ἐπὶ σταφυλῇ σταφυλή, σῦκον δ'ἐπὶ σύκῳ.

Tasso clearly had this passage in mind when, in the *Gerusalemme
Liberata*, he described the trees in that garden which the enchantress

1. ll. 117–21, transl. E. V. Rieu.

Armida had created on one of the Fortunate Islands, beyond the Pillars
of Hercules, and to which she had conveyed Rinaldo:

> The trees no whirlwind felt, nor tempest smart,
>   But ere their fruit drop off, the blossom comes,
>   This springs, that falls, that ripeneth and this blooms.
>
> The leaves upon the self-same bough did hide
> Beside the young the old and ripened fig,
> Here fruit was green, there ripe with vermeil side,
> The apples new and old grew on one twig,
> The fruitful vine her arms spread high and wide
> That bended underneath their clusters big,
>   The grapes were tender here, hard, young and sour,
>   There purple ripe, and nectar sweet forth pour.[1]

Spenser imitated this in his description of the Garden of Adonis:

> There is continuall spring, and haruest there
> Continuall, both meeting at one time:
> For both the boughes doe laughing blossoms beare,
> And with fresh colours decke the wanton Prime,
> And eke attonce the heauy trees they clime,
> Which seeme to labour vnder their fruits lode.[2]

The descriptions of Tasso and Spenser are more 'literary' than those
of some later poets, but, here at any rate, both of them felt, I think,
that Homer's fiction had been proved to be no stranger than fact.
It was certainly without any recollection of Homer or of Tasso that
the unscholarly and comparatively unbookish Saint-Amant composed,
during one of his voyages, his sonnet entitled *L'Autonne des Canaries*,
which concludes:

> L'orange en mesme jour y meurit et boutonne,
> Et durant tous les mois on peut voir en ces lieux
> Le printemps et l'esté confondus en l'autonne.[3]

Full of witty expatiations on such 'paradoxes', further from the
manners of Tasso and of Spenser and nearer to that of Marvell, are

---

1. Canto XVI x–xi, in Fairfax's translation.
2. *FQ*, III vi 42.
3. *Œuvres Complètes*, ed. Livet, 1855, I 393. The sonnet was first printed in
Saint-Amant's *Troisième partie des Œuvres*, 1649.

portions of Waller's poem *The Battle of the Summer Islands* (the name given to the Bermudas after Sir George Somers had been shipwrecked there in 1609), which I agree with Margoliouth in thinking that Marvell had certainly read in the 1645 edition of Waller's *Poems*. This little poem of some 220 lines, divided into three cantos, and presumably suggested by some report which had reached England, is a kind of mock-heroic, describing a battle between the islanders and two whales which had been cast upon their coast. It was almost certainly with Waller's whales in his memory that Marvell wrote

> Where he the huge Sea-Monsters wracks,
> That lift the Deep upon their Backs.

The actual description of the battle, which occupies the second and third cantos, is tedious, being too deficient in those touches of burlesque and hyperbole which the mock-heroic requires, but the first canto, describing the climate and vegetation of the Bermudas, has some delightful passages very much in Marvell's manner.

> Bermudas, walled with rocks, who does not know?
> That happy island where huge lemons grow,
> And orange trees, which golden fruit do bear,
> The Hesperian garden boasts of none so fair;
> Where shining pearl, coral, and many a pound,
> On the rich shore, of ambergris is found.[1]

From this passage Marvell may well have derived his orange trees (in the lines already quoted) and also, later in the poem, his ambergris:

> And makes the hollow Seas, that roar,
> Proclaime the Ambergris on shoar.

Waller, too, celebrates the 'eternal spring' of the Bermudas (possibly, though by no means certainly, with Spenser's 'continuall Spring and harvest' in mind), and, like Homer, Tasso and Spenser, dwells on the 'paradox' that fruit and blossom appear together:

> For the kind spring, which but salutes us here,
> Inhabits there, and courts them all the year.
> Ripe fruits and blossoms on the same trees live;
> At once they promise what at once they give.

Although I do not feel certain that Waller actually had Homer, Tasso

1. *Poems*, ed. Thorn Drury, I 66.

and Spenser, all of them or any of them, in mind, I seem to perceive in such a passage as this (as also in the earlier one, with its 'Hesperian garden') a fascinating interaction between ancient fable and the reports of contemporary travellers: fact and fiction melting into and modifying one another, the old familiarising and integrating the new and, at the same time, reacquiring from it the charm of novelty; literature and life, books and experience, literary reminiscence and fresh visual perception all combining in that manner which is so characteristic of so much that is best in seventeenth-century poetry, above all, in Marvell's. Elsewhere in this first canto Waller exploits the contrasts his subject affords in a witty, hyperbolical and slightly burlesque manner which (although he was writing before Cleveland's poems had been printed) one might be inclined to call Clevelandish, and which has much affinity with what I have called the Clevelandish passages in *Appleton House*. Indeed, since his poem on the Bermudas makes it almost certain that Marvell had been impressed by this poem of Waller's, it may well have been Waller as well as Cleveland who had suggested to him some of the new and amusing possibilities he had exploited in earlier poems.

> The lofty cedar, which to heaven aspires,
> The prince of trees! is fuel for their fires;
> The smoke by which their loaded spits do turn,
> For incense might on sacred altars burn;
> Their private roofs on odorous timber borne,
> Such as might palaces for kings adorn.
> The sweet palmettos a new Bacchus yield,
> With leaves as ample as the broadest shield,
> Under the shadow of whose friendly boughs
> They sit, carousing where their liquor grows . . .

> Tobacco is the worst of things, which they
> To English landlords, as their tribute, pay.
> Such is the mould, that the blessed tenant feeds
> On precious fruits, and pays his rent in weeds . . .
> Nature these cates with such a lavish hand
> Pours out among them, that our coarser land
> Tastes of that bounty, and does cloth return,
> Which not for warmth, but ornament, is worn.

I have suggested that it was Sylvester who first introduced into

English poetry those 'artificial' descriptions of nature, of which Marvell, in *Appleton House* and elsewhere, has given us some particularly delightful examples. I will conclude my examination of some of the fascinating combinations of 'traditionality' and 'originality' in this poem with some remarks on a famous and beautiful stanza behind which, so far as I have been able to discover, we may perceive once more, ultimately if not directly, the fertilising influence of Sylvester and also, it may be, of an earlier version of a certain passage in Du Bartas's poem. After his witty description of the Garden that had been laid out 'in the just Figure of a Fort' Marvell continues (sts. XLI–XLIII):

> Oh Thou, that dear and happy Isle
> The Garden of the World ere while,
> Thou *Paradise* of four Seas,[1]
> Which *Heaven* planted us to please,
> But, to exclude the World, did guard
> With watry if not flaming Sword;
> What luckless Apple did we tast,
> To make us Mortal, and The Wast?
>
> Unhappy! shall we never more
> That sweet *Militia* restore,
> When Gardens only had their Towrs,
> And all the Garrisons were Flowrs,
> When Roses only Arms might bear,
> And Men did rosie Garlands wear?
> Tulips, in several Colours barr'd,
> Were then the *Switzers* of our *Guard*.
>
> The *Gardiner* had the *Souldiers* place,
> And his more gentle Forts did trace.
> The Nursery of all things green
> Was then the only *Magazeen*.
> The *Winter Quarters* were the Stoves,
> Where he the tender Plants removes.
> But War all this doth overgrow:
> We Ord'nance Plant and Powder sow.

It seems to me by no means unlikely (and, if so, it would be an interesting reminder of that leisured literary community in and out of

---

1. Marvell again mentions the 'four Seas' of Britain in *Last Instructions to a Painter*, l. 762 and in *A Dialogue between the Two Horses*, l. 61.

which Marvell's best poetry was written) that this whole passage was *immediately* suggested by a not very good poem which Mildmay Fane, second Earl of Westmorland (of the second creation), included among the few secular poems which form the second part of his *Otia Sacra*, a collection of poems, mainly religious, which he had privately printed in 1648 and of which he presented copies to his friends and relations, among them, one cannot but think, to his brother-in-law the Lord General Fairfax. This poem, which is entitled *Anglia Hortus*, begins:

> The Garden of the world, wherein the Rose
> In chief Commanded, did this doubt propose
> To be resolv'd in; Whether sense to prise
> For umpire to Create it Paradise.

The third and fourth lines can only be construed as 'which of the five senses should be chosen as umpire to proclaim the Garden of the World as Paradise?', which does not make very good sense, but Fane's general meaning is (as the context reveals) 'In virtue of its delighting which of the five senses should the Garden of the World be proclaimed Paradise?' After each of the five senses has been equally delighted, the poem concludes:

> And thus dispos'd, whilst every Sense admires,
> 'Tis sensless t' plant 'mongst Roses, Thistles, Briars.

The title and contents of the poem suggest that it was written after the outbreak of the Civil War, which had begun to plant 'thistles and briars' in the English garden, and I think it very likely that it was this not very good poem of the Lord General's brother-in-law which gave Marvell the phrase 'the Garden of the World', the idea of England as a garden wasted by civil war, and, at the same time, reminded him of something in Sylvester's *Du Bartas* and also, perhaps, of something in Shakespeare.

To begin with that phrase 'the Garden of the World': although, as I think, it came to Marvell from Fane, Fane was not the first to employ it; it had been used by Giles Fletcher in the third stanza of the elegy on Prince Henry which he contributed to the volume *Epicedium Cantabrigiense*, 1612: before Prince Henry's death England had been

> The Garden of the world, whear nothing wanted,
> Another Paradise, that God had planted.[1]

1. *Poetical Works of Giles and Phineas Fletcher*, ed. F. S. Boas, I 266.

Shakespeare had also used something very like it[1] in the last Act of
Henry V (ii 36–7):

>   this best garden of the world,
>   Our fertile France;

and in the Epilogue to that play (ll. 6–7):

>   Fortune made his sword,
>   By which the world's best garden he achieved.

It may be that Shakespeare was the inventor of the phrase, but, if so,
I think it was almost certainly suggested to him by a similar phrase
in Du Bartas's poem, either in Sylvester's translation (of which the
passage in question seems to have been first published in 1598, the
probable date of *Henry V*) or in an earlier version, which was almost
certainly in his mind when he was writing *Richard II*. At the conclusion
of the Third Part of the Second Day of the Second Week, entitled
The Colonies, Du Bartas inserts a panegyric on France, which Sylvester,
with a few necessary modifications, adapts into a panegyric on England. The relevant portions of it are as follows:

> *All-hail (dear* ALBION) *Europ's Pearl of price,*
> *The Worlds rich Garden, Earths rare Paradise:*
> *Thrice-happy Mother, which ay bringest forth*
> *Such Chiualry as daunteth all the Earth*
> *(Planting the Trophies of thy glorious Arms*
> *By Sea and Land, where ever* Titan *warms) . . .*
> *Fenç't from the World (as better worth then That)*
> *With triple Wall (of Water, Wood and Brass)*
> *Which never Stranger yet had powr to pass;*
> *Save when the Heav'ns have, for thy hainous Sin,*
> *By som of Thine, with false Keys let them in.*[2]

It may well have been Sylvester's 'the Worlds rich Garden' which
suggested to Shakespeare his 'world's best garden' and 'best garden
of the world' in *Henry V* and either or both of them (but more probably Sylvester, who was more *read*, and more able to be read than

---

1. It might, I suppose, be maintained that there is a subtle but important
difference between 'the garden of the world', *hortus mundi*, as denoting something
absolutely *sui generis*, and 'this best garden of the world', or 'the world's best garden',
as denoting something which, although at the top of its *genus*, is not *sui generis*.

2. ed. 1621, p. 283.

Shakespeare) who led Giles Fletcher and Fane and Marvell to describe England as 'the Garden of the World'. And Sylvester's 'Earths rare Paradise' and

> Fenc't from the World (*as better worth then That*)
> *With triple Wall* (*of Water, Wood and Brass*)

may well have been in Marvell's mind when he wrote

> Thou *Paradise* of four Seas,
> Which *Heaven* planted us to please,
> But, to exclude the World, did guard
> With watry if not flaming Sword.

But it is also possible that another passage may have been echoing in Marvell's memory:

> This royal throne of kings, this scept'red isle,
> This earth of majesty, this seat of Mars,
> This other Eden, demi-paradise,
> This fortress built by Nature for herself
> Against infection and the hand of war,
> This happy breed of men, this little world,
> This precious stone set in the silver sea,
> Which serves it in the office of a wall
> Or as a moat defensive to a house
> Against the envy of less happier lands,
> This blessed plot, this earth, this realm, this England,
> This nurse, this teeming womb of royal kings,
> Fear'd by their breed and famous by their birth,
> Renowned for their deeds as far from home,
> For Christian service and true chivalry,
> As is the sepulchre in stubborn Jewry,
> Of the world's ransom, blessed Mary's Son—

this passage, and also, perhaps, the phrase of the Gardener's servant in a later scene (III iv 43) about 'our sea-walled garden, the whole land'. I think there can be no doubt that in this famous passage in Gaunt's speech Shakespeare was also indebted to Du Bartas's panegyric on France at the end of *The Colonies*—not, however, in Sylvester's version, which had not appeared at the time when he was writing *Richard II*, but in a translation of that panegyric which had been printed side by side with the original by John Eliot in his *Ortho-epia Gallica*,

1593, a book for which there is other evidence that Shakespeare was familiar. Eliot, unlike Sylvester, who has here generalised the particular

> (*Planting the Trophies of thy glorious Arms*
> *By Sea and Land, where ever* Titan *warms*),

retains Du Bartas's allusion to the prowess of French chivalry in the crusades, which Shakespeare (who, moreover, probably had enough French to read the original) has transferred to the chivalry of England:

O Fruitfull *France*! Most happie Land, happie and happie thrice!
O pearle of rich *European* bounds! O earthly Paradice!
All haile sweet soile! O *France* the mother of many conquering knights,
Who planted once their glorious standards like triumphing wights,
Vpon the banckes of *Euphrates* where *Titan* Day-torch bright
Riseth, and bloodie swords unsheathd where *Phoebus* drounds his light.[1]

> O mille & mille fois terre heureuse & feconde!
> O Perle de l'Europe! O Paradis du Monde!
> France, ie te saluë, ô mere des guerriers,
> Qui iadis ont planté leurs triomphants lauriers
> Sur les rives d'Euphrate, & sanglanté leur glaive
> Ou la torche du iour & se couche & se leve . . .
> Tu as pour bastions & deux monts, & deux mers.

It was, I think, certainly Eliot's 'O earthly Paradise!' (Du Bartas: 'O Paradis du monde!') which inspired Shakespeare's 'this other Eden, demi-paradise', just as it was almost certainly Sylvester's 'the Worlds rich Garden' which inspired his later 'world's best garden' and 'best garden of the world'.

The preceding discussion, including the attempt to determine the time relation between passages in Shakespeare and the versions of Du Bartas by Eliot and Sylvester, does not seem to me to have been irrelevant either to a consideration of *Appleton House* or of Marvell's

---

1. 1593, Y[4].
For the suggestion that Sylvester was the probable originator of the phrase 'the Garden of the World' I am indebted to the Rev. A. S. T. Fisher, from whom a reply to an enquiry of mine, which had been printed in *TLS*, 7 November 1952, appeared in the same paper on 28 November. For the information about Eliot's *Ortho-epia Gallica* I am indebted to Mr J. W. Lever, who kindly wrote to me personally, and by whom an article on Shakespeare and Eliot appeared in *Shakespeare Survey* VI, April 1953.

poetry in general. In order to understand how much of our earlier poetry came to be written, it is necessary to liberate oneself from the modern and romantic conception of originality as something done out of one's own head, and to try to understand the theory and practice of the Renaissance doctrine of imitation. Even a poet so tremendous and so 'original' as Shakespeare could be inspired to one of his finest utterances by a very humble and pedestrian translation of Du Bartas, just as he was later inspired to some of the most memorable utterances in his tragedies (including Macbeth's great outburst at the sight of his blood-stained hands) by recollections of Seneca. It is true that in such passages he has transformed almost out of recognition the original sources of his inspiration, but without those sources the passages we admire would not have been there, or—what amounts to the same thing —would have been quite different. During the sixteenth and seventeenth centuries lesser poets were continually providing what might be called literary raw material for greater poets. And many good poets enabled other equally good or better poets (such as Marvell) to achieve new and original arrangements—suggested to them, as I have expressed it, new and amusing things to do. Without Fane and Sylvester, possibly without Shakespeare and Eliot, the first stanza in the passage we have been considering would almost certainly never have been written, and the two delightfully and unmistakably Marvellian stanzas that follow would almost certainly never have been written but for the new and amusing possibilities that had been suggested to Marvell by Cleveland. And just as the whole poem would never have been written but for Marvell's residence with Fairfax at Nunappleton, even so, without all that Nunappleton symbolised in the way of cultivated leisure and literary tradition the whole poem is inconceivable. Finally, it is perhaps worth remarking that, although I have spent much time, and have led others to spend much time, in discovering the origin of the phrase 'the Garden of the World', it is only Marvell who, by means of context and emphasis, has made that phrase memorable—so much so that it had perhaps never occurred to any previous reader that he did not invent it. (The two examples in *Henry V* are quite unmemorable and can, as it were, only be discovered with the aid of a magnifying glass.) Here, as always in poetry, it is the *impression* that matters: if a poet gives the impression of originality, originality is what he has achieved, however deeply indebted to earlier writers he may be shown to have been.

Upon Appleton House contains more than its fair share (over a hundred examples in 776 lines) of those clumsy inversions for the sake of rhyme and those line-filling 'did's', 'do's', and 'does's' which make one wish that Marvell had written less often with what Scott, praising Byron's *Cain*, called 'the negligent ease of a man of quality' and had displayed a more Popish zeal for 'correctness'. Even in the two delightful stanzas last quoted there are, apart from inversions, three of these irritating expletives:

> And Men *did* rosie Garlands wear . . .

> And his more gentle Forts *did* trace . . .

> But War all this *doth* overgrow.

It would be easy to multiply examples, but I will limit myself to two where Marvell almost seems to touch bottom and to achieve something like the style of the very baldest of *Lyrical Ballads*: one of the nuns says to the 'blooming Virgin Thwates':

> But much it to our work would add
> If here your hand, your Face we had
>
> (st. XVII)

and

> And (for I dare not quench the Fire
> That me does for your good inspire)
>
> (st. XVIII)

Sometimes a mixture of inversion and carelessness produces almost impenetrable obscurity:

> The double Wood of ancient Stocks
> Link'd in so thick, an Union locks,
> It like two *Pedigrees* appears,
> On one hand *Fairfax*, th'other *Veres*.
>
> (st. LXII)

Margoliouth takes 'union' to be the subject: if that is so, I think we must alter the punctuation of the first two lines, for the only thing in this passage about which I feel absolutely certain is that 'so thick an Union' forms a single phrase:

> The double Wood of ancient Stocks,
> Link'd in, so thick an Union locks.

The meaning would then be: 'There is a "union", an inter-communi-
cating line of trees, between the two parallel woods of ancient oak,
linked into them and locking them so closely ("thick") together that
the double-wood looks like two pedigrees'. I am doubtful, however,
whether 'union' here can mean what Margoliouth would have it mean
(i.e. more or less what it means in modern plumbing), and I am also
doubtful about 'link'd in'. I rather think that Marvell meant no more
than 'the double-wood is linked in so thick an union that it looks
like two pedigrees', and that he added the tautology and confusing
'locks' (=locks itself) merely because he wanted a rhyme for 'Stocks'.
There are also a few places where the past participle has been leng-
thened, an archaism which, like the inversions and the expletives, is
out of harmony with the natural and colloquial manner of the poem
as a whole:

When larger sizèd Men did stoop	(l. 29)
Of those wild Creatures, callèd Men	(l. 102)
Our *Orient* Breaths perfumèd are	(l. 109)
When we have prayèd all our Beads	(l. 121)

Even the beauty of that most beautiful poem *The Garden* is marred
by inversions and expletives, which, since I would conclude what I
have to say about Marvell's poetry with *nil nisi bonum*, I will antici-
patingly notice here. *Inversions*: 'themselves amaze' (l. 1); 'How far these
Beauties Hers exceed!' (l. 22); 'where s'eer your barkes I wound,/No
name shall but your own be found' (ll. 23–4); 'The *Gods*, that mortal
Beauty chase' (l. 27); 'that She might Laurel grow' (l. 30); 'from
pleasure less' (='from lesser pleasure') (l. 41). *Expletives* (often with
inversion): '*Does* prudently their Toyles upbraid' (l. 6); 'While all
Flow'rs and all Trees *do* Close' (l. 7); 'Still in a Tree *did* end their race'
(l. 28); '*did* after *Syrinx* speed' (l. 31); 'Upon my Mouth *do* crush their
Wine' (l. 36); 'Into my hands themselves *do* reach' (l. 38); '*Does* streight
its own resemblance find' (l. 44); 'My Soul into the boughs *does* glide'
(l. 52); '*Does* through a fragrant Zodiack run' (l. 68). It is because there
are so many inversions that they give the impression of having been
resorted to for the sake of a too easy rhyme. Had they been used more
sparingly, some of them might be justified by the emphasis they throw
upon particular words:

> When we have *run* our Passions heat,
> Love *hither* makes his best retreat

(ll. 25–6, where 'hither' can perhaps scarcely be regarded as an inversion). Except for the 'did's' and 'does's' there are not, I think, in *The Garden* any words that are mere passengers, mere line-fillers and syllable-fillers and syllable-suppliers; nevertheless, as I have observed before, Marvell's expletives and (as I am tempted to call them) his lazy inversions counteract to some extent that impression of *mastery* produced by the concentration and unsuperfluousness of his language. In fact, it must be admitted that Marvell's verse is sometimes no more careful and (alas!) no more distinguished than that of his patron the Lord General. If this amateur, this unprofessional, this society, this coterie poetry had its great virtues, it also had its characteristic defects. It was written for an audience not sufficiently critical of *minutiae*, and it is on the observance of innumerable *minutiae* that absolute success in the art of poetry depends.[1]

1. [It seems likely that if Kitty W. Scoular's *Natural Magic: Studies in the Presentation of Nature in English Poetry from Spenser to Marvell* (Oxford, 1965) had appeared before J. B. Leishman's death, he would have referred to her treatment of *Upon Appleton House.*   J.B.]

Nowhere is that balance between the conceptual and the visual, between the dialectical and the pictorial or descriptive, which is so characteristic of Marvell, more perfectly exemplified than in *The Garden*, which, it seems reasonable to suppose, was composed about the same time as *Appleton House*. But while *Appleton House* is primarily a descriptive poem, *The Garden* is primarily an argumentative or dialectical one; and, since the argument which it develops has recently received much attention, often, as it seems to me, with insufficient observance of that balance between seriousness and light-heartedness which distinguishes the poem, and also with some failure to perceive what other seventeenth-century poems *The Garden* does and does not resemble, it may be as well to begin with some prose (and perhaps rather prosaic) analysis of the nine stanzas in which Marvell has arranged his octosyllabic couplets.

I. Those who toil for military, civic or poetic honours are crowned only with the leaves of a single tree (palm, oak or bay), but here all the flowers and all the trees offer us the garlands of repose.

II. Only here are innocence and quiet to be found. Their plants, unlike those which supply the garlands of ambition, are given only in the places where they grow. Society, in comparison with this delicious solitude, is merely barbarous.

III. This lovely green excites more desire than the white and red in any woman's cheeks, but lovers, if they will, carve their mistress's name on these trees that so excel her in beauty: the only names I will ever carve upon them shall be their own.

IV. Apollo only pursued Daphne in order that she might turn into a laurel, and Pan Syrinx in order that she might turn into a reed.

V. Fruits offer themselves to me and flowers ensnare me.

VI. But my mind withdraws from the lesser pleasures of the senses into that happiness which is within itself, and there, transcending those external objects that are mirrored within it as terrestrial things are counterparted in the ocean, it creates other worlds and rejects all the visible creation in favour of those green, innocent and primal thoughts that come to it in a green shade.

VII. My soul leaves the body and glides like a bird into the trees, where it prepares itself for yet longer flight.

VIII. Such was the state of Adam in Paradise, before the creation of Eve. That, however, was a state of happiness too great for a mortal, and he was not allowed to enjoy it for long.

IX. How could such hours be reckoned but by a sundial made of flowers and herbs?

With conscious paradox and hyperbole, with an inimitable combination of jest and earnest, seriousness and light-heartedness, Marvell is here maintaining at least four more or less paradoxical propositions:

(1) The superiority of the contemplative to the active life.

(2) The superiority, because more favourable to contemplation, of solitude to society.

(3) The superiority, for the same reason, of the beauty of gardens to the beauty of women.

(4) The superiority of the invisible to the visible and of the inner world created by the mind to the external world perceived by the senses.

The argument of his poem might also be expressed, less abstractly, as follows: the only perfect human life we know of was that of Adam, before the creation of Eve; but through weakly yielding to her charm he sinned and fell. While Adam was alone, his only sensual or sensuous pleasures were the sight and smell and taste of flowers and fruits, and these could not distract him from, nay, rather their very mildness and unwithholdingness left him free, impelled him to seek, the higher pleasure of conversing with God.

In an interesting and stimulating essay on 'The Argument of Marvell's "Garden" '[1] Professor Frank Kermode seems to me to reveal an insufficient awareness of what, when all deductions and qualifications have been made, I may call the uniqueness of Marvell's poem, and, at the same time, to make far too much of an antithesis,

1. In *Essays in Criticism*, II, no. 3 (July 1952), 225 ff.

based on superficial or imaginary resemblances, between what he would have us regard as two *genres* of seventeenth-century poetry: poems in which gardens are praised as places apt for love, and poems in which they are praised as places apt for contemplation. For, while poems, or passages in poems, praising gardens as places apt for love are as old as the *Roman de la Rose*, as old as Petronius (*dignus amore locus*), the first poem distinguishably and memorably celebrating what Professor Kermode would call the Philosopher's Garden is Marvell's. The chief source of what seem to me the errors and confusions in Professor Kermode's essay is probably the fact that he, like some other writers upon Marvell, has persuaded himself that, because Fairfax translated it, Saint-Amant's poem *La Solitude* must have exerted a far greater influence upon Marvell's poetry than it actually did, and that it is far more like Marvell's poetry than it really is.[1] I have already insisted on the fundamental differences between *La Solitude* and *Appleton House* and upon the fact that the only significant resemblance between them is that they may both be regarded as what I have called 'catalogues of delights'. But between *La Solitude* and *The Garden* even that resemblance is absent, and the only link between the two poems is that the word 'solitude' occurs in both. *The Garden* is not, like *La Solitude*, a catalogue of delights, and *La Solitude* is not, like *The Garden*, an argument. *La Solitude* is in no sense argumentative or dialectical, but essentially evocative and romantic, and consists, as I have said, 'of a loosely related series of leisurely and expansively described scenes and images which a mood may "feed upon" '. On the other hand, between *The Garden* and *Appleton House* there are some real affinities, and stanzas from the shorter poem might well have been incorporated at various places in the longer one. Nevertheless, while there are certain dialectical or argumentative passages in *Appleton House*, passages in which the visual and the conceptual, the dialectical and

1. The first writer to suggest that Marvell's poetry had been influenced by Saint-Amant's seems to have been Edward Bliss Reed, in an article on 'The Poems of Thomas Fairfax', *Transactions of the Connecticut Academy of Arts and Sciences*, XIV, July 1909, 237–90. Assuming that Marvell wrote all (or most) of his 'nature' poems at Nunappleton, Reed declared: 'That these poems were inspired not only by the beauty of Nunappleton, but by its owner's love and appreciation of poetry, there can be little doubt. We may go even further, and see in Marvell's nature-poems some hints from Saint-Amant. Marvell's verse is richer and deeper; where Saint-Amant is vague in his descriptions or conventional in his thought, Marvell is concrete and original; for it is the Englishman, and not the Frenchman, who uses *le mot précis*, and yet Saint-Amant's theme—to lose oneself in Nature—is the theme of *The Garden* and of the finest lines in *Appleton House*' (p. 248).

the descriptive, are combined in much the same way as in *The Garden*, *Appleton House* still remains primarily a descriptive poem, a catalogue of delights, while in *The Garden* description is throughout subordinated to argument, is essentially illustrative. I say 'subordinated to argument', although it is probable that for most readers, who delightedly encounter it for the first time in *The Golden Treasury*, *The Garden* seems primarily a descriptive poem, and that the chief impression it leaves upon them is a pictorial or visual one. It is, I think, above all the purely descriptive and visual fifth stanza, which stands in the exact middle of the poem (four stanzas before it and four after it), that has contributed to produce this, for many readers, abiding impression:

> What wond'rous Life is[1] this I lead!
> Ripe Apples drop about my head;
> The Luscious Clusters of the Vine
> Upon my Mouth do crush their Wine;
> The Nectaren, and curious Peach,
> Into my hands themselves do reach;
> Stumbling on Melons, as I pass,
> Insnar'd with Flow'rs, I fall on Grass.

This stanza, it seems worth remarking, is strikingly reminiscent of some lines (by which it may well have been suggested) in one of the most notable descriptions of a *locus amoenus* in ancient poetry, that passage at the end of Theocritus's seventh Idyll (The Harvest-home) which describes how the three wayfarers, having reached Phrasidamus's farm, lay down on beds of rushes and vine leaves in a place where poplars and elms murmured overhead, a spring flashed near by, and the air was filled with the sound of cicadas and tree-frogs, larks and finches, doves and bees:

> All nature smelt of the opulent summer-time, smelt of the season of fruit. Pears lay at our feet, apples on either side rolling abundantly, and the young branches lay splayed upon the ground because of the weight of their damsons.[2]

It is, I think, mainly because of the Theocritean glow and colour

1. 'Is this': to this Thompson (1776, III 413), with or without MS authority, silently emended the 'in this' of 1681, an emendation accepted (silently again) by Grosart and several other modern editors. I cannot but think that 'is this' must be the authentic reading, and I cannot imagine any really convincing defence of the appropriateness of 'in this'.

2. ll. 143–6, Loeb translation.

radiated from this motionless centre of the poem that many (perhaps most) readers of *The Garden* fail to perceive, or perhaps only come to perceive much later, that there is an argument continuously progressing beneath a surface of description. Marvell, one might almost say, is arguing in images. In fact, the more closely one considers his poem, the more deeply aware one becomes, both in manner and in matter, of its uniqueness.

If it is to be classified at all, it belongs to two often overlapping *genres*, the 'Replies' and the 'Paradoxes'. As a Reply it cannot, indeed, like Crashaw's *Answer for Hope* in reply to Cowley's *Against Hope* or Strode's *Against Melancholy* in reply to Fletcher's 'Hence, all you vaine Delights', be regarded as a reply to any particular poem, but only as a general reply to those innumerable poems and passages in poems which, from the time of Petronius, had celebrated either the garden or the *locus amoenus* as a *dignus amore locus*. As a Paradox, it would seem to be, even in the most restricted and popular sense of that term, essentially original; for, so far as I am aware, neither the central paradox, the superiority of solitude to society (as distinct from the superiority of country life to that of the city or the court, a well-established Horatian and Virgilian theme that can scarcely be regarded as paradoxical), nor the subsidiary paradox, the superiority of natural to feminine beauty, had ever been poetically elaborated before. Generations of poets had declared that the white and red of roses was as nothing in comparison with the white and red in their mistress's cheeks, but no poet before Marvell had ventured to declare that

> No white nor red was ever seen
> So am'rous as this lovely green.[1]

1. Similarly, it seems likely that many poets before Marvell had declared that it was cruel of lovers to carve their mistresses' names on trees: Mrs Katherine Philips ('the Matchless Orinda') certainly did so in a poem written long before Marvell's poems were printed, 'Upon the Graving of her Name upon a Tree in Barn-Elms Woods' (*Caroline Poets*, ed. Saintsbury, I 583):

> Alas, how barbarous are we,
> Thus to reward the courteous Tree
> Who its broad shade affording us,
> Deserves not to be wounded thus!
> See how the yielding bark complies
> With our ungrateful injuries!
> And seeing this, say how much the
> Trees are more generous then men,
> Who by a nobleness so pure,
> Can first oblige, and then endure

Nevertheless, the manner (as distinct from the matter) of this subsidiary paradox of Marvell's may be compared with Donne's

> I can love her, and her, and you and you,
> I can love any, so she be not true;[1]

or

> Love built on beauty, soone as beauty, dies,
> Chuse this face, chang'd by no deformities.[2]

Since, however, Marvell's poem is not merely a paradoxical pane-gyric on solitude but a celebration of the State of Innocence, it is possible (though not absolutely necessary) to establish connections between it and the very earliest records of our cultural and religious inheritance. For the Christian and Old Testament conception of the State of Innocence, of the unfallen Adam, has affinities with the ancient Greek and Roman conception of a Golden Age.

Among the ancient Greeks it was an article of belief that perfect justice and holiness were to be found only among certain barbarous peoples at the extreme edge of the earth. For, although here and there appeared philosophers who believed in progress and looked back upon barbarism, the general and popular belief did not see mankind as continually progressing, but rather as having fallen further and further away from an original state of virtue and happiness. This belief, merely implied in that often-repeated Homeric phrase 'such as men are now' (οἷοι νῦν βροτοί εἰσίν), finds its clearest expression in Hesiod, who, in the *Works and Days* (ll. 109–201), describes five races of men: those of the Golden Age, who lived like the gods, without labour or sorrow, until they finally perished from the earth; those of the Silver Age, who were destroyed by Zeus because they failed to honour the gods; those of the Brazen Age, who destroyed themselves in war; those of the Heroic Age, the heroes and demi-gods who fought at Troy and Thebes, some of whom are still living at the ends of the earth, where Cronos rules over them; and, finally, those of the Iron

---

Marvell, though (and here it seems unlikely that he had had any predecessor) went one better, and added:

> Fair Trees! where s'eer your barkes I wound,
> No Name shall but your own be found.

Cleveland also had something of this capacity to go one better, to keep the ball longer in the air, but he seldom exercised it with Marvell's tact and taste.

1. *The Indifferent*, ll. 8–9.
2. *Elegie II (The Anagram)*, ll. 27–8

Age, to which Hesiod himself belongs, men who never rest from labour and sorrow by day and from perishing by night.

It was during and after the Alexandrine period, when the πόλις, the city-state, had been replaced by large cities no longer able to satisfy in the same way the lives of all their citizens, that passages describing, on the one hand, the Golden Age itself and, on the other hand, the life of shepherds or of simple husbandmen, as being least unlike that of the Golden Age, become frequent in ancient literature. In Latin poetry, among the most memorable descriptions of the Golden Age itself, the age of 'unlaborious earth and oarless sea', are those of Ovid (*Amores*, III viii 35 ff.), Tibullus (I iii), and Seneca (*Hippolytus*, 483–564, *Octavia*, 377 ff.). As celebrations of, as it were, vestigial remains of the Golden Age we have the slightly idealised shepherds of Theocritus in their Sicilian landscape and the still more idealised shepherds of Virgil's Eclogues in their imaginary Arcadia; to which may be added the celebrations, in Virgil's *Georgics* (II 458 ff.) and in various passages in Horace, of simple husbandmen as inheritors and transmitters of those *mores prisci* through which Rome had become great.

Common to nearly all classical descriptions of the Golden Age is the insistence that there was no ploughing, no mining (and hence no weapons and no war), no enclosure of lands and no 'tempting' of the sea with ships. One of the most elaborate and representative of these descriptions is that of Tibullus, in the third elegy of his first book, where the poet, having fallen sick in Phaeacia, begs his friend Messalla not to cross the Aegean without him, since, if he should die, there will be no relative or friend at hand to perform his funeral rites.

How well lived folk in olden days when Saturn was the king, before the earth was opened out for distant travel! Not as yet had the pine-tree learned to swim the blue sea wave or surrendered the spreading sail to belly before the wind; nor, seeking gain in unknown lands, had the vagrant seaman loaded his bark with foreign wares. That was a time when the sturdy bull had not bent his neck to the yoke, nor the tamed horse champed the bit. No house had doors; no stone was planted on the land to set fixed boundaries to men's estates. The very oaks gave honey; and with milky udders came the ewes unbidden to meet the careless swain. Then were no marshalled hosts, no lust of blood, no battles; no swords had been forged by the cruel armourer's ruthless skill. But now that Jupiter is Lord, there are wounds and carnage without cease; now the sea slays, and a thousand ways of sudden death.[1]

In the Latin poets of antiquity a description of the Golden Age is frequently (one might almost say, generally) no more than a kind of rhetorical figure, introduced to illustrate and support a proposition which may itself be no more (and, one may add—since everything depends on what the poet makes of it—no less) than a rhetorical commonplace. Here, for example, Tibullus begins with the famous commonplace (as old as Homer) on the evil of dying without funeral rites; proceeds to another ancient commonplace, that of sea-faring as an example of human presumption or, as we might say, of 'tempting Providence', and then introduces a description of the Golden Age as a time when sea-faring was unknown. Ovid, in the eighth elegy of the third book of the *Amores*, introduces his description of the Golden Age by means of a more facetious transition: he has been rejected as a lover in favour of a rich knight who has gained his wealth and rank as a soldier, so Ovid celebrates the Golden Age as a time when mining, metals, weapons and war were unknown. In another elegy of Tibullus's (II iii) there is at least the germ of a topic which I have not found elsewhere in descriptions of the Golden Age by ancient poets—the suggestion, merely, that in the Golden Age not only fields but women were unenclosed. The starting-point of this elegy is that Tibullus's mistress, whom he calls 'Nemesis', is staying in the country: this leads him to declare that he will follow the example of Apollo and turn countryman (Apollo had tended the flocks of Admetus), and this leads to praise of rural simplicity, especially as it was in the 'days of old', and to condemnation of urban luxury and avarice. It is at l. 71 that Tibullus associates these 'days of old' (*olim*: he does not specifically say that he is describing the Golden Age) not merely with the unenclosed field, but with the unenclosed woman:

> Tunc, quibus aspirabat Amor, praebebat aperte
> mitis in umbrosa gaudia valle Venus.
> nullus erat custos, nulla exclusura dolentes
> ianua. si fas est, mos precor ille redi.

(Then, to those on whom Love breathed, a gentle Venus openly proffered her pleasures in the shady vale. There was no watchman, no door to exclude the anguished. If it be not wrong to do so, I pray for that custom's return.)

1. ll. 35-50, Loeb translation.

I have not found any other example of this topic in ancient descriptions of the Golden Age. For the Ancients in general, it would seem, love was free enough in the world they knew, and they did not need to look back longingly to some greater freedom in a Golden Age; but for many Renaissance poets the Golden Age became first and foremost an age of free love, just as for the classical poets it had been primarily an age of unmined earth and 'untempted', or 'unattempted', sea. The most famous of these Renaissance celebrations of the *bella età dell'oro* was that Chorus in Tasso's *Aminta* (translated by Daniel with the title *A Pastoral* and appended to the *Delia* Sonnets in the 1601 edition of his *Works*), which declared that the tyrant Honour was then unknown and that whatever pleased was right, but Tasso had been preceded by some forty years by that finest of Renaissance Latin poets Johannes Secundus. In the following passage from the seventh elegy of his first book, a poem on the betrothal of his Julia to another, Secundus is partly imitating and, to some extent, parodying both the elaborate description of the Golden Age in Tibullus's Messala elegy and the short passage about the 'days of old' in Tibullus's Nemesis elegy. For Tibullus in his Messala elegy the unattempted sea had been the *fons et origo* of his whole evocation of the Golden Age, but for Secundus it is merely, together with the unlaboured earth and undivided fields, a piece of conventional decoration. For him the primary characteristic of the Golden Age is not the oarless sea but the doorless house, which he associates with the unguarded mistress and unfettered love. In his Messala elegy Tibullus had introduced this doorless house merely incidentally, in association with the undivided fields:

> Non domus ulla fores habuit, non fixus in agris,
>   qui regeret certis finibus arva, lapis.

It was no doubt this almost casual allusion to doors (*fores*) which led Secundus to associate the description of the Golden Age in the Messala elegy with the description of the 'days of old' in the Nemesis elegy, a description which seems to culminate in the evocation of unexcluded, unprohibited and uninhibited love:

> nullus erat custos, nulla exclusura dolentes ianua.

If my supposition is correct, it was this casual and, so far as I am aware, unique piece of witticism and waggery on the part of Tibullus which, through Secundus, so profoundly modified and, as it were, *de-moralised* for many succeeding poets the whole classical conception of the Golden Age.

> Quam bene priscorum currebat vita parentum,
>   Ingenuae Veneris libera sacra colens!
> Nondum conjugii nomen servile patebat,
>   Nec fuerat divis adnumeratus Hymen.
> Passim communes exercebantur amores
>   Omnibus, et proprii nescius orbis erat.
> Ense maritali nemo confossus adulter
>   Purpureo Stygias sanguine tinxit aquas.
> Anxia non tenuit custodis cura puellam,
>   Nulla erat invisis clausa domus foribus.
> Nec sacer agricolis stabat lapis arbiter agro,
>   Trabsque procellosum nulla secabat iter.
> At postquam domibusque fores, foribusque subivit
>   Clavis, et aequoreas navita sprevit aquas,
> Non dubitans animam tenui concredere ligno,
>   Externas fragili puppe secutus opes,
> Discretique novo jacuerunt limite campi,
>   Indixit leges et sibi quisque novas:
> Scilicet ex illo sensit fera jura, jacetque
>   Clausa pedem dura compede serva Venus . . .
> Tempora, si fas est, iterum primaeva redite,
>   Falciferoque iterum sub sene mundus eat.
> Inscia tunc rastri, tunc vomeris inscia curvi,
>   Sponte sua segetem terra benigna feret,
> Et repetent iterum desertas numina terras,
>   Et fruar, O, longum tutus amore meo!

(How happily passed that life of our ancestors which practised the free rites of ingenuous Venus! The servile name of marriage was not yet current and Hymen not yet numbered among the gods. Love everywhere was made by all in common, and the world was ignorant of property. No adulterer, pierced by a husband's sword, purpled the Stygian waters with his blood. The young girl was not confined by a guardian's anxious care; no house was closed by hateful doors; no boundary stone, sacred object to their tillers, stood in fields; no vessel clove the stormy path. But from the time when houses were furnished with doors and doors with keys, and the sailor, not fearing to trust his life to a slender beam, braved the watery main, seeking foreign wealth in fragile bark, and fields lay separate with new-placed bounds—from the time when each first submitted himself to laws, Venus too felt cruel decrees and, feet locked in savage fetters, lies a slave . . . Return, if it may be, primeval ages, and let the world pass once more beneath the scythe-bearing ancient's sway! Ignorant then of rake, ignorant of curved plough-share, kindly earth will yield harvest of her own free will, divinities will seek once more the abandoned earth, and I in safety shall enjoy, O long, my love!)

Secundus, whose poems were enormously popular, would seem to have been the Renaissance originator of this witticism, this piece of waggery, about the unenclosure of love and women in the Golden Age. Be that as it may, it certainly, as we say, 'caught on'. Carew, for example, at the beginning of his famous *Rapture*, after inviting his Celia to fly with him to that 'Loves Elizium' whose ultimate source is probably the conclusion of that important elegy of Tibullus I have quoted from,[1] tells her not to fear that 'Gyant, Honour', whom Tasso had exorcised in the *Aminta*, and who, he assures her, is not, as was once thought, of divine origin,

> but a weake modell wrought
> By greedy men, that seeke to enclose the common,
> And within private armes empale free woman.[2]

And Randolph, in *Upon Love fondly refus'd for Conscience sake*, may have been partly elaborating upon Carew and partly, so to speak, re-inspired by Secundus when he wrote

> It was not love, but love transform'd to vice
>   Ravish'd by envious Avarice,
> Made women first impropriate; all were free.
>   Inclosures mans Inventions be.
> I' th' golden age no action could be found
>   For trespasse on my neighbours ground:
> Twas just with any Fayre to mix our blood;
>   The best is most diffusive good.[3]

---

1. This passage had also been imitated by Secundus in the second of his *Basia* and from Secundus by many poets of the Pléiade.
2. *Poems*, ed. Dunlap, p. 49.
3. *Poems*, ed. Thorn Drury, pp. 128-9.

Marvell's *Garden*, celebrating—not unseriously, and yet not wholly seriously, but with much conscious paradox and hyperbole—on the one hand, the Christian and Old Testament Age of Innocence and, on the other hand, the superiority of solitude to society, including the society of women, may indeed be incidentally regarded, and may well have been incidentally intended, as a reply to these various neo-classical celebrations of the Golden Age as the Age of Free Love and of Gardens and other *loci amoeni* as places 'apt for love'. It should, however, be regarded primarily as a continuation, with much of the conscious paradox and hyperbole which distinguishes so many seventeenth-century poetic debates for and against Inconstancy, Melancholy, 'Fruition', Hope, and so forth, of that very ancient philosophic and theological debate on the respective benefits of society and solitude, the active and the contemplative life. This debate is at least as old as Plato, who in the *Republic* declared that the philosopher must be compelled, by the penalty of being ruled by men worse than himself, to forsake from time to time the supreme pleasure of contemplation in order to take his turn in governing the state. The Stoics in the main followed Plato in this respect, and declared that their virtuous man could never be discharged from the duty of labouring for the public good; the Epicureans, on the other hand, taught that the wise man would abstain from public affairs. It was generally supposed, however, that the ancient philosophers had on the whole recommended a life of retirement;[1] this was partly because nearly all the ancient philoso-

---

1. This, certainly, was the opinion of Sir William Temple in his essay *Upon the Gardens of* Epicurus; *or, of Gardening*. Temple's essay, it is true, was written, as the title informs us, 'In the Year 1685', more than thirty years later than Marvell's poem; nevertheless, we may perhaps assume that Temple's knowledge of ancient literature and philosophy was very much what Marvell's had been when he wrote his paradoxical praise of solitude in *The Garden*. After praising Horace for refusing to become Secretary to Augustus, Temple continued (*Works*, 1720, I 175):

> But all the different Sects of Philosophers seem to have agreed in the Opinion of a Wise Man's abstaining from Publick Affairs, which is thought the Meaning of *Pythagoras's* Precept, to *abstain from Beans*, by which the Affairs or Publick Resolutions in *Athens* were managed. They thought that sort of Business too gross and material for the abstracted Fineness of their Speculations . . . But above all, they esteemed Publick Business the most contrary of all others to that Tranquillity of Mind, which they esteemed and taught to be the only true Felicity of Man.

> For this reason *Epicurus* passed his Life wholly in his Garden; there he Studied, there he Exercised, there he Taught his Philosophy; and indeed, no other sort of Abode seems to contribute so much, to both the Tranquillity of Mind, and Indolence of Body, which he made his Chief End. The Sweetness of Air, the

phers agreed that, although the active life might be necessary and expedient, the life of contemplation was better and higher, and partly because the eclectic Seneca, whose influence during the Middle Ages and the Renaissance was immense, had, though he professed himself a Stoic, nevertheless declared that, when the state was past cure, the wise man might retire into solitude and work for posterity.

This debate had been continued, though in a somewhat different form, by the Fathers of the Christian Church and by the Schoolmen in their attempts to decide upon the true place of hermitism and monasticism in the life of the Church. The view which finally prevailed was that which had been expressed at the beginning by St Augustine and St Gregory and which was subsequently elaborated by Aquinas: namely, that although the contemplative life was in a sense higher, as being more like the life to come, it was nevertheless optional, was not a life which all Christians were called upon to lead, and must at least be preceded by the active life.

Since every scholar must have been familiar with this age-long debate, it is perhaps a little remarkable that among the numerous collections of paradoxes, both in prose and verse, that were published during the sixteenth and seventeenth centuries the theme of Solitude *versus* Society or the contemplative *versus* the active life, does not seem to appear. For had it not been almost thrust upon the notice of Renaissance scholars by Petrarch's *De Vita Solitaria*, the longest and most elaborate of all celebrations of the life of retirement, contemplation and study? And Petrarch, though he continually appeals to Christian precedent and often expresses specifically Christian beliefs and ideals, is writing primarily as a scholar and humanist, and might have been expected to engage the attention of later scholars and humanists more closely than seems to have been the case. Petrarch refers several times to St Ambrose, in one of whose letters (no. XLIX), written in A.D. 390 to Sabinus, Bishop of Placenza, a letter from which Petrarch quotes, there are some remarks about the baneful impingement of Eve upon Adam's solitude which might surely have been expected, sooner or later, to provide some Italian writer of *Capitoli* or some English 'metaphysical'

Pleasantness of Smells, the Verdure of Plants, the Cleanness and Lightness of Food, the Exercises of Working or Walking; but above all, the Exemption from Cares and Solicitude, seem equally to favour and improve both Contemplation and Health, the Enjoyment of Sense and Imagination and thereby the Quiet and Ease both of the Body and Mind.

poet with a topic for slightly irreverent wit. Mary, declares St Ambrose, was alone when the Angel addressed her, alone when the Holy Ghost came upon her, alone when she conceived Christ.

> Peter was alone when the mystery of the sanctification of the Gentiles all over the world was made known to him. Adam was alone, and he fell not, because his mind adhered to God. But when the woman was joined to him he lost his power of abiding by the celestial precepts, and therefore he hid himself when God walked in Paradise . . . From whence it appears that it is when alone that we offer ourselves to God, that we open to Him our souls, that we put off the cloak of fraud. Adam was alone when placed in Paradise; alone also when made in the image of God: but when cast out of Paradise he was not alone. The Lord Jesus was alone when he redeemed the world; for it was no herald or messenger, but the Lord Himself Who redeemed His people, although He, in Whom the Father always dwells, can never be alone. Let us also then be alone, that the Lord may be with us.[1]

I do not know whether St Ambrose was the first theologian to declare so explicitly that Adam lost his sanctity with his solitude, nor do I know whether the topic was treated with any significant emphasis by his successors. Donne, whom it would not have been surprising to find treating the topic with irreverent wit in the days of his youth, treated it very much in the manner of St Ambrose (though he does not refer to him) in the second of the two parts into which he later divided the sermon preached at the Hague in December 1619 on the calling of Simon and Andrew. Donne begins this second part with a consideration of Christ's words 'Follow me', which leads him to speak of the virtue of humility and the sin of pride, which, he declares, began with company and with Eve:

> Comparatively *Adam* was better then all the world beside, and yet we finde no act of pride in *Adam*, when he was alone. Solitude is not the scene of Pride; The danger of pride is in company, when we meet to looke upon another. But in *Adams* wife, *Eve*, her first act (that is noted) was an act of Pride, a hearkning to that voyce of the Serpent, *Ye shall be as Gods*. As soone as there were two, there was pride.[2]

1. *The Letters of S. Ambrose*, in *A Library of Fathers*, Oxford 1881, pp. 317–18.
2. *Sermons*, ed. Potter and Simpson, II 295, ll. 282 ff.

No doubt many other preachers and theologians, besides Donne, had repeated these reflections which St Ambrose may or may not have been the first to express. Sooner or later, however, it was surely inevitable that these or similar reflections should lead some medieval clerk or some sixteenth- or seventeenth-century wit to remark that, as soon as Eve was joined to Adam, the serpent made up three. Nevertheless, this surely inevitable witticism, whether or no it had occurred to anyone before, does not seem to have found its way into print until 1668, in the seventh stanza of that charming poem beginning 'Hail, old *Patrician* Trees' in Cowley's essay *Of Solitude*:

> Oh Solitude, first state of Human-kind!
>   Which blest remain'd till man did find
>   Even his own helpers Companie.
> As soon as two (Alas) together joyn'd,
>   The Serpent made up Three.[1]

Were it not for the fact that the *Several Discourses by way of Essays, in Verse and Prose* did not appear in print until the 1668 edition of Cowley's *Works*, one might have been tempted to suppose that this stanza had been the starting-point, the initial inspiration of Marvell's *Garden*, just as two stanzas from poems in Cowley's *The Mistress* had almost certainly provided the initial inspiration for *The Definition of Love* and *To his Coy Mistress*.

---

1. *Works*, 1684, Qqq3ᵛ (p. 94). Cowley, it is true (and, for that matter, Marvell), had been somewhat fumblingly and unmemorably anticipated by William Habington in his poem *To Zephirus*, whom he begs to waft himself and Castara to some beautiful and uninhabited coast:

> Thus Paradise did our first Parents Wooe,
> To harmless sweets, at first possest by two.
> And o're this second, weele usurpe the throne;
> *Castara* weele obey and rule alone.
> For the rich vertue of this soyle I feare,
> Would be depraved, should but a third be there.

(*Poems*, ed. Allott, p. 58. The poem was first printed in Habington's *Castara*, 1634.) It is only because of the faint gleam of wit in the last line that one can speak of anticipation, for Habington, although he is being hyperbolical, is being no more paradoxical than Spenser or Milton or any sixteenth- or seventeenth-century imaginer of a Golden Age. 'Should but a third be there': it is, I suppose not impossible that this may have suggested to Cowley the paradoxical witticism that, if a second was there, a third was bound to follow, and that this third would be no other than the serpent.

Such was that happy Garden-state,
While Man there walk'd without a Mate:
After a Place so pure, and sweet,
What other Help could yet be meet!
But 'twas beyond a Mortal's share
To wander solitary there:
Two Paradises 'twere in one
To live in Paradise alone.

Although this piece of wit does not seem to have been suggested to Marvell by any previous *poet*, he is here treating with a slightly irreverent wit, with, one might even say, a certain waggishness, what may well have been almost a theological commonplace, treating it with a kind of wit (hyperbolical, paradoxical, surprising, slightly shocking) not dissimilar from that which Donne had applied to more scholastic concepts—as when, for example, he declared that his mistress possessed the more than angelic power of reading thoughts directly, or that the Countess of Bedford was a divinity, to be apprehended partly by reason and partly by faith. During the seventeenth century such theological wit was often indulged in even by the gravest and most orthodox—partly, perhaps, because so much of their reading and thinking was theological, and partly because they were speaking to or writing for persons whom they could depend upon to take what they said exactly as they meant it. No one, for example, would ever have accused King James of insufficient respect for what he and his contemporaries regarded as the Word of God; yet King James, according to Archdeacon Plume, once declared that 'Dr Donns uerses were like ye peace of God, they passed all understanding'.[1] Only those who are very secure in their faith can afford to jest about it, as Chaucer could afford to jest about Courtly Love and about learning and about much else that he held dear—a fact which, as C. S. Lewis observed, has led many modern readers to suppose that he was what the French call *un vrai business man* and that his spokesman in the *Parlement of Foules* is the Duck. Modern readers, rooted in a totalitarian, or increasingly totalitarian, society and no longer habitually aware of any distinction between things temporal and things eternal, either do not realise, or too often forget, how wide an area of play, of *Spielraum*, our older writers, especially those of the seventeenth century, were able to

1. In a notebook in the Plume Library at Maldon, MS 30, folio 17 verso: see a letter from Percy Simpson *TLS*, 25 October 1941.

permit themselves. This is especially true of poets such as Donne and Marvell, who wrote their poems, not for the world at large, but for circulation among friends, whom they could depend upon to make all necessary qualifications and allowances and to admire the art and the wit. The last-quoted stanza should alone be sufficient to prevent us from taking Marvell's *Garden* too seriously, from supposing that Marvell regarded it as a full and sufficient expression of his then attitude to the relation between the contemplative and the active life—or, for that matter, to female society! His position and attitude is much more like that of a defendant or respondent in some academic debate, saying, with all the wit and eloquence at his command, all he can find to say for or against the position he has been selected to defend or to oppose.

Nevertheless, although in this poem Marvell is being deliberately paradoxical and hyperbolical, he is not being so in the riotous and almost burlesque manner of many of the Italian *Capitoli*, or many of the paradoxes in the prose collections, of some of Donne's Elegies and *Songs and Sonets*, or of his own *Character of Holland*. Marvell's paradox (his central paradox, as distinct from such a subsidiary paradox as that trees are more desire-exciting than women), that the contemplative life is superior to an active life because more like that of the unfallen Adam, is not really *in pari materia* with Donne's paradox that it is better to marry an old and ugly woman than a young and handsome one because the former's face can never change for the worse. The paradox which Marvell, with such an exquisite mingling of seriousness and light-heartedness, is here maintaining is the great, the eternal, paradox of which Aristotle was aware when he recognised that θεωρία, the life of pure contemplation, although often incompatible with the exercise of those faculties and the performance of those duties which are necessary for the preservation of human society, was nevertheless the most divine kind of life and that, in spite of those who tell us to be content to think mortal thoughts and to leave immortal thoughts to the gods, we should strive so far as possible to make ourselves immortal (ἐφ' ὅσον ἐνδέχεται ἀθανατίζειν) by living in and through the exercise of that intellect (νοῦς) which is the most potent element within us and which, small though it be, 'in power and dignity far surpasses all the rest';[1] the paradox of which Aquinas was aware when, elaborating upon Aristotle, he declared that, although the *vita contemplativa* was *non proprie humana sed superhumana*, it was nevertheless the noblest kind of life because it

1. *Nicomachean Ethics*, X vii (1177^b).

contained some pledge and foretaste of that immortal felicity which man was promised.

Marvell's poem may perhaps best be regarded as a graceful tribute, more sustained and serious than two stanzas in *Appleton House* with which it has some affinity, to his patron the Lord General Fairfax, who had for a time, but only for a time, exchanged a life of action for one of retirement and contemplation. In *Appleton House*, after the beautiful passage about 'the Garden of the World' that had been wasted by civil war, Marvell had reflected that there walked in the garden of Nunappleton one who, had it pleased God and himself, might have made the Garden of England flourish like his own:

> But he preferr'd to the *Cinque Ports*[1]
> These five imaginary Forts:
> And, in those half-dry Trenches, spann'd
> Pow'r which the Ocean might command.

> For he did, with his utmost Skill,
> *Ambition* weed, but *Conscience* till.
> *Conscience*, that Heaven-nursed Plant,
> Which most our Earthly Gardens want.
>
> (sts. XLIV–V)

in *The Garden*, we may say, Marvell has written a more sustained and unqualified panegyric upon the life Fairfax had chosen, although he, like his patron, was well aware that the active life too had its place and its necessity. For that the Lord General, although he delighted in his solitude and retirement, did not regard it as more than temporary, is a fact of which we are reminded by the words of his cousin, Brian Fairfax, in the Dedicatory Epistle to his posthumously published edition of the Lord General's *Short Memorials*:

---

1. H. M. Margoliouth and Hugh Macdonald, in their notes on this passage, declare that Fairfax was never Lord Warden of the Cinque Ports, and assume that the allusion to the Cinque Ports was quite arbitrarily introduced to match the 'five imaginary Forts'; but, as Mrs E. E. Duncan-Jones has pointed out in a letter to *TLS* (11 November 1955), 'all powers appertaining to the Lord High Admirall of England and Lord Warden of the Cinque Ports' had, in February 1650, been assigned to the Council of State, of which Fairfax was a member, and whose meetings he continued to attend until he resigned his commission in the following June. Marvell, therefore, is alluding to the *share* which Fairfax had had in the powers of Lord Warden of the Cinque Ports, and also, as Mrs Duncan-Jones has further pointed out, in the powers ('Pow'r which the Ocean might command') of Lord High Admiral.

The retired part of his Life gave him greater Satisfaction than all his former Victories, when he lived quietly at his own House at *Nun-Appleton* in *Yorkshire*; always earnestly wishing and praying for the Restitution of the Royal Family, and fully resolved to lay hold on the first good Opportunity to contribute his part towards it; which made him always lookt upon with a jealous eye by the Usurpers of that time.[1]

Some time after the death of his famous cousin (who was considerably older than himself) Brian Fairfax had celebrated this retired life at Nunappleton (recalling, it may well be, the post-Restoration years as well as the 1650's) in a poem entitled *The Vocal Oak. Upon the cutting down of the woods at Nun-Appleton*. After alluding (like Marvell in *Appleton House*) to the days when Nunappleton was a nunnery and declaring that it could tell many 'pretty stories' of the 'vestal virgins', and after recalling, in a passage reminiscent of Marvell's poem *Upon the Hill and Grove at Bill-borow*, how the Lord General had preserved its companions from the axe, the oak speaks of its great master's delight in 'this pleasant place':

> Where twenty years' retirement pleased him more
> Than all the trophies he had won before.
> Oft would he bring a book, and sit him down,
> Less glorious in arms than in his gown;
> All ages past, and persons that are gone,
> Were not, to me who saw them, better known.
> He read diviner things than Druids knew,
> Such mysteries were then revealed to few;
> For his chief study was God's sacred law,
> And all his life did comments on it draw.
>
> As Israel's king at last lay by his sword,
> And took the sacred harp to praise his Lord,
> Like some religious hermit now he seem'd,
> By all the world (least by himself) esteem'd.
> Fain would I hear him tell what he had done,—
> How many battles fought, as many won;
> When all the fields and villages around
> Heard his victorious drums and trumpets sound;
> When all these woods did echo forth his praise,
> And wish'd, t'adorn his head, we'd all been bays.[2]

---

1. *Short Memorials of Thomas Lord Fairfax. Written by Himself.* 1699, p. vii.
2. This, together with some other poems by Brian Fairfax, will be found on pp. cxxi–v of G. W. Johnson's *Memoirs of the Reign of Charles I*, 1848, vol. I.

I return to what I have called that central and eternal paradox which Aristotle first clearly formulated and which Aquinas Christianised. Man is both human and divine, or potentially divine; although, as human, he must attend to 'his station and its duties', he must also, as potentially divine, cherish so far as possible the divine spark within himself and recognise, even if he cannot always pursue it, that the life of contemplation is higher and better than the life of action. The life of contemplation is indeed the final justification of the life of action, since, as Aristotle said, we are only unleisurely in order that we may be at leisure (ἀσχολούμεθα γὰρ ἵνα σχολάζωμεν), understanding leisure, σχολή, not as mere relaxation but as a kind of festival or celebration in which we may achieve what the Shorter Catechism describes as man's chief end, namely, to glorify God and to enjoy him for ever. It is this central and eternal paradox that seems to have been revealed with fresh force and clarity to all who knew him by the life of the Lord General Fairfax. No man, when he recognised its authority, responded with more alacrity to the call of action; no man, when the time for action had passed or had been suspended, recognised more clearly the essential superiority of the life of contemplation, or embraced it more wholeheartedly and happily. It was in this man's society, and, as I cannot but think, chiefly for him, that Marvell wrote his panegyric on solitude and contemplation in *The Garden*: seriously, because the life of contemplation was divine; delightedly and delightfully, because it was the highest delight of which man was capable; and yet, at the same time, light-heartedly (with witty allusions to the metamorphoses of Daphne and Syrinx and to the banefulness of Eve), because, for such a being as man in such a world as the present one, the life of contemplation could seldom be more than an interlude and might at any time be interrupted by the claims, ultimately and eternally lower, immediately and temporally higher, of action. Is not, perhaps, the vibration and the iridescence, the delightedness and the delightfulness, which interpenetrates so many of these poems which, as I think, Marvell wrote during his two years' sojourn at Nunappleton—their continuous vibration, as distinct from that forgetful and exclusive luxuriance in a particular mood which characterises so much romantic poetry, between seriousness and light-heartedness (as an electric spark vibrates between the positively and negatively charged terminals of an induction coil)—is not this, perhaps, a reflection of Marvell's continuous awareness of what I have called the 'Paradox', of his awareness that what he was enjoying, though indeed a foretaste of man's highest felicity, was but a temporarily conceded joy? Even as the society and the civilisation in and out of which they were written, and of which to many they have seemed the most gracious flower, itself existed but for a season and a time—as a suggestion, perhaps, of something that might be.

I will conclude these reflections on *The Garden* with an examination of the sixth and seventh stanzas, since for most modern readers both their language and their allusions (especially those of the sixth) seem to require some explanation and commentary.

> Mean while the Mind, from pleasure less,
> Withdraws into its happiness:
> The Mind, that Ocean where each kind
> Does streight its own resemblance find;
> Yet it creates, transcending these,
> Far other Worlds, and other Seas;
> Annihilating all that's made
> To a green Thought in a green Shade.

ll. 1–2. 'From pleasure less': Marvell's clumsy inversion, here as often elsewhere, has produced an unintended ambiguity; he does not mean, as, according to normal syntax, he might be (and has been) supposed to mean, that the mind has grown less through pleasure, has been diminished through pleasure, but that the mind withdraws from the lesser pleasure of the senses into the greater pleasure, or rather, into the happiness, that is within itself. Marvell is here employing—consciously, I think—the Aristotelian and scholastic distinction between pleasure ($\dot{\eta}\delta o\nu\dot{\eta}$) and happiness ($\epsilon\dot{\upsilon}\delta\alpha\iota\mu o\nu\dot{\iota}\alpha$). Happiness, Aristotle declares, is a virtuous activity of the mind and spirit ($\psi\upsilon\chi\hat{\eta}s$ $\dot{\epsilon}\nu\dot{\epsilon}\rho\gamma\epsilon\iota\alpha$ $\kappa\alpha\tau$ $\dot{\alpha}\rho\epsilon\tau\dot{\eta}\nu$, *Eth. Nic.* 1098a, 15), and the highest kind of virtue or excellence that man can attain to is the exercise of intellect ($\nu o\hat{\upsilon}s$), not upon practical matters, but in some kind of contemplation, having affinity with that which we must suppose to be the chief activity of the gods. Happiness therefore, concludes Aristotle, must be some kind of contemplation ($\theta\epsilon\omega\rho\dot{\iota}\alpha$ $\tau\iota s$, 1178b, 8).

ll. 3–8. 'And there, transcending those external objects that are mirrored within it as terrestrial things are counterparted in the ocean, it creates other worlds and rejects all the visible creation in favour of those green, innocent and primal thoughts that come to it in a green shade.'

There is no need to comment upon the ancient belief that all terrestrial creations had their counterparts in the ocean (and also in the

heavens), a belief which Marvell, although he has used it for a simile,
may well, like Sir Thomas Browne,[1] have regarded as a 'vulgar error'.

> Annihilating all that's made
> To a green Thought in a green Shade.

Whether we understand 'annihilating all . . . to' as 'regarding all as
nothing in comparison with' or as 'reducing all to' does not greatly
matter: what does matter is that we should not suppose that Marvell
is writing merely impressionistically, as a modern poet, perhaps, might
write of a 'blue thought in a blue sky', using 'blue' in 'blue thought'
in a manner that might be described either as paradoxical, idiosyn-
cratic, or affected. A poet who should write of a 'black thought in a
black night', exploiting the common metaphorical sense of 'black', not
forcing upon it a metaphorical sense which it does not normally
possess, would be nearer to Marvell's procedure, for Marvell, in
'green Thought', is using 'green' in the metaphorical sense which was
still almost as common as the literal. 'Green', like Latin *viridis*, meant
not merely green in colour, but youthful, fresh, lively, vigorous; also
(and perhaps still more frequently) tender, innocent, or (a metaphor,
presumably, from unripe fruit) immature. Today the metaphorical

---

1. *Pseudodoxia Epidemica*, III xxiv. Cleveland, as Professor Pierre Legouis has
noticed, had made a characteristic use of the belief in his elegy on Edward King, in
the volume to which Milton contributed *Lycidas*:

> Some have affirm'd that what on earth we find
> The sea can parallel for shape and kind:
> Books, arts, and tongues were wanting, but in thee
> Neptune hath got an Universitie.

In Sylvester's *Du Bartas*, which everyone read, there is a very quaint and elaborate
passage on the subject (First Week, Fifth Day, ed. 1621, p. 92):

> Seas haue (as well as Skies) Sun, Moon, and Stars:
> (As well as Aire) Swallows, and Rooks, and Stares:
> (As well as Earth) Vines, Roses, Nettles, Millions,
> Pinks, Gilliflowrs, Mushroms, and many millions
> Of other Plants (more rare and strange then these)
> As very Fishes living in the Seas:
> And also Rams, Calfs, Horses, Hares, and Hogs,
> Wolves, Lyons, Vrchins, Elephants, and Dogs,
> Yea Men and Mayds: and (which I more admire)
> The Mytred Bishop, and the Cowled Fryer:
> Whereof, examples (but a few yeers since)
> Were showen the *Norways*, and *Polonian* Prince . . .
> And, as if *Neptune*, and fair *Panopé*,
> *Palæmon, Triton*, and *Leucothoé*,
> Kept publike Roules, there is the *Calamary*;
> Who, ready Pen-knife, Pen and Ink doth cary.

sense, very much simplified and vulgarised, survives only in the now almost obsolete, or obsolescent, phrase 'he's very green', as applied to a young freshman or a young recruit. (It was in more common use when the once very popular account of the adventures of that Oxford freshman Mr Verdant Green first appeared.) The phrase 'green Shade' may well have been suggested to Marvell by Virgil, who in his ninth Eclogue (ll. 19-20) makes Lycidas exclaim:

> quis humum florentibus herbis
> spargeret aut viridi fontis induceret umbra?

'who would strew the turf with flowery herbage, or curtain the springs with green shade?' But Virgil had also spoken of the 'green' or flourishing youth of Euryalus:

> Euryalus forma insignis viridique iuventa,[1]

and of the 'green old age' of Charon:

> iam senior, sed cruda deo viridisque senectus.[2]

I do not think, though, that *viridis* ever meant, as did English *green* 'innocent', or (in a much more complex and less denigrative sense than in the now almost obsolescent modern metaphor) 'immature'. Of these specifically English senses the *Oxford Dictionary* has some useful illustrative quotations: Barnabe Googe, *Eglogs* (1563), 'Eche thyng is easely made to obaye, whyle it is yong and grene'; Cornwallis, *Essays* (1601), 'The world in his greenest time lay in the arms of ignorance'; the Preface to the Authorised Version of the Bible (1611), 'In that new world and greene age of the Church'. To these might be added many examples from Shakespeare: for example, Pandulph to the Dauphin in *King John* (III iv 145), 'How green you are and fresh in this old world!'; Cleopatra's recollection of

> My salad days,
> When I was green in judgment;

> (I v 73-4)

Paulina's indignant description of Leontes's

> Fancies too weak for boys, too green and idle
> For girls of nine.

> (*Winter's Tale*, III ii 182-3)

---

1. *Aen.* V 295.   2. *Aen.* VI 304.

In the beautiful opening lines of the poem *On the Kings Birth-day*, which, although it is included in Ben Jonson's *The Underwood* (no. LXXXI), is probably by Sir Henry Wotton, to whom it is ascribed in two Bodleian manuscripts and in the *Reliquiae Wottonianae*, there is a play upon, an exploitation of, the literal and metaphorical senses of 'green' and 'gray' similar to Marvell's exploitation of the literal and metaphorical senses of 'green' in the passage we are considering

> Rowse up thy selfe, my gentle Muse,
> Though now our greene conceits be gray.

In Marvell's line the metaphorical sense of green is modified by the literal and the literal sense by the metaphorical: his thought is as green and innocent as the thoughts of Adam among the innocent, the newly created greenery of the Age of Innocence. Marvell has also, though less strikingly and profoundly, less completely and exhaustively, exploited the literal and metaphorical meanings of 'green' in *The Mower's Song*, which begins:

> My Mind was once the true survey
> Of all these Medows fresh and gay;
> And in the greenness of the Grass
> Did see its Hopes as in a Glass;
> When *Juliana* came, and She
> What I do to the Grass, does to my Thoughts and Me;

and which concludes:

> And thus, ye Meadows, which have been
> Companions of my thoughts more green,
> Shall now the Heraldry become
> With which I shall adorn my Tomb;
> For *Juliana* comes, and She
> What I do to the Grass, does to my Thoughts and Me.

Professor Kermode, in the interesting essay to which I have already alluded, has professed to find a resemblance between this sixth stanza of *The Garden* and two stanzas in Saint-Amant's poem *Le Contemplateur*, which, like *La Solitude*, was also written at Belle-Ile-en-Mer, and dedicated to the Bishop of Nantes, who had converted Saint-Amant from Huguenotism to the Catholic faith. It contains a few descriptive stanzas reminiscent of *La Solitude*, but many more of rather conventional religion, and as a whole is greatly inferior to its justly more

celebrated companion. Looking down at the sea, the poet recalls Noah
and the Flood, and how Noah's tears for the sins of the world, instead
of increasing the waters, caused them to recede. A dove flying past
him reminds him of the one that returned to Noah with the sprig of
olive. He then exercises his sense upon objects of 'lesser stuff', tries,
like a natural philosopher, to penetrate the secrets of nature, but finds
even the mystery of the ebb and flow of the tides too much for him.

> Tantost, faisant agir mes sens
> Sur des sujets de moindre estofe,
> De marche en autre je descens
> Dans les termes du philosophe;
> Nature n'a point de secret
> Que d'un soin libre, mais discret,
> Ma curiosité ne sonde;
> Ses cabinets me sont ouvers,
> Et, dans ma recherche profonde,
> Je loge en moy tout l'univers.

> Là, songeant au flus et reflus,
> Je m'abisme dans cette idée;
> Son mouvement me rend perclus,
> Et mon ame en est obsedée.
> Celuy que l'Euripe[1] engloutit
> Jamais en son coeur ne sentit
> Un plus ardent desir d'apprendre;
> Mais quand je veux bien l'esplucher,
> J'entens qu'on n'y peut rien entendre,
> Et qu'on se pert à le chercher.[2]

It seems to me that between these two stanzas and the sixth stanza of
Marvell's *Garden* the differences are fundamental, the resemblances (if
they really exist) merely accidental. Saint-Amant 'descends' from the
Book of Revelation to the Book of Creation, from Biblical or theological recollections (Noah and the dove) to questions of 'natural
philosophy'. This is quite unlike Marvell's procedure, who 'ascends',
or 'withdraws', from the lesser pleasure of perception into the greater

---

1. Saint-Amant is presumably referring to the ancient tradition (Procopius, *De
Bello Gothico*, viii 6, 20) that Aristotle died of grief because he was unable to solve
the mystery of the tides and currents of the Euripus.
2. *Œuvres Complètes*, ed. Livet, Paris 1855, I 32.

pleasure (or rather, happiness) of contemplation. In fact, Saint-Amant's
notion of 'contemplation' is much looser and more popular, much less
technically philosophic, than Marvell's.

Nevertheless, although Professor Kermode's attempts to find
parallels between Marvell's poetry and Saint-Amant's seem to me unconvincing, I think he is almost certainly right in perceiving in the
seventh stanza of *The Garden* a conscious or unconscious recollection of
Spenser.

> Here at the Fountains sliding foot,
> Or at some Fruit-trees mossy root,
> Casting the Bodies Vest aside,
> My Soul into the boughs does glide:
> There like a Bird it sits, and sings,
> Then whets, and combs its silver Wings;
> And, till prepar'd for longer flight,
> Waves in its Plumes the various Light.

This image of the soul as a bird had almost certainly come to Marvell,
through Spenser, from Castiglione, who, towards the end of his book
The Courtier, in a passage of what may be called popular Platonism,
describes how the lover can ascend from the beauty of his mistress to
a contemplation of universal beauty, but admits that the ascent is
difficult and that few are able to make it:

> Wherefore such as come to this love, are like to yong birdes
> almost flush, which for all they flitter a litle their tender winges,
> yet dare they not stray farre from the nest, nor commit themselves
> to the winde and open weather.[1]

This passage, together with the whole discussion of which it forms a
part, was certainly in Spenser's mind when he wrote his *Hymne of
Heavenly Beautie*, of which this is the fourth stanza:

> Beginning then below, with th'easie vew
> Of this base world, subiect to fleshly eye,
> From thence to mount aloft by order dew,
> To contemplation of th' immortall sky,
> Of the soare faulcon so I learne to fly,
> That flags awhile her fluttering wings beneath,
> Till she her selfe for stronger flight can breath.

1. *The Courtier*, transl. by Sir Thomas Hoby, Everyman's Library, p. 318.

It is hard not to suppose that the last line of this stanza was in Marvell's memory when he wrote: 'And, till prepar'd for longer flight.' Marvell, like Milton and unlike Donne, did not disdain the poetry of 'sage and serious Spenser', although, even at its most sage and serious, his own poetry is interpenetrated by a wit such as we scarcely ever find in Spenser or in Milton, but which has some affinity with Donne's. From all his English predecessors, from Spenser to Cleveland, Marvell was able to learn something, and from all these lessons and suggestions to produce something inimitably his own.

ALPHABETICAL TABLE OF
MARVELL'S POEMS QUOTED
OR DISCUSSED

INDEX

DUE